FROMMER'S

EasyGuide

TO

NAPLES, SORRENTO & THE AMALFI COAST

By
Stephen Brewer

Easy Guides are ✦ Quick To Read ✦ Light To Carry
✦ For Expert Advice ✦ In All Price Ranges

FrommerMedia LLC

FROMMER MEDIA LLC

ISBN 978-1-62887-192-0 (paper), 978-1-62887-193-7 (e-book)

Editorial Director: Pauline Frommer
Editor: Pauline Frommer
Production Editor: Lynn Northrup
Cartographer: Liz Puhl
Photo Editor: Dana Davis
Indexer: Maro Riofrancos

For information on our other products or services, see www.frommers.com.

Frommer Media LLC also publishes its books in a variety of electronic formats. Some content that
appears in print may not be available in electronic formats.

Manufactured in the United States of America

5 4 3 2 1

FROMMER'S STAR RATINGS SYSTEM

Every hotel, restaurant and attraction listed in this guide has been ranked for quality and value. Here's what the stars mean:

★ Recommended
★★ Highly Recommended
★★★ A must! Don't miss!

AN IMPORTANT NOTE

The world is a dynamic place. Hotels change ownership, restaurants hike their prices, museums alter their opening hours, and buses and trains change their routings. And all of this can occur in the several months after our authors have visited, inspected, and written about these hotels, restaurants, museums, and transportation services. Though we have made valiant efforts to keep all our information fresh and up-to-date, some few changes can inevitably occur in the periods before a revised edition of this guidebook is published. So please bear with us if a tiny number of the details in this book have changed. Please also note that we have no responsibility or liability for any inaccuracy or errors or omissions, or for inconvenience, loss, damage, or expenses suffered by anyone as a result of assertions in this guide.

CONTENTS

ABOUT THE AUTHOR

Stephen Brewer has been exploring and enjoying Naples and the Amalfi Coast for almost 30 years, writing about the region for magazines and travel guides. He also writes frequently about other parts of Italy and Europe for Frommer's.

ABOUT THE FROMMER'S TRAVEL GUIDES

For most of the past 50 years, Frommer's has been the leading series of travel guides in North America, accounting for as many as 24% of all guidebooks sold. I think I know why.

Though we hope our books are entertaining, we nevertheless deal with travel in a serious fashion. Our guidebooks have never looked on such journeys as a mere recreation, but as a far more important human function, a time of learning and introspection, an essential part of a civilized life. We stress the culture, lifestyle, history, and beliefs of the destinations we cover, and urge our readers to seek out people and new ideas as the chief rewards of travel.

We have never shied from controversy. We have, from the beginning, encouraged our authors to be intensely judgmental, critical—both pro and con—in their comments, and wholly independent. Our only clients are our readers, and we have triggered the ire of countless prominent sorts, from a tourist newspaper we called "practically worthless" (it unsuccessfully sued us) to the many rip-offs we've condemned.

And because we believe that travel should be available to everyone regardless of their incomes, we have always been cost-conscious at every level of expenditure. Though we have broadened our recommendations beyond the budget category, we insist that every lodging we include be sensibly priced. We use every form of media to assist our readers, and are particularly proud of our feisty daily website, the award-winning Frommers.com.

I have high hopes for the future of Frommer's. May these guidebooks, in all the years ahead, continue to reflect the joy of travel and the freedom that travel represents. May they always pursue a cost-conscious path, so that people of all incomes can enjoy the rewards of travel. And may they create, for both the traveler and the persons among whom we travel, a community of friends, where all human beings live in harmony and peace.

Arthur Frommer

THE BEST OF NAPLES & THE AMALFI COAST

T ravelers have been coming to Campania to enjoy the good life ever since Emperor Tiberius discovered the pleasures of Capri and his fellow Romans built lavish villas around the Bay of Baiae, outside present-day Naples. Modern-day travelers still descend in search of a little slice of heaven, and, of course, they find it in spades: at posh resorts along the Amalfi Coast, in glamorous hideouts on Capri, at the sybaritic spas of Ischia.

The Amalfi Coast and Capri are fabled seaside playgrounds, and if sun and sea are the draws, you'll probably be delighted to discover the islands of Ischia and Procida and the relatively undiscovered Cilento coast, too.

Beautiful coastlines and glamorous lifestyles aside, the region hits you full throttle with all sorts of other pleasures and diversions. Naples, for starters, is maybe Italy's most intense urban concoction. The city is a fascinating and perplexing place where you'll encounter treasures of the ancient world, medieval churches, and a labyrinth of laundry-hung lanes and sunny piazzas. The ruins of the classical world surround the city—most famously at Pompeii and Herculaneum, just southeast around the bay; at Paestum, farther south; and to the east, in Capua and Benevento. For a weird encounter with the ancients, just hop on a train for the trip west to Pozzuoli. This Greco-Roman seaside city is at the edge of a strange landscape that's littered with ruins and potholed with volcanic vents still hiss and steam.

It can all make your head spin, so brace yourself, because that's what traveling in this part of the world is all about. Here's how to get the most out of the experience.

THE best TRAVEL EXPERIENCES

o **Walking Through Old Naples:** Everything is over the top in Italy's third-largest city. Dark, brooding lanes open to palm-fringed piazzas, and laundry-strewn tenements stand cheek by jowl with grand palaces and medieval churches. Little kids dart around street stalls, and old crones hang out windows to hoist their groceries in baskets past crumbling facades. A wander through Quartieri Spagnoli or anywhere else in the old city is like witnessing street theater, and a surefire exhilarating experience. See chapter 4.

The famed rock outcroppings of Faraglioni, Capri.

o **Swanning Around Capri:** You have to approach this enchanting, glamorous beauty just the right way. Come on a hurried day trip and you'll be corralled through the Gardens of Augustus and just herded into a boat for a quick row through the Blue Grotto. Instead, spend a night, or more. Enjoy the spectacle of a sunset from the little cove below the *faro* (lighthouse). Wake up to a chorus of birdsong in the scented pines. Swim in the shadow of the Faraglioni rocks. You'll soon fall under the island's spell. See chapter 7.

o **Arriving in Naples by Boat:** At some point in your wanderings—returning from Capri or Ischia, maybe—you'll savor the pleasure of gliding into the bay, with a sea breeze at your back and the spectacle of the city spread out ahead of you. Mt. Vesuvius looms to the east, Castell d'Ovo greets you on the seafront, Castell Sant'Almo looks down from the top of the Vomero hill, dozens of church domes pierce the skyline. You'll know what they mean when they say, "See Naples and die." See chapter 4.

o **Wandering Down Ancient Roman Lanes in Pompeii:** It almost gives you shivers to share space with the doomed residents of this lively, boisterous Roman port where life ended so abruptly on August 24, A.D. 79. No other ancient town has been brought to light so completely. With just a little imagination, the remarkably well-preserved remains of shops, villas, brothels, and baths will whisk you right back to the days when you might have zipped along the tufa-stone streets in a chariot. See chapter 5.

o **Riding a Bus Along the Amalfi Coast:** Forget about your Walter Mitty fantasies of climbing behind the wheel of a Lamborghini and revving up the engine. Instead, board the bus and leave the driving to a well-seasoned pro. That's the best way to savor one of the world's most fabled coastlines and its famous cornice, justifiably known as the "Road of 1,000 Bends." Even with someone else at the wheel, you'll be on the edge of your seat as you hug the vertical cliffs and cross deep gorges, though the bluest sea you've ever set eyes upon is a soothing tonic. See chapter 6.

- **Eating the Best Pizza in the World:** A lot of folks in Campania claim they invented pizza, with everyone from Neapolitans to villagers in the mountains behind the Amalfi Coast stepping up to take credit. Little matter. Chefs throughout the region have perfected the art of making a wafer-thin crust, topping it with sun-kissed tomatoes and cloud-like mozzarella, and baking the pie to perfection. You're in for a taste sensation, whether you encounter the local specialty at legendary but humble Pizzeria Da Michele and Pizzeria Gino Sorbillo in old Naples or Da Gigino Pizza a Metro in Vico Equense, where it's dished up by the meter. See chapters 4 & 6.

THE best RUINS

- **The Temples of Paestum:** You'd have to go all the way to Greece to top the spectacle of these three ancient beauties rising above fields of wild roses south of Salerno. Greek colonizers crafted the elegant, remarkably well-preserved columns and porticos out of honey-colored stone in the 6th-century B.C., showing off their perfect sense of proportion. The outpost even has a delightful mascot, the figure of a young man taking a swan dive into a rushing stream from the so-called Tomb of the Diver, now in the treasure-filled archeological museum. See chapter 8.

- **The Anfiteatro Campano of Santa Maria Capua Vetere:** Spartacus, leader of the famous 1st-century slave revolt, was among those who sparred in the second-largest coliseum in the Roman world. Most of the gleaming marble and golden travertine has been carted off over the centuries, but generous sweeps of arches, seating, and columns evoke the roar of 60,000 spectators as gladiators and beasts did battle in the 170m (558-ft.) long arena. See chapter 9.

The Anfiteatro Campano of Santa Maris Capua Vetere.

- **Pompeii and Herculaneum:** When Mt. Vesuvius blew its top in A.D. 79, ash, molten lava, and ooze preserved these two remarkable time capsules to make ancient times stand still. Frescoes, temples, villas, and arenas elicit plenty of oohs and ahhs, but most moving are the tidbits of everyday life. Charred wood fittings and staircases in Herculaneum give you the impression the householders have just stepped out for a flask of wine, while stone storage boxes in the *apodyterium* (changing room) at the Terme Suburbane in Pompeii invite you to stash your toga and sandals and settle into the *caldarium* (hot bath) for a long, soothing soak. See chapter 5.

o **Trajan's Arch in Benevento:** "Use it or lose it" could be the motto of this magnificent gateway that commemorated the opening of the Via Traiana, a quick route to the Roman port of Brindisi. For many centuries the handsome monument, carved with the accomplishments of the emperor for whom it's named, came in handy as the main gate in the city walls, surviving earthquakes and barbarian invasions. See chapter 9.

o **The Campi Flegrei (Phlegraean Fields):** A day on this volcanic seaside peninsula just west of Naples will make your head spin with images of hedonism, villainy, and ancient lore. Here, amid volcanic landscapes that hiss, steam, bubble, and spew, Caligula road his horse across the bay on a floating bridge of boats, Caesar relaxed with Cleopatra in a lavish seaside villa, and the Cumaean Sibyl passed on messages from Apollo. It doesn't take too much imagination to coax this colorful past out of the marketplace in Pozzuoli, the villas in Baiae, and other copious ruins and natural phenomena. See chapter 5.

THE best PLACES TO GET WET

o **Bagno della Regina Giovanna (Queen Giovanna's Bath) at Punta del Capo:** A swim in this rock-sheltered cove of clear water, reached on a path through citrus and olive groves, comes with a history. The tranquil pool was once the private harbor of the ancient Roman Villa of Pollio Felice. You can step through the ruins at the top of the cliff and daydream about a *quinquereme*, an ancient galley, full of dignitaries pulling up beside you as you swim your laps. See chapter 6.

o **Spiaggia Grande and Fornillo, Positano:** You won't be alone, but who cares when the scenery is as spectacular as this? The pastel-hued houses, tiled domes, and soaring cliffs of one of the world's most beautiful seaside towns are especially picturesque when seen from the water. So swim out from the crowds on shore, turn on your back, and float in the warm water and enjoy the view. See chapter 6.

o **Faraglioni and Marina Piccola, Capri:** These fabled bathing spots are a far cry from silky tropical beaches, but that hasn't stopped Liz Taylor, Jackie O., Mariah Carey, and countless other stars and notables from taking the plunge. If the celebrity connections don't win you over, the glorious island scenery and mesmerizing light will. How's the water? It's so tempting that the emperor Tiberius couldn't resist tossing his guests into the surf from the cliff-side terraces of his villa. See chapter 7.

o **Ischia's Thermal Baths:** You don't have to be a millionaire to live like a sybarite on the island of eternal youth. Dozens of bathing establishments will pamper you in style, letting you soak in heated pools, packing you in hot mud, and massaging out your knots and kinks. In a close contest, Parco

Spiaggia Grande as seen from the sea.

Termale Negombo takes the prize for the most beautiful of them all, with 12 pools tucked into luxuriant gardens next to beautiful San Montano Bay. See chapter 7.

THE best MUSEUMS & MONUMENTS

- **Museo Archeologico Nazionale, Naples:** Dusty, gloomy galleries are filled with some of the great treasures of the ancient world. Crowd pleasers are the frescoes, mosaics, statues, and titter-inducing pornography from Pompeii, but save some enthusiasm for the similarly impressive Ercole Farnese, a huge statue of Hercules unearthed at the Baths of Caracalla in Rome. See chapter 4.

- **Pio Monte della Misericordia, Naples:** Caravaggio's sumptuous 1607 "Seven Acts of Mercy" takes center stage in this small octagonal chapel. The tempestuous artist had a fondness for gambling, prostitutes, young boys, rowdiness, and drunkenness, and his stormy disposition comes through in his dark, moody, and chaotic canvas. You'll probably only be able to spot six acts of mercy, but there's a trick. See chapter 4.

- **Chiesa di San Michele, Capri:** You're in for a jolt when you step into this plain-looking church on a quiet square in Anacapri. The entire floor is awash in hand-painted, technicolor tiles depicting the expulsion of Adam and Eve from the Garden of Eden. Head up the spiral staircase for a bird's-eye view of the scene, making sure to pick out the bestiary of exotic creatures surrounding the doomed couple. See chapter 7.

- **Castello Aragonese:** More than 17,000 souls once crowded into this lofty redoubt perched atop a rock hundreds of feet above the waves and a refuge

Reggia di Caserta.

since the ancient Greeks built fortifications in the 5th century B.C. Monasteries, churches, humble houses, and watchtowers, in various states of repair, line the lanes and squares, and a bracing walk on the ramparts is one of the island's great thrills. See chapter 7.

o **Reggia di Caserta, Caserta:** For Bourbon King Carlo III, it was "the bigger the better" when it came time to build a new palace. The largest royal residence in the world, intended to make Versailles look like a frumpy bungalow, was a white elephant by the time it was finally completed in the mid–19th century. But the grandeur of the place is certainly impressive and extends into the vast gardens, awash with lavish waterworks. See chapter 9.

o **Certosa di San Lorenzo, Padula:** No simple hermit's cave for these monks: This massive Carthusian monastery has 320 halls, 52 staircases, 100 fireplaces, 13 courtyards, and 41 fountains. Most impressive of all is the main cloister, the largest in the world, where two levels of porticos supported by a forest of columns surround 1.2 hectares (3 acres) of lawns and gardens. See chapter 8.

THE best FOR FAMILIES

o **Getting into the Christmas Spirit in Naples:** Is there a kid anywhere who doesn't love Christmas? And the inner kid in you probably feels just the same way. Well, every day is Christmas on Via San Gregorio Armeno in Naples, where craftspeople specialize in *presipi,* nativity scenes. No humble mangers here: Wood and ceramic figures—not just Jesus, Mary, and Joseph, and the other old standbys, but soccer stars and pop idols, too—inhabit fantastical worlds where animated cattle lull, water wheels spin, and lights twinkle in village squares. The world's largest *presepe* is on permanent display at the city's hilltop Museo di San Martino. See chapter 4.

o **Exploring Capri:** The enchanted isle has been the scene of lots of grown-up shenanigans, but there's plenty to entice young visitors, too. Some great swimming aside, even getting around can be a ball: riding the funicular from the port at Marina Grande up to Capri Town, taking a bus alongside the sheer drop-offs along the cornice to Anacapri, ascending to the top of Monte Solaro in the chairlift, being rowed into the Grotto Azzurra. Plus, scampering up and down the hundreds of steps and navigating steep paths that the rest of us consider to be a workout is mere child's play. See chapter 7.

o **Going Underground in Naples:** There's more to Naples than meets the eye, and kids will love ferreting out the hidden city beneath the streets. Where else could they explore Roman cisterns converted to World War II bomb shelters? The catacombs of San Gennaro are a similarly eerie world of frescoed burial niches, while below the church of San Lorenzo Maggiore is a big surprise: a Greco-Roman market and streets lined with bakeries and shops. See chapter 4.

o **Getting Around by Boat:** The family car will be seem like a boring old buggy once kids experience the regional transport. On a clear day, sitting on a boat deck and chugging down the Amalfi Coast or out to the islands can seem like a thrilling sea voyage. (Whenever you have the time, forgo the speedier hydrofoils, on which seating is indoors only.) For good sports who aren't too travel weary, even the ride around the bay from Naples to Pompeii on the Circumvesuviana railway, beneath Naples on the subway, or along the Amalfi Drive on the bus can be joy rides. See chapter 5.

THE best TOWNS & NEIGHBORHOODS

o **Pozzuoli, West of Naples:** A storied past, ancient monuments (including those of a magnificent marketplace and amphitheater), volcanic landscapes, and sweeping sea views to the islands of Ischia and Procida make Pozzuoli a lot more interesting and appealing than a scrappy suburban town has any right to be. Adding to the lore of the place is screen legend Sophia Loren, who was born here in 1934. See chapter 5.

o **Spaccanapoli, Naples:** Gird your loins, watch your wallet, and forget about a map as you plunge into the narrow, laundry-strung lanes and clamorous squares of the heart of old Naples. Street vendors push fried snacks and religious statues, and a neighborhood chorus chirps away above you on hundreds of apartment balconies. Lofty, too, are the domes of dozens of churches and the glass arcades of 19th-century Galleria Umberto I, one of the world's first shopping malls, anchoring the southwest corner of the neighborhood. See chapter 4.

o **Ravello, Amalfi Coast:** Sorry, Positano and Amalfi, you're beauties, too, but top prize for prettiest town on what many scenery buffs consider to be the world's most beautiful coastline goes to this heavenly aerie. It's all about the ethereal light that lends the palaces and gardens a transcendent otherworldliness. Add the views, like those from the gardens of the Villa Cimbrone, where you'll have the dizzying sensation of being suspended between sea and sky. See chapter 6.

o **Sant' Angelo, Ischia:** The otherwise laid-back island gets a bit showy with this spectacle of a town, a little cluster of colorful houses clinging to a huge rock formation off the southern coast. Adding another splash of drama is nearby Fumarole beach, where it's a

A clothesline-draped street in Spaccanapoli, Naples.

local tradition for picnickers to bury their food in the sand and let underground vapors roast a meal to perfection. See chapter 7.

o **Corricella, Procida:** The stack of tall, pastel-hued houses rising up from the ramshackle quay has inspired painters, photographers, and filmmakers (*Il Postino*, the 1994 classic, was shot here)—and charmed droves of scenery-saturated island-hoppers as well. All of tiny Procida is pretty as a picture, and so small you can walk across the island in about an hour. Doing so means immersing yourself in a romantic world of crumbling palaces, sun-baked squares, and overgrown gardens, catching glimpses of the sparkling blue sea along the way. See chapter 7.

THE best RESTAURANTS

o **Pizzeria Da Michele and Pizzeria Gino Sorbillo, Naples:** It's a toss-up who makes the best pizza in Naples—half the residents say Michele, the other half Sorbillo. Both places are wait-in-line no-frillers, and each is a mandatory stop. Michele makes just two varieties, margherita and marinara (toppings are for snobs, say the guys behind the counter), while Sorbillo defiantly turns out topping-laden masterpieces that include the Quattro Stagione (Four Seasons), with its quadrants of mushrooms, salami, prosciutto, and cheese. See p. 81 and 82.

o **Rosiello, Posilipo, Naples:** It's a bit of a trek out to this hilltop retreat, but a meal on the terrace is one of the city's great treats. Waiters will guide you through the fresh-that-day offerings. Just about all are from the sea just below—the light-as-a-feather seafood risotto is the stuff of dreams—and the restaurant's own vegetable plots on the hillside—*scialatielli con melanzane e provola,* fresh pasta with eggplant and local cheese, is like everything else here, elegant and simply delicious. See p. 79.

o **Addio Riccio, Capri:** It's hard to imagine the good life getting much better than it does with a feast on this airy terrace above the sea. Waiters hurry around with heaping platters laden with just-caught seafood, introducing you to such delights as urchin roe. But remember what Mom told you about swimming on a full stomach, because you'll want to take the plunge from the wave-washed swimming platforms below. See p. 187.

o **Pulalli Wine Bar, Capri:** One of the best hideaways on an island famous for them is perched in the clock tower high above the busy Piazzetta. The cozy terrace supplies far-ranging looks across the white town below, but you can't live on views alone. Enhance the moment with a good selection of wine, cheeses, and a few special dishes. See p. 187.

o **Don Alfonso 1890, Sant'Agata sui Due Golfi, near Sorrento:** A garden next to the swimming pool is an idyllic setting for a lazy summer lunch, but that's only part of the equation. The Iaccarino family's vegetable plot and a network of local suppliers provide the ingredients for a meal in which even the homegrown tomatoes seem like exotic fruits, and simple ravioli filled with farmhouse cheese could pass as an offering to the gods. See p. 131.

THE best LUXURY RETREATS

o **Hotel Santa Caterina, Amalfi:** Nothing about this seaside lair is pretentious or overly posh. The much-expanded villa is just plain transporting, set in lemon groves against sea-meets-sky horizons. Lots of ceramic tiles, a smattering of antiques, and sea-view terraces grace guest rooms that are comfortable without being over the top—though a private beach reached on a James Bond–worthy elevator most welcomingly is. See p. 151.

o **Grand Hotel Cocumella, Sorrento:** Monks built this cliff-top monastery centuries ago so they could lead simple, spiritual lives out of harm's way from pirate raids. Their luxuriant, orange-scented gardens and magical blue sea vistas are still otherworldly, and their cells have been combined and fitted out with lots of contemporary style, all creating a little bit of heaven on earth. See p. 122.

o **Capri Palace, Anacapri, Capri:** Some of the suites tucked into private gardens with their own swimming pools are fit for royals, but even toned-down guest quarters geared to the rest of us are soothing, beautifully done digs. A lovely pool surrounded with loungers and lawns is an oasis of calm on the busy island, and a spiffy beach club is just a short shuttle ride away. See p. 184.

o **Grand Hotel Vesuvio, Naples:** Acres of shiny parquet, handsome old prints, fine linens, and classic furnishings deliver boatloads of old-world glamour. Enhancing the Grand Tour–worthy experience are the views of the bay, the Castel dell'Ovo, and Mt. Vesuvius. And take heart: Off-season rates and the occasional special offer brings the memorable pleasure of a stay here almost within reach. See p. 76.

THE best AFFORDABLE GETAWAYS

o **Costantinopoli 104, Naples:** A stay in this 19th-century Art Nouveau palace that once belonged to a marquis delivers a one-of-a-kind Neapolitan experience. Some of the dark decor befits an out-of-luck royal, but blue skies and fresh air are plentiful—the best rooms open directly off a sprawling roof terrace, and a small bean-shaped pool is set in a palm-shaded courtyard. See p. 77.

o **Hotel Piazza Bellini, Naples:** The archaeological museum is just outside the door of this centuries-old palace, where a cool contemporary redo takes the edge off city life. An outdoor living room fills the cobbled courtyard, and rooms are minimalist chic with warm hardwood floors and neutral tones accented with warm hues. See p. 78.

o **La Fenice, Positano:** A private beach is the pride and joy of some the most exclusive and expensive on the Amalfi Coast, but this little parcel of heaven clinging to a cliff on the outskirts of Positano has one, too. Even without that amenity, or the sparkling pool in the garden, the charming and simple terraced rooms would be a delight, tucked away along shaded walkways and stone stairways that descend the hillside amid lemon groves and grape vines. See p. 137.

o **Hotel della Baia, San Montano Beach, near Lacco Ameno, Ischia:** At this pleasant seaside getaway surrounded by lime trees and myrtle, you might be tempted to hang out on your bougainvillea-filled terrace. But you'll have to fend off double-barreled distractions. One of the island's best beaches is just down the road, and a garden-laced park with 12 thermal pools is right next door. See p. 201.

o **La Locanda del Mare, Paestum:** No need to rush away from the Greek ruins when these stylish, whitewashed bungalows tucked into a pine forest are just down the road. Topping off the long list of perks is the sparking blue sea and 14km (9 mi.) stretch of sand at the end of the garden path. See p. 223.

NAPLES & THE AMALFI COAST IN CONTEXT

Y ou may well be coming to this region in search of
beautiful coastlines and idyllic islands. Who's to blame
you? Of course, you'll find plenty of scenery-filled
retreats, and much, much more.

Given the presence of Pompeii and Herculaneum, it's no surprise
that these lands are also rich in the traces of ancient civilizations,
and those magnificently preserved Roman cities are just the beginning. Paestum, the even older Greek city, is just to the south, while
ruins at Capua, Benevento, and elsewhere throughout the region
attest to thousands of years of civilization in the lands the Romans
called the *Campania felix,* or fertile countryside.

A LOOK AT THE PAST

Campania's long and complex history is drama-soaked, and as you
travel around the region you'll encounter emperors, tyrants, gladiators, pirates, and enlightened kings and queens. No need to turn
your trip into a history lesson, but encountering these characters,
and the monuments they left behind and the cultures they influenced, is one of the real pleasures of being here and sheds a lot of
light on the present day. This chapter will help you understand why.

Who Was Who

As you travel around the region you will encounter a confusing
litany of names—Samnites, Oscans, Longobards. All these cultures
have left a mark, and here, in brief, is who they were.

THE GREEKS

In 750 B.C., the Greeks founded the city of Cuma (p. 91), on a peninsula west of present-day Naples. Cuma was the first Greek city of
Magna Grecia—the Greek cities outside the mainland—and from
there colonists expanded into the region. Their settlement in Naples
is marked by an agora and shops below the church of San Lorenzo
(p. 68). They also left the marketplace in Pozzuoli (p. 86), from
around 531 B.C. Their presence is most strikingly seen at Paestum
(p. 218), where around 600 B.C. they created some of the most

beautiful temples to survive from the ancient world. Traces of a Greek city also remain in Velia (p. 229), founded in 540 B.C.

Greeks won two major battles in Cuma against the Etruscans, one in 524 B.C. and the other in 474 B.C. But weakened by these fights, the Greeks could not resist the Samnite invasion in the 5th century B.C.

THE ETRUSCANS

While the Greeks colonized Campania's coast, the Etruscans colonized the rich interior plains around Capua (p. 239), which they founded in the 9th century B.C., and continued to move south into the hinterland around Paestum. They, too, were weakened by their fights for supremacy in the region against the Greeks, so when the Samnites began their expansion, the Etruscans soon succumbed.

THE SAMNITES

These mountain warriors, with an economy based on sheep husbandry, established a flourishing civilization in Benevento (p. 244) around the 5th century B.C., and continued moving toward the coast.

Samnite attacks against Greeks and Etruscans were successful: They took Capua in 424 B.C. and Cuma 3 years later. Their influence quickly expanded to other cities, Pompeii, and Herculaneum among them, and gave birth to a new civilization, the Oscans (see below).

Etruscan sculpture.

Samnites of Benevento, in the meantime, came into opposition with the Romans who, by the 4th century B.C., had started their expansion southward. This led to the three famous Samnite wars. It took Rome from 343 B.C. to 290 B.C. to overcome the Samnites.

THE LUCANIANS

Another Italic mountain population, the Lucanians, began to migrate toward the coast. They took over Paestum in 400 B.C., but soon merged with the Greek population into the cultural melting pot that became the Oscans.

THE OSCANS

The Samnites merged culturally with Etruscans and Greeks, giving birth to a new civilization, the Oscans. The Oscans made

Emperor Nero (pictured) had a mansion in Baia on the Amalfi Coast.

their capital in Capua and eventually shifted their support to Rome during the Empire's conquest of Campania.

THE ROMANS

The Romans quickly moved into the region, settling into Paestum by 273 B.C., Beneventum by 268 B.C., then Salerno and Puteoli (modern-day Pozzuoli) by 194 B.C. A network of roads linked these cities to the capital. Chief among them was the Appian Way, leading from Rome to Capua and Benevento, then all the way to Brindisi, the gateway to the eastern Mediterranean.

In exchange for the allegiance of local peoples to the Republic, Rome bestowed upon them Roman citizenship, with the right to vote and decide on public affairs (but with the obligation of military service). This was one of the ways in which Campania was completely Romanized, though its agriculture-based economy was slowly supplanted by the production from Africa and Spain, leading to a strong local recession. By the time the empire ended in A.D. 395, the rich plains of Capua and Paestum had been abandoned and were malarial. The population was forced to settle new villages up in the mountains, and the situation would not improve dramatically until the 20th century.

THE LONGOBARDS

With the end of the Roman Empire, barbarians swept in. The Goths from the north invaded the region in 410, while Vandals from Africa sacked and destroyed Capua in 456. The Longobards, a warlike central European tribe, had taken over the interior by 570. The Byzantines who inherited the remnants of the Roman Empire struggled to maintain power, but eventually lost, keeping only the harbors of Naples, Sorrento, and Amalfi.

The role of monasteries in preserving classical culture was invaluable. Much later (in the 13th century), the Abbey of Monte Cassino, in northern Campania, would be the home of the greatest philosopher-theologian in Europe, St. Thomas Aquinas.

In the second half of the 8th century, the Longobard prince Arechi II moved his court from Benevento to Salerno, causing increasing tension between the two towns, which resulted in civil war and the splitting of the Longobard realm into two independent principalities in 849. This marked the beginning of the end for the Longobards. By the 10th century, Capua had become an independent principality, and Amalfi had become independent from the Byzantines, gaining strength and power on its own as a maritime commercial republic.

THE SARACENS

By the 9th century, the Saracens—Arab mercenaries who had established a beachhead in Sicily—were attacking and sacking towns along the coast of Campania. The once-prosperous coast became deserted as residents sought refuge in the hills and the countryside. Some of the towns were then reborn, often in more defensive locations and surrounded by heavy fortifications.

THE NORMANS

Things changed with the arrival of the Normans, who reintroduced the concept of central government and unity in southern Italy. Their first base was Aversa, near Naples, established in 1029, and from there they rapidly expanded their conquest to Capua in 1062, Amalfi in 1073, and Salerno in 1076. Salerno was the Normans' capital until they annexed Naples in 1139 and then proceeded south to take Sicily.

Under the Normans, Salerno became a splendid town and a center of culture and learning, with a famous medical school. Benevento, on the other hand, became a papal stronghold in the mid–11th century and stayed so, with a couple of brief interludes, until the unification of Italy in 1860.

THE ANGEVINS

When the Norman stronghold loosened, power eventually passed to the Angevins, another French dynasty. By the mid–13th century, the Angevins had established a flourishing capital in Naples, but the interior was ravaged by poverty. Bandits established themselves in the hills and attacked travelers on the roads. The legacy of these centuries of stagnation and lawlessness persists to this day.

THE SPANISH

By the early 1500s, Naples and the region were under Spanish rule. Extraction of taxes and the imposition of authoritarian rule were onerous. Philip IV called Naples "a gold mine, which furnished armies for our wars and treasure for their protection." The main events of Spanish rule were revolts against it. Meanwhile, in 1656, the great plague raged through the region, killing an estimated half the population of Naples.

THE BOURBONS

After almost three decades of Austrian rule, Naples regained its independence in 1734, with the arrival of Carlo di Borbone, of the royal Bourbon line of French origin. Carlo and the Bourbons revitalized the kingdom, improving roads, draining marshes, and creating new industries—such as the silk manufacturers in San Leucio (p. 238), the ceramic artistry in Capodimonte (p. 72), and the cameo and coral industries in Torre del Greco (p. 109).

MODERN TIMES

After a brief period of Napoleonic rule, followed by the return of the Bourbons, the region was poised for rebellion. Between the French, the Spanish, and the Austrians, tyrannical thugs, and enlightened princes, the region and the rest of Italy had had enough. Thanks to the efforts of Camillo Cavour (1810–61) and Giuseppe Garibaldi (1807–82), the kingdom of Italy was proclaimed in 1861. Victor Emmanuel (Vittorio Emanuele) II of the House of Savoy, king of Sardinia, became the head of the new monarchy.

Unfortunately, the new kingdom spelled disaster for Campania's economy: The northern government imposed heavy taxes, and the centralized administration paid little attention to local differences and needs. This killed the burgeoning industry that had been developing with the Bourbons' paternalism and protection. Only coastal regions, with a solid agricultural base, were spared rampant poverty and unemployment.

World War II

World War II took a serious tool on the region. It was heavily bombarded to rout the Germans in preparation for the Allied landing on September 8, 1943, when 55,000 Allied troops stormed ashore in a long arc from Sorrento to Paestum. The Nazis set up a desperate resistance, retreating slowly for long months just north of Caserta along the Garigliano River. This involved one of the war's most notorious battles, the several-months-long siege of Monte Cassino, which left the ancient monastery a heap of rubble. The Nazis destroyed as much as they could during their retreat, sacking and vandalizing everything—even the most important section of the Naples State Archives was burned.

In September 1943, Allied forces arrived in Naples. Other towns' insurrections resulted in horrible massacres; men and women organized guerrilla groups against the Nazis, hiding out in the mountains and hills and striking mostly at night, while the Allies bombarded their towns and cities. After many hard months of fighting, Campania was finally freed in June 1944.

The Postwar Years

In 1946, Campania became part of the newly established Italian Republic—although Naples had shown its preference for keeping the monarchy in a postwar referendum—and reconstruction began. Even though ravaged Italy succeeded in rebuilding its postwar economy and became one of the world's leading industrialized nations, Campania was slow to recover. Hindering development was the terrible destruction that the region had suffered, as well as the plague of corruption and the increasing influence of the Camorra, Campania's Mafia-like organization.

The great earthquake (about a 7 on the Richter scale) that shook the region on November 23, 1980, was another setback. More than 3,000 people died, especially in the provinces of Avellino and Salerno, and the destruction and economic hardship the quake caused were enormous.

To the Present

The regional government has had a twofold mission in recent decades: to fight crime and corruption and to place a focus on Campania's artistic treasures. A walk through Naples, with its artistic and historical attractions, illustrates the success of the latter. The war against crime is an ongoing battle that will have little effect on visitors to Naples and the region.

ART & ARCHITECTURE IN CAMPANIA

Campania's fertile lands bear the traces of many civilizations. Most famous are some of Italy's best-preserved monuments from antiquity, and most notably the superb Greek temples at Paestum and the preserved Roman cities of Pompeii and Herculaneum. You'll also find medieval castles and towns, Norman-Sicilian (or Arab-Norman) architecture, and a treasure trove of Renaissance and baroque art and monuments.

The Greeks & Etruscans

The Greeks and the Etruscans introduced their artistic styles to Campania as early as the 9th century B.C. Greek ruins are thick on the ground, from the ruins of **Cuma**—the first Greek colony in Italy—to the wonderful temples of **Paestum** and the acropolis of **Velia.** The region's jewelry and metalwork bear the mark of Etruscan influence. Influences of both the Greeks and the Etruscans show up in the marvelous statues from the Sanctuary of the Goddess Matuta in **Santa Maria Capua Vetere** (p. 239) and in superb wall paintings from tombs you'll see in the archaeological museums of Naples, Capua, and Paestum.

The Romans

Like savvy home buyers of today, Romans had a fondness for seaside real estate where they could build lavish villas and take a break from the work and politics of the capital. **Herculaneum, Pompeii, Oplontis, Boscoreale,** and **Baiae** were choice spots. The Romans flaunted their flair for public monuments in the amphitheater in **Capua Vetere** and in the triumphal arch in **Benevento.**

The Middle Ages

The cathedrals of **Capua, Salerno,** and **Amalfi** are the richest examples of medieval art in Campania, and the bronze doors at Salerno and Amalfi are some of the finest workmanship to come down from the period. Scenery aside, some of the most transporting sights along the Amalfi Coast are the medieval cloisters of **Amalfi's cathedral** (p. 149), **Ravello's Villa Rufolo** (p. 158), and **Sorrento's Chiesa di San Francesco** (p. 120), bringing together Arab and Sicilian influences. Among the region's cloisters, though, the ones at the **Certosa di San Lorenzo** (p. 224) in Padula is the blockbuster, primarily for its size—the columned porticos surround 1.2 hectares (3 acres) of lawns and gardens. In Naples, Cosimo Fanzago (1591–1678) created cloisters for the **Certosa di San Martino** (p. 69), a grand assemblage of statue-lined porticoes facing a broad lawn.

Renaissance & Baroque

The Renaissance exploded in Naples, as it did everywhere in Italy. Among the famous artists who came to the city from Tuscany to execute lucrative commissions was Donatello (1386–1466), the great Florentine sculptor—his graceful tomb of Cardinal Rinaldo Brancaccio in the **Chiesa di Sant'Angelo a Nilo** (p. 63) is an impressive concoction more than 11m (38 ft.) high. Another outsider with enormous influence was the tempestuous Caravaggio (1571–1610). His sumptuous canvases, with their realistic portrayals of saints and martyrs and dramatic use of light, have become emblematic of the city's emotion-filled baroque style. His dark, moody, and chaotic "Seven Acts of Mercy" altarpiece is in the chapel of the **Pio Monte della Misericordia** (p. 68), and his "Flagellation of Christ" makes the trek out to the **Capodimonte gallery** (p. 72) especially worthwhile.

Neapolitan painters were an especially drama-prone group. Belisario Corenzio (1558–1643), whose color-saturated frescoes cover the **Cappella del Monte di Pietà** (p. 58), was ringleader of the so-called Cabal of Naples. The triumvirate also included the painters Jusepe de Ribera and Batistello Caraciollo, and they dealt with competitors for the city's lucrative commissions by running the lucky ones out of town and poisoning the others. For the **Certosa di San Martino** (p. 69), Ribera (1591–1652) did paintings of martyrdom and suffering that were said to be the "poetry of the repulsive." By 1700, the undisputed head of Neapolitan painting was Francesco Solimena (1657–1747), a wealthy duke and conventional painter who compensated for his lack of genius with flamboyance. His colorful frescoes are in the **Basilica di San Paolo Maggiore** (p. 57), **Chiesa del Gesù Nuovo** (p. 59), and **Chiesa di San Domenico Maggiore** (p. 61). Luca Giordano (1634–1705), a Neapolitan who made his name as a court painter in Spain, returned home to enjoy fame and fortune for his work in **Chiesa dei Girolamini** (p. 59) and **Chiesa di San Gregorio Armeno** (p. 62).

The Capodimonte gallery.

Art & Architecture in Campania

A TASTE OF CAMPANIA

For the Italians, food has always been one of life's great pleasures. This seems to have been the case even from the earliest days, judging from the banqueting scenes in Etruscan tombs. Romans, of course, were especially famous for knowing how to put on a good banquet. Hosts went out of their way to outdo one another with exotic treats. Flamingo tongue, anyone?

While we can only imagine the lavish feasts served in the villas of Baiae, Boscoreale, and other toney ancient Roman resorts around the Bay of Naples, we're familiar with regional cuisine that's a lot more mundane. Americans, especially, associate southern Italian cooking with spaghetti and clam sauce or with *ragù* (meat sauce), meatballs, pizzas, and fried calamari. That's because so many Neapolitans moved to the New World, opened restaurants, and adapted their repertoire to some surefire mainstays to suit their customers' tastes. In your travels you'll discover that the cuisine is a lot more varied and refined. Even something as ordinary as tomato sauce is an entirely different creation here, where tomatoes are a taste sensation all their own. In the countryside, a mountain tradition shows up in dishes flavored with **truffles** and cakes made with **chestnuts.** Pork and wild boar take precedence over fish and seafood, mostly because savvy diners insist on freshness—if the fish you're eating could not have leapt out of the sea onto your plate, it's not really fresh. And fresh is what you should expect from restaurants on the Amalfi Coast and the islands.

Dining Basics

Dining hours tend to be later in Campania than in the United States and the U.K: Lunch is between 1:30 and 4pm and dinner between 8:30 and 11pm. Restaurants will rarely open before 12:30pm or 7:30pm, and often they'll only be setting up at that time.

Although you are not obliged to eat every course, a typical meal starts with an *antipasto*, or appetizer, followed by a first course (*primo*) of pasta or rice. This is followed by a second course (*secondo*) of meat or fish, and/or a vegetable side dish or a salad (*contorno*). Italians finish a meal with cheese (*formaggio*), or a piece of fruit (*frutta*), and, of course, coffee (*caffè*). They'll have dessert (*dolce*) only occasionally, often opting instead for a gelato at a nearby ice-cream parlor. Ordering a cappuccino after lunch or dinner is a social blunder: Cappuccino is a breakfast or midmorning drink. Instead,

A trattoria in Naples.

The Passeggiata

This time-honored tradition takes place nightly in every town in Italy, and is an especially honored tradition in the south. Shortly after 6pm, men and women, young and old alike and dressed in their best, stroll before dinner in the town center, usually through the main piazza and surrounding streets. Often members of the same sex link arms or kiss each other in greeting. There's no easier way to feel a part of everyday life in Italy than to make the passeggiata part of your evening routine, too.

have an espresso. That's what you'll get when you say "Un caffè, per favore," or, to make it a double, "un caffè doppio."

American-style **fast food** is replaced here by specialized restaurants that serve at the counter: *Spaghetterie* serve a large variety of pasta dishes, and they are usually youth-oriented hangouts; *pizza a metro* and *pizza a taglio* are casual pizza parlors, where slices of pizza are sold by size or weight, with limited or nonexistent seating. A *tavola calda* (literally, "hot table") serves ready-made hot foods you can take away or eat at one of the few small tables. A *rosticceria* is the same type of place; you'll see chickens roasting on a spit in the window. *Friggitoria* (frying shops) sell deep-fried vegetables, rice balls (*arancini*), and deep-fried calzones.

For a quick bite, you can also go to a **bar.** Although bars in Italy do serve alcohol, they function mainly as cafes. *Al banco* is the price you pay standing at the bar counter, while *al tavolo* means you are charged two to four times as much for sitting at a table where you'll be waited on. Bars serve local pastries, *panino* sandwiches on various kinds of rolls, and *tramezzini* (white-bread sandwich triangles with the crusts cut off).

A **pizzeria** is a restaurant specializing in individual pizzas, usually cooked in a wood-burning oven. Pizzerias will also sometimes serve pasta dishes, and, typically, the menu includes an array of appetizers as well. A full-fledged restaurant is called an **osteria,** a **trattoria,** or a **ristorante.** Once upon a time, these terms meant something—osteria meant basic, trattoria meant casual full meals, and ristoranti meant fancy. Nowadays, fancy restaurants often call themselves trattorie to cash in on the charm factor, trendy spots use osteria to show they're hip, and simple, inexpensive places sometimes tack on ristorante to ennoble themselves.

The **enoteca** is a marriage of a wine bar and an osteria; you can sit and order from a list of good local and regional wines by the glass while snacking on appetizers or eating from a full menu featuring local specialties. Relaxed and full of ambience, these are great spots for light, inexpensive lunches—or simply recharging your batteries.

The *pane e coperto* (**bread and cover charge**) is a 1€ to 4€ cover charge that you must pay at most restaurants for the mere privilege of sitting at a table. To request the bill, say, "Il conto, per favore" (eel *con*-toh, pore fah-*vohr*-ay).

A tip of 15% is usually included in the bill these days, but if you're unsure, ask, "È incluso il servizio?" (ay een-*cloo*-soh eel sair-*vee*-tsoh?).

At many restaurants, especially larger ones and in cities, you'll find a *menu turistico* (tourist's menu), sometimes called *menu del giorno* (menu of the day) or *menu à prezzo fisso* (fixed-price menu). This set-price menu usually covers all meal incidentals—cover charge and 15% service charge—along with a first course (*primo*) and second course (*secondo*), and sometimes even a drink. It almost always offers an abbreviated selection of pretty common-place dishes and should not be confused with the *menu dégustazione* (tasting menu) that more elegant gourmet restaurants offer. Wherever you eat, it's a good idea to forego the menu entirely and put yourself in the capable hands of your waiter.

Pasta, Mozzarella & Pizza

The stars of Campanian cuisine are so well known that they're almost national symbols. They say a lot about the abundance of what the Romans called *Campania felix,* or fertile countryside, still one of Italy's most productive agricultural regions.

Famous for the quality of their **pasta** since the 16th century, the many mills of the Monti Lattari, at the beginning of the Sorrento Peninsula, are counted among the best producers of pasta in the world (the ones in Gragnano are particularly renowned). The pasta here is still *trafilata a bronzo* (extruded through bronze forms), a procedure that leaves the pasta slightly porous, allowing for a better penetration of the sauce for tastier results (as opposed to steel forms, which makes the pasta perfectly smooth).

This region created the kinds of pasta that we eat today—penne, fusilli, rigatoni, and so on, each type strictly defined: Spaghetti is thicker than vermicelli, and both are thicker than capellini.

The warm plains of Campania are also home to the rare native buffalo that graze on the plains of the provinces of Caserta and Salerno. Campanians have made **mozzarella** with delicious buffalo milk for centuries and look with disdain on what the rest of us know as mozzarella, the similar cheese made with cow's milk. In this region they call that *fiordilatte* (literally, "flower of milk"). Indeed, once you've tasted the real **mozzarella di bufala,** with its unique delicate flavor and lighter texture, you might also look down on regular mozzarella as being inferior. It's delicious as is, or in a *caprese,* a simple salad of sliced mozzarella, fresh tomatoes, and basil seasoned with extra-virgin olive oil.

Putting together the wheat, the mozzarella, and the third famous produce of this region, the tomato, Neapolitans one day invented **pizza.** The unique local tomatoes—especially those produced on the slopes of Mt. Vesuvius—have basically no seeds: Imagine a tomato with no central cavity (no spongy white stuff, either), but filled with fruit meat, flavorful and juicy. These are the *pomodorini* or small tomatoes of Mt. Vesuvius. Obviously the result couldn't be anything but a hit, and pizza quickly spread from Naples throughout the world.

Dough and tomatoes are the key ingredients of Neapolitan pizza, and cheese is an option. If you ask for a Neapolitan pizza in Naples, you'll be offered a "marinara": a thick, puffy crust that is crunchy on the outside and covered with fresh tomatoes, olive oil, and oregano, with no cheese at all. What Romans and the rest of Italy call Neapolitan pizza (*pizza Napoletana*), with tomatoes, cheese, and anchovies, is referred to here in Naples as "Roman pizza" (à la Romana).

The second-most traditional pizza in Naples is the *margherita*. Named after Margherita di Savoia, queen of Italy, who asked to taste pizza during a stay at the Palazzo Reale (Royal Palace) in Naples, the pizza bears the colors of the Italian flag: basil for the green, mozzarella for the white, and red for the tomatoes. The new pizza met with immediate favor, eventually surpassing the popularity of its older counterpart. Pizza evolved with the addition of a large variety of other toppings, but purist pizzerias in Naples (such as Pizzeria Da Michele, p. 81) serve only these two types. In Naples, you can also taste *pizza fritta.* This wonderful creation is served only in truly old-fashioned places, where a double round of pizza dough is filled with ricotta, mozzarella, and ham, and deep-fried in a copper cauldron of scalding olive oil. It arrives as puffy as a ball. As you poke into it, the pizza flattens out, allowing you to delve into the delicious (though not exactly cholesterol-free) dish.

Antipasti e Contorni

Over the centuries, poverty prompted Campanians to create some delicious, simple dishes out of basic ingredients. Check out the *antipasti* buffet of any good restaurant in the region, and you'll find a variety of tasty concoctions made from what's usually been readily available in the region: vegetables and seafood. They might be as straightforward as marinated vegetables, or sautéed clams and mussels toasted in a pan with garlic and olive oil. A short list of regional favorites to look for also include *polipetti in cassuola* or *affogati,* squid cooked with a savory tomato-and-olive sauce inside a small, terra-cotta casserole; *zucchine a scapece,* sliced zucchini sautéed in olive oil and seasoned with tangy vinegar and fresh mint dressing (the same preparation is sometimes used for eggplant); *involtini di melanzane,* a roll of deep-fried eggplant slices, filled with pine nuts and raisins, and warmed up in a tomato sauce; and *friarelli,* a local vegetable that is a cousin to broccoli but much thinner, usually served sautéed with garlic and chili pepper—it's traditionally paired with local sausages.

Soups & Primi

One of the most surprising and delicious combinations you'll come across here is the delicious *zuppa di fagioli e cozze,* beans and mussels soup, a staple on menus south of Naples and on Capri. Another local soup is the *minestra maritata,* a thick concoction of pork meat and a variety of fresh vegetables. The simple comfort food *pasta e patate* (pasta and potatoes smothered with cheese) will surprise you by how tasty it is. At the other end of the spectrum,

The Scoop on Gelato

Gelato is the Italian version of ice cream. It is milk- or egg white–based, with cream used only for certain flavors, and contains less sugar than American ice cream. This makes it much easier to digest, and, in general, less caloric—especially the fruit flavors, which are made with fresh fruit (technically, these are usually water-based, making them *sorbetto*, or sorbet).

You can choose to eat your gelato from a cone (*cono*) or a cup (*coppetta*); the number of flavors you get depends on the size (two scoops for the small and up to four for the large). Locals often ask for a dollop of whipped cream (*panna*) on top: Specify if you don't want it: "senza panna" (sen-zah pan-nah).

Here are some important tips to help you spot the best gelato parlors:

o The bar or parlor bears a sign saying PRODUZIONE PROPRIA or PRODUZIONE ARTIGIANALE, which means it is made fresh, in small batches, and from fresh, mostly local, ingredients (no large-scale industrial production).

o Avoid overly bright colors—no neon green for pistachio, for instance, or bright yellow for lemon. Natural colors are off-white for banana, pale green for pistachio, and white for lemon.

o The flavors on offer include seasonal fruits, such as peach, apricot, and watermelon in summer, and orange, mandarin, and chocolate in winter.

o They tend to be gelato specialists: Gelato is all they sell, or at least, the section devoted to it is substantial, with a large cold counter well in view.

Another cold treat is a *granita*, a close cousin to a slushie. A classic granita is made from frozen lemon juice (made from real lemons, of course) or coffee, but other flavors are sometimes available. Coffee-flavored granite are usually served with *panna*. You'll also see street carts selling shaved ice with flavored syrup, also called granite. It's a good and refreshing treat, but not quite the same thing.

the elaborate *sartù*, a typical Neapolitan baked dish made with seasoned rice, small meatballs, sausages, chicken liver, mozzarella, and mushrooms, matches the labor intensity of its preparation with the satisfaction of eating it.

Local pasta includes *scialatielli*, fresh, eggless flat noodles served with sautéed seafood (*ai frutti di mare*). Fusilli is served with all the region's traditional sauces: *con le vongole* (with clams), *zucchine e gamberi* (shrimp and zucchini), or *al ragù,* a sauce in which many kinds of meat are cooked with tomatoes. Cooks in the region would be shocked that it needs to be said, but any good restaurant makes its own pasta, usually with grain from a local and well-vetted mill.

Secondi

The cuisine of Naples—shared by most of Campania's coast—focuses on seafood. The *frittura* (*fritto misto* elsewhere in Italy) of shrimp and calamari is a staple, as is *fragaglie,* with very small fish. Large fish is served grilled, with a tasty dressing of herbs and olive oil; *all'acqua pazza*, poached in a light broth made of a few tomatoes and herbs; or *alle patate*, baked over a bed of thinly sliced potatoes. You might also find fish *al sale,* baked in a salt crust to retain its moisture and flavors. *Zuppa di pesce* is the expensive specialty of some kitchens, but much more common and equally delicious are the *polpi affogati* or *in cassuola,* squid or octopus slowly stewed with tomatoes and parsley.

This isn't beef country, like Tuscany is, though one of the specialties you'll encounter when you travel inland is *brasato,* beef slowly stewed with wine and vegetables. You might also come across beef *alla pizzaiola,* a beef cutlet sautéed in olive oil and cooked with fresh tomatoes and oregano. *Braciola di maiale* is a pork cutlet filled with prosciutto, pine nuts, and raisins, rolled, and cooked in a tomato sauce. *Coniglio all Ischitana,* rabbit baked with wine and black olives, is a menu staple on Ischia, especially once you get off the coast and into the mountains.

Sweets

If Sicilians are famous for having a sweet tooth, Neapolitans come in a close second. Naples is famous for its *pastiera,* a cake traditionally prepared for Easter but so good that it is now offered year-round in most restaurants. Whole-grain wheat is soaked, boiled, and then used to prepare a delicious creamy filling with ricotta and orange peel in a thick pastry shell.

Another famous dessert is *babà,* a soft, puffy cake soaked in a sweet syrup with rum and served with pastry cream. The famous *sfogliatelle* (flaky pastry pockets filled with a sweet ricotta cream) are so good with typical Neapolitan coffee that you will never again settle for coffee and a doughnut back home. A specialty from Conca dei Marini on the Amalfi Coast is *sfogliatella Santa Rosa,* filled with pastry cream and *amarene* (candied sour cherries in syrup) instead of ricotta, invented by nuns at the 14th-century Convento di Santa Rosa.

Each town in Campania has some kind of sweet specialty, so you can happily munch your way through the region: *ravioli al limone,* filled with a lemon-flavored ricotta mixture, from Positano; the *Sospiri* (Sighs)—also called *Zizz'e Nonache* (Nuns' Breasts)—dome-shaped small, pale pastries filled with lemon cream from Maiori and Minori; and *dolcezze al limone,* puff pastries filled with lemon-flavored cream from Sorrento.

And Some Vino to Wash It All Down

Italy is the largest wine-producing country in the world, with more than 1.6 million hectares (4 million acres) planted with vineyards. Grapes were cultivated as far back as 800 B.C., probably introduced by the Greeks, and wine has been produced ever since. However, it wasn't until 1965 that laws were enacted to guarantee consistency in winemaking and to defend specific labels. Winemakers must apply for the right to add "D.O.C." (*Denominazione di Origine Controllata*) on their labels, and only consistently good wines from specific areas receive this right. The "D.O.C.G." on a label (the "G" means *Garantita*) applies to even better wines from even more strictly-defined producing areas. Vintners who are presently limited to marketing their products as unpretentious table wines—*vino da tavola*—often expend great efforts lobbying for an elevated status as a D.O.C.

Of Campania's five provinces, Benevento has the largest number of D.O.C. wines, including the *Aglianico del Taburno, Solopaca, Guardiolo, Sannio, Sant'Agata dei Goti,* and *Taburno.* Avellino is the viniculture star with three D.O.C.G. wines: the earthy red *Taurasi* and two whites, *Greco di Tufo* and *Fiano di Avellino.*

Other D.O.C.s to look for in the region are *Falerno,* from Caserta; *Campi Flegrei,* from the area around Pozzuoli; *Furore,* from the Amalfi Coast; *Castel San Lorenzo,* from Salerno; and *Galluccio* and *Asprino d'Aversa,* from Salerno.

Just because a wine isn't D.O.C. doesn't mean it should be shunned. From the volcanic soil of Mt. Vesuvius comes the amber-colored *Lacrima Christi* **(Tears of Christ),** while the whites of Capri and the reds and whites of Ischia complement an island meal.

Other Drinks

Campania also excels at the preparation of *rosolio,* sweet liquor that is usually herb- or fruit-flavored, prepared according to recipes passed down by families for generations. The most famous is *limoncello,* a staple in lemon-growing Capri and Sorrento. Travelers either come away with a nostalgic affection for the drink, or, especially those who prefer their alcohol stiff and not sweet, a lifelong aversion to anything lemony. Recipes for the concoction have been passed down through families for generations. Restaurants in Naples, along the Amalfi Coast, and on Capri often make their own versions, and *limoncello* is these days almost as much a national beverage as Campari. Taking second billing to *limoncello* in the rosolio lineup, but no less praiseworthy, are *nanassino,* made with prickly pears; and *finocchietto,* made with wild fennel.

WHEN TO GO

The best months for a visit are **April to June** and **September to October.** Temperatures are usually mild, and the crowds aren't nearly as intense as they can be at the height of the summer. If you plan on spending time on the beach, think about May and September, when you can be assured of decent weather and warmer waters and seaside resorts still won't be as crowded and expensive as they are in high season. Starting in mid-June, the summer rush begins at the seaside resorts; from **July to August,** the coast teems with visitors. **Mid-August** is the busiest, as the entire country goes on vacation around the holiday of **Ferragosto,** on August 15. While the cities tend to be deserted at this time—in Naples, Benevento, Caserta, and Salerno many restaurants and shops will be padlocked—the seaside towns and island resorts buzz with activity. The interior never gets really crowded, though summer temperatures can be hot and you might find many businesses closed during the August exodus to the seaside and mountains. From **November to Easter,** attractions outside of Naples often go to shorter winter hours, and many hotels and restaurants along the Amalfi Coast and on Capri and Ischia close.

Weather

Campania enjoys four well-defined seasons. Winters are mild, spring and fall are pleasant, and summers are hot. July and August are very hot, especially in low-lying areas. The high temperatures begin in Naples in May, often lasting until sometime in October. For the most part, though, the humidity is lower in Campania than it is, say, in Washington, D.C., so high temperatures don't seem as oppressive. In Naples, temperatures can stay in the 90°F (30°C) range for days, but nights are often comfortably cool.

Winters are mild by the sea, with temperatures averaging 50°F (10°C). It gets much colder in the interior and the mountains, where it can snow. Precipitation tends to be rare in summer but increases abruptly in the fall, which tends to be the wettest season.

Holidays

Banks, government offices, post offices, and many stores, restaurants, and museums are closed on the following **national holidays:** January 1 (New Year's Day), January 6 (Epiphany), Easter Monday, April 25 (Liberation Day), May 1 (Labor Day), June 2 (Republic Day), August 15 (Ferragosto/ Assumption of the Virgin), November 1 (All Saints' Day), December 8 (Feast of the Immaculate Conception), December 25 (Christmas Day), and December 26 (Santo Stefano). Roman Catholic holidays are deeply felt in Campania. Closings are common on **feast days** honoring the patron saint of each town and village, when processions are organized through the historic district and around the town's main church or cathedral. In Naples, September 19 celebrates the Feast of St. Gennaro; in Salerno, September 21 celebrates the Feast of St. Matteo; and Amalfi celebrates the Feast of St. Andrea on June 27 and November 30.

Campania Calendar of Events

JANUARY

Il Presepe nel Presepe (Manger in a Manger), Morcone. Villagers transform a hamlet near Benevento into a version of Bethlehem and open their homes to visitors. January 3.

Epiphany celebrations, region-wide. Epiphany festivities include numerous fairs and processions celebrating the arrival of the Three Kings at Christ's manger. January 6.

Festival Internazionale della Canzone Napoletana ed Italiana (International Festival of Italian and Neapolitan Song), Capua. This 3-day event gathers performers and music lovers for a celebration of Italian folk music, both new and traditional. End of January.

FEBRUARY

Carnival, region-wide. Just before Lent, most towns, big and small, put on parades and histrionic pageants. Some of the best are in *Capua. Paestum* also stages a great parade and dance shows. Usually during the week before Ash Wednesday.

MARCH & APRIL

Pasqua (Easter), region-wide. Celebrations include several events: Processions for the benediction of the symbolic palm—usually olive tree branches—take place on the Sunday before Easter Sunday; Stations of the Cross processions (reenacting Jesus' ascent to Golgotha) are staged on Holy Friday; and Easter Sunday is marked by special religious celebrations. Various dates between end of March and April.

Pasqua a Sorrento (Easter in Sorrento), Sorrento. These Easter celebrations last a whole week; religious processions and concerts are scheduled in the town's cathedral and in the delightful cloister of San Francesco. Other processions take place on the night of Holy Thursday through Holy Friday in the towns surrounding Sorrento: Meta, Piano di Sorrento, and Sant'Agnello. Week before Easter.

Processione dei Misteri (Procession of the Mysteries), Procida. A procession of scenes from the Passion of Christ sculpted by local craftspeople is one of the most famous traditional religious events in Campania. The tableaux depict the betrayal of Judas, the Last Supper, and other events, and this island tradition since 1627 also features large statues of Christ and the Madonna. Holy Thursday night into Holy Friday morning.

MAY

Feast of San Costanzo, Marina Grande, Capri. This day honors St. Costanzo, who died in Capri on his way to Constantinople around A.D. 677 and whose remains long afterward protected islanders from pirate attacks. May 14.

Maggio dei Monumenti (Monuments in May), Naples. The *centro storico* (old city center) comes alive for a week of concerts and special openings of private collections and monuments normally closed to the public. Last week of May.

JUNE

Historic Regatta of the Maritime Republics, Amalfi. Each of Italy's four historical towns—Genova, Pisa, Venice, and Amalfi—take turns hosting this annual regatta. Amalfi's turn comes around again in 2017. First Sunday in June.

Concerti al Tramonto, Anacapri. The Villa San Michele is the setting for spectacular sunset concerts (classical and jazz). www.villasanmichele.eu. June through August.

Il Trionfo del Tempo e del Disinganno (The Triumph of Time and Enlightenment), provinces of Caserta and Benevento. A festival of medieval, Renaissance, and baroque music presents high-quality performances in little-known historical buildings, some of which are not usually open to the general public. trionfo.altervista.org. Second half of June through the end of August.

Leuciana Festival, Caserta. A rich program of musical, theatrical, and dance performances are staged in the Reggia and in the scenic Belvedere di San Leucio. www.leuciana.org. June through August.

JULY

Sagra del Limone (Lemon Fair), Massa Lubrense. Walks in the countryside, farm visits, and culinary events celebrate the local fruit. First weekend in July.

Benevento Citta' Spettacolo, Benevento. The ancient Roman theater is the venue for a full-fledged summer season of opera and drama. July through August.

Festival Ville Vesuviane, Ercolano. Popular Italian singers perform at the splendid villas of the Miglio d'Oro, the stretch of some 122 elegant villas the 18th-century Bourbon court built at the foot of Mt. Vesuvius. Throughout July.

Ischia Film Festival, Ischia. The island where the great director Luchino Visconti summered screens some 100 films from more than 20 countries. www.ischiafilmfestival.it. One week in July.

Neapolis Festival, Naples. Rock always has devoted fans, and this 2-day festival showcases some of the best groups in Italy and the world. www.neapolis.it. July.

Ravello Festival, Ravello. The romantic garden of Villa Rufolo and the striking new Auditorium Niemeyer are among the settings of the internationally renowned festival of classical music, jazz, dance, and the visual arts. Make reservations well in advance. www.ravellofestival.com. July through September.

Festa del Mare, town of Ischia. A procession of boats floats across the harbor beneath the illuminated Castello Aragonese to celebrate the Festival of Sant'Anna. July 26.

AUGUST

Festival of the Assunta, Positano. Villagers reenact those perilous 9th- and 10th-century days when pirates regularly raided the coast and the Madonna was called upon time and again to miraculously intervene on the town's behalf. August 14 and 15.

Incontri Musicali Sorrentini (Sorrentine Musical Encounters), Sorrento. The peaceful cloister of the church of St. Francis hosts 3 weeks of classical concerts. August through September.

Music in the Cloister, Amalfi. The splendid Chiostro del Paradiso of Amalfi's cathedral is the evocative settings for concerts. Usually on Fridays at 9pm from the beginning of August to mid-September.

Musica negli Scavi Archeologici, Ercolano. Classical concerts are staged amid the ruins of Herculaneum and in the 18th-century Villa Campolieto. August through September.

Sagra della Sfogliatella di Santa Rosa, Conca dei Marini. The guest of honor is the local version of *sfogliatella,* the most famous of Neapolitan pastries, filled here with pastry cream and *amarene* (candied sour cherries in syrup). August.

Surrentum Grandi Eventi, Sorrento. The beautiful Villa Fiorentino is the setting for dance, theater, and music performances. www.festivaldellospettacolo.it. August.

Settembre al Borgo (September in the Village), Casertavecchia. For 10 days, the medieval *borgo* comes alive with music and other performances. www.casertamusica.com. End of August to the beginning of September.

SEPTEMBER

Festa di Piedigrotta, Naples. The famous song "O Sole Mio" was presented at this festival for the first time in 1898, and traditional music still fills squares around the city. First 2 weeks in September.

Ischia Jazz Festival, Ischia. Jazz musicians and fans come to the island from around the world. www.ischiajazz.com. Usually first week of September.

Santa Maria della Libera, Capri. A grand procession honoring island patron St. Costanzo is accompanied by music and fireworks. The Sunday closest to September 12.

NOVEMBER

Feast of St. Andrew, Amalfi. The town honors its patron and protector of fishermen with a dash from the beach up the steps of the cathedral—a rigorous jaunt in itself, all the harder since runners carry a heavy statue of the saint on their shoulders. Townsfolk then present the saint with offerings of fish (fresh and carved) and enjoy a fireworks display. November 30.

DECEMBER

Sagra della Salsiccia e Ceppone (Sausage and Bonfire Fair), Sorrento. About 91kg (200 lb.) of delicious local sausages are barbecued over a huge fire then consumed with large quantities of the local wine. December 13.

Divers' Procession to Grotta dello Smeraldo, Conca dei Marini. Scuba divers swim from the beach to an underwater manger inside the Grotta dello Smeraldo. December 24 and January 6.

Live Manger, Belvedere di San Leucio, Caserta. The 18th-century hamlet turns the clock back with nativity reenactments and seasonal music. December 25 to January 6.

Sagra della Zeppola (Feast of the Zeppola), Positano. Celebrants ring in the New Year by feasting on *zeppolas,* delicious fried sweet pastries, and dancing on the beach of Marina Grande as fireworks explode overhead. December 31 through January 1.

SUGGESTED ITINERARIES

3

S o, you have a week, maybe even two, to explore one small slice of Italy. That's great, but beware. Like other parts of Italy, Naples and its surroundings—the Amalfi Coast, the islands floating offshore, the mountains and coasts to the south, the inland towns—can be deceptive. Though you're tackling just one region, there is so much to see and do, so many experiences to have and character-filled hotels to hide out in, and so much food to sample that you'll feel pressed no matter how much time you have. That's not a problem, just a testament to the allure of this sun-kissed part of the world.

Consider how much there is to see and do, but don't feel overwhelmed, just enthused, by the prospects. Naples, Italy's third-largest city, is a pleasure to explore. Aside from enjoying the riveting street theater that passes for everyday life, you'll also discover museums and churches packed with riches. To the west are the weird volcanic landscapes and evocative ancient ruins of the Campi Flegrei, the Phlegraean Fields. To the east along the bay are two of the world's most famous and best-preserved ancient cities, Herculaneum and Pompeii, and the volcano that doomed them, Vesuvius. Just beyond them is the beautiful Sorrento Peninsula and the Amalfi Coast, two of the world's most beguiling seaside getaways. A triumvirate of enchanting islands, Capri, Ischia, and Procida, float alluringly in the Bay of Naples. To the south of the Amalfi Coast is Paestum, where some of the best-preserved Greek temples in the world stand proudly amid fields of wildflowers. Inland from Naples is yet another treasure, often bypassed—the Reggia of Caserta, a white elephant of a palace that's larger and maybe even a little grander than Versailles. As if that's not enough, nearby are the Roman ruins of Capua and Benevento. And there's a lot more in between.

How to take it all in? The following itineraries show you how to enjoy our favorite places at a reasonable pace. You might want to speed up, or slow down, or make your own discoveries. Keep in mind that throughout most of the region, distances are fairly short, so you can settle in at one base for a few days and see quite a bit from there. Wherever you end up going, we suggest you use public transportation. Trains, boats, and buses make it easy to get around. Sailing around the Bay of Naples or up and down the Amalfi Coast on a ferry is part of the fun of being here. If you have any notion of sportily zipping along a seaside *corniche,* you'll be stopped in your tracks, literally, once you hit the traffic-choked Amalfi Drive in summer. Take heart: The scenic trip along the coast on the public bus is one the world's most inexpensive thrill rides.

IF YOU HAVE ONLY 1 WEEK

A week? So much to see, so little time. Well, that's more time than a lot of folks have in the region, so let's make the most of it. Pressed as you'll be to cover a lot of turf, remember to slow down a bit just to linger, because that's one of the best things to do in this part of the world.

Day 1: Naples ★★

I'm giving you two days in Naples, but you'll want to divide and conquer. See the city in halves, the old center first, the more salubrious waterfront and heights the next day. Start by plunging into the part of the Historical Center east of Via Toledo that's often called **Spaccanapoli.** Not only will the chaotic, noisy, laundry-hung lanes immerse you in Neapolitan life, but there's a church or two on every block to introduce you to the city's rich artistic legacy. In just a few hours, you can step into three of the finest, all near each other.

Begin in Piazza Dante and follow Via Pont d'Alba east to Via dei Tribunali, the cobbled street that was the main artery of the Greek and Roman city. In fact, you will descend into the *scavi* (excavations) of the marketplace of the Greek city, Neapolis, at your first stop, the basilica of **San Lorenzo Maggiore** (p. 68). Not only will you be transported to the ancient world, but this is also the finest medieval church in the city, with beautiful cloisters. Just a couple of blocks farther along is **Pio Monte della Misericordia** (p. 68), an octagonal chapel with the dark, moody, and chaotic "Seven Acts of Mercy" altarpiece by the greatest 17th-century painter of them all, Caravaggio. Head back west a couple of blocks to what might be the most delightful street in Naples, **Via San Gregorio Armeno** (p. 63), where shop windows are jammed with nativity scenes, *presepi.* Pickpockets along the street are up to unholy misdeeds, so watch your wallet. The church of **San Gregorio Armeno** (p. 62) is a baroque extravaganza with acres of candlelit gilt and frescoes by Luca Giordana, one of many Neapolitan masters whose lives were as colorful as their works. Okay, those are enough churches for one day. Now head back to Via dei Tribunali for a late lunch at **Pizzeria Gino Sorbillo** (p. 82) to taste for yourself why Neapolitan pizza is considered the best in the world.

Naples & the Amalfi Coast

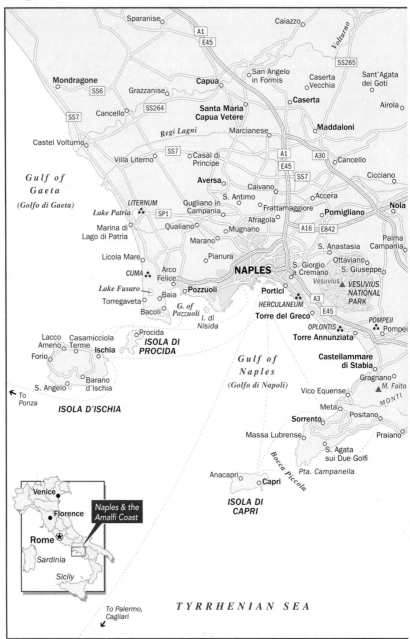

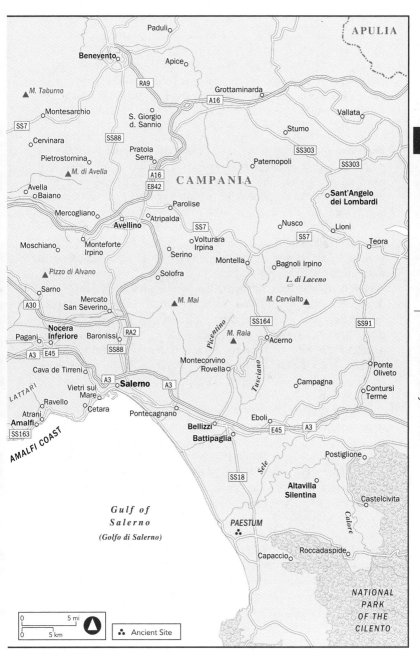

Paduli

APULIA

Benevento

Apice

M. Taburno

RA9

Grottaminarda

A16

Montesarchio

S. Giorgio
d. Sannio

Vallata

SS7

Stumo

Cervinara

SS88

SS303

Pietrostornina

Pratola
Serra

Paternopoli

SS303

M. di Avella

A16

CAMPANIA

E842

Avella
Baiano

Parolise

Sant'Angelo
dei Lombardi

Mercogliano

Atripalda

Avellino

SS7

Nusco

Lioni

Moschiano

Monteforte
Irpino

Volturara
Irpina

Teora

SS7

Serino

Montella

Bagnoli Irpino

Pizzo di Alvano

Solofra

L. di Laceno

Sarno

Mercato
San Severino

M. Mai

M. Cervialto

A30

SS164

SS91

Nocera
Inferiore

Baronissi

RA2

M. Raia

Pagani

Acerno

A3 E45

SS88

Montecorvino
Rovella

Cava de Tirreni

A3

Campagna

Ponte
Oliveto

LATTARI

Vietri sul
Mare

Salerno

A3

Contursi
Terme

Ravello

Cetara

Pontecagnano

Atrani

Eboli

Amalfi

Bellizzi

E45

A3

SS163

AMALFI COAST

Battipaglia

Postiglione

Gulf of
Salerno

(Golfo di Salerno)

SS18

Altavilla
Silentina

Castelcivita

PAESTUM

Sele

Calore

Capaccio

Roccadaspide

NATIONAL
PARK
OF THE
CILENTO

Picentino

Tusciano

0   5 mi

0   5 km

Ancient Site

31

Via del Sole will take you north to the **National Archeological Museum** (p. 65) and its treasure trove of frescoes, statuary, and other finds from Pompeii and elsewhere in the ancient world. The museum is open until 7:30, so you have time to browse at your leisure. You might find that the Farnese statues from the Baths of Caracalla in Rome are as riveting as the Pompeii finds. When you can't focus on another bit of antiquity, you're well-poised for dinner in nearby Piazza Bellini, at **La Stanza del Gusto** (p. 79) or one of the other restaurants on this square filled with outdoor cafes.

Day 2: Naples ★★

Begin day 2 with a cup of coffee at **Gran Caffè Gambrinus** (p. 83). No need to pay extra money to sit down—even standing at the ornate, mirrored bar, a throwback to more extravagant times, is a pleasure. Outside the door is **Piazza del Plebiscito** (p. 56). This vast expanse of paving stones is a good introduction to some of the city's greatest public spaces and monuments, many of them nearby. Take a look at the front of the **Palazzo Reale** and the other neoclassical facades that surround it, then walk backward between the two kings on horseback in the middle of the square (ensured to bring good luck).

Now head inland past the ornate facade of **Teatro San Carlo** (p. 56), the world's oldest opera house, from 1737, to the **Galleria Umberto I** (p. 53), for a walk through the glass-roofed arcades lined with shops and cafes. Leave through the eastern arcade so you'll be close to **Piazza Municipio,** to stop for a look at the remarkable seaside **Castel Nuovo** (p. 52). This is a fantasy of a medieval storybook castle with a moat, crenellations, and a white-marble Triumphal Arch squeezed between two turrets.

It's a pleasant seaside walk of about a mile west from here to one more regal stop, **Castel dell'Ovo** (p. 52), and lunch—or you can take the handy N1 bus from Piazza Municipo to the corner Via Morelli and walk about 5 minutes from there. The outrageously picturesque castle is wedged onto a tiny island, **Borgo Marinaro,** and surrounded by fishermen's houses, many of which are now restaurants. **Zi Teresa** (p. 80) is an old favorite, where you can enjoy a seafood lunch on a terrace next to bobbing boats.

An after-lunch stroll takes you through the pleasant **Chiaia** neighborhood to the Parco Margherita funicular stop for the uphill ride to **Villa La Floridiana** (p. 71). Salons glisten with a stash of priceless ceramics, and the lush gardens with turtle-filled ponds and fake ruins that frame city views are ideal for relaxing for an hour or so. Just along the hilltop are Castel San Elmo and the adjacent San Martino monastery. The sweeping views across the city bring Neapolitans up here for a sunset stroll, but if you have the stamina, the **Museo Nazionale di San Martino** (p. 70) is open until 7:30 and shows off everything from paintings and royal barges to the world's largest nativity scene.

From the nearby Morghen station, a funicular will take you back down to Montesanto, in the middle of the old city. That puts you temptingly close to dinner at **Nennella** (p. 81), a local favorite for home-style Neapolitan cooking.

Day 3: Sorrento ★★★

No need to get up at the crack of dawn; Sorrento is only an hour from Naples on the convenient Circumvesuviana railroad. Once there you can enjoy a leisurely afternoon after you settle into your hotel. Unpack. You'll be staying in Sorrento and taking day trips from there. Then I suggest jumping into some cool water: Take the bus out to **Bagno della Regina Giovanna** (Queen Giovanna's Bath; p. 122) at Punta del Capo and swim in a little cove beneath the ruins of a Roman villa. Come evening, you'll want to join Sorrentines in a passeggiata through the old city center, with some time for pre-dinner lingering in a cafe in Piazza Tasso.

Day 4: Day Trip to Amalfi & Ravello ★★★

Time to explore farther afield. Take a boat to **Amalfi** (p. 117) to experience the sight of the rocky coast from the sea, and once there spend a couple of hours or so seeing the exotic, Arabesque cathedral and walking through the mazelike town. An almost mandatory stop is **Pasticceria Pansa,** on Piazza Duomo, for a *delizia al limone.*

Then take the bus up to **Ravello** (p. 155), to stroll in the gardens and gaze up and down the coastline—but begin with lunch at **Cumpa' Cosimo** (p. 161), where Netta Bottone accompanies her heaping pasta platters with a kiss on the cheek. You'll do a bit of walking in Ravello, but the view from the **Belvedere Cimbrone** (p. 158), where you'll feel suspended between sea and sky, should revitalize you for the trip home. Take the bus back down to Amalfi, and switch there to the Sorrento-bound bus. The trip up the narrow, cliff-hugging road is a thrill ride, and you might notice just how worn out the armrests are from all those tight grips of nervous hands. Grab a seat on the left-hand side to best enjoy the epic vistas of cliffs and sea.

Day 5: Day Trip to Pompeii or Herculaneum ★★★

Get back onto the Circumvesuviana railroad for the trip to **Pompeii** (p. 97), 25 minutes north around the bay. If you've been to Pompeii before, visit **Herculaneum** (p. 97) instead (about 40 minutes on the Circumvesuviana). If you haven't been to either, Pompeii provides the more sensational experience. Whichever you choose, plan to arrive mid- to late-morning, so you won't feel too rushed and can poke around the astonishing, ruined ancient cities at your leisure.

Day 6: Capri ★★★

Board a morning ferry for the short crossing to Capri. This leaves you the afternoon to settle in, relax, and do a bit of exploring—a walk along

Naples & the Amalfi Coast in 1 or 2 Weeks

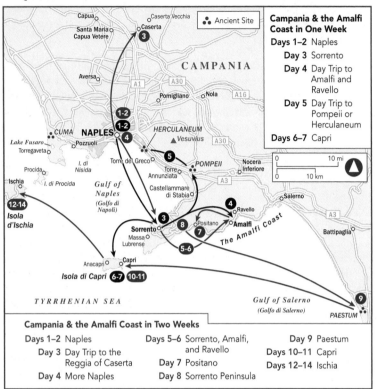

Campania & the Amalfi Coast in One Week

Days 1–2 Naples
Day 3 Sorrento
Day 4 Day Trip to Amalfi and Ravello
Day 5 Day Trip to Pompeii or Herculaneum
Days 6–7 Capri

Campania & the Amalfi Coast in Two Weeks

Days 1–2 Naples	Days 5–6 Sorrento, Amalfi, and Ravello	Day 9 Paestum
Day 3 Day Trip to the Reggia of Caserta	Day 7 Positano	Days 10–11 Capri
Day 4 More Naples	Day 8 Sorrento Peninsula	Days 12–14 Ischia

the pine-shaded paths out to **Punta Tragara** (p. 177) and the much-photographed **Faraglioni** rock spires (p. 177) is a good introduction to the beauty of the island. Next, an evening *aperitivo* in Capri Town's Piazzetta shows off the island's worldly sheen.

Day 7: Capri ★★★

Spend the morning of day 2 visiting **Villa San Michel**e (p. 182), with its beautiful gardens and transporting views. You don't want to rush things on Capri, but if you get there by 10 am or so you might miss the crowds of day-trippers. Follow the visit with a ride to the top of **Monte Solaro** (p. 182) on the chairlift. Then it's time to indulge in one of the island's great pastimes, lunch and a swim at one of the beach clubs (*stabilimenti balneari*). Top choice is **La Fontelina** (p. 188), tucked into the base of the Faraglioni. Lunching, lazing, and swimming will happily fill the rest of your final day.

CAMPANIA & THE AMALFI COAST IN 2 WEEKS

Two weeks—so much better than one! You'll have all that much more time to explore and better appreciate this rich region.

Days 1 & 2: Naples ★★

The itinerary suggested in "If You Have Only 1 Week," above, will help you plan days 1 and 2, but you have two extra days to see the city and its surroundings.

Day 3: Day Trip to the Reggia of Caserta

Next up is a visit to the magnificent royal palace just inland, **Reggia of Caserta** (see p. 232). **Caserta** is only 30 minutes by train from the central station in Naples, and trains arrive in the town center, next to the entrance of the palace built for the Bourbon kings of Naples and the largest royal residence in the world. A mid-morning arrival gives you time to spend a few hours in the palace and gardens and enjoy lunch just outside the palace grounds on the patio of **Antica Hostaria Massa** (p. 238). Then get on a train for the 10-minute trip to **Santa Maria Capua Venere** (p. 239) for a look at the magnificent amphitheater, second in size only to the Coliseum in Rome. From there you can take a train directly back to Naples.

Day 4: More Naples

Spend a good part of the day roaming around the Capodimonte district, north of the center. The metro doesn't go out there, but the R4 bus from

Reggia of Caserta.

in front the Archeological Museum will deliver you to the front door of the **Museo e Gallerie Nazionale di Capodimonte** (p. 72). Begin with a walk through the galleries, where standouts include "The Flagellation of Christ," by Caravaggio, and part of an admirable contemporary collection, Andy Warhol's iconic "Mt. Vesuvius." I'm also quite fond of the depiction of wild beasts setting upon San Gennaro by Artemisia Gentileschi (1593–1656), the only successful female artist of the Neapolitan baroque. That painting will set the stage for your encounter with the saint in the **Catacombs of San Gennaro** (p. 71), about a 10-minute walk east of the museum. On the way, make a stop for lunch at **Trattoria da Luisa,** a neighborhood favorite just outside the museum's Porta Grande entrance at Via Sant'Antonio a Capodimonte 19 (© **081-449766;** open daily noon to 3pm and 7 to 11pm). Gennaro is among those interred in frescoed underground burial niches from the 2nd to 11th centuries. The R4 bus will take you back to the Archeological Museum in about 25 minutes.

Days 5 & 6: Sorrento, Amalfi & Ravello ★★★

Follow the itinerary suggested in "If You Have Only 1 Week," above, for days 5 and 6 of your visit.

Day 7: Positano ★★★

Head back down the coast to **Positano** (p. 133). You can take the bus ride down this beautiful coastline every day and never tire of the views. From Positano's main bus stop (it's the second one in town, coming from Sorrento), follow the warren of lanes down past the majolica-domed **Collegiata di Santa Maria Assunta** until you come to the beach at **Marina Grande.** From there, follow Via Positanesi d'America, a cliff-side pedestrian promenade, around a small cape to the slightly more relaxing beach of **Fornillo.** The lemon-scented terrace of **Pupetto** (p. 139) is a great spot for a leisurely light lunch. That might spill over into some beach time, or better yet, walk back to Marina Grande and rent a boat to poke along the cove-studded coast. By the time you pull back into port, Positano should be coming back to life after the afternoon lull. Walking back up through town to the bus stop along the shop-lined lanes will be like navigating your way through a crowded souk. Head back to Sorrento for the night.

Day 8: Sorrento Peninsula ★★

Take the bus to **Sant'Agata sui Due Golfi** for an eyeful of views up and down the coast, and true to the two gulfs part of the name, across the Gulf of Naples and the Gulf of Sorrento. The best outlooks are from the **Convento del Deserto,** on a hillside about a kilometer (half a mile) outside town. Hop the bus again to **Marina del Cantone** (buses run fairly often), with a nice strip of beach backed by a few restaurants. A good spot for lunch is waterfront **Maria Grazia** (p. 131), leaving you some beach time before getting the bus back to Sorrento.

Day 9: Paestum ★★

How you get to Paestum will depend on the time of year. If boats are running between Sorrento and Salerno (check www.alicost.it), the quickest and most pleasant route is by ferry to Salerno, with a transfer there to the Paestum train; the entire trip will take you a little over 2 hours. Another fairly quick route is via the Circumvesuviana train to Pompeii with a transfer from the Circumvesuviana station to the mainline train station (about a 20-minute walk or short cab ride) for the train to Paestum; this trip, too, takes a little over 2 hours. Spending the night in Paestum leaves a good stretch of the afternoon free to roam around the ruins

Certosa di San Giacomo.

of the magnificent Greek temple and see the archeological museum at leisure, with some time on the nearby beaches as well. Cap the day with dinner at **Il Granaio dei Casabella** (p. 223).

Days 10 & 11: Capri ★★★

On the morning of day 10, take the train back to Salerno and transfer there to the hydrofoil to Capri. See "If You Have Only 1 Week," above, for suggestions on how to spend time on the island.

On day 11, when you'll be moving onto Ischia, schedule a mid-afternoon boat so you can enjoy some extra time on Capri. You can probably arrange for your hotel to transfer your bags to the dock so you're free to roam. A good sendoff would be walk around the fringes of Capri Town through the **Giardini di Augusto** (p. 174) and into the cloisters of the **Certosa di San Giacomo** (p. 174) for more of those heart-stopping views. Time permitting, make the trek along the southern shore for a lunch at **Grottelle** (p. 186), tucked into the seaside cliffs. Just be sure to allow at least an hour for the walk back to Capri Town and the funicular trip down to Marina Grande.

Days 12–14: Ischia ★★★

Your late afternoon arrival leaves time to settle into your hotel and engage in one of the island's favorite evening pastimes: lingering over the local wine at the cafes that line the seafronts of all the coastal towns.

Devote the next day to exploring the island on the efficient bus network. The entire circuit of the island only takes an hour and a half, with buses running in either direction about every half-hour. Your first stop is **Ponte Ischia** and the remarkable **Castello Aragonese** (p. 193), a heavily fortified citadel atop an offshore rock where you can wander down medieval lanes and along breezy ramparts. Follow up the visit with lunch at **Da Ciccio** (p. 202), just across from the walls, before heading south to the pretty seaside village of Sant'Angelo, tucked into the flanks of another rocky outcropping. From the harbor, hop aboard one of the boats to make the short trip out to surrounding coves, where hot springs bubble up under the sea and the sand gets so hot that crafty cooks bury their food for a beach roast. The final stop is **Villa La Mortella** (p. 196), outside Forio, with its magnificent gardens. La Mortella is not open on Monday, Wednesday, and Friday, so it may be necessary to work this stop into the next day instead.

Your final day is given over to relaxation. Spend the better part at **Parco Termale Negombo** (p. 199), where you can climb in and out of 12 hot-spring–fed swimming pools, spend time on the beautiful, adjacent San Montano beach, and get out of the sun beneath a canopy of exotic vegetation. The park is near Villa La Mortella, so if you didn't see those gardens the day before, take time out from the lounging for a visit. If you've already seen the gardens and can tear yourself away from the waters, you can also visit **La Colombaia** (p. 196), the exotic seaside villa of film director Luchino Visconti.

CAMPANIA & THE AMALFI COAST FOR FAMILIES

Kids, like their parents, will never be bored in this region, where they can spend most of their time outdoors. Beaches, castles, cool ruins, sea caves, and all sorts of other wonders provide a jam-packed and fun itinerary. Even getting around—on boats, trains, funicular, and chairlifts—can be a ball.

Days 1 & 2: Ischia ★★

This family-friendly island, ringed with good beaches, is a great place to launch a vacation with kids. On the first day, take your young traveling companions for a swim day unlike any they've ever had before at **Parco Termale Giardini Poseidon** (p. 198), one of island's famous thermal parks, with 22 swimming pools fed from underground volcanic springs. Pools have whirlpools, waterfalls, and all sorts of other gizmos, and there's a nice beach, too, along with snack bars and cafes. A lot of Italian families spend an entire day here, and you'll have a hard time tearing your kids away. When you do manage to do so, take a walk around the harbor in nearby Forio.

The kids will probably beg you to go back to the water park, but they'll forget all about it once they set their eyes on the **Castello Aragonese** (p. 193). The offshore citadel, connected to the rest of the island by a bridge, is sort of a fantasy castle from Harry Potter, Treasure Island, and Robin Hood all rolled into one. Let the adventure begin with the climb up the massive 16th-century ramp (a far more exciting way to approach than on the elevator);

Ponte Ischia.

inside are courtyards, twisting alleyways, mysterious stone staircases, and breezy ramparts hundreds of feet above the surf. Lunch at the cafeteria of the **Monastero Hotel** (p. 201) inside the walls. For an afternoon swim, the **Spiaggia dei Pescatori** is just west of the castle. Follow that up with a walk along the seafront into Ponte Ischia, where a stop at **De Maio** (p. 203), the island's temple of gelato, fortifies the troops.

Day 3: Capri ★★★

Take the morning boat from Ischia so you'll have most of day 3 on Capri. From Capri Town, walk out to **Punta Tragara** and then scramble down the steps to the base of the **Faraglioni.** You might want to get your feet wet here, but the beach at **Marina Piccola** is better suited to young swimmers. You can get there via shuttle boat from the Faraglioni, but the walk along the south side of the island is a scenic adventure and a good workout, with a climb back up the stairs to Punta Tragara and a descent again to the beach at Marina Piccola on Via Krupp (sometimes closed due to falling rocks, in which case take Via Mulo).

Day 4: Anacapri (on Capri) ★★★

Kids love the short trip across the heights from Capri Town, on the bus zipping and skirting sheer drop-offs along the narrow cliff road between the two towns. Once there, take the chairlift up and down the slopes of **Monte Solaro,** pausing at the top to admire the views across the island and the gulf to the mainland. Back at the bottom, take Via Giuseppe Orlandi to **Pizzeria Materita** (p. 187) for a delicious (and kid-friendly) lunch. After lunch, step into **Chiesa di San Michele** and climb the circular staircase to the gallery for a bird's-eye view of the floor below, in which majolica tiles depict a scene that many young visitors will be familiar with: the expulsion of Adam and Eve from the Garden of Eden. Kids will especially enjoy picking out the exotic beasts that surround the couple. Now it's time to visit the island's most justifiably popular attraction. Buses marked GROTTA AZZURA leave from well-marked stops near the chairlift terminal. They deposit you at a busy dock, where you climb into a boat to be rowed through what might be the world's most famous sea cave. Back on terra firma, a small beach near the dock is ideal for a splash.

Day 5: Sorrento ★★★

As with most trips in the region, traveling by ferry or hydrofoil is half the fun. Let the kids take it easy for the rest of the day. They, and you, will enjoy the leisurely amble through the car-free old town, with stops at the pretty **cloisters of San Francesco** and the **Villa Communale gardens** across the street. An evening walk takes you down the path and steps to **Marina Grande** (p. 120), where kids will probably want to get their feet wet before sitting down to a waterside dinner at **Il Delfino** (p. 125). Frequent bus service whisks you back to the center of town.

Day 6: Day Trip to Pompeii ★★★

From Sorrento, Pompeii is just 25 minutes away on the Circumvesuviana train. Kids will be able to coax a vivid picture of ancient life out of the copious ruins. They'll probably be especially fascinated by the remnants of everyday life: the water fountains, the marble counters from which snacks were sold, the bakeries, laundries, and baths. *Note:* The plaster casts of the victims in the Forum grain warehouse might upset younger children, but older ones will be riveted. You might also want to monitor their encounters with the sexually explicit frescoes and other erotica. Bring snacks and plenty of water; and slather the kids in sunscreen.

Day 7: Day Trip to Amalfi ★★★

Take the boat to Amalfi, a real joy ride alongside cliffs and green hillsides tumbling into the sea. With your help, the remnants of old piers and vaulted shipyards of Amalfi's **Arsenale Marinaro** will help young visitors envision the days when the little town was the center of one of the world's most powerful maritime republics. The glorious mosaic and marble facade and fanciful Arabesque cloisters of the **Duomo** might turn them into architecture buffs. They can admire the cathedral while enjoying a snack in one of the cafes in Piazza Duomo at the foot of the monumental staircase, and follow it up with a scoop at **Gelateria Porto Salvo.** The trip back to Sorrento on the cliff-hugging coast road is also a thrill, one of the most exciting bus rides anywhere. Try to get seats on the left side for the best sea views.

Day 8: Naples ★★

From Sorrento, take a morning boat to Naples. The city, with its seaside castles and hilltop fortresses, looks spectacular from the water. While Naples has the reputation of being a Gomorrah, kids will probably enjoy the busy street life and colorful scenery. Begin at the **Archeological Museum,** where the frescoes and other finds from Pompeii are a nice follow-up to the visit to the ruins. Young museumgoers will also enjoy a quick look at the huge Farnese statues from the Baths of Caracalla in Rome. **Pizzeria Gino Sorbillo** on Via dei Tribunali is just a 10-minute walk away, and a late lunch there introduces the family to what many connoisseurs consider to be the best pizza in the world. Then it's underground, into **Napoli Sotterranea** (p. 65), from an entrance nearby at Vico Sant'Anna di Palazzo; guides lead visitors through huge cisterns and tunnels that the ancient Romans dug beneath their city. Back in the light, Christmas comes early on **Via San Gregorio Armeno** (p. 63), where shop windows are filled with some of the most elaborate *presipi* (nativity scenes) you and the kids will ever see. For a final dinner in the region, it's hard to beat the Borgo Marinaro for atmosphere—many restaurant terraces there provide sea views and a look at the towers and crenellations of medieval **Castel dell'Ovo.**

Campania for Families & Romantics

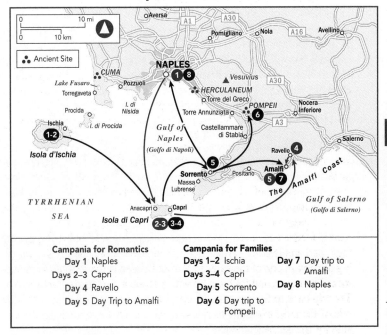

Campania for Romantics	Campania for Families	
Day 1 Naples	Days 1–2 Ischia	Day 7 Day trip to Amalfi
Days 2–3 Capri	Days 3–4 Capri	
Day 4 Ravello	Day 5 Sorrento	Day 8 Naples
Day 5 Day Trip to Amalfi	Day 6 Day trip to Pompeii	

CAMPANIA FOR A WHIRLWIND ROMANCE

Here are some of places most likely to have any heart beating faster in less than a week.

Day 1: Naples ★★

Time was, "See Naples and Die" evoked the city's beauty and charms, and the City on the Bay can still set the heart aflutter. For a romantic hideaway, it's hard to top the **Grand Hotel Vesuvio** (p. 76), with its knockout views of the bay, the Castel dell'Ovo, and Mt. Vesuvius. Another less obvious contender is the hillside **Hotel San Francesco al Monte** (p. 77), where the former monks' cells look across the city to the bay and the sky-high monk's garden is carved out of the cliff.

Ironically, churches are some of the most romantic spots in the city, so spend a pleasant afternoon in the old city stepping in and out of them. **San Lorenzo Maggiore** (p. 68) is the most beautiful medieval church and cloisters in Naples. Boccaccio (author of *The Decameron*) supposedly first laid eyes on his muse, Maria d'Aquino, here on Holy Saturday

41

1338, and it was love at first sight. He nicknamed Maria *La Fiametta* (Little Flame), wooed her with verse, and eventually won her over. It's an atmospheric 10-minute stroll west from there to **Chiesa di Santa Chiara** (p. 60), rooted in a kindly but decidedly unromantic gesture: King Robert the Wise founded the church and convent in 1343 as a place for his wife, Sancha, to retreat from him and the world. True to the queen's wishes, the frescoed and tiled cloister is still the most peaceful hideaway in the city.

A late-afternoon walk through the seaside Villa Communale gardens is a perfect prelude to dinner with views of boats bobbing on the moonlit bay in **Borgo Marinaro** (I recommend **Zi Teresa,** p. 80).

Santa Maria Monteoliveto in Naples.

Days 2 & 3: Capri ★★★

Capri is famous for instilling romance. Just think of the old Frank Sinatra hit, "My Heart's on the Isle of Capri." A balcony at the **Hotel Punta Tragara** (p. 177) overlooking the rocks of the **Faraglioni** (p. 177) or a terrace with a sea view at the **Capri Palace** (p. 184) should stir even the stoniest heart. A morning arrival from Naples on day 2 allows you time to check in and find your way, via steps from Punta Tragara or a launch from Marina Piccola, to **La Fontilena** (p. 188), for lunch accompanied by a pitcher (or two) of fruit-loaded sangria, the house drink. An after-lunch treat is a swim at the base of the iconic Faraglioni.

Spend the next morning in the magnificent gardens of the **Villa San Michele** (p. 182) in Anacapri. Then it's time for another seafood feast, this time at **Addio Riccio** (p. 187), perched on a cliff next to the Grotta Azzurra. Like yesterday's drill for taking it easy, lunch is followed by lounging on the club's rooftop sun deck and swimming from the platforms below. When it's time to move on, follow the **Sentiero die Forini (Path of the Forts;** p. 184) along the coast to the far western end of the island, where a cocktail at the **Lido di Faro** (p. 189) comes with a sunset view.

Day 4: Ravello ★★★

Seascapes along the Amalfi Coast have been tempting travelers ever since Ulysses had to dodge the alluring call of the Sirens. The coast is littered with romantic hideaways, but for a heart-stopping setting, it's hard to top (literally) sky-high **Ravello,** the next place you'll stay. Take the boat from Capri to Amalfi, and from there continue by bus or taxi up to town (even chugging up the green hillside on a bus is a nice ride). There, the old-world **Palumbo** (p. 160) and the more contemporary **Palazzo Avino** (p. 159) occupy centuries-old palaces with top-of-the-world views. Once you settle in you don't need to venture far—at **Villa Rufolo** (p. 158), the exotic Moorish cloisters are the starting point for a wander along pathways through rare plantings to breezy lookout points. Even more spectacular is the **Belevedere at Villa Cimbrone** (p. 158), perched between the sea and sky. Dinner on the terrace at **Rossellinis** (p. 160) tops off a day of otherworldly experiences.

Day 5: Day Trip to Amalfi

Take a ride down to **Amalfi** and have a coffee and pastry in one of the cafes in Piazza Duomo, where you'll have a view of the mosaic-clad facade of the **Duomo.** Then climb the stairs for a closer look, and step into the Moorish **Cloister of Paradise.** It's hard to resist a wander through Amalfi's maze of porticos and narrow lanes, but sooner or later find your way to the **Santa Caterina Hotel,** a decadent getaway on the coast just outside of town. A long lunch there at the seaside **Ristorante Al Mare** (p. 153), followed by a swim, is the perfect way to spend a final afternoon on the coast.

CAMPANIA'S CLASSICAL RUINS

Few other places are as littered with remnants of the ancient past, and that's saying something in history-soaked Italy. Pompeii and Herculaneum, those windows to Roman life, were relatively new towns in the region when they were buried by an eruption of Mt. Vesuvius in A.D. 79. Ancient Greeks established their first colony on mainland Italy at Cuma in the 8th century B.C. and built magnificent temples at Paestum in the 6th century B.C. Quite literally, in whatever direction you strike out in this region, you're likely to come across remnants of the ancient past.

Day 1: Naples ★★

Naples is a convenient base for day trips to ancient sites around the bay and into the hinterlands the Romans called the *Campania felix,* or fertile countryside. You'll be staying in a Naples hotel through day 5, and you'll start your explorations at the **Archeological Museum** (p. 65), one of the finest in the world. A visit should fill the better part of the day. Among the showstoppers are frescoes and mosaics of Pompeii and the colossal "Toro Farnese," the world's largest-known sculpture from antiquity, carved from a single piece of marble. Among the many finds are frescoes and pottery from villas elsewhere around the bay at Boscoreale, Stabiae, and Cuma. The decent audio-guide makes the collections a bit less overwhelming.

Day 2: Day Trip to Campi Flegrei

Line 2 of the Metropolitana (subway) or the Cumana railroad will deliver you to **Pozzuoli** (p. 86), where a long but satisfying day of exploration begins. This ramshackle seaside suburb is littered with ancient sights. The subway or train leaves you near the **Serapeo,** the Greek and Roman marketplace. The Roman **amphitheater** is about a 10-minute walk from there along a well-marked route inland along Via Sacchini. From there it's another 10 minutes along the Via Solfatara to the entrance to the **Solfatara,** the hissing, bubbling volcanic crater that the ancients thought was an entrance to the underworld.

Return to the Serapeo and continue by subway to **Baiae** (p. 89), where Julius Caesar, Nero, and other Roman elite once relaxed and debauched in lavish villas. After a stop for lunch at **Il Tucano** (p. 93), you'll be forti-fied for a walk among the ruins of villas and baths that now litter a hill-side in the Parco Archeologica di Baiae. Much of the ancient town is underwater, preserved as the **Parco Archeologico Sommerso di Baiae (Underwater Archeological Park of Baiae);** tour operators offer cruises in glass-bottom boats, or if you want to get wet, on snorkel and diving tours (see p. 91). The massive 16th-century **Castello di Baia Museo** shows off statuary and other artifacts from Baiae and the surrounding region in the **Archeologico dei Campi Flegrei,** including two nympha-eums, statue-lined porches from the villa of Emperor Claudius that were rescued from the sea floor.

Day 3: Day Trip to Santa Maria Capua Vetere

The Romans knew this as Capua (not to be confused with the modern city of the same name); it's about 30 minutes from Naples by frequent train service. Once there, you can follow the famous Appian Way (the stretch through town is known as **Corso Appia),** passing the **Arco di Adriano (Hadrian's Arch)** and the remains of a **Roman house.** The **amphithe-ater** was the second largest in the Roman world after the one of the capi-tal, and it's looking quite good for its 2,000 years. The next stop is the **Museo Archeologico dell'Antica Capua,** a 15-minute walk south. The main attraction here is the adjacent Mitreo, a well-preserved cult temple to the sun god Mitreo. All in all, these sights should take no more than 2 hours to see.

Buses connect Santa Maria Capua Vetere with **Capua** (p. 239), the ancient harbor the Romans called Casilinum, though they run infre-quently, so you might want to make

A mosaic from Pompeii in the Archeologi-cal Museum.

Campania's Classical Ruins

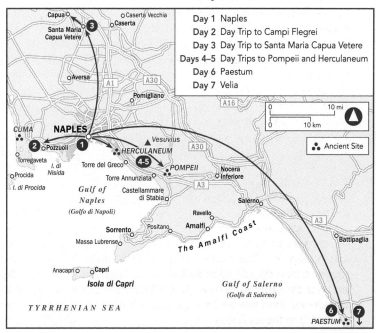

Day 1 Naples
Day 2 Day Trip to Campi Flegrei
Day 3 Day Trip to Santa Maria Capua Vetere
Days 4–5 Day Trips to Pompeii and Herculaneum
Day 6 Paestum
Day 7 Velia

the 10-minute trip by taxi. What will capture your attention here are the Madri in the **Museo Campano** (see p. 244). These statuettes of women with swaddled infants in their arms were offerings to an ancient deity known as Mater Matuta. After lunch in one of the pizzerias in and around Piazza Duomo, you might want to add some medieval architecture to the mix with a 15-minute trip out to the **Basilica di Sant'Angelo in Formis** (p. 243; buses leave from the train station). This vaguely Moorish landmark is built atop a temple to Diana and completely covered in Byzantine frescoes. From Sant' Angelo in Formis you can catch a train back to Naples.

Days 4 & 5: Day Trips to Pompeii & Herculaneum

Devote the next two days to **Pompeii** and **Herculaneum,** seeing each on separate outings. Pompeii, with its gridlike streets and public buildings, provides the overview of a large Roman town, while Herculaneum, with its better-preserved houses and artifacts, offers an evocative glimpse into day-to-day life—many of the houses in Herculaneum retain their second floors, making them seem more like residences than ruins.

You can reach both sites on the Circumvesuviana railway from Piazza Garibaldi in Naples. Herculaneum is about 20 minutes from Naples, and

Pompeii is about 40 minutes. When leaving Pompeii, if you have an hour's worth of energy left, you might also want to make a stop at Oplontis, one stop east (toward Naples) on the Circumvesuviana. **Villa di Poppea** (p. 109), a short walk from the train station, is one of the largest Roman villas ever uncovered and retains frescoes, mosaics, and extensive servants' quarters. The villa is just down Via Sepolchri from the station.

Day 6: Paestum ★★★

By train, it's a little under an hour and a half from Naples to **Paestum,** where three magnificent and well-preserved, golden-hued Greek temples stand amid fields of wildflowers. Plan on a late-morning arrival so you can settle into a hotel, have lunch, and spend the rest of the day exploring the temples and other ruins that include parts of the circuit of massive defensive walls; you can climb them for views over the ruins and coast. In the site's **archaeological museum,** the star of the show is the sole figure of a young man taking a swan dive into a rushing stream, from the so-called Tomb of the Diver. He might inspire you to do some swimming of your own from Paestum's long, sandy beach.

Day 7: Velia ★

It's an hour by bus from Paestum to the ruins of this once-great city, 43km (26 miles) south. **Velia** (p. 229) is not nearly as well preserved as Paestum, but some portions of walls, a stretch of pavement arched by the impressive **Porta Rosa** (Pink Gate), and fragments of a bath and theater are evocative remains of what was once a great center of philosophy. You can be back in Paestum by mid-afternoon and, with the region's efficient transport, move on to your next destination from there.

NAPLES

I n Naples, Mt. Vesuvius looms to the east, the fumaroles of the Campi Flegrei hiss and steam to the west, and the isle of Capri floats phantomlike across the gleaming waters of the bay. But for all the splendor and drama of this natural setting, one of Italy's most intense urban concoctions is the real show. Naples shoots out so many sensations that it takes a while for visitors to know what's hit them.

Everything seems a bit more intense in Italy's third-largest city, the capital of the south. Dark brooding lanes open to palm-fringed piazzas. Laundry-strewn tenements stand cheek by jowl with grand palaces. Medieval churches and castles rise above the grid of streets laid out by ancient Greeks. No denying it, parts of the city are squalid, yet its museums are packed with riches. Dozens of churches are not only architectural masterpieces and showcases of a long artistic tradition, but they're also rich in the endlessly fascinating stories of artists and patrons that unfold behind almost every doorway in this city.

It seems that most of life here transpires on the streets, so you'll witness a lot. The pace can be both leisurely in that southern way, and amazingly hectic. When you partake—in a meal, in a passeggiata, or just in a simple transaction—you'll notice the warmth, general good nature, and a sense of fun. You get the idea—but you won't really, until you experience this fascinating, perplexing, and beguiling city for yourself.

ESSENTIALS

Arriving

BY PLANE Naples's **Aeroporto Capodichino** (www.gesac.it; © **081-789-6259** or 081-789-6255), is only 7km (4 miles) from the city center. It receives flights from Italian and European cities, plus a few intercontinental flights. From the airport, you can take a taxi into town (make sure it is an official white taxi with the Naples municipal logo); the flat rate for the 15-minute trip to the train station is 16€, and 19€ to Molo Beverello (for ferries to the islands). There is a convenient bus service to Piazza Municipio and Piazza Garibaldi called the Alibus, run by the **ANM bus company** (www.anm.it; © **800-639525;** 3€ one-way from ticket desk, 4€ onboard). The bus runs every 30 minutes from the airport (6:30am–11:50pm) and from Piazza Municipio (6am–midnight).

BY TRAIN Naples is on the main southern rail corridor and is served by frequent and fast **train service** from most Italian and European cities and towns. InterCity (IC) trains make limited stops, and AltaVelocità (AV) trains are high-speed express trains. Regular trains take between 2 and 2½ hours between Rome and Naples, while the AV train takes only 87 minutes, making it by far the best method of transport between the two cities. The fare is 44€ one-way, but varies, and specials are often available, as are lower rates for advance booking. The same journey on an IC train will cost about 22€. Unfortunately for travelers trying to save money, IC trains run with less frequency than AV trains do, making cheaper transport quite inconvenient at times. Eurail pass holders should note that AV trains require a reservation and an extra fee (10€). Contact **Trenitalia** (www.trenitalia.it; ✆ **892021**) for information, reservations, and fares.

The city has two main rail terminals: **Stazione Centrale** at Piazza Garibaldi, and **Stazione Mergellina** at Piazza Piedigrotta. Most travelers will arrive at Stazione Centrale. Nearby, on Corso Garibaldi, is **Stazione Circumvesuviana Napoli-Porta Nolana** (www.vesuviana.it; ✆ **800-053939**), the starting point for commuter lines serving the Vesuvian and coastal area south of Naples, including Sorrento, Pompeii, and Ercolano.

BY CAR Although driving *in* Naples is a nightmare, **driving** *to* Naples is easy. The Rome-Naples autostrada (A2) passes Caserta 29km (18 miles) north of Naples. The Naples–Reggio di Calabria autostrada (A3) runs by Salerno, 53km (33 miles) north of Naples.

BY FERRY Boats run between Naples and Catania, Messina, and Palermo in Sicily; Cagliari in Sardinia; and other Mediterranean ports. The city is also connected by ferry to the islands of Capri, Ischia, and Procida, as well as to Sorrento and towns along the Amalfi Coast. Most boats arrive and depart from the Porto Molo Beverello at the edge of the historic district. Other ferry ports are Mergillina, to the west of the center, and Pozzuoli, farther west.

Getting Around

The **Metropolitana** (subway) has two lines: line 1 from Piazza Dante to the Vomero and beyond, and line 2 from Pozzuoli to Piazza Garibaldi and beyond. Several new stations have opened in recent years, with more underway. You can also use the urban section of the **Cumana** railroad from Montesanto, which is convenient to Mergellina and other coastal locations north of the city center. Handy **bus** routes include the R lines (R1, R2, R3, R4), with frequent stops at major tourist attractions, and the electric minibuses (marked E) that serve the historic district. **Funiculars** take passengers up and down the steep hills of Naples. The Funicolare Centrale (www.metro.na.it; ✆ **800-568866**) connects the lower part of the city to Vomero. Daily departures (6:30–12:30am) are from Piazzetta Duca d'Aosta just off Via Roma. Be careful not to get stranded by missing the last car back. One-way fare for the subway, buses, and funiculars is 1.50€; daily tickets (Biglietto Giornaliero)

The Fontana del Nettuno near City Hall.

are 4.50€, good until midnight the day they are validated; and weekly tickets (Biglietto Settimanale) are 15.80€. You can purchase tickets at newsstands, tobacco shops, and from machines in most metro and funicular stations and at some bus stops; you must validate tickets in the electronic ticket machines in stations or on the bus. For more information on buses and subways, visit http://unico campania.it.

Taxis are an excellent, relatively inexpensive way to get around the city, and are very reliable and strictly regulated. Official taxis are painted white and marked with COMUNE DI NAPOLI. Inside the cab, you'll find a sign listing official flat rates to the seaports, central hotels, and major attractions; don't fret if your driver doesn't use the meter—*not* using the meter is legal for all rides that have established flat rates. Taxis do not cruise but are found at the many taxi stands around town, or, for an extra 1€ surcharge, can be called by phone (© **081-444444** or 081-555-5555).

As for **driving** around Naples, we have one word: *Don't.* If you're tempted, take a look at the cars on the street. In the rest of Italy, even the simplest models are kept in pristine condition; here, cars look like they've been used in demolition derbies. Car theft is so common that some rental agencies will not extend coverage to drivers planning to go to Naples.

Walking is an excellent way to get around the city center, where sights are fairly close together, but remember: For Neapolitan drivers, red lights are mere suggestions; cross busy streets carefully, and stick with a crowd if possible. Always look both ways when crossing a street, because a lot of drivers scoff at the notion of a one-way street. The zebra stripes (white lines) in the street, indicating where pedestrians have the right of way, mean absolutely nothing here.

Visitor Information

The **Ente Provinciale per il Turismo,** Piazza dei Martiri 58 (© **081-410-7211;** bus: 152), is open Monday to Friday 9am to 2pm, with another office at Stazione Centrale (© **081-268779;** Metro: Garibaldi; Mon–Sat 9am–7pm). The AASCT (www.inaples.it) maintains two tourist information points: Via San Carlo 9 (© **081-402394**) and Piazza del Gesù (© **081-551-2701**); both are open daily (Mon–Sat 9:30am–6:30pm; Sun 9:30am–2pm). Any of these offices can give you a free map, an essential piece of equipment when navigating Naples.

The Neighborhoods in Brief

Where should you stay and where are the major attractions? Read on.

Chiaia Naples cleans itself up a bit in this seaside and hillside enclave that stretches from Piazza del Plebiscito west along the bay, skirting the seaside park, Villa Communale. By day, strollers follow the bay along the Lungomare di Chiaia all the way to similarly genteel Mergellina. Come evening, crowds head inland for a passeggiata along Via Chiaia. To join them, just move along with the flow west from Piazza Plebiscito.

Citta Antica (Historical Center) This warren of many tight lanes, a few avenues, and some boisterous piazzas is also known as the Decumani, and just as often as Spaccanapoli (that's the name of the street that runs straight through the center of the neighborhood, as it has ever since the Greeks established a colony here). Roughly, the heart of Naples extends north from seaside Castel Nuovo to the Museo Archeologico Nazionale, and east from Via Toledo and Quartieri Spagnoli to the Porta Nolona Fish Market. Anchoring the southwest corner of this neighborhood are two of Naples' grandest landmarks, which stand opposite each other just off the Piazza Trieste e Trento. The stately Teatro San Carlo is one of the world's finest opera houses, resplendent with gilded stucco and plush red velvet. Galleria Umberto I is one of the world's first shopping malls, a beautiful late-19th-century concoction of domes and steel girding, where commerce transpires in style on beautifully tiled promenades beneath glass arcades.

Piazza Garibaldi No need to linger in this decidedly unsavory quarter of grungy streets and some decidedly unsavory denizens. The train station is here, as is a station of the Circumvesuviana line for Pompeii and Sorrento. Descend into the flashy subway station for the metro and Circumflegrea line. The perpetually torn-up piazza is also a stop on many bus and tram lines, but you'll need to summon the ancient oracle of Cumae to find the right stop—short of her, check with the friendly folks in the tourist office in the train station if they're on duty.

Quartieri Spagnoli This is the real Naples, where age-old rituals of city life hang on— just like the laundry that perpetually hangs across the narrow streets. It's not street life you're witnessing, but just plain Neapolitan life, because everything seems to transpire in narrow, gridlike streets wedged between Via Toledo on the east and the San Martino hill on the west. Residents talk to one another from balconies, guys in T-shirts lower baskets from windows and haul up cigarettes, and kids play amid street stalls selling everything from fish to votive candles. If it all gets to be a bit much, just keep heading south (toward the bay) and you'll emerge in airy, semicircular Piazza del Plebiscito, where the huge Chiesa di San Francesco di Paola, copied on the Pantheon in Rome, faces the Palazzo Reale (p. 56).

Santa Lucia and the Seafront It's been a while since anyone but yachters set sail from this old fishermen's quarter made famous by the song. Neapolitans come here to stroll along seaside Via Mazzuro Sauro and Via Partenope (both closed to traffic) and gaze across the bay toward Capri. The nautical atmosphere cranks up a notch or two once you cross the bridge to Borgo Marinari, the little island where old houses huddle alongside Castel dell'Ovo (p. 52). In a case of moving up in the world but staying in the same neighborhood, Neapolitan rulers built other castles and palaces of increasing grandeur near the shore. From the sea-girt Castell d'Ovo they moved onto the Castel Nuovo, then Bourbon kings used the 17th-century Palazzo Reale on Piazza Plebiscito as one of their several residences. These regal addresses hold down a breezy precinct of other grand public monuments and one extremely handy presence, the Molo Beverello, the hub of the region's ferry network.

Vomero Life in Naples never really becomes too gentrified, but it calms down quite a bit in the hilltop enclave of the Napoli *bene* (the city's middle and upper classes). Aside from fresh air and spectacular

4

Essentials

NAPLES

views, this quarter of elegant 19th- and early-20th-century villas (plus one too many banal apartment houses) has two big draws: Castel Sant'Elmo (p. 69), and Certosa di San Martino (p. 69), a huge monastery that was founded in the 14th century and expanded in the early 17th century into the hilltop landmark that's visible from throughout the city. The trip up here from the center is on the Centrale and Montesanto funiculars.

[FastFACTS] NAPLES

Consulates The **U.S. Consulate** is on Piazza della Repubblica 1 (http://naples.usconsulate.gov; ☏ **081-583-8111;** Metro: Mergellina, tram: 1). Consular services are open Monday to Friday 8am to noon. The **Canadian Consulate,** at Via Carducci 29 (www.canada.it; ☏ **081-401338;** Metro: Amedeo), is open Monday to Friday (9am–1:30pm). Citizens of Australia and New Zealand need to go to the embassies or consulates in Rome. British subjects should contact the U.K. embassy in Rome, Via XX Settembre 80a (http://ukintaly.fco.gov.uk; ☏ **06-4220-0001**).

Drugstores Several pharmacies are open weekday nights and take turns staying open on weekend nights. A good one is located in the Stazione Centrale (Piazza Garibaldi 11; ☏ **081-440211;** Metro: Piazza Garibaldi).

Emergencies If you have an emergency, dial ☏ **113** to reach the police. For medical care, dial ☏ **118,** but only in an emergency. To find the local Guardia Medica Permanente, ask for directions at your hotel.

Laundry & Dry Cleaning Self-service laundromats are few and far between in Naples; your best bet is a *tintoria* (dry cleaner) or a *lavanderia* (dry cleaner and laundry service). Two good, centrally located choices are **Lavanderia Speedylava** at Via della Cavallerizza a Chiaia 18 (☏ **081-422405**) and **Lavanderia Suprema** on Via Vannella Gaetani 10 (☏ **081-764-3356**).

Mail The **Central Post Office (Ufficio Postale)** is at Piazza Matteotti (☏ **081-428-9585;** bus no. R3 to Piazza Matteotti).

Maps You can buy a good map with a *stradario* (street directory) of Naples at any newspaper stand in town (most carry the reliable **Pianta Generale** by N. Vincitorio); if you prefer something smaller, buy the excellent, foldable, credit card–size **Mini-City,** sold at museum shops in town (try the shop at Palazzo Reale).

Safety The Camorra-related crime for which Naples is infamous will have little bearing on your visit. Street crime is another story, and it's best to err on the side of caution in this city with catastrophically high unemployment, a big drug problem, and lots of dark, empty streets. If you have a money belt, by all means use it. Also use common sense. *Do not* carry a lot of cash, wear expensive jewelry, walk around with a fancy camera hanging from your neck, place your smartphone on cafe tables, or plunge down dark, deserted lanes at night. *Do* leave your valuables in a safe at your hotel (most rooms are equipped with them). When going out for a meal or excursion, carry only as much cash as you are going to need and only the credit card you will be using, and leave the others behind (including your debit/cash cards unless you need to make a withdrawal). Do not carry a wallet in your back pocket, of course, or even in your inside jacket pocket, where someone brushing against you can easily get to it. When walking, carry any bags on the side away from the street to thwart thieves whizzing past on motorbikes. Beware of pickpockets in crowds and on the subways and commuter trains—they're crafty. The Circumvesuviana stop at Piazza Garibaldi is prime turf for quick-handed thieves who prey on tourists carting bags from the main station to the commuter line that serves Sorrento. Be mindful of your bags at all times.

EXPLORING NAPLES

As large as Naples is, it's easy to get to the sights you want to see on foot, allowing you to experience one of the city's greatest allures—its street life. Clustered on and near the seafront are three royal residences, Castel Nuovo, Castel dell'Ovo, and Palazzo Reale, as well as two of the city's finest outdoor expanses, Piazza del Plebiscito and the seaside gardens of the Villa Communale. The magnificent **Teatro San Carlo** and **Galleria Umberto I**, a grand 19th-century shopping arcade, are just inland off Piazza Trento e Trieste. From there, Via Toledo/Via Roma leads north. To the west is the Quartieri Spagnoli, a neighborhood of tightly packed narrow lanes, while to the east, just beyond Piazza Dante, is the atmospheric historical center of the city, where many of the churches you want to see face airy piazzas. At the northern end of Via Toledo, about a 10-minute walk beyond Piazza Dante, is the celebrated Archaeological Museum.

Santa Lucia & the Seafront

Castel dell'Ovo ★★ CASTLE   As every Neapolitan knows, the poet Virgil placed an egg under the foundations of the city's outrageously picturesque seafront fortress (Castle of the Egg); when it broke, a great disaster would befall the city. Considering earthquakes, eruptions of nearby Mt. Vesuvius, plague outbreaks, and World II bombings, it's probably safe to assume the egg is no longer intact. The castle is enchanting even without such legends, squeezed onto a tiny island the Greeks first settled almost 3 millennia ago. Built over the foundations of the villa of the Roman emperor Lucullus, it was a royal residence from the 13th through 20th centuries. The little lanes beneath the thick walls are lined with the houses of Borgo Marinaro, a former fisherman's haunt where the ground floors of the quaint house are now occupied by pleasant bars and pizzerias. For Neapolitans, a walk across the stout bridge onto the island is a favorite Sunday afternoon outing.

The Castel dell'Ovo.

Borgo Marinari (off Via Partenope). ✆ **081-795-4593.** Free admission. Mon–Sat 8am–6pm; Sun 8am–2pm. Bus: 152, C25, 140, or E5 to Via Santa Lucia.

Castel Nuovo ★ CASTLE/MUSEUM Now that the Giotto frescoes that once decorated this palace's chapel have faded away, you can forgo a visit to the fairly uninspired staterooms and collection of painting and sculpture from defunct churches and settle for admiring this medieval sea-girt beauty from the

The Galleria Umberto I.

outside. As you do so, consider the plight of prisoners who once shared their dungeons with crocodiles imported from Egypt for the express purpose of snacking on the doomed souls. The best view is from the Piazza Municipio, where you can take in the castle's towers, crenellations, and the white-marble Triumphal Arch of Alfonso I of Aragona squeezed between two turrets, erected when Alfonso took control of the city in 1443. It's a splendid example of early Renaissance architecture.

Piazza Municipio. © **081-795-2003.** Admission to staterooms and collections 5€. Mon–Sat 9am–7pm. Bus: R1 or R2.

Fontana del Nettuno ★★ LANDMARK Neapolitans have enjoyed these water-spouting lions and sea monsters since 1600, though they might have a hard time finding them. The marble showpiece—dolphins, tritons, and the sea god Neptune himself—has been carted from one end of the city to the other, from Piazza del Palazzo Reale to square after square on the way to the fountain's current lodging, off Via Medina near City Hall. In spite of their mobility, the smooth basins and water-splashed statuary are a lovely and soothing presence amid the city grime, and little wonder. They're partly the work of Pietro Bernini, whose greatest creation is the Fontana della Barcaccia at the bottom of the Spanish steps in Rome. His more famous son, architect and sculptor Lorenzo Bernini, was in the fountain business, too, and designed the Fontana dei Quattro Fiumi in Rome's Piazza Navona.

Piazza Municipio (off Via Medina). Metro: Via Toledo. Bus: 140, N1, N3, R1, or R2.

Galleria Umberto I ★★ LANDMARK Shopping malls have only gone downhill since elegant glass-and-iron landmarks like this were all the rage in the late 19th century. The cafe and shop-lined gallery modeled after the older Galleria Vittorio Emanuele II in Milan saw its best days in the years leading up to World War I, though Neapolitans are once again waking up to the pleasures of shopping and socializing beneath the glass dome and four glass vaulted wings. If the place works its magic on you, as it is sure to do, dip into *The Gallery,* a novel by John Horne Burns (1916–53) about American GIs in Naples after World War II. Much of the action transpires in the Galleria, though the sad, poignant vignettes and dire views of the human condition might not be the best advertisement for an upbeat shopping experience. Another Liberty-era construction of the era, **Galleria del Principe di Napoli,** is off Piazza Cavour near the Archaeological Museum (Metro: Piazza

Exploring Naples

Basilica di San Paolo
  Maggiore **12**
Cappella del Monte
  di Pietà **20**
Cappella Sansevero **9**
Castel Capuano **16**
Castel dell'Ovo **27**
Castel Nuovo **22**
Castel Sant'Elmo **30**
Catacombs of
  San Gennaro **1**
Certosa di San Martino **28**
Chiesa dei Girolamini **18**
Chiesa del Gesù Nuovo **5**
Chiesa di San Domenico
  Maggiore **8**
Chiesa di San Giovanni
  a Carbonara **15**
Chiesa di San Gregorio
  Armeno **10**
Chiesa di Sant'Angelo
  a Nilo **7**
Chiesa di Santa Chiara **6**
Chiesa di Santa Maria
  di Monteoliveto **4**
Fontana del Nettuno **21**
Galleria Umberto I **23**
Il Duomo **13**

Museo Archeologico
  Nazionale **3**
Museo d'Arte
  Contemporanea
  Donna Regina **14**
Museo e Gallerie
  Nazionale di
  Capodimonte **2**
Museo Nazionale
  di San Martino **29**
Napoli Sotterranea **11**
Palazzo Reale **25**
Piazza del Plebiscito **26**
Pio Monte della
  Misericordia **17**
San Lorenzo
  Maggiore **19**
Teatro San Carlo **24**
Villa Comunale **32**
Villa La Floridiana **31**

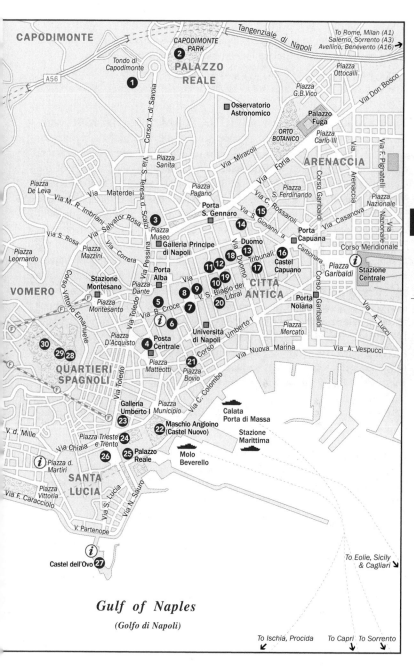

Gulf of Naples

(Golfo di Napoli)

To Ischia, Procida   To Capri   To Sorrento

Cavour). The adjacent church of Santa Maria di Constantinopoli got in the way of expanding the gallery into a four-winged cross shape like the more famous Galleria Umberto, but the vaults and domes are impressive testaments to the city's efforts to clean itself up after the devastating cholera epidemics of the 1880s. Today the gallery houses more offices than it does shops.

4 entrances: To the right off Via Toledo as you come from Piazza del Plebiscito, Via Giuseppe Verdi, Via Santa Brigida, and Via San Carlo. Bus: R2 or R3 to Piazza Trieste e Trento.

Piazza del Plebiscito ★★ ARCHITECTURAL SITE   The most beautiful square in Naples is an airy expanse surrounded by a remarkably elegant assemblage of neoclassical landmarks: the refined facade of the Royal Palace; the 19th-century church of San Francesco di Paola, a bland replica of the Roman Pantheon, and the Palazzo della Prefeturra, once a royal guest house. Rather ironically, the grandiose church honors one of the most pious and humble men in the saintly roster, who, even as a child, was dressed in pint-sized sackcloth habits and spent most of his life fasting in caves. Domes, pediments, columned porticoes, and majestic, curving colonnades suggest all the grandeur of classical Greece—just as Murat, the 19th-century king of Naples, intended them to do when he designed the square to honor his brother-in-law, the Emperor Napoleon. It's little wonder the square was named to commemorate a great moment of democratic enlightenment, the 1863 plebiscite (popular vote) that made Naples part of the new Kingdom of Italy. Two Neapolitan kings survey the cobblestones from the backs of their steeds: the forward-thinking **Carlo III** (1716–88) and the plotting and treacherous **Ferdinando I** (1423–94). It's said you will be blessed with good fortune if you turn your back to the Palazzo Reale, close your eyes, and walk backward between the two kings.

Off Piazza Trieste e Trento (btw. Via Chiaia and Via C. Console). Bus: R2 or R3 to Piazza Trieste e Trento.

Royal Palace (Palazzo Reale) ★ MUSEUM   If your decorating tastes lean toward royal pomp, you'll love following a designated route (accompanied by a dry audio commentary) through some 30 grandiose yet strangely vacuous rooms where Neapolitan royalty ruled and entertained in the 18th and 19th centuries. You won't miss too much if you give this pompous old pile a miss, though it's hard not be impressed by the sweep of the marble double staircase, the opulent Teatrino di Corte (the private theater), and the ridiculously large, tapestry-hung Hall of Hercules (the ballroom). Most seductive of all are the manicured private gardens, tucked away above the city and the Bay of Naples; those, you can enter for free.

Piazza del Plebiscito 1. www.palazzorealenapoli.it. ✆ **081-580-8111.** Admission 4€; courtyard and gardens free. Thurs–Tues 9am–7pm. Bus: R2 or R3.

Teatro San Carlo ★★★ ARCHITECTURAL SITE   The great Naples-born tenor Enrico Caruso (1873–1921) only appeared once at his hometown's sumptuous opera house, in 1901, when he was booed off the stage and vowed never to return. Other performers and composers have been more fortunate. The world's oldest opera house, inaugurated on November 4, 1737, has welcomed Rossini, Bellini, Verdi, Puccini, and a veritable who's-who of opera greats. For much of the 19th century, the 1,379-seat house, with what are claimed by many to be the finest acoustics in the world, was the center of the opera world. Composers have clamored to have their works debut on the stage, singers consider the chance to perform in the plush auditorium a career maker, and audiences gush. Even the French novelist Stendhal abandoned his usual dark realism in favor of flowery praise, "There is nothing in all Europe, I won't say comparable to this theatre, but which gives the slightest idea of what it is like . . . it dazzles the eyes, it enraptures the soul. . . ." You can become enraptured with the magnificent red-and-gold interior on a guided tour (in Italian or English), or better yet, at a performance (see "Entertainment & Nightlife," later in this chapter), to see the building in its full glory.

Via San Carlo 93. www.teatrosancarlo.it. © **081-797-2111.** Guided tours 6€, Mon–Sat 10:30am, 11:30am, 12:30pm, 2:30pm, 3:30pm, 4:30pm; Sun 10:30am, 11:30am, and 12:30pm. Ticket office hours: Mon–Sat 10am–7pm; Sun 10am–3:30pm. Bus: R2 or R3 to Via San Carlo.

Villa Comunale ★★ PARK/GARDEN   There was a time when was the public was only allowed into the seaside gardens of the royal family once a year, on September 8, the Fiesta di Piedigrotta. That changed with the proletarian sentiments that swept in with the unification of Italy in 1869, and a good thing, too. Following the paths through greenery and past statues and fountains for a km (1/2 mile) or so from Piazza Vittoria on the east to Piazza della Repubblica on the west is one of the city's great delights. The Bay of Naples shimmers along the southern flanks, and many of its denizens—octopi, squid, sea urchins, and other creatures indigenous to the bay—now reside in tanks at the Anton Dohrn Zoological Station. The renowned German naturalist established the one-room aquarium in 1874. A popular antiques market takes over a corner of Villa Communale on the third and fourth weekends of each month from 8:30am to 1pm; contact the tourist office (p. 49) for details.

Park: Piazza Vittoria. Daily 7am–midnight. Aquarium: © **081-583-3111.** Free admission. Tues–Sun 9am–5pm. Bus: C82 or R2.

Citta Antica (Historical Center)

Basilica di San Paolo Maggiore ★ CHURCH   Two Corinthian columns braced precariously against the facade of one of Naples' oldest places of worship are all that remains from the 1st-century Temple of Discori, honoring the twins Castor and Pollux, founding gods of the Greek city of Neapolis. The temple became a Christian place of worship in the 8th century, was massively overhauled in the 16th century, and richly redecorated at the height of the baroque, around 1700. By then, Francesco Solimena was at the top of his game—immensely wealthy, a baron, and the undisputed head of the

Neapolitan school of painting. His self-assurance shows through in the sacristy, awash in the frescoes that are his masterwork. Massimo Stanzione, a master of the previous century, painted the "Stories of the Lives of Saint Peter and Saint Paul" in the nave, but only a fragment of these rich, complex, and vastly superior works remains; the rest were blown to smithereens during Allied bombings in World War II.

Via San Paolo (off Via dei Tribunali, opposite Piazza San Gaetano). © **081-454048.** Free admission. Daily 8am–noon and 5–7pm. Metro: Piazza Cavour.

Cappella del Monte di Pietà ★ MUSEUM   The Monte di Pietà, literally, "mountain of pity," was a charitable organization set up in 1539 to make interest-free loans to the indebted poor. Quite fittingly, flanking the doorway are sculptures of Charity and Security by Pietro Bernini (1562–1629), father of Lorenzo, the more famous sculptor and architect. Inside the church, florid and color-saturated ceiling frescoes depicting scenes from the life of Jesus are by Belisario Corenzio (1558–1643), who was every bit as colorful as his work. A competent but mediocre artist whose talent was no match for that of other masters, Corenzio decided the best way to deal with his rivals was to kill them. When Guido Reni (1575–1642), the Bolognese master of the high baroque, came to Naples in 1621 to work on the Chapel of San Gennaro in the Duomo, Corenzio hired an assassin to do away with him. The hit man fatally wounded Reni's assistant by mistake, but the artist got away, fleeing town in fear for his life. Corenzio then formed the so-called Cabal of Naples, a notorious triumvirate that also included the painters Jusepe de Ribera and Batistello Caraciollo. They would destroy the works of interlopers who accepted commissions they thought were rightfully theirs, sometimes even poison their competitors, or simply harass them to the point that remaining in Naples was impossible. Corenzio worked well into his 80s and died by the sword, either pushed from a scaffold or poisoned.

Via Biagio dei Librai 114. © **081-580-7111.** Free admission. Sat 9am–7pm; Sun and holidays 9am–2pm. Bus: C57 or R2. Metro: Dante.

Cappella di Sansevero ★★ MUSEUM   Only in Naples would a room as colorful, fanciful, mysterious, beautiful, and macabre as this exist. Prince Raimondo di Sangro of Sansevero remodeled his family's funerary chapel in the 18th century, combining the baroque style then in fashion with his own love of complex symbolism and intellectual quests. Neapolitan sculptor Giuseppe Sanmartino crafted "Christ Veiled Under a Shroud," in which a thin transparent covering seems to make Christ's flesh look even more tormented and his suffering greater. (Antonio Canova, the Venetian sculptor, came to Naples to see the work a century later and said he would give 10 years of his life to have created something so beautiful.) The prince's father lies beneath a statue of "Despair on Disillusion," in which a man disentangling himself from a marble net suggests a troubled soul and mind seeking relief—provided by the winged boy who represents intellect. Prince Raimondo's mother, who died at age 20, lies beneath a statue of "Veiled Truth," in which a woman holds a broken tablet, symbol of an interrupted life; her veil in this case suggesting the unfulfilled promise she took to the grave with her. Raimondo himself is surrounded by colorful floor tiles arranged in a complex maze, symbol of the quest to unravel the secrets of life. Downstairs are two skeletal bodies in which the circulatory systems are perfectly preserved and brightly colored, allegedly with the injection of a substance the prince devised (and the subjects are probably not, as legend has it, the prince's unwilling servants, whom he supposedly sacrificed in the interest of science).

Via Francesco De Sanctis 19 (near Piazza San Domenico Maggiore). www.museosansevero.it. ℂ **081-551-8470.** Admission 7€. Mon and Wed–Sat 10am–6:30pm; Sun 10am–2pm. Closed May 1 and Easter Monday. Metro: Dante.

Chiesa dei Girolamini ★ CHURCH   Behind this somber Renaissance facade directly opposite the Duomo is one of the hidden treasures of Naples. Around two quiet courtyards are a church, chapels, convent, and a library that were a blank canvas for the city's artists throughout the 17th and 18th centuries. Especially prominent are frescoes and paintings by Luca Giordano (1634–1705), a Neapolitan who made his name as a court painter in Spain, then returned home to enjoy his fame and fortune. He spent large amounts of money supporting younger artists, and here and in other Neapolitan churches he claimed to have given the public what they wanted, with his colorful renderings of well-known biblical subjects. His "Jesus Ejects Moneylenders from the Temple" near the entrance may well have served as a KEEP OUT sign to those who once gathered in the dark corners of churches to conduct nefarious business. His "St. Nicholas Saving Three Innocents from a Vat" was a surefire crowd pleaser of the time. The saint, who has become synonymous with Santa Claus, was especially popular in Naples because of his frequent interventions on behalf of sailors in peril at sea. In this canvas, Nicholas restores three young victims to life after they have been chopped up and thrown into a pickling vat. The church's splendid library, the Quadreria, was much in the news recently when it was discovered that a curator was looting the shelves of their invaluable manuscripts and carting them off by the truckload; many have been recovered.

Via dei Tribunali. ℂ **081-292316.** Free admission. Mon–Sat 9am–1pm and 4–7pm; Sun 9am–1pm. Library: Via Duomo 142. ℂ **081-449139** or 331-426-7772. Free admission. Sat 9:30am–1pm and 3–6pm. Other days by appointment only; call ℂ **331-426-7772.** Bus: R1, R2, R3, or R4. Metro: Dante.

Chiesa del Gesù Nuovo ★ CHURCH   One of the most famous facades in Naples has not brought good luck to those who live behind it. The princes of Salerno built what was once their palace in 1470, requesting that the facade be done in *bugnato a punta di diamante*, or ashlar, a technique that uses stones that are regularly cut to create a perfectly uniform appearance. The princes lost the palace a century later due to their political shenanigans, and the Jesuit order bought it and converted the stately salons into a church. The Jesuits, too, were evicted in due time, but not before enlivening the interior with opulent frescoes and marblework. On the interior facade wall is a fresco by Francesco Solimena (1657–1747) that's as dramatic as the exterior. Solimena was a conventional painter who compensated for his lack of genius with flamboyance. His "Expulsion of Heliodorus from the Temple" is a colorful swirl of flowing draperies and swirling robes in which God sends a horseman and two angelic, sword-brandishing youths to thwart Heliodorus as he attempts to steal the treasure of the Temple of Jerusalem. The altar of the chapel of the Visitation is the final resting place of Naples' most popular modern saint, Giuseppe Moscatti (1880–1927), a devoutly religious physician and biochemist famous in his lifetime for his ability to heal impossible cases. The so-

The Church of Gesù Nuovo.

called "Holy Physician of Naples" is believed to still be working miracles. The ill and injured often throng to his shrine seeking his help, and it's said that many have been cured on the spot. In the piazza outside the church is another soothing presence, the Guglia dell'Immacolata. The so-called "plague column," decorated with scenes from the life of Mary and topped with her statue, was completed in 1750 to celebrate deliverance from plagues as well as earthquakes, eruptions, and any other calamity likely to befall the city.

Piazza del Gesù. www.gesunuovo.it. ✆ **081-557-8111.** Free admission. Mon–Sat 7am–1pm and 2:15–7:30pm; Sun 7am–1:45pm and 4:15–7:30pm. Bus: R1, R2, R3, or R4. Metro: Dante.

Chiesa di Santa Chiara ★ CHURCH   Despite its vast light-filled interior and unabashedly cheerful cloisters, the church of Naples' 13th- to 15th–century French rulers, the House of Anjou, is steeped in a stormy past. It's not a sign in a good marriage when a wife's only desire is to be a nun, but that's what Queen Sancha, second wife of Robert the Wise, wanted, so the king founded Santa Chiara in 1343 as a place for her to retreat from the world. Robert's tomb is in the nave; the poet Boccaccio eulogized him as "unique among kings of our day, friend of knowledge and virtue." His granddaughter Joan was crowned queen here in 1343, launching an enlightened reign nonetheless marred with plotting, intrigue, the murder of a husband, and her own demise at 56, when she was smothered with pillows. Her body was thrown into a deep well on the grounds of Santa Chiara and, once retrieved, denied Christian burial because of her heretical anti-papal views; instead, she was laid to rest in an unmarked grave under the church floor. During World War II, Allied bombers laid waste to most of the church's colorful frescoes, though a few fragments remain in the reconstructed nave. Other frescoes line the walls of the delightful **cloisters,** where columns are decorated with colorful Mallorca tiles. This is one of the most refreshing corners of Naples, and well worth the 5€ admission fee if you've been walking around the old city and need some peace and quiet.

Church: Via Santa Chiara 49. ℭ **081-797-1235.** Free admission. Mon and Wed–Sat 7:30am–1pm and 4:30–8pm. Cloisters and museum: Admission 5€. Mon and Wed–Sat 9:30am–5:30pm; Sun 10am–2:30pm. Metro: Dante.

Chiesa di San Domenico Maggiore ★ CHURCH   Walking through the seat of Dominican friars in Naples is a little like unraveling a puzzle. Even the facade is hidden from view, facing an inner courtyard, while another church, the 10th-century San Michele Arcangelo a Morfisa, is tucked away amid 26 chapels. The Dominicans built their mother church between 1283 and 1324, expanding a monastery that was already famous throughout Europe as the seat of the University of Naples. St. Thomas Aquinas taught theology at the university in the 1270s. In the chapel of St. Nicholas, he was supposedly observed levitating in front of an image of Christ on the crucifix, engaged in poignant conversation. When Christ asked him, "You have written well of me, Thomas. What reward would you have for your labor?" the tearful Thomas responded, "Nothing but you Lord." The accomplishments of the order come to light in the sacristy, where ceiling frescoes by baroque master Francesco Solimena (1657–1747) detail the "Triumph of Faith over Heresy by the Dominicans." On a three-sided, double-tiered gallery beneath the colorful images rest 45 coffins containing the mortal remains of members of the House of Aragon. Among them is Ferdinand I, king of Naples from 1423 to 1494. He is treated with greater respect than he showed his enemies, whom he murdered, embalmed, dressed elaborately, and showed off to his guests. A grand marble staircase at the rear of the church descends to Piazza San Domenico, one of Naples's most beautiful squares. The vast space is graced by the Guglia San Domenico, an intricately carved marble spire erected between 1658 and 1737 in gratitude for the end of the plague. Topping the monument is a statue of Spanish-born St. Dominic, who founded the Dominican order in 1216 and famously counseled his followers "to have charity, to guard humility, and to make treasure out of poverty."

Piazza San Domenico Maggiore (off Via San Biagio dei Librai). ℭ **081-459188.** Free admission. Daily 8.30am–noon and 3:30–7pm. Metro: Piazza Cavour.

Chiesa di San Giovanni a Carbonara ★ CHURCH   A sweeping double staircase ascends to a lofty entry porch, a fitting way to approach the final resting place of two of the city's more colorful citizens. Giovanni Caracciolo (1372–1432), often known as Sergianni, lies for eternity in a tomb by Leonardo da Besozzo in a circular chapel awash in frescoes and rare majolica flooring. Caracciolo, prime minister and lover of Queen Joan of Naples, amassed great wealth and so much power that he virtually controlled the finances and politics of the kingdom. All was well until 1432, when the aging queen, possibly tired of Caracciolo's endless machinations, ordered four of her knights to stab him to death in Castel Capuano. Rather ironically, three marble knights hold aloft his handsomely sculpted sepulcher. Joan's brother, King Ladislaus (1377–1414), sealed the doom of the House of Anjou when he died young without a legitimate heir, allegedly of uninhibited and unceasing sexual activity. He rests in a skyscraper of a tomb in which he sits astride a horse at the apex of many tiers of statuary, including life-size statues of him sitting next to his sister Joan. The name of the church comes from its location atop a medieval garbage dump, where refuse was burned, *ad carbonarum.*

Via San Giovanni a Carbonara 5 (5 short blocks east of the Duomo). ✆ **081-295873.** Free admission. Mon–Sat 8am–noon and 4:30–8:30pm; Sun 8am–2pm. Metro: Piazza Cavour.

Chiesa di San Gregorio Armeno ★★ CHURCH   When nuns fleeing persecution in Asia Minor came to Naples in the 8th century, they brought with them the relics of St. Gregory, an Armenian bishop. Over the centuries they built suitable surroundings for the saint, who now rests in a sumptuous baroque church that bursts at the seams with gold leaf, a beautiful wooden ceiling, and elaborate marble carvings. Stepping into the church, described as "a room of paradise on earth," is like walking into one of the elaborately nativity scenes, *presepi,* that vendors sell up and down the street outside. Neapolitan master Luca Giordano tells the story of the nun's flight with their precious cargo in a series of dramatic frescoes, "The Embarkation, Journey and Arrival of the Armenia Nuns with the Relics of St. Gregory" (1671–84). Gregory, however, is upstaged by one of the nuns, Santa Patrizia, whose dried blood is said to liquefy every Tuesday. The cloisters are an oasis of tranquility. Nothing disturbs the peace but the splashing of a fountain topped with a statue of Jesus meeting the Good Samaritan as dolphins and sea horses look on.

Via San Gregorio Armeno 44 (btw. Via San Biagio dei Librai and Via dei Tribunali, 3 short blocks west of Via Duomo). Free admission. Daily 9:30am–noon. Metro: Piazza Cavour.

Chiesa di Santa Maria di Monteoliveto (aka Sant'Anna dei Lombardi) ★★ CHURCH   What was once the largest monastic complex in Italy is a fraction of its former size, tucked behind the main post office and a police station. The church's greatest treasures, three canvases by the painter Caravaggio (see "Bad Boy with a Brush" box, p. 67), were destroyed when the church collapsed after an earthquake in 1805. Even so, some of Naples' great Renaissance sculptures still decorate the chapels. Among them is a remarkable terra-cotta sculptural grouping of eight life-size figures surrounding the lifeless body of Christ, "Mourning the Death of Christ" (1492), by Guido Mazzoni (1445–1518). The sculptor was a court favorite in Ferrara, where he crafted a similar lamentation for Duke Ercole d'Este. The work came to the attention of the duke's brother-in-law, King Alfonso of Aragon, who brought Mazzoni to Naples. Alfonso barely had time to enjoy the emotion-wracked, grieving figurers Mazzoni sculpted for him (they happen to

EVERY DAY IS christmas IN NAPLES

Among the many delights of Naples are the *presepi*, nativity scenes that pop up everywhere, any time of the year and, not surprisingly, come out in force at Christmastime. Figures are carved in wood or fired in ceramic. Mainstays are Mary, Joseph, the infant Jesus, the donkey, the Wise Men, and angels, though the Neapolitan repertoire often expands to soccer stars and other celebrities. The settings are often a lot more elaborate than a humble manger: medieval town squares, rusticated villages with thatched cottages and spinning waterwheels, elaborate caves that look like some troglodyte fantasy. The **Museo di San Martino** (Largo San Martino 8; ✆ **081-578-1769;** admission 6€; open Thurs–Tues 8:30am–7:30pm) shows off the world's largest *presepe*, an 18th-century concoction with hundreds of figures and objects; it's the museum's most popular display, and it's thronged at Christmastime. You can piece together your own scene with a walk down **Via San Gregorio Armeno,** where year-round, dozens of shops sell figures beginning at about 15€. You can also buy a complete scene for anywhere from 100€ well into five digits, or have one specially made with figures of your family and favorite celebrities (as many Neapolitans do). As you peruse these holy scenes, be aware that pickpockets flock to the street like sheep to a Bethlehem hillside with the unholy intent of preying on distracted gawkers glued to shop windows. Among the most reputable shops are **Gambardella Pastori,** Via San Gregorio Armeno 40 (✆ **081-551-7107); Giuseppe Ferrigno,** Via San Gregorio Armeno 10 (✆ **081-552-3148);** and **Amendola,** Via San Gregorio Armeno 51 (✆ **081-551-4899).**

bear an exacting likeness to the Aragonese royal family). He fled Naples in 1495 as the armies of King Charles VIII of France approached the city. King Charles, meanwhile, was so smitten with the sculptures that he whisked Mazzoni away to Paris, where he worked for the rest of his life. The most extensive frescoes of painter, architect, and man of letters Giorgio Vasari are in the Old Sacristy. The Tuscan is best-known for his gossipy biographies of Renaissance artists, *Lives of the Most Excellent Painters, Sculptors, and Architects*, but here he covered the entire ceiling with colorful paintings depicting the meaning of faith. Beneath them are similarly delightful inlaid wood panels by the monk Fra Giovanni da Verona (1457–1525). The Fontana di Monteoliveto, the most beautiful baroque fountain in Naples, is in the pretty square out front.

Piazza Monteoliveto 44 (off Via Monteoliveto, 1 block east of Via Toledo/Via Roma). ✆ **081-551-3333.** Free admission. Daily 9am–6pm. Bus: R1, R2, R3, or R4. Metro: Dante.

Chiesa di Sant'Angelo a Nilo ★ CHURCH

The powerful Brancaccio family wanted only the best, as seen in this handsome church with a striking red and gray facade they commissioned, completed in 1385. Thinking ahead of the impression he might make for eternity, family luminary Cardinal Rinaldo Brancaccio hired Donatello, the great Florentine Renaissance sculptor, to create his tomb. Donatello and a partner, Michelozzo, rented a workshop in Pisa for the job, to be close to the marble quarries of Carrara as well as near a seaport from which they could more easily ship the completed piece to Naples. Donatello executed a graceful relief of the Assumption of the Virgin that is set amid statues, other reliefs, coats of arms, and, of course, the tomb itself, atop of which is a supine statue of the cardinal resting in the company of two angels. All told, the assemblage, completed around 1428, is 11.6m (38 ft.) high and 4.6m (15 ft.) wide. By comparison, the statue in the square out front that gives the church its name is a relatively modest affair, a Greek-Roman tribute to the Egyptian god Nile. The bearded old fellow is surrounded by babies who represent the river's tributaries.

Piazzetta Nilo (off Via Benedetto Croce). Free admission. Mon–Sat 8:30am–1pm and 4:45–7pm; Sun 8:30am–1pm. Bus R2. Metro: Piazza Cavour.

Il Duomo Cattedrale di Santa Maria Assunta ★★ CATHEDRAL

Three times a year—the first Saturday in May, September 19, and December 16—all of Naples squeezes into the great cathedral that King Carlo I d'Angio dedicated to San Gennaro in the 13th century. On these dates the dried blood of the city's patron saint liquefies, or sometimes doesn't. Not doing so foretells terrible events for Naples, such as an outbreak of the plague in 1528 or the earthquake in 1980 that killed 2,000 residents. The rest of the year the blood is kept in a vault inside an altar in the **Canella di San Gunnar,** where a reliquary houses the head that soldiers of the Emperor Diocletian severed from the rest of the bishop's body around 305.

Within the cathedral are Naples' two oldest remaining places of worship. The **Capella di Santa Restituta** served as the city's 4th-century basilica and is supported by a forest of columns from a Greek temple, and the **Capella di San Giovanni in Fonte** was a 5th-century baptistery; if you crane your neck and squint (binoculars or a telescopic lens come in handy) you can make out some endearingly rendered frescoes in the dome, including one showing Christ's miracle of the loaves and fishes.

The Cathedral of Santa Maria Assunta.

Via del Duomo 147. ✆ **081-449097.** Free admission to the cathedral, but the archaeological zone is 3€. Mon–Sat 8am–12:30pm and 4:30–7pm; Sun 8am–1:30pm and 5–7:30pm. Metro: Piazza Cavour.

Museo d'Arte Contemporanea Donna Regina (MADRE) ★ ART

MUSEUM It's not New York's Guggenheim or London's Tate Modern, but the sprawling **Palazzo Regina** in the middle of medieval and baroque Naples provides a dramatic counterpoint for works by such contemporary artists as

Anish Kapoor, Richard Serra, and Jeff Koons. Painter Francesco Clemente, who was born in Naples but made his reputation on the international art scene, creates an illusionary experience in two rooms he's decorated with colorful tile floors and frescoes replicating ancient symbols of the city. Conceptual sculptor Anish Kapoor has transformed a room into a white cube with rich blue pigments on the floor that seem to draw you into the bowels of the earth; he also designed the entrance to the Monte S. Angelo subway station just outside the city center to resemble his version of Dante's entrance to the underworld (and perhaps sympathizing with riders that commuting can indeed be hell). Across town, the **Palazzo delle Arti Napoli,** or PAN (Via dei Mille 60; palazzoartinapoli.net; *(C)* **081-795-8604**) houses rotating exhibitions of contemporary art.

Via Settembrini 79 (btw. Via Duomo and Via Carbonara). www.madrenapoli.it. *(C)* **081-1931-3016.** Admission 7€ Wed–Sun, free Mon. Mon and Wed–Sat 10:30am–7:30pm, Sun 10:30am–11pm. Bus: E1. Metro: Cavour.

Napoli Sotterranea ★★ ARCHEOLOGICAL SITE   Guided tours of the city's ancient waterworks are wildly popular and a surefire hit with kids. Some 2,000 years ago, Romans dug huge cisterns beneath the city and connected them with a system of tunnels. Neapolitans used the ancient water supply well into the 19th century, when some cholera outbreaks necessitated purer sources. The emptied cisterns came in handy as quarries, as part of an escape route from the Palazzo Reale, then as bomb shelters during World War II (some of the wartime furnishings and graffiti remain in place). Adding to the mix is a Greek theater that's been unearthed amid the subterranean network. Tours last about 90 minutes, include English commentary, and usually meet at Piazza San Gaetano 68, on Via dei Tribunali near the church of San Lorenzo (Metro: Dante); sometimes they meet in front of Café Gambrinus in Piazza Trento e Trieste. Exit points vary a bit, too, but usually you'll climb out of the dark up a long staircase and emerge into the courtyard of an ordinary-looking apartment house (a good illustration of this city's many age-spanning layers). Aside from climbing stairs, you'll also be asked to squeeze through a very tight passage (not recommended for the claustrophobic or the overweight).

Vico S. Anna di Palazzo, 52. www.lanapolisotterranea.it. *(C)* **081-296944.** Admission 9.30€, 6€ for children under 10. Tours in English are scheduled daily, year-round, at 10am, noon, and 2 and 4pm.

National Archaeological Museum (Museo Archeologico Nazionale) ★★★ MUSEUM   The echoey, dusty, gloomy galleries of the run-down Palazzo degli Studi provide one of the world's great time-travel experiences, from grimy modern Naples back to the ancient world. Two treasure troves in particular should not be missed. The superb **Farnese Collection** of Roman sculpture shows off the pieces snapped up by the enormously wealthy Roman Cardinal Alessandro Farnese, who became Pope Paul III (1543–49) and was at the top of the Renaissance game of antiquity hunting. His remarkable collection was inherited by Elisabetta Farnese, duchess of

Parma, who married Philip V of Spain and whose son and grandson became kings of Naples and brought the collection here in the 18th century. Among Cardinal Farnese's great prizes was the magnificent **Ercole Farnese,** a huge statue of Hercules unearthed at the Baths of Caracalla in Rome. The superhero, son of Zeus, is tuckered out, leaning on his club after completing his 11th Labor. He looks a bit troubled, and who can blame him? After slaying monsters and subduing beasts, he's just learned he has to go into the fray again, descend into Hell, and bring back Cerberus, the three-headed canine guardian. It's a magnificent piece, powerful and wonderfully human at the same time. The colossal **"Toro Farnese,"** 4m (13 ft.) high, is the world's largest-known sculpture from antiquity and is carved out of a single piece of marble. This prize was also unearthed at the Baths of Caracalla, and Cardinal Farnese hired

The famed Toro Farnese sculpture.

a team of Renaissance masters, Michelangelo among them, to restore it, piecing together bits and pieces here and there. The intricate and delicate work depicts one of mythology's greatest acts of satisfying revenge, when the twin brothers Amphion and Zethus tied Dirce—who had imprisoned and mistreated their mother, Antiope—to the horns of a bull that dragged her to her death.

On the mezzanine and upper floors are mosaics, frescoes, and bronzes excavated from Pompeii and Herculaneum. Seeing these everyday objects from villas and shops hauntingly brings the ruined cities to life, as they show off the residents' tastes and preoccupations. Some, such as baking equipment and signage, are quite mundane, touchingly so; many, such as the bronze statues of the "Dancing Faun" (on the mezzanine), the "Drunken Faun" (top floor), and five life-size female bronzes known as "Dancers" (top floor) show off sophisticated artistry. Most of the mosaics, on the mezzanine, are from the House of Faun, one of the largest residences in Pompeii. The million-plus-piece floor mosaic, "Alexander Fighting the Persians," depicts the handsome, wavy-haired king of Macedonia astride Bucephalos, the most famous steed in antiquity, sweeping into battle with King Darius III of Persia, who's looking a bit concerned in his chariot. The **Gabinetto Segretto** (Secret Room; also on the mezzanine) displays some of the erotica that was commonplace in Pompeii. Some works are from brothels, among them frescoes that show acts lively yet predictable and some bestial (literally, as in Pan copulating with a

BAD BOY WITH A brush

The painter Caravaggio arrived in Naples in 1606, fleeing authorities in Rome after he killed a man in a fight over a debt. With his taste for gambling, prostitutes, young boys, rowdiness, and drunkenness, the tempestuous artist must have felt right at home in colorful Naples. The city was then the second largest in Europe after Paris, with 350,000 inhabitants, more than a few of whom shared Caravaggio's predisposition for recklessness. His sumptuous canvases, with their realistic portrayals of saints and martyrs and dramatic use of light, have become emblematic of the city's emotion-filled baroque style. Three Caravaggio works are in Naples.

The dark, moody, and chaotic "Seven Acts of Mercy" altarpiece is in the chapel of the **Pio Monte della Misericordia,** Via Tribunali 253 (☎ **081-446944;** Metro: Dante), a fraternity founded by nobles in 1601 to loan money to the poor. As you pick out the merciful acts—St. Martin in the foreground giving his cloak to the beggar is easy (clothing the naked)—you'll probably only detect six. But look again at the scene of the old man sucking at the breast of the young woman: That counts as two, visiting prisoners and feeding the hungry. Classicists might recognize the pair as the Roman Cimon, who was sentenced to death by starvation; his daughter, Pero, secretly suckled him, and this act of family honor won him his release. It's open Thursday to Tuesday 9am to 2pm; admission is 5€.

Located in the **Capodimonte gallery** (p. 72), the "Flagellation of Christ" depicts two brutish tormentors whipping a nearly naked Christ with almost rote determination ("another day, another flagellation"); a third is in the foreground, preparing his scourge to join in the action. Lighting emphasizes the arms in action and Christ's twisted, suffering body, providing an almost-hard-to-witness depiction of cruelty in action. This is one of two flagellation scenes Caravaggio painted while he was in Naples (he did this one originally for a family chapel in the Church of San Domenico).

The "Martyrdom of St. Ursula" hangs in the **Palazzo Zevallos Stigliano** (Via Toledo 185; ☎ **081-425011;** Metro: Montesanto), the lavish headquarters of the Banco Intesa Sanpaolo. Ursula appears relatively unfazed as the king of the Huns, from whom she has just refused an offer of marriage, shoots an arrow into her breast at point-blank range (given that, as legend has it, the 11,000 virginal handmaidens accompanying Ursula on a pilgrimage had just been beheaded, she could not have been terribly surprised at the cruel reaction of her jilted suitor). Caravaggio himself looks on from the background. This was his last painting and the last image we have of him, for he died of fever while returning to Rome a couple of months later. The *palazzo* is open Tuesday to Sunday 10am to 6pm (Sat until 8); admission is 4€.

goat) and others include phallus-shaped oil lamps and huge phalluses placed at doorways to suggest fertility and good fortune. We might titter at the bulges under togas and a fresco from Herculaneum's House of Papyri showing a gent weighing his huge member, but they weren't necessarily intended to be pornography and rather suggest the libertine attitudes of the time.

Piazza Museo 19. http://cir.campania.beniculturali.it/museoarcheologiconazionale. ☎ **081-442-2149.** Admission 10€. Daily 9am–7:30pm. Metro: Museo or Cavour.

Pio Monte della Misericordia

★★★ CHAPEL Caravaggio's 1607 "Seven Acts of Mercy" (see "Bad Boy with a Brush" box, above) takes center stage in this small octagonal chapel that once served as headquarters of a charitable institution of seven noblemen who fostered good works and offered interest-free loans to the poor and needy. The seven-sided table where they met remains in place, as does the secret gallery from which they could spy into the church below—which happens to look directly onto Caravaggio's masterpiece. Works by several Neapolitan followers of Caravaggio also hang in the rooms. So do canvases by Bolognese master Guido Reni (1575–1642), who came to Naples in the 1620s to undertake lucrative commissions. It may be poetic justice that his portrait of St. Mark and other rich canvases are standouts amid works by the local artists who quite literally ran him out of town.

Caravaggio's "Seven Acts of Mercy."

Via dei Tribunali 253. www.piomontedellamisericordia.it. ⓒ **081-446944.** Admission 7€, 5€ seniors and those under 25, 14€ families of 2 adults and up to 3 children. Thurs–Tues 9am–2.30pm. Metro: Dante.

San Lorenzo Maggiore ★★★ CHURCH

The most beautiful of Naples' medieval churches seems to inspire great literature. Petrarch, the medieval master of Italian verse, lived in the adjoining convent in 1345, and it was here on Holy Saturday 1338 that Boccaccio (author of *The Decameron*) supposedly first laid eyes on his muse, Maria d'Aquino. The daughter of a count and countess but rumored to have been the illegitimate daughter of Robert of Anjou, king of Naples, Maria was married but preferred refuge in a convent to life with her debauched husband. For Boccaccio, it was love at first sight; he nicknamed her La Fiametta (Little Flame), wooed her with his romantic epic "Filocoppo," and eventually won her over and convinced her to become his mistress (she jilted him for another man a few years later). You can ponder 14th-century romance as you stroll through the delightful cloisters, then descend a staircase to witness more of the city's multilayered history: Ongoing excavations have unearthed streets from the Greco-Roman city lined with bakeries and shops, porticoes, an entire covered market, and an early Christian basilica.

Piazza San Gaetano, Via Tribunali 316. ⓒ **081-290580.** Free admission to church. Mon–Sat 8am–noon and 5–7pm. Excavations: Admission 4€. Mon–Sat 9:30am–5:30pm; Sun 9:30am–1:30pm. Metro: Piazza Cavour.

Piazza Garibaldi

Castel Capuano ★ CASTLE   Neapolitans have lived with this fortress in their midst since the 12th century, when the Norman Guglielmo I d'Altavill (William I, aka "The Bad"), the second king of Sicily, found it necessary to fortify the adjacent Porta Capuana. The gate guarded the road to and from Capua, a then-important city that had just become part of William's uneasy kingdom. Over the centuries the castle has been a royal residence, a prison, and the seat of the civil courts, which remained here until a recent move to less atmospheric quarters in the city's shiny new Civic Center. A wide flight of steps in the medieval courtyard leads to the some of the frescoed court chambers.

Via Concezio Muzy (off Via dei Tribunali). Free admission. Daily 9am–6pm (hrs. vary). Metro: Piazza Garibaldi.

Vomero

Castel Sant'Elmo ★ CASTLE   The Spanish gave this star-shaped fortress atop Vomero Hill its present appearance in the 16th century, taking advantage of a strategic position high above the city that is the reason to come up here: The castle still offers the best 360-degree views in town.

Via Tito Angelini. ℭ **081-578-4120.** Admission 4€. Wed–Mon 8:30am–9:30pm. Metro: Vanvitelli and then bus V1 to Piazzale San Martino.

Certosa di San Martino (Carthusian Monastery) ★★ MONASTERY The Carthusian monks who took up residence high atop Vomero Hill in 1368 obviously knew something of the good life. Their view is still the best in Naples, across the city and the bay to Mt. Vesuvius. Over the next several centuries they hired the city's best artists to embellish their surroundings.

San Lorenzo Maggiore from the front.

Foremost among them was the fractious architect and sculptor Cosimo Fanzago (1591–1678), who created the piece de la resistance, an enormous central courtyard/cloisters. Fanzago was lucky to be alive, having once fled the city after being sentenced to death for supporting a peasant revolt. He spent his last 30 years laboring on the cloisters and executing fine marble inlays in the monastery church, while at the same time suing his Carthusian benefactors for underpayment. His cloister is a masterpiece of the baroque, a grand assemblage of statue-lined porticoes facing a broad lawn. Lest the monks get too comfortable in their earthly surroundings, a gallery of skulls reminded them of their inevitable fate. As if to reinforce the point, in surrounding chapels the Spanish painter Jusepe de Ribera (1591–1652) executed several of his ghoulish scenes of martyrdom and suffering, so realistically portrayed with wounds, wrinkles, and writhing agony that he's been said to partake in "the poetry of the repulsive." His dark "Pieta," a masterpiece full of light and shadow, hangs above an altar glittering with lapis lazuli in the Cappella del Tesoro. Overhead, in a ceiling fresco by Luca Giordano, the widow Judith holds aloft the head of her oppressor, the Assyrian general Holfrenes, whom she has just beheaded—a classic story of modesty trumping power that is a little hard to swallow in such opulent surroundings. As you wander through the vast monastery, now housing the collections of the Museo Nazionale di San Martino (see below),

One of the gallery of skulls from Certosa di San Martino.

it's easy to see why the city's royal administrators were so appalled by the monks' lavish lifestyle that they threatened to cut off state subsidies.

Largo San Martino 8. ✆ **081-578-1769.** Admission 6€. Thurs–Tues 8:30am–7:30pm; ticket booth closes 90 min. earlier. Closed Jan 1 and Dec 25. Metro: Vanvitelli and then bus V1 to Piazzale San Martino. Bus: C28, C31, or C36 to Piazza Vanvitelli. Funicular: Centrale to Piazza Fuga or Montesanto to Morghen.

Museo Nazionale di San Martino ★★ MUSEUM   The gleaming white monastery of San Martino (see above), high atop the Vomero hill, is the city's beacon, visible from just about anywhere. So it's only fitting that within its thick walls is a repository of all things Neapolitan—paintings, prints, sculpture, historical artifacts, and the standout, the *presepi* (nativity scenes) for which the city has an undying affection (see "Every Day Is Christmas in Naples" box, p. 63). St. Francis of Assisi allegedly commissioned the first *presepe* in the 13th century, and Naples elevated the scenes to high art, bolstered by the patronage of King Charles III in the 18th century. As you'll see, city craftsmen went to town, carving figures in wood and firing them in ceramics, fitting them with tailored clothing, and setting the Holy Family and their retinue on typical Naples streets. None outshine the 750-piece Cuciniello Presepe, equipped with a lighting system that simulates the cycle of a day from dusk to nightfall and so big it occupies an entire side of the former monastery kitchens. Even larger is the full-size model of the Great Barge used by King Charles of Bourbon in the 1700s, housed amid other models and artifacts that honor the city's role as a maritime power. The Gothic cellars are filled with sculpture, including an astonishing St. Francis of Assisi by

Giuseppe Sanmartino, who so artfully crafted "Christ Veiled Under a Shroud" in the Cappella di Sansevero.

Largo San Martino 8. © **081-578-1769.** Admission 6€. Thurs–Tues 8:30am–7:30pm; ticket booth closes 90 min. earlier. Metro: Vanvitelli and then bus V1 to Piazzale San Martino. Bus: C28, C31, or C36 to Piazza Vanvitelli. Funicular: Centrale to Piazza Fuga or Montesanto to Morghen.

Villa La Floridiana & Museo Nazionale della Ceramica Duca di Martina ★★ MUSEUM   When King Ferdinand I returned to Naples in 1815 after ten years of exile, he brought with him a Italian/Spanish wife, Lucia Migliaccio, the duchess of Floridia. Their wedding, only a few months after the death of Ferdinand's first wife, Queen Marina Carolina of Austria, created an international scandal. The duchess did not care for court life or for Naples, and Neapolitans didn't care for her, so Ferdinand bought her a gift—this magnificent retreat on the Vomero hill with lush gardens and views that would make anyone surrender to the city's charms. The villa now houses the ceramics collection of another noble Neapolitan, Placido de Sangro, the duke of Martina. The 6,000 pieces he collected in his late 19th-century travels are arranged around the gracious rooms as they were once shown off in the duke's palace. A Chinese drummer on horseback, medieval glass, and porcelain from Meissen and Naples' own Capodimonte potteries (see below) look as if the duke had just been through with a duster. Among the items is King Ferdinand's walking stick, with a glass top that contains a portrait of Lucia; it used to be said this was the only way the powerless, morganatic queen would ever appear in court. Sketches by 18th-century Neapolitan artists hang on the walls.

Via Cimarosa 77. © **081-578-8418.** Admission 2€. Wed–Mon 8:30am–2pm; ticket booth closes 1 hr. earlier. Bus: C28, C32, or C36. Funicular: Chiaia to Cimarosa. Metro: Vanvitelli.

Pieces from the Museo Nazionale della Ceramica Duca di Martina.

Farther Afield

Catacombs of San Gennaro (St. Januarius) ★ RELIGIOUS SITE   San Gennaro's head is in the duomo, but the rest of him is in his namesake two-story underground cemetery, used from the 2nd through 11th centuries. Some of the city's earliest frescoes (those from Pompeii aside) are here, including one depicting a haloed San Gennaro with Mt. Vesuvius on his shoulders. Even earlier is a charming 2nd-century scene with Adam and Eve and a portrait of a family, with figures of each of the three members added over the years when their times came. Guides (most speaking English) will lead you down the wide aisles past the frescoed burial niches and early basilicas carved from the *tufa* rock, providing fascinating insights into the city's long past—with a special nod to Sant'Agrippino, a 3rd-century bishop once interred here, who is almost as popular among Neapolitans as San Gennaro.

Via Capodimonte 13. www.catacombedinapoli.it. © **081-744-3714.** Admission 8€. Tours Mon–Sat on the hour 10am–5pm; Sun 10am–1pm. Bus: 24 or R4.

National Museum & Gallery of the Capodimonte (Museo e Gallerie Nazionale di Capodimonte) ★ MUSEUM Italy has many better art collections, and the trip here inevitably involves a change of buses or a taxi ride. That said, there's plenty to lure you out to the former hunting preserve of the Bourbon kings. For one, the *bosco reale* (royal woods) are one of the few parks in Naples, and sharing the greenery with picnicking families can be a refreshing change of scenery. The core of the collection is from Elisabetta Farnese, the duchess of Parma who handed down the family's paintings to her children and grandchildren after she became Queen of Spain, and they in turn brought them back to Italy when they became kings of Naples. By the time the works got here, many of the best had found their way into other collections; what remains includes a roster of the greatest Italian and Northern masters, but often secondary works. In fact, the two standout pieces here have nothing to do with the Farneses. Caravaggio executed his dramatic "Flagellation of Christ" for Naples' Church of San Domenico Maggiore (for more on Caravaggio in Naples, see the "Bad Boy with a Brush" box, p. 67), and it was brought here in the 1970s, not long after another Caravaggio was stolen from an oratorio in Palermo. In the contemporary galleries hangs Andy Warhol's "Mount Vesuvius," an almost-corny comic-book depiction of an eruption that renders the mountain as an age-old icon of volatility. If you've found other royal palaces around town fairly empty, it's because many of the furnishings are upstairs here, in the Royal Apartments. There's enough Sèvres and Meissen to put together a royal feast of epic proportions. Some of the pieces, the Capodimonte ceramics, were fired right here on the grounds throughout the 18th century.

Palazzo Capodimonte, Via Miano 1; also through the park from Via Capodimonte. http://cir.campania.beniculturali.it/museodicapodimonte. © **081-749-9111.** Admission 7.50€; 6.50€ after 2pm. Thurs–Tues 8:30am–7:30pm. Bus: R4 (from the Archaeological Museum).

ORGANIZED TOURS

You might have enjoyed CitySightseeing tours in other cities, but CitySightseeing Napoli (www.napoli.city-sightseeing.it; © **081-551-7279**) is not a surefire hit. As in all cities, the company runs double-decker bus tours that allow you to hop off at sights then get back on. In Naples, the company operates several routes—two around the city center and one along the bay (your ticket allows you to use any of them). The city center tours are not of great use, since much of what you want to see is squirreled away in the historic center on narrow pedestrian-only streets and alleys, and the buses only skirt the areas you'll want to explore on foot. The farther-flung tour, along the bay out to Posillipo, is a breezy excursion geared toward scenic glimpses of the seafront; it's a nice/good value outing even if you never get off the bus—provided you would rather sit back and enjoy the scenery rather than see churches and museums. The company also operates a Shuttle Bus (5€), a minivan that makes a circuit of the historic center with stops at the Duomo, Archaeological Museum, and churches of Santa Chiara and Gesu Nuovo. If mobility is an issue, this might be helpful, but otherwise you can walk between these sights in 10 minutes. All tours depart from Piazza Municipio/Parco Castello with varying stops along the way, depending on the route. Tickets are valid for 24 hours on all lines and can be purchased onboard for 22€ for adults, 11€ for children ages 6 to 15, and 66€ for a family (2 adults and 3 children 18 and under).

Passes

The confoundingly complex **Campagnia Artecard** (www.campaniartecard. it; © 800-600601 or 06-3996–7650) can actually save you some money if you plan to make the rounds of churches, museums, and archeological sites. Depending on which version you buy, the card gives you free admission to two or three attractions, discounted admission (as much as 50%) to a great number of others, free access to public transportation, and discounts to a number of participating shops and restaurants. The pass comes in seven different versions (21€–34€) for use in Naples and/or the surrounding region. One option you might want to consider is the 3-day Tutta la Regione pass, because it covers Herculaneum and Pompeii as well as the Naples museums; for 32€ you get free transport within Naples and on the Circumvesuviana line (out to Herculaneum and Pompeii) as well as free admission to two sights and a 50% discount on others. A 34€ version provides free admission to five sights but no transport. Within Naples, the 3-day 21€ pass gives you free admission to three sights, a 50% discount on a fourth, and free transport on subways and buses—so again, it's a not a huge money saver, but you will save a few euros. To see which sites qualify for free or 50% admission, go to the website listed above. (These include all of the sites most tourists come to Naples and its surroundings to see.)

The Artecard is for sale at all participating sites and museums, and at the Campania Artecard stand at the Napoli Centrale train station.

WHERE TO STAY

Where you stay in Naples makes a difference—as in, enjoyable stay versus "I never want to set foot in this hellhole again." You want a safe neighborhood close to the sights, and our suggestions below meet that criterion. Some good business-oriented hotels have opened near the train station, but this area is not very convenient or, for that matter, particularly savory after dark. Naples hotels often post special Internet rates on their websites, especially in summer, which is low season in the city.

Naples Hotels & Restaurants

RESTAURANTS ◆

Europeo di Mattozzi **9**
La Campagnola **4**
Nennella **11**
Pizzeria Da Michele **6**
Pizzeria Gino Sorbillo **5**
Rosiello **17**
Squistezze/La Stanza del Gusto **3**
Tandem **7**
Zi Teresa **16**

HOTELS ■

Art Resort Gallery Umberto **13**
Chiaia Hotel de Charme **14**
Costantinopoli 104 **1**
Decumani Hotel de Charme **8**
Grand Hotel Vesuvio **15**
Hotel Il Convento **12**
Hotel Piazza Bellini **2**
San Francesco al Monte **10**

Ferry Terminal
ⓘ Tourist Information
Ⓕ═══Ⓕ Funiculars

0 ———— 1/4 mi
0 ———— 500 m

RIONE ALTO

ARENELLA

Via B. Cavallino
Via D. Fontana
Via P. Castellino
Via Altamura

Piazza Musil
Piazza Medaglie d'Oro
Piazza d. Artisti
Piazza Fanzago
Via Camaro
Stadio Collana
Piazza Quattro Giornale
Via L. Giordano
Via Bernini
Piazza Vanvitelli

SOCCAVO

Via Epomeo
Viale Traiano
Via Giustiniano
Tangenziale di Napoli
A56

Via Cilea
Via Scariatti
Via Belvedere
Via Cimarosa
Via A. Falcone
Corso Europa
Via Tasso

CHIAIA

Stazione Corso Vitt. Emanuele
Corso Vitt. Emanuele
Via Crispi
Piazza Amedeo
Via Schipa
Via A. D'Isernia
Villa Pignatelli

FUORIGROTTA

To Pozzuoli, Cuma, & Phlegrean Fields
Via Terracino
Via Leopardi
Via Consalvo
Ferrovia
Via Manzoni
Cumana
Stazione Mergellina ⓘ
V. Piedigrotta
Piazza d. Repubblica
Riviera di Chiaia
Via Francesco Caracciolo

Stazione Fuorigrotta
Via Lepanto
Viale Augusto
Viale G. Cesare
Piazza Sannazzaro
Terminal Aliscafi (Hydrofoil)

Via Orazio

Via Campegna
Via Manzoni
Via Petrarca
Via Posillipo

POSILLIPO

Palazzo Donn'Anna
17

To Ischia, Procida | To Capri | To Sorrento | To Eolie

Expensive

Grand Hotel Vesuvio ★★★   Old-world glamour holds sway in this famed waterfront hostelry that pampers the rich and famous and provides a Grand Tour–worthy experience (with all the 21st-century amenities, including a spiffy spa and small indoor pool). Expanses of shiny parquet, handsome old prints, fine linens on the firm beds, and classic furnishings give the large, bright, and very comfortable guest rooms a sophisticated yet understated polish. The big perk, though, is the view of the bay, the Castel dell'Ovo, and Mt. Vesuvius outside big glass doors that open to balconies off many of the rooms and suites. You'll get the same eyeful from the bright salon where a lavish breakfast buffet is served, and from the rooftop restaurant. High-season prices are geared to the pocketbooks of celebrities and dignitaries, though off-season rates and the occasional special offer brings the memorable experience of a stay here within reach of the rest of us.

Via Partenope 45 (off Via Santa Lucia by Castel dell'Ovo). www.vesuvio.it. ℂ **081-764-0044.** 160 units. 180€–460€ double. Most rates include buffet breakfast. Parking 25€. Bus: 152, 140, or C25. **Amenities:** 2 restaurants; bar; fitness center and spa; pool (for a fee); room service; smoke-free rooms; Wi-Fi (free).

Moderate

Art Resort Gallery Umberto ★   As if the location were not dramatic enough, an upper floor of accommodations in the city's 1890s Art Nouveau-style glass shopping arcade is almost over-the-top with plush interiors. The painted headboards, swag draperies, and gilded furniture are not for minimalists, but for a Neapolitan experience it's hard to beat the dash of theatricality, or the location (none better for shoppers). Many of the rooms face the interior of the *galleria* (but are just below the glass roof, so quite bright), while others look out over an adjoining piazzetta, and a choice few have small balconies. All guests can enjoy the large interior terrace high above the tile-floored arcades far below.

Galleria Umberto 1. www.artresortgalleriaumberto.it ℂ **081-497-6224.** 16 units. 120€–135€ double. Rates include buffet breakfast. Parking 20€ in nearby garage. Bus: R2. **Amenities:** Bar; concierge; free Wi-Fi in lobby and some rooms.

Chiaia Hotel de Charme ★   With its bright shops and bars, spiffy, pedestrian-only Via Chiaia may be the city's friendliest address, and this warmly decorated inn that ranges across two floors of an old nobleman's residence does the location justice. Some smaller rooms face interior courtyards and have snug, shower-only bathrooms, while many of the larger ones on the street side (with double panes to keep the noise down) have large bathrooms with Jacuzzi tubs. Decor throughout is sufficiently traditional and regal to suggest the palazzo's aristocratic provenance, and services are more wholesome than they were when the place was an upscale brothel. Pastries and snacks are laid out in the sitting room in the afternoon and evening, the buffet breakfast is generous, and the staff is good at recommending restaurants and providing directions.

Via Chiaia 216. www.hotelchiaia.it. ℂ **081-415555.** 33 units. 145€–185€ double. Rates include buffet breakfast. Parking 18€ in nearby garage. Bus: R2. **Amenities:** Bar; concierge; free Wi-Fi in lobby and some rooms.

Costantinopoli 104 ★★ A 19th-century Art Nouveau palace that once belonged to a marquis is set in a palm-shaded courtyard that's mere steps from the archeological museum but a world removed from the noisy city—there's even a small swimming pool for a refreshing dip. Contemporary art and some stunning stained glass grace a series of salons; some rooms are traditionally done with rich fabrics and dark wood furnishings, others are more breezily contemporary, and some spread over two levels. The choicest rooms are on the top floor and open directly off a sprawling roof terrace—a magical retreat above the surrounding rooftops and definitely what you should ask for when booking.

Via Santa Maria di Costantinopoli 104 (off Piazza Bellini). www.costantinopoli104.com. ℂ **081-557-1035.** 19 units. From 140€ double. Rates include buffet breakfast. Parking 25€. Metro: Museo. **Amenities:** Pool; room service; Wi-Fi (free).

Decumani Hotel de Charme ★★ The heart-of-Naples neighborhood outside the huge portals can be gritty, but these are sprucely regal lodgings, on the *piano nobile* of the palazzo of the last bishop of the Bourbon kingdom, Cardinal Sisto Riario Sforza. Guest rooms surround a vast, fresco-smothered ballroom-cum-breakfast room; all have plush draperies and fabrics and a few antique pieces complementing shiny hardwood floors and timbered ceilings. Larger rooms include small sitting areas and face the quiet courtyard, while many of the smaller, street-facing doubles share small terraces with the adjoining rooms.

Via San Giovanni Maggiore Pignatelli 15 (off Via Benedetto Croce, btw. Via Santa Chiara and Via Mezzocannone). www.decumani.it. ℂ **081-551-8188.** 22 units. 135€–150€ double. Rates include breakfast. Parking 25€ in nearby garage. Metro: Piazza Dante. **Amenities:** Wi-Fi (free).

San Francesco al Monte ★★ This ex-Franciscan convent just above the Spanish quarter and halfway up the San Martino hill makes the monastic life seem pretty appealing. The hillside location is a handy refuge above the fray but an easy walk or funicular ride away from the sights, and views from all the rooms and several airy glassed-in and outdoor lounges sweep across the city to the bay. The monastic tenants left behind a chapel, a refectory, secret stairways, and all sorts of atmospheric nooks and crannies (one houses an elaborate nativity scene), and their cells have been combined into large, tile-floored guest rooms, all with sitting areas, and some sprawling suites. In the contemplative, sky-high monk's garden, shaded walkways are carved out of the cliffside and a swimming pool and outdoor bar are delightful un-monastic perks.

Corso Vittorio Emanuele 328. www.sanfrancescoalmonte.it. ℂ **081-423-9111.** 45 units. 135€–225€ double. Rates include buffet breakfast. Parking 25€. Metro: Piazza Amedeo; Montesanto or Centrale funiculars to Corso Vittorio Emanuele. **Amenities:** Restaurant; bar; pool; room service; Wi-Fi (free).

4

NAPLES — Where to Stay

Inexpensive

Hotel Il Convento ★   If you want to experience a slice of Neapolitan life—as in laundry flapping outside your window—this is the place for you. While the narrow Spagnoli streets outside teem with neighborhood color and busyness, a 17th-century former convent provides all sorts of cozy ambience, with lots of wood beams, brick arches, and terracotta floors. Two rooms are real retreats, with their own planted rooftop terraces, and two others spread over two levels. Main artery Via Toledo is just 2 short blocks away, taking the edge off comings and goings at night. An eager staff will steer you to neighborhood restaurants and shops.

Via Speranzella 137/a. www.hotelilconvento.com. 🕿 **081-403977.** 14 units. 85€–110€. Rates include buffet breakfast. Parking 15€ in nearby garage. Bus: R2 to Piazza Municipio. Small pets allowed. **Amenities:** Bar; fitness room and sauna; room service; Wi-Fi (free).

Hotel Piazza Bellini ★★   The archaeological museum and lively Piazza Bellini are just outside the door of this centuries-old palace, but a cool contemporary redo softens the edges of city life. An outdoor living room fills the cobbled courtyard, and the rooms, which range across several floors, are minimalist chic with warm hardwood floors, neutral tones with warm-hued accents, sleek surfaces that make plenty of space for storage, Philippe Starck chairs, and crisp white linens. Some of the rooms have terraces and balconies, a few are bilevel, and some with limited views are set aside in an "economy" category—but rates for any room in the house are reasonable and make this mellow haven an especially good value.

Via Costantinioli 101. www.hotelpiazzabellini.com. 🕿 **081-451732.** 48 units. 100€–160€ double. Metro: Piazza Dante or Piazza Cavour. **Amenities:** Bar; concierge; Wi-Fi (free).

A room at the Hotel Piazza Bellini.

WHERE TO EAT

Neapolitans love to eat, and you'll love dining here, too. What's not to like about a cuisine in which pizza is a staple? Other dishes to look out for include *mozzarella in carrozza* (fried mozzarella in a "carriage"), in which mozzarella is fried between two pieces of bread and topped with a sauce of the chef's design, often with tomatoes and capers; *gnocchi alla sorrentina,* little pockets of potato pasta filled with mozzarella and topped with tomato sauce; *ragu,* a sauce of several meats cooked for hours and served atop pasta, of course, or in a bowl with thick slices of bread; *parmigiana di melanzane* (eggplant parmigiano), yes, the now-ubiquitous dish of fried eggplant, tomato sauce, mozzarella, parmigiano, and basil originated here; *crocchè di patate* (fried potatoes, pronounced "croquet"), mashed with herbs, cheese, sometimes salami, lightly coated in breadcrumbs and fried; and *pasta e fagioli,* beans and pasta, nothing could be more Neapolitan. Think, too, of seafood—any kind, especially *cozze,* mussels, often served *alla marinara* (simmered in tomato sauce); and *polpette,* succulent little meatballs.

For a sampling of street food—especially the above mentioned *crocchè di patate* and *arancini,* fried rice balls—stop by the stand on the ground floor of **Matteo,** a venerable pizzeria at Via Tribunali 94 (© **081-455262**), open Monday to Saturday 9am to midnight.

Expensive

Rosiello ★★★ NEAPOLITAN/SEAFOOD   It's a cab ride or long bus trip out to this retreat, on a hilltop above the sea in swanky and leafy Posillipo, but the trip is worth it. Ask your hotel to make reservations and help arrange transport, because a meal on the terrace here is one of the city's great treats. Everything comes from the waters at your feet or the restaurant's extensive vegetable plots on the hillside; even the cheese is local. These ingredients find their way into seafood feasts that might include risotto *alla pescatora* (with seafood) and *pezzogna all'acquapazza* (fish in a light tomato broth), but even a simple pasta here, such as *scialatielli con melanzane e provola* (fresh pasta with local cheese and eggplant), is elegant and simply delicious.

Via Santo Strato 10. www.ristoranterosiello.it. © **081-769-1288.** Main courses 10€–25€. Thurs–Tues 12:30–4pm and 7:30pm–midnight (May–Sept open daily). Closed 2 weeks each Jan and Aug. Bus: C3 to Mergellina (end of line), and then 140.

Squistezze/La Stanza del Gusto ★★ CREATIVE NEAPOLITAN Chef Mario Avallone prepares some of the most innovative food in town, and he offers it two ways: In a casual, ground-floor cheese bar/*osteria* (Squistezze) and in a simple-but-stylish upstairs restaurant. Downstairs, daily offerings are written on blackboards and include the best lunch deal in town—a main course of the day, dessert, wine, water, and coffee for 13€. Or you can pair cheese and *salumi* (cured meats) with carefully chosen wines or what is probably the city's largest selection of craft beers (the staff makes suggestions) or tuck into hearty salads and several unusual specialties, such as *arancino di* *mare,* a fresh take on classic fried rice balls, in this case concealing a core of fresh seafood. Upstairs, locally sourced ingredients find their way into dishes that you'll probably want to enjoy on one of several tasting menus that start at 35€; choose one that includes the *variazione di baccalà,* an amazing presentation of salt cod prepared in several different ways.

Via Santa Maria di Costantinopoli 100. www.lastanzadelgusto.com. ⓒ **081-401578.** Main courses (upstairs restaurant) 14€–20€. Tues–Sat noon–11:30pm; Sun noon–3pm. Upstairs restaurant Tues–Sat 7–11pm. Closed 3 weeks in Aug. Metro: Piazza Dante or Museo.

Moderate

Europeo di Mattozzi ★★ NEAPOLITAN/PIZZA/SEAFOOD Just about all Neapolitans rank this attractive center-of-town eatery as a favorite, and the walls—covered with copper pots, framed photos, and oil paintings—provide welcoming surroundings that suggest that dining here is serious business. Even connoisseurs claim the pizzas are some of the best in town, and if one of the large pies doesn't suffice as a starter, choose from *zuppa di cannellini e cozze* (bean and mussel soup) or *pasta e patate con provola* (pasta and potatoes with melted local cheese). Seafood *secondi* are the house specialties and include *ricciola all' acquapazza* (a local species in a light tomato and herb broth) and *stoccafisso alla pizzaiola* (dried codfish in a tomato, garlic, and oregano sauce). Reservations are a must on weekends.

Via Marchese Campodisola 4. ⓒ **081-552-1323.** Main courses 12€–18€. Mon–Wed noon–3:30pm; Thurs–Sat noon–3:30pm and 8pm–midnight. Closed 2 weeks in Aug. Bus: R2 or R3 to Piazza Trieste e Trento.

Tandem ★ NEAPOLITAN Take a seat in the simple room or the pleasant little terrace on the lane outside and linger over the house specialty, *ragu.* A lot of Neapolitans drop by the friendly, almost-funky little room and terrace for their fix of this city staple, which comes in two varieties, meat (three or four kinds, slow-cooked) or vegetarian, which is a bit of a desecration. It's served over spaghetti or a choice of other pasta, or by itself with thick slices of bread for dunking, along with carafes of the house wine.

Via Paladino 51. www.ristorantetandemragu.it. ⓒ **081-407-4833.** Reservations recommended Fri–Sat. *Secondi* 10€–18€. Mon–Fri noon–3:30pm and 7–11:30pm, Sat–Sun noon–4pm and 7–midnight. Metro: Piazza Dante.

Zi Teresa ★★ NEAPOLITAN/SEAFOOD Neapolitans know the Borgo Marinaro tourist traps to avoid, but they flock to this bright room in the shadow of Castel dell'Ovo to soak in the sea views while enjoying reliably fresh fish and seafood. This 125-year-old institution is wildly popular for family gatherings, thanks to huge platters of seafood grills and *fritturra mista* that can nourish large groups. The natty decor has a nautical twist, and if that doesn't make the point, the fleet of boats bobbing next to the huge terrace will.

Via Borgo Marinaro 1. www.ziteresa.it. ⓒ **081-764-2565.** Main courses 9€–20€. Tues–Sat 12:15–11:30pm, Sun 12:15–5:30pm. Bus: 152, C25, 140, or E5 to Via Santa Lucia.

On top of their many other sterling qualities, Neapolitans make delicious sweets and desserts. Delicious, clam-shaped *sfogliatelle,* filled with ricotta cream and topped with powdered sugar, is the city's unofficial pastry, available at bars and in pastry shops all over the city. *Il baba* are little cakes soaked in a rum or *limoncello* syrup and often filled with cream; *delizia al limone* (delicious lemon) consists of sponge-cake soaked with lemon or *limoncello* syrup, filled with lemon pastry cream, and iced with lemon-flavored whipped cream; and dark, flourless *torta Caprese,* topped with powdered sugar, is the chocolate cake of choice.

Scaturchio, Piazza San Domenico Maggiore 19 (www.scaturchio.it;

✆ **081-551-7031**) makes some of the best *sfogliatelle* in town and also serves excellent coffee. Another popular stop for a coffee (the hazelnut cream is a city favorite) and a sweet treat is **Il Vero Bar del Professore** at Piazza Trieste e Trento, 46 (ilverobardelprofessore.com, ✆ **081-403041**). Naples's ice cream parlors dispense some of the best gelato in the country; **Gelateria della Scimmia,** Piazza della Carità 4 (✆ **081-552-0272**) is a mandatory stop. The city's revered temple of chocolate, **Gay-Odin,** has elegant shops throughout the city, dispensing chocolate *cozze* (mussels) and chocolate-wrapped coffee beans alongside much-lauded gelato; a convenient central outlet is at Via Benedetto Croce 61 (www.gay-odin.it; ✆ **081-551-0794**).

Inexpensive

La Campagnola ★★ NEAPOLITAN   A lot of students, professors, and neighborhood regulars eat at this plain, homey wine shop/trattoria almost every day, or at least stop by for a glass of the house wine and a plate of fried artichokes or one of the other appetizers. The chalkboard menu changes daily and includes Neapolitan home-style favorites like *parmigiano di melanzane* and *vitello limone.* The pizzas are excellent, too, perfect for starters, and a meal ends with a plate of *zeppole* (fried donuts), courtesy of the house.

Via Tribunale 47. ✆ **081-459034.** Main courses 7€–10€. Wed–Tues noon–3pm and 7–11pm. Metro: Dante.

Nennella ★ NEAPOLITAN   No one here is going to stand on formality, but the guys at this Spagnoli favorite will make you feel like one of the neighborhood regulars who crowd into the tent-covered terrace or plain white room for the satisfying home cooking. Stick to the specials, listed on a board and recited by one of the busy waiters—*pasta e patate* (pasta and potatoes), maybe some fried fish or roasted pork, and salads of fresh greens. Even when accompanied by wine, a meal here won't cost more than 12€ or 15€.

Vico Lungo Teatro 103–105. ✆ **081-414338.** Main courses 6€–8€. Mon–Sat noon–3pm and 7–11pm. Metro: Montesanto.

Pizzeria Da Michele ★★ PIZZA   According to about half the residents of Naples, this no-frills, zero-ambience place serves the best pizza in town—the other half would vote for Pizzeria Gino Sorbillo (see below). Take a number at the door and prepare to wait for a table, as the place is always packed.

But you won't have to wait long for one of the enormous and simply delicious pizzas that come in just two varieties, *margherita* or *marinara* (toppings are for snobs, say the guys behind the counter); they emerge from the oven in a mere 20 seconds, an act of wizardry that keeps the tables turning quickly. No credit cards accepted.

Via Sersale 1. www.damichele.net. ✆ **081-553-9204.** Pizza 4€–5€. Mon–Sat 11am–11pm. Metro: Garibaldi.

Pizzeria Gino Sorbillo ★★ PIZZA
Don't let the crowds out front put you off, and don't let one of the other pizza places on Via Tribunali lure you in (a couple of others, also confusingly called Sorbillo, have been set up by other family members). Just make your way through the crowd, give your name to the friendly, bemused woman with the clipboard, and

A crowd waits to get into Pizzeria Gino Sorbillo.

enjoy the partylike atmosphere on the street out front as you wait for a table. The wait is never as long as you think it might be, and once inside you'll probably be ushered to the vast, upstairs dining room where a long menu of pizzas is accompanied by a palatable house wine. This attractive place is the Ritz compared to serious contender Pizzeria Da Michele (see above). The Quattro Stagione (Four Seasons) pizza defies Michele's no-topping policy with its quadrants of mushrooms, salami, prosciutto, and cheese.

Via Tribunali 32. www.sorbillo.it. ✆ **081-033-1009.** Pizza 4€–5€. Daily noon–3:30pm and 7–midnight. Metro: Dante.

SHOPPING

Via Toledo and **Galleria Umberto I** still hold their own as mainstays of Naples shopping, though the clothing and accessories shops tend to be a little less elegant than those in **Chaia.** There, big Italian fashion names have outlets along the Riviera di Chiaia, Via Calabritto, Via dei Mille, Via Filangeri, Via Poerio, and Piazza dei Martiri. On the subject of labels, street vendors sell knockoffs, carrying on a long tradition in this city that was famous for counterfeiting as early as the 17th century. Be aware, though: Police are cracking down on the trade to protect the legal rights of designers and holding buyers as well as sellers culpable. You run the risk of a fine, and might also be nabbed for transporting illegal goods when coming through customs at home.

You're much better off picking up one of the handcrafted goods for which the city is justly famous. Heading the list are *presepi,* the nativity scenes crafted and sold along **Via San Gregorio Armeno** (see "Every Day Is Christmas in Naples" box, p. 63). Another shop selling handcrafted figurines is **La Scarabatto,** in the historic center at Via die Tribunali 50 (www.lascarabattola. it; *©* **081-291735**), where the delightful output includes traditional Neapolitan folk figures and contemporary ceramics. In Chaia, some venerable standbys known for their handmade wares are **Marinella,** Via Riviera di Chiaia 287 (www.marinellanapoli.it; *©* **081-764-4214**), for colorful ties; **Aldo Tramontano,** Via Chiaia 149 (www.tramontano.it; *©* **081-414837**), for handbags; and **Mario Talarico,** Vico Due Porte a Toledo 4/b (mariotalarico.it; *©* **081-401979**), for umbrellas.

A branch of Italy's big bookstore chain, **La Feltrinelli** (www.lafeltrinelli. it), is located in the train station and is a good stop for English-language books and maps; it's open daily 7am to 9pm. **Bowinkel,** near the seafront at Via Santa Lucia 25 (www.bowinkel.it; *©* **081-764–0739**), is the city's most venerable purveyor of vintage prints.

The boisterous **Mercato di Porta Nolano** stretches around Piazza Nolano, just south of the train station (metro: Porta Nolano). Stalls burst with seafood and local produce and all manner of other foodstuffs; they operate daily, until 6pm Monday through Saturday and 2pm on Sunday (pickpockets have a field day here, so watch your belongings). Every third Saturday and Sunday of each month from 8am to 2pm (except in Aug), a *fiera antiquaria* (antiques fair) is held in the Villa Comunale di Napoli on Viale Dohrn.

Opening hours for stores in Naples are generally Monday to Saturday from 10:30am to 1pm and from 4 to 7:30pm.

ENTERTAINMENT & NIGHTLIFE

Neapolitans make the best of balmy evenings by passing the time on cafe terraces. Top choice is the oldest cafe in Naples, with a Liberty-style interior from the 1860s, the elegant **Gran Caffè Gambrinus,** Via Chiaia 1, in Piazza Trento e Trieste (*©* **081-417582**). Another very popular spot is **La Caffetteria,** Piazza dei Martiri 25 (*©* **081-764-4243**), great for evening *aperitivi.*

OPERA & CLASSICAL MUSIC   The venerable **Teatro San Carlo,** Via San Carlo 98 (www.teatrosancarlo.it; *©* **081-797-2412** or 081-797-2331), stages world-class opera, along with dance and orchestral works, Tuesday through Sunday, December through June. Tickets cost between 30€ and 100€.

The **Centro di Musica Antica Pietà dei Turchini,** Via Santa Caterina da Siena 38, at the base of the Vomero hill near the Vittorio Emanuele funicular stop (www.turchini.it; *©* **081-402395**), is a music conservatory that is well known for its concerts of early music, though the repertoire extends to other music as well. Concerts are held in the church of Pietà dei Turchini, beneath paintings by some of Naples' great baroque masters, and in an adjoining hall that was once an orphanage where the young charges were instructed in singing and musical composition. Among the star pupils were Alessandro Scarlatti (1660–1725) and Giovanni Pergolesi (1710–36).

Another great venue is the **Associazione Alessandro Scarlatti,** Piazza dei Martiri 58 (www.associazionescarlatti.it; *©* **081-406011**), which stages

The Teatro San Carlo.

chamber music concerts at Castel Sant'Elmo and other venues; tickets prices range from 15€ to 25€.

Trianon Viviani, near the train station (metro Garibaldi) at Piazza Vincenzo Calenda 9 (www.teatrotrianon.it; ℂ **081-225-8285**), focuses on traditional Neapolitan song and theater; the concert season usually starts in April, with performances Thursday through Sunday, but check the theater for changes in the programs.

BARS & CLUBS   This is a port, a cosmopolitan city, and a university town all rolled into one, so the Neapolitan nighttime scene is eclectic and lively. **Piazza Bellini,** near the university at the edge of the historical center, is an especially lively destination. *Enoteche,* or wine bars, provide a good choice of wines by the glass and by the bottle, along with a bit of food and usually a relaxed atmosphere. Some top choices are quiet **Berevino,** Via Sebastiano 62 (ℂ **081-060-5688;** closed Mon); **Enoteca Belledonne,** Vico Belledonne a Chiaia 18 (www.enotecabelledonne.com; ℂ **081-403162;** closed Sun), with a local Chiaia vibe; chic, stark **Barril** (Via Giuseppe Fiorelli 11); and **Trip** (Via Giuseppe Martucci 64; www.tripnapoli.com; ℂ **081-1956-8994**), with its welcoming overstuffed couches.

Kestè, near the university at Largo San Giovanni Maggiore 26 (www.keste. it; ℂ **081-551-3984**), is a dance club and bar with a huge terrace where you can observe the youth of Naples peacocking around. On the more elegant end of the scale is **Chez Moi,** just off Chiaia's Piazza Amedeo on Via del Parco Margherita 13 (ℂ **081-407526**), a hotel bar with an intimate 1970s vibe that makes you think Austin Powers might saunter over and say "Groovy, baby." The unappealingly named **Tongue** (maybe a reference to what's going on around you on the dance floor?), Via Manzoni 202 (ℂ **081-769-0888**) in Posillipo is a popular disco with a mix of gays and straights.

AROUND NAPLES

Whe n you've come to grips with Naples, and realized that for all its grime and noise the city is a pretty grand and fascinating place, you might be ready to venture into its similarly atmospheric surroundings. It's easy to do so, on trains that whisk you west and east along the bay. To the west are the weird volcanic landscapes and evocative ancient ruins of the Campi Flegrei, the Phlegraean Fields. To the east are two of the world's most famous and well-preserved ancient cities, Herculaneum and Pompeii, and the volcano that doomed them, Vesuvius. You can visit any of these fabled places easily on a day trip and be back in Naples in time for a passeggiata and dinner.

THE CAMPI FLEGREI (PHLEGRAEAN FIELDS) ★★

On this seaside peninsula just west of Naples, volcanic vents steam and hiss (the name Phlegraean Fields is from the Greek, "Burning Fields"), and ruined villas testify to ancient hedonism. Whatever drama natural phenomena and mere mortals fail to provide, mythic characters and oracles seem to spring to life and pick up the slack. Our alphabet was invented here, when the Latin language officially adopted the characters used for written communication in Cuma. Nero murdered his mother, the ambitious and villainous Agrippina, outside Baiae, the Palm Beach of the ancient world, where Caesar relaxed and Hadrian breathed his last. Moonlike landscapes are interspersed with lush hillsides carpeted with olive groves and orange and lemon orchards, adding an eerie beauty to the mix.

Getting There

A day exploring this strange, mythic landscape begins in seaside Pozzuoli, reached from Naples by Line 2 of the Metropolitana (subway) or via the Cumana Railroad (www.unicocampania.it; ✆ **800-053939**), starting from Piazza Montesanto. From Pozzuoli, SEPSA buses run to the nearby sights: Baia, Solfatara, and Lago d'Averno, and Cuma (www.sepsa.it; ✆ **081-735-4965**).

Pozzuoli ★★

32km (14 miles) W of Naples

Screen legend Sophia Loren was born in this seaside town in 1934, contributing a bit of color to a place already well steeped in lore. The Greek colony of Dicearchia, founded in 530 B.C., became the Roman Puteoli in 194 B.C. You will soon sniff out the origin of the name—from the Latin *putere,* "to stink," from the sulfurous springs surrounding the town. Or possibly, and a little more kindly, the name comes from the Greek *pyteolos,* or "little well." Roman emperors preferred the harbor to the one at Partenope (Naples). Among them was Caligula, who performed his famous stunt at Puteoli: He rode his horse across a floating bridge of boats to Baiae, defying the soothsayer who said he had "no more chance of becoming emperor than of riding a horse across the Gulf of Baiae."

Puteoli was also a busy hub for cargo ships from all over the Roman world, and dockworkers unloaded grain from Sicily and other outposts of the empire and reloaded them with marble, mosaics, and other exports. Among the voyagers who disembarked here was St. Paul, sometime around A.D. 60. He'd sailed across the Mediterranean from Caesarea, in present-day Israel, where he'd been imprisoned. From Puteoli he traveled up the Appian Way to Rome to stand trial for alleged crimes in Asia Minor and was later freed. As Paul recounted the visit in the Bible, "The next day a wind began to blow from the south, and in two days we came to the town of Puteoli. We found some believers there who asked us to stay with them a week. And so we came to Rome."

The town also became famous for *pozzolana,* volcanic ash that reacts with water to form a substance like concrete that allowed engineers to build the huge dome of Rome's Pantheon. The barbarian Alaric destroyed the Roman town in A.D. 410, but the acropolis, on a tufa-stone promontory pushing into the sea, continued to be inhabited throughout the Dark Ages. This storied past, the ancient monuments, volcanic landscapes, and sweeping views over the sea and the islands of Ischia and Procida make Pozzuoli a lot more interesting and appealing than an otherwise scrappy suburban town has any right to be. Unless you have a yen to dive through the underwater ruins at Baiae or consult the Sybil at Cuma, you can get a good sense of the Campi Flegrei without venturing beyond Pozzuoli.

The ruins at Pozzuoli.

Phlegraean Fields

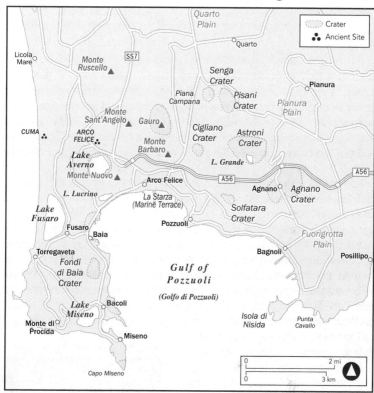

Anfiteatro Flavio (Flavian Amphitheater) ★ RUINS More than 20,000 spectators could squeeze into the many rows of seats in this theater from the last part of the 1st century, the third-largest arena in the Roman world. So much remains that it seems like a crowd is about to mill in for the next gladiatorial show. The handiwork of the theater's engineers, who also built the Coliseum in Rome, includes subterranean staging areas with "mechanics" that hoisted wild beasts up to the field of slaughter and pumped in water to flood the arena for mock naval battles. Among the unfortunate victims of the sophisticated works was Januarius, or San Gennaro, the patron saint of Naples. A painting by Artemisia Gentileschi (1593–1656), a surprisingly successful female artist of the Neapolitan baroque, shows the composed bishop withstanding the attacks of a ferocious boar. Actually, the saint didn't have much to worry about. According to legend, the beasts released to devour him fell submissively at his feet. Gennaro was later beheaded on the crater floor of the nearby Solfatara volcano. Gentileschi's painting, "The Martyrdom of San Gennaro at Pozzuoli," is in the collection of the Museo e Gallerie Nazionale di Capodimonte in Naples (see p. 72).

Via Nicola Terracciano 75. www.cir.campania.beniculturali.it. © **081-526-6007.** Admission 4€ (also includes Serapeo, Parco Archeologica di Baia, Catello di Baia, and Scavi di Cuma, and is valid 2 days). June–Sept Wed–Mon 9am–7pm; Oct–May Wed–Mon 9am–4pm, last admission 3pm.

Serapeo ★ RUINS   The discovery of a statue of the Greco-Egyptian god Serapis in the 18th century led to centuries of confusion. Serapis was a popular cult figure in the ancient world, a master of abundance and resurrection. A Serapeum, or temple to the god, was a fixture of many Greco-Roman cities—though not, as was once believed, in Puteoli. Instead, the statue stood in a niche of a magnificent marketplace, where shops surrounded a marble-floored, arcaded courtyard. In the middle was a *tholos,* a raised round meeting hall decorated with sea creatures. Another mystery arose when 19th-century antiquarians discovered that columns in the marketplace were riddled with holes drilled by mollusks, a sign they had once been underwater. Subsequent investigations revealed that the site has a long history of ups and downs, a phenomenon known as "bradyseism." Slow subsidence over long periods allows water to rush in, then the ground rises above sea level again—by as much as 6 feet in a decade, making living in Pozzuoli a fairly shaky business. In fact, a series of uplifts in the 1980s forced the evacuation of the town, damaged 8,000 buildings, and raised the seabed to the point that the harbor can no long accommodate large craft. As you wander around the site, you can see the telltale little holes in the marble columns that were once submerged in water.

The otherworldly landscape of Solfatara.

Center, follow signs. www.cir.campania.beni-culturali.it. © **081-526-6007.** Admission 4€ (also includes Anfiteatro Flavio, Parco Archeologica di Baia, Catello di Baia, and Scavi di Cuma, and is valid 2 days). Wed–Mon 9am–1 hr. before sunset.

Solfatara ★★ PARK   The ancients called this dormant volcano just 2km (1¼ miles) above Pozzuoli "Forum Vulcani" and believed it to be the residence and workshop of the god Vulcan and an entrance to Hades. It's easy to see why: Lunar landscapes hiss, steam, bubble, and spew sulfurous clouds, and the ground beneath your feet can feel as hot as, yes, hell. Despite all the bubbling, steaming, and the heavy stench of sulfur, the volcano has not erupted since 1198. It's quite safe to walk around the caldera floor on

The Campi Flegrei (Phlegraean Fields)

AROUND NAPLES

the well-marked paths, observing steaming fumaroles, breathing in the vapors, and taking in the ancient mysteries. For sheer drama, look up the slopes to the Bocca Grande, or Big Mouth, where fumaroles continually release steam at temperatures that reach 160°C (320°F). Meanwhile, in the middle of the crater, lakes of gassy mud sizzle at 250°C (482°F).

Via Solfatara 161. www.solfatara.it. © **081-526-2341.** Admission 6€. Daily 8:30am–1 hr. before sunset.

Baia ★

6km (4 miles) SW of Pozzuoli

Many of the villas and thermal baths of this ancient spa town are now under-water, though enough remains on terra firma to suggest the grandeur of ancient Baiae (the modern town dropped the final "e"). Julius Caesar, Nero, and other Roman elite once relaxed and debauched in Baiae's large villas, equipped with swimming pools and other luxuries. Seneca the Younger, the 1st-century philosopher and man of letters, called the place a "vortex of lux-ury" and a "harbor of vice." The poet Ovid said it was "a favorable place for love-making," while Horace chimed in, "No bay on Earth outshines pleasing Baiae." The town takes its name from Baio, the navigator of Odysseus, who is said to be buried somewhere in Baia.

Ancient Baiae was the select retreat of an elite few, more luxurious than Herculaneum or Capri, other nearby retreats where wealthy Romans escaped the summer heat at home. Only Stabiae (see p. 111), east across the Bay of Naples, came close to creating such a paradise on earth. Under Augustus (reigned 27 B.C. to A.D. 14), Baiae became even more exclusive as imperial property. The town was also famed for its thermal baths, fed by sulfur springs that were believed to have medicinal properties. Some of the more salacious moments of Roman infamy transpired at Baiae—not that the location really had much to do with these events, but simply because some especially amoral and hedonistic Romans spent a lot of time in Baiae. This is where, according to legend that probably obscures the factual record, the emperor Nero tried to kill his mother, Agrippina, by contriving to have a ceiling crash down on her bed. When that didn't work, he arranged to have her boat rammed at sea, but she swam ashore. The thwarted emperor finally sent a henchman to Baiae to stab the doomed woman. Poster girl for the town's debauchery may have been the much-maligned and, allegedly, sexually insatiable Messalina, third wife of the emperor Claudius. She is said to have snuck out of her Baiae villa in dis-guise at night to work at the town's brothel under the name She Wolf.

Castello di Baia ★★ HISTORIC SITE/MUSEUM   One of the most impressive landmarks in a town steeped in legend is the work of the Ara-gonese kings of Naples of the 16th century. Their massive complex of thick walls and defensive moats rises from a wave-buffeted headland that was once topped with the villa of the emperor Nero (whether or not he really lit his garden by burning Christians dipped in oil is a matter of debate). The sea-facing battlements Neapolitan royalty built were meant to deter Barbary pirates from North Africa who would pillage coastal towns and take captives to sell into the Ottoman slave market. This was an age-old practice on these shores that went back to Roman times, when a fortress at Baiae kept a lookout for Cretan pirates raiding the coast for victims to auction off at the slave market on Delos.

Castello di Baia.

More importantly, the unassailable stronghold, with its sweeping views of the bay, also ensured protection from the French navy, whose ships didn't stand a chance of sailing past the lookouts to land troops and invade Naples. The fortifications are largely the work of military mastermind Francesco di Giorgio Martini (1439–1502), who designed scores of fortresses for the enlightened duke Frederico di Montefeltro of Urbino. The castle that Martini built here at Baiae long served the Austrian, Spanish, and Bourbon rulers of the kingdom of Naples. Some of the vast rooms now house the **Museo Archeologico dei Campi Flegrei ★**, showing off statuary and other artifacts from Baiae and the surrounding region. Most enchanting are the two nymphaeums, delightful, statue-lined porches that were once equipped with lavish fountains; one is said to have been from the villa of Emperor Claudius and rescued from the sea floor.

Via Castello 39. www.cir.campania.beniculturali.it. ✆ **081-523-3797** or 848-800288. Admission 2.50€, or combined ticket 4€ (also includes Serapeo and Anfiteatro Flavio in Pozzuoli, Zona Archeologica in Baia, and Scavi di Cuma, and is valid 2 days). Tues–Sun 9am–1 hr. before sunset.

Parco Archeologica di Baia (Archeological Park of Baia) ★

ARCHEOLOGICAL SITE   Ruins of temples, villas, and bathing establishments litter three grassy terraces above the bay. The ruins are not especially well marked, nor are they well preserved (the town was sacked by Muslim raiders in the 8th century and abandoned altogether around 1500 because of rampant malaria). Not much is known about who might have lived where, though it's believed that a pile of stones near the top of the site may have been the villa of Julius Caesar. He popped up to Rome for a meeting of the senate on the Ides of March in 44 B.C. and the rest is history. His houseguest at the time was Cleopatra. Enough remains of the Terme di Baiae to show just how large and elaborate the bathing complexes were. Several of these baths are erroneously called temples: The Temple of Mercury and the Temple of Venus were actually huge baths with vast domed swimming pools, while the Temple of Diana was probably a domed casino. The pleasure of a visit to the ruins is just to wander, coming upon fragments of marble friezes, columned walkways, patches of mosaic flooring, faded frescoes that have been left to the elements, and the arcades of what is believed to have been a theater.

Much of the ancient town is underwater, preserved here. Mosaic flooring, statuary, fish ponds, columns, and other ruins litter the seabed amid bubbling geysers and flourishing flora. You can view this undersea world on dives, by snorkeling, or on trips on glass-bottom boats. Dive centers and boat tours operate out of shops along the port and Via Lucullo in Baia; expect to pay about 10€ for a boat trip, 20€ for a snorkeling tour, and 35€ for a guided dive. The office of the Area Protteta di Baia (www.areamarinaprotettabaia.eu; ✆ 081-523-2739) can provide more information and a list of tour operators; it's at Via Lucullo 94.

Via Sella di Baia 22, Bacoli. www.cir.campania.beniculturali.it. ✆ 848-800228. Admission free weekdays, Sat–Sun combined ticket 4€ (also includes Serapeo and Anfiteatro Flavio in Pozzuoli, Castello di Baia, and Scavi di Cuma, and is valid 2 days). Tues–Sun 9am–1 hr. before sunset.

Lago d'Averno (Lake Avernus) ★

5km (3 miles) N of Baia

This placid lake just north of Baia, barely 2km (1 mile) around and fringed with orange groves, fills the 60m (213 ft.) depths of the crater of an extinct volcano. If the legends are true, the lake was once so vaporously lethal (possibly from gas-emitting underwater vents) that the name derives from a Greek word meaning "without birds," because winged creatures flying over the waters would plunge to their deaths. The Cumaean Sibyl (see below) is said to have ferried Aeneas, son of Aphrodite, across the lake, where he discovered the River Styx, the Gateway to Hades. In the 1st century B.C., Emperor Agrippa had a canal dug to connect the lake with the sea, providing safe harbor for Roman ships. A couple of centuries later, the Romans built the lakeside **Temple of Apollo ★**, a huge thermal complex covered with a dome almost as large, but not as long lasting, as the one on the Pantheon in Rome; a large section of the well-weathered facade attests to the former grandeur. Time was you could get to nearby Cuma via the Grotta di Cocceio (Cocceio's Cave), a straight tunnel 1km (½ mile) long and wide enough for a chariot to pass. Agrippa had the tunnel constructed as part of his defense systems, and it was passable for almost 2,000 years, until World War II bombs caused a section to collapse.

Cuma ★

7km (4½ miles) NW of Lago d'Averno

The Greeks founded their first colony on mainland Italy at Cuma in the 8th century B.C., and Cuma grew into an important town as the center of Greek farming operations throughout Campania. The settlers soon discovered they had a helpful neighbor: the Cumaean Sibyl, who, according to legend, passed on messages from Apollo. The god told Sibyl he would grant her one wish. She took a handful of sand and said she wanted to live as many years as the

Gone to the Dogs

One attraction you can count your blessings you won't be seeing on a tour of the Campi Flegrei is the once famous Grotta del Cane (Cave of the Dogs). In the days of the 18th- and 19th-century Grand Tour, the little cave at the eastern edge of the region, just outside Pozzuoli, was a mandatory stop on the itinerary of just about any traveler, including Goethe and Mark Twain. To demonstrate how dangerous volcanic gases could be, guides would suspend dogs over vents where carbon dioxide would build up. The poor beasts would soon fall unconscious, and the fortunate ones would be revived in the cold waters of a nearby lake. The gruesome sideshow eventually fell out of favor and the cave, maybe dug by ancients as a sudatorium (sweat chamber), is now off limits to visitors and dogs.

number of grains she held. Then came the catch: Apollo wanted her virginity in return. Sibyl refused, so Apollo gave her long life but he didn't give her eternal youth. So, over the centuries she withered away. She eventually became so small she could be kept in a jar, then only her voice remained—handy for uttering a last request, "I want to die." The Sibyl's chamber became a big draw for advice-seekers from around the ancient world, though for the Romans the town wasn't much more than a pleasant backwater with a famous oracle. A road between Rome and Naples, the Via Domitiana, passed right through Cuma, and in the 1st century A.D. the **Arco Felice ★★** was cut through a hillside to accommodate chariots and wagons. Traffic still passes through the beautifully engineered arch, clattering across the original cobblestones.

The largest of the Campi Flegri's volcanic lakes is semicircular **Lago Fusaro ★**, a km (½ mile) south of Cuma, separated from the sea by a narrow strip of sand dunes. The ancients called the lake *Acherusia Palus*, or the "Infernal Swamp." Writers of antiquity unflatteringly called the lake a "billowing and tempestuous lagoon" and a "muddy expanse of sea." Even so, they also saw the strategic importance of the sheltered waters, and in the 1st century A.D., Roman engineers dug a channel to the sea so they could harbor vessels in relative safety. The Roman statesman Servilius Vatia built a now-ruined villa overlooking the lake, and in 1782 Bourbon king of Naples Ferdinando IV had Neapolitan architect Carlo Vanvitelli build a hunting and fishing lodge on a little islet, the **Casina Reale ★★**. The little palace is still a stunning presence as reflections of the pink, polygonal facade shimmer on the still lake waters. In the airy, view-filled salons Ferdinando entertained royalty and artists, among them Rossini and Mozart. The king took a great interest in oyster cultivation and fish farming, and Neapolitans were soon relishing the plump oysters plucked from the lake waters, nourished by thermal springs and known as the "fruits of the gods." On the shoreline opposite the villa is the *barraccone,* a large pavilion where boats and fishing equipment were stored, and a *cassone,* where fish were kept alive in reed containers until they were ready to be sold. You can see the exterior of the palace and outbuildings, but they are open for special functions only.

Scavi di Cuma (Ruins of Cuma) ★ ARCHEOLOGICAL PARK   The inner chamber of the famous Sibyl of Cuma is at the end of a long, narrow trapezoidal tunnel cut through volcanic stone—131.5m (432 ft.) long, some 5m (16.5 ft.) high, and as wide as 2.4m (8 ft.) across. All in all, it's a mighty impressive entrance that can still send chills down the spine and probably reassured supplicants they were about to hear something gravely important. Among them, allegedly, was Aeneas, who asked to be shown the way to the underworld so he could receive his father's wise counsel. That's how he ended up on the waters of Lake Avernus (see above). Also in these ancient landscapes just outside the entrance is a Tempio di Apollo (Temple of Apollo), supposedly built by Daedalus, best known as the creator of the maze of the Minotaur in Crete. As legend has it, Daedalus and his son Icarus were eventually locked in the maze but escaped using wings that Daedalus had built. Icarus flew too close to the sun and crashed into the sea, and heartbroken Daedalus came to Cuma and built this temple. Nearby are the remains of what was once the Tempio di Giove (Temple of Jupiter), later converted into a Christian basilica. An altar and baptismal font stand amid the ruins.

Via Montecuma. www.cir.campania.beniculturali.it. © **081-854-3060.** Admission 2.50€ or combined ticket 4€ (also includes Serapeo and Anfiteatro Flavio in Pozzuoli, Zona Archeologica in Baia, and Castello di Baia and is valid 2 days). Daily 9am to 1 hr. before sunset.

Where to Eat

Il Tucano ★ SEAFOOD/PIZZA   These white and powder-blue rooms seem as fresh as the sea out front, though they go back to the 1920s, when the place was known as Trattoria Miramare. A nice seafood menu, with fresh shellfish from the bay, carries on the tradition. Even so, the standouts are the oversized Neapolitan pizzas, as big as your table and often topped with shrimp and other seafood.

Via Molo di Baia 40, Baia. © **081-854-5046.** Main courses 10€–18€. Pizza 3€–8€. Tues–Sun noon–midnight.

VESUVIUS ★★

Towering, pitch-black Mt. Vesuvius looms menacingly over the Bay of Naples. The volcano has erupted periodically since the day of doom, August 24, A.D. 79, when it buried Pompeii and Herculaneum in eruptions that released 100,000 times the thermal energy of the Hiroshima bomb. Less violent eruptions occurred in 1631, in 1906, and most recently on March 31, 1944. Mt. Vesuvius is the only active volcano on mainland Europe, though another formidable volcanic summit, taller and more active Mt. Etna, is only 560km (335 miles) away, on the east coast of Sicily. More to the point, given the mountain's unleashed destructive power and the millions who live around its slopes, Vesuvius is one of the most potentially deadly volcanoes in the world.

The mountain still puffs steam every once in a while, just to keep everybody on their toes. Volcanologists and geologists say that given the historic record, a major eruption is likely in the relatively near future. That is, it's a question of *when* rather than *if* the mountain will blow its top again, putting the 3 million people who live around the Bay of Naples at considerable risk. Especially vulnerable are the 600,000 residents who live in the so-called "red zone," in the path of flowing lava and rocks that are expected to hurl through the sky at 100 mph.

It might sound like a dubious invitation, but it's possible to visit the rim of the crater's mouth. As you look down into its smoldering core, you might recall that, a century before the A.D. 79 eruption that buried Pompeii, the escaped slave Spartacus, who boldly led an uprising against his Roman captors, hid in the hollow of the crater, which was then covered with vines.

Getting There

The most convenient way to visit Vesuvius by public transportation from Naples or Sorrento is on the **Circumvesuviana railway** (www.vesuviana.it; ✆ **800-053939** toll-free in Italy) train to the Ercolano Scavi, where you can catch Vesuvio Express (www.vesuvioexpress.info) minivans to the parking lot below the summit. Fares for the vans are 10€ round-trip, plus you'll pay another 10€ for admission to the park. Buses run about every 45 minutes daily from 9:30am and the last bus makes the run up the mountain about 2 hours before the park closes. The trip up and down the mountain only takes about 20 minutes each way. You can also take the Circumvesuviana to the Pompei Scavi station, where you have two options. **Busvia del Vesuvio** (www.busvia delvesuvio.com; ✆ **340-935-2616**) takes a bumpy back road up the mountain in a 4WD vehicle and drops you at the summit parking lot; round-trip fare is 22€, including park admission, and runs April to October daily from 9am to 3pm, sometimes later in July and August. Buy tickets at the train station. **Tram Via del Vesuvio** (Vesuvius Trolley Tram) also makes the trip up the mountain from a terminus near the train station; round-trip fare is 12€, plus park admission. Whichever way you travel from Pompeii, allow about 40 minutes each way and at least 1½ to 2 hours at the top.

By car, take the Torre del Greco exit from the A3 autostrada and follow the signs to Vesuvio. The road ends in the parking lot below the summit, where you'll pay 2.50€ to park. A taxi from Naples costs a flat rate of 90€ round-trip, including a 2-hour wait.

Visitor Information

The **Parco Nazionale del Vesuvio** (www.parconazionaledelvesuvio.it; ✆ **081-865-3911**) maintains trails and other visitor facilities. All transportation gets you only as far as the park entrance at 1,017m (3,337 ft.) in altitude. At a ticket

One way you won't be making the ascent up the mountain is on the old Mt. Vesuvius funicular that used to climb to the summit from Pugliano, near Ercolano. It opened to great fanfare in 1880, when the song "Funiculì, Funiculà" was written to commemorate the event. Everyone from Connie Francis and the Grateful Dead to Mario Lanza and Luciano Pavarotti have recorded the jaunty tune. The great composer Johann Strauss found himself embroiled in a copyright lawsuit when, hearing the melody on a trip to Italy in the 1890s, he mistook it for a Neapolitan folk tune and incorporated the music into one of his works, *Aus Italien*. Alas, the little cable car has been less long-lived. The eruption of 1944 wiped out the tracks and sealed its fate, as the ascent by road was by then more practical.

booth here you'll pay 10€ to continue on a fairly steep trail to the summit or explore the mountainside on other trails, none of which are wheelchair accessible. The entrance fee also includes admission to the observatory at 608m (1,994 ft.), the oldest such seismological/volcanological institution in the world, dating from 1841. The park is open daily, November through March 9am to 3pm; April to May 9am to 5pm; June through August 9am to 6pm; and Sept and October 9am to 5pm. The trail to the crater closes in extreme weather.

What to See & Do

The menacing mountain is the centerpiece of 8,482-hectare (20,959-acre) **Parco Nazionale del Vesuvio (Vesuvius National Park)** ★★★. The park has laid out nine summit trails, each of them highlighting the fascinating lava flows and other geology underfoot all around you. Placards along the way explain the unique microenvironment of the volcanic summit, including many species of orchids and some other amazingly tenacious vegetation. The ticket office hands out maps of the routes, also available in short version on the website, which range from easy 1-hour strolls to strenuous 8-hour hikes.

Trail number 5, Gran Cono, is the classic ascent to the top. A moderately difficult uphill walk of about half a mile leads from the parking area and ticket office near the summit to the 230m (754-ft). deep crater. The walk takes about 20 minutes, but forego any notions of being alone in empty volcanic landscapes—cafes and souvenir stands line the route. A guide will lead you around the rim, 650m (2,132 ft.) in diameter. Make sure the guide who approaches you is a bona fide ranger and not a shill looking for a tip; the guide service is free with the price of admission and mandatory. Wear sneakers, since the lava underfoot can be hard on the feet, and bring a sweater or jacket, because it can be windy and surprisingly chilly on the heights. Once at the top, the view across Naples and the bay to the islands is so mesmerizing you might just forget how menacing Vesuvius really is. As a reminder,

explosive SIGHTINGS

The only written record from a witness of the A.D. 79 eruption of Vesuvius are two letters that magistrate and author Pliny the Younger wrote long after the event. He witnessed the spectacle from the town of Misenum, 21km (13 miles) west across the bay from Pompeii. His uncle, scholar and statesman Pliny the Elder, died while trying to rescue a friend and his family from Stabiae, near Pompeii. As commander of the navy, the elder Pliny requisitioned a boat from the imperial fleet to cross the bay on his ill-fated mission. Mission accomplished, according to some accounts, the craft attempted to head back to Misenum, and passengers, crew, and slaves strapped pillows to their heads to soften the blow of rocks falling on them. But the captain was unable to buck the winds and leave shore, and the asthmatic Pliny soon succumbed to fumes. From the safety of Misenum, his nephew witnessed a plume of ash and fumes that shot as high as 33km (19 miles), resembling, he wrote, "a (Mediterranean) pine more than any other tree. Like a very high tree the cloud went high and expanded in different branches . . . sometimes white, sometimes dark and stained by the sustained sand and ashes." He also wrote of "black and horrible clouds, broken by sinuous shapes of flaming wind."

American soldiers and airmen stationed at the Pompeii Airfield at the foot of the mountain got a good look at another Vesuvian eruption that began on March 18, 1944, raining hot ash and small rocks on their helmets and tents. They were soon forced to evacuate, leaving behind 88 airplanes. When they returned to the base, they found the planes would never fly again, their engines clogged with ash and the fuselage riddled with holes from flying rocks. Unlike Pliny solitarily recording the events of A.D. 79, the Americans had their cameras at the ready. You can see fascinating footage at www.dailymotion.com/video/x2rhfez.

Considering the power of these past eruptions, you have to agree with a 19th-century visitor to the area, German philosopher Friedrich Nietzsche, who observed, "Live in danger. Build your cities on the slopes of Vesuvius."

consider that before the A.D. 79 eruption, the mountain was more than twice as tall as its current 1,282m (4,206 ft.).

Osservatorio Vesuviano (Vesuvius Observatory) ★★ HISTORIC SITE/MUSEUM   Bourbon king of Naples Ferdinando II established this observation post to monitor Vesuvius in 1841. Two scientists on duty at all times continue to keep as eye on seismic and geochemical activity within the mountain, while guides show visitors around a collection of instruments and volcanic rocks and other well-done exhibits that provide a fascinating and terrifying look at Vesuvius and other volcanoes. One room shows off records of current rumblings within the mountain, while sophisticated photography captures shots from deep within the crater.

Via Osservatorio 14. www.ov.ingv.it. ℂ **081-610-8483.** Free admission as part of park entrance fee. Mon–Sat 9am–4pm (from 9:30am Sept–Mar).

POMPEII & HERCULANEUM

On that fateful day, August 24, A.D. 79, the people of Pompeii, a prosperous fishing town, and Herculaneum, a resort just down the coast, watched Mt. Vesuvius hurl a churning column of gas and ash high into the sky. It was only a matter of time before flows of superheated molten rock coursed through the streets of Herculaneum and ash and pumice buried Pompeii. In Herculaneum, volcanic debris quickly hardened into a layer of rock that fossilized everything—furniture, wooden beams, clothing, skeletons, graffiti, mosaics; in Pompeii, ash and rock fragments buried structures under a layer as deep as 12 meters (20 feet), preserving everything beneath it through the centuries.

Terrifying indeed for the ill-fated townsfolk, but lucky for us, the layers of ooze and ash preserved Pompeii and Herculaneum as time capsules. Pompeii is much more extensive than Herculaneum, with more to see, while Herculaneum provides an easier-to-manage, less crowded experience. You could see both in one day, and you might want to consider doing so if your time in the region is limited. However, get a good rest the night before, because seeing the sights involves a lot of walking and they can easily overwhelm you with sensory overload—you'll be seeing a lot and taking in an enormous amount of information in a short amount of time. With its gridlike streets and extensive remains, Pompeii provides an overview of a large Roman town, while Herculaneum, with its better-preserved houses and artifacts, gives an evocative glimpse into day-to-day life. Ideally, devote a day to each. If you have to choose between the two, Pompeii provides the more sensational experience.

Essentials

GETTING THERE The **Circumvesuviana Railway** (www.vesuviana.it; © **800-053939**) runs between Naples and Sorrento every half-hour from Piazza Garibaldi, with stops at the excavations. For Herculaneum, get off at Ercolano/Scavi (*scavi* means "archeological excavation"). Herculaneum is about 20 minutes from Naples and 50 minutes from Sorrento; the entrance is about 10 blocks from the station. Pompeii is about 40 minutes from Naples and 30 minutes from Sorrento; exit the train at Pompei-Scavi (note that the modern spelling

Statue of Roman Proconsul Marcus Nonius Balbus at Herculaneum.

drops the last "i" of the ancient name). The entrance is about 45m (150 ft.) from the station.

To reach either by **car** from Naples, follow the *autostrada* A3 toward Salerno. If you're coming from Sorrento, head east on SS. 145, where you can connect with A3 (marked NAPOLI). Then take the signposted turnoffs for Pompeii and Herculaneum.

LOGISTICS Hours for both excavation sites are the same: April to October, they are open daily 8:30am to 7:30pm and November to March daily 8:30am to 5pm (last admission 90 min. before close); admission to Pompeii is 13€, and entrance to Herculaneum is 11€. A cumulative ticket (22€) will grant you access to both as well as to Oplontis, Boscoreale, and Stabia (see below) and is good for three consecutive days. You can purchase it at the Circumvesuviana Railway Station, Piazza Garibaldi, in Naples, or at the sites. Unless you're a real archaeology buff, Pompeii and Herculaneum will probably supply your fill of ancient cities. Nearby Oplontis, Boscoreale, and Stabia (see below) are fascinating (especially the villas at Oplontis and Stabia), but what you see there doesn't compare to the wonders of Pompeii and Herculaneum. Both sites can be crowded in the mornings, especially in July and August, when tours often arrive in force. However, crowds tend to thin out by early afternoon.

The ticket offices at both provide free maps and good, detailed booklets that will guide you through the sites. Inside the entrances at both you'll find **bookstores,** where you can purchase additional guidebooks to the ruins (available in English, complete with detailed photos). Audio guides are good accompaniments to your visits. You can rent them at both sites for 6.50€, 10€ for two people (but sharing is not a particularly good idea), with a kids' version for 4€. Pompeii has a cafeteria inside the archeological zone, which is handy for sandwiches and beverages. At Herculaneum there's a good cafe/cafeteria just outside the entrance. You can store your luggage at both sites (also at the train station in Pompeii), making it possible to work in a visit if you're traveling between Naples and Sorrento and the Amalfi Coast.

If you're visiting the sites on a sunny day, wear sunscreen and bring along a bottle of water. For both sites, visit www.pompeiisites.org.

Herculaneum (Ercolano)

10km (6 miles) SE of Naples

Excavations began at Herculaneum in the early 18th century and continue to this day, with the fairly recent discovery of a beached boat full of desperate souls trying to make an escape by sea. Another 300 skeletons were found in vaulted stone boathouses on what would have been the town's beach; they were huddled in the shelters waiting to board boats and sail to safety when they were killed instantly by the poisonous vapors of a wall of heated gas and rock that swept through the town at 100 mph. Although many questions about Herculaneum remain unanswered, it's known for certain that this town was

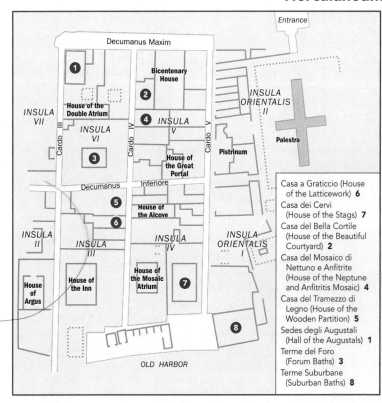

Entrance

Decumanus Maxim

❶

Bicentenary
House

❷

INSULA
ORIENTALIS
II

INSULA
VII

House of the
Double Atrium

Cardo III

INSULA
VI

Cardo IV

❹ INSULA
V

Cardo V

Palestra

❸

Decumanus
Inferiore

House of
the Great
Portal

Pistrinum

INSULA
II

INSULA
III

❺

House of
the Alcove

❻

INSULA
IV

INSULA
ORIENTALIS
I

House
of
Argus

House of
the Inn

House of
the Mosaic
Atrium

❼

❽

OLD HARBOR

Casa a Graticcio (House
of the Latticework) **6**

Casa dei Cervi
(House of the Stags) **7**

Casa del Bella Cortile
(House of the Beautiful
Courtyard) **2**

Casa del Mosaico di
Nettuno e Anfitrite
(House of the Neptune
and Anfitritis Mosaic) **4**

Casa del Tramezzo di
Legno (House of the
Wooden Partition) **5**

Sedes degli Augustali
(Hall of the Augustals) **1**

Terme del Foro
(Forum Baths) **3**

Terme Suburbane
(Suburban Baths) **8**

5

AROUND NAPLES | Pompeii & Herculaneum

about a third of the size of Pompeii, with a population of about 4,000, and wealthier, a glitzy seaside resort for elite Romans. Herculaneum didn't have much commerce or industry and its streets were lined mostly with elegant villas, along with a few apartment blocks for poor laborers and fishermen.

If only the same could be said for modern Ercolano, a grimy, workaday suburb that you'll probably be eager to rush through. Bright spots are the hundred of so summer villas at the foot of Mt. Vesuvius, where members of Naples' 18th-century Bourbon court used to while away the hot summer days. They line the so-called **Miglio d'Oro ★,** the Golden Mile, along Corso Resina between the archeological excavations and the town of Torre del Greco. Most now house offices or stand empty, but you can step into one of them, **Villa Campolieto,** Corso Resina 283, for a look at a couple of salons and the gardens; there you can pick up an audio guide that will steer you around the exteriors of a couple of other mansions on the street. The visit to Villa Campolieto (www.villevesuviane.net; ✆ **081-732-2134**) is 3€, 6€ with the audio guide. It's open Tuesday through Sunday 10am to 1pm.

SCAVI DI ERCOLANO (HERCU-LANEUM ARCHEOLOGICAL AREA) ★★★

The ruins of Herculaneum give the unsettling impression of a ghost town from which residents have only recently walked away. Many of the houses retain their second floors, making them seem more like residences than ruins. The volcanic mud that covered Herculaneum during the eruption of Vesuvius in A.D. 79 quickly hardened to a hard, rocklike material. While making excavations difficult, this semi-rock protected the structures underneath, and rather remarkably preserved wooden beams and floors along with furnishings, clothing, and household objects. The ruins provide a wealth of rich and intriguing detail about building techniques, architecture, and domestic decoration in Roman times, and, of

Mosaic-laden baths at Herculaneum.

course, about daily life. Seeing the charred wood, staircases, and double-height houses here instill the sense of being in a real town, unlike a sense of remote detachment you might experience in Pompeii and other ancient ruins. From the Ercolano-Scavi station, follow the signs for the scavi for about 10 blocks down the main street, Via IV Novembre; the entrance is about a 10-minute walk from the station. Plan to spend at least 2 hours at the site.

DECUMANUS MAXIMUS   The excavations stretch from the town's main street to what was once the shoreline (now a kilometer to the west); the rest of the Roman town remains inaccessible beneath the buildings of modern Ercolano. Decumanus Maximus is lined with shops, some of them still sporting advertisements and price lists. One of the discoveries along this street was a crucifix, proof that Christianity had already come to Herculaneum by the time of the eruption.

TERME DEL FORO (FORUM BATHS)   Elegant mosaics of fish, dolphins, and other sea creatures decorate the town's largest and grandest bath complex, with several entrances that include, of course, those for men and women. Enough of the men's section, the **Terme Maschili,** remains to show the full range of facilities: a latrine, changing room lined with benches and shelves for stashing sandals and personal effects, and an exercise room. You can still make out the *frigidarium* (cold bath), to the left, and the *tepadarium* (tepid bath), to the right. Once patrons had gone through these ablutions they could settle into the *caldarium* (hot bath) for a long, soothing soak. In the smaller but similarly elaborate **Terme Feminili,** a mosaic of a naked Triton decorates the floor of the changing rooms.

SEDES DEGLI AUGUSTALI (HALL OF THE AUGUSTALS) The Augustals were priests of a cult to Augustus, founder and first emperor of the Roman Empire (reigned 27 B.C. to A.D. 14). These rooms, with marble floors and elaborate wall paintings, did justice to their elite status. Their custodian died in his sleep, in a small room that's still furnished with the bed where his skeleton was found.

CASA DEL TRAMEZZO DI LEGNO (HOUSE OF THE WOODEN PARTITION) Behind a perfect facade is a rarity in Roman houses, a double atrium. It probably just means that at some point the owner scraped together enough money to buy adjoining houses and merge them. He obviously worked hard: The house is named for a well-preserved wooden screen that separated part of the atrium from the *tablium,* a little room that served as an office.

CASA DEL BELLA CORTILE (HOUSE OF THE BEAUTIFUL COURTYARD) The namesake courtyard seems almost medieval, with a wide stone staircase ascending to a landing on the second floor. Three skeletons that have been placed here are presumed to be those of a mother, father, and daughter trapped on the beach as they tried to flee.

CASA DEL MOSAICO DI NETTUNO E ANFITRITE (HOUSE OF THE NEPTUNE AND ANFITRITIS MOSAIC) A bright blue mosaic of the sea god and his nymph is just one of many elaborate decorations in this house, whose owner probably operated the remarkably well-preserved shop next door. Carbonized wooden racks hold amphorae and masonry jars that were found on the counter, still filled with broad beans and chick peas when they were unearthed.

CASA A GRATICCIO (HOUSE OF THE LATTICEWORK) The is one of the very few examples of working-class housing that has survived from antiquity; the name-giving lattices, though cheaply made of interwoven cane and plaster, are remarkably well preserved.

CASA DEI CERVI (HOUSE OF THE STAGS) One of the most elegant houses in town had terraces and porticos overlooking the sea. Decorations say much about its fun-loving inhabitants: Frescoes depict cheerful and playful cherubs, while courtyards were filled with statues of drunken satyrs and an inebriated, peering Hercules. The house is named for a statue of dogs attacking a pair of innocent, noble-looking deer, perhaps a commentary on the cutthroat politics and hard-edged social echelons of the Roman world.

VILLA DEI PAPIRI One of the grander seaside villas housed a huge library of 1,000-odd papyrus scrolls, badly charred but intact when they were uncovered during excavations (they're now in the library of the Palazzo Reale in Naples). The onetime home of Julius Caesar's father-in-law, consul Lucius Calpurnius Piso Caesoninus (100 B.C.–43 B.C.) has also yielded a treasure trove of nearly 90 magnificent bronze and marble sculptures, Roman copies of Greek originals that are now housed in the Archeological Museum in Naples. Most famous among them is a sculpture of Pan, the half-man, half-goat god of shepherds and flocks, caught in this marble having sex with a nanny goat. The oddly humane scene was unearthed in the 18th century but was thought to be so licentious that it was locked away in the cellars of a royal palace. As one early English observer put it, the statue was too indecent to describe and should be thrown into the crater of Vesuvius. Fortunately, it wasn't, and since the early 19th century, randy Pan has been one of the Archeological Museum's most cherished prizes.

TERME SUBURBANE (SUBURBAN BATHS)   Another bath complex shows off state-of-the art sophistication, with marble floors and benches and an elaborate underfloor heating system in which heat generated by wood fires circulated through a maze of conduits. In the *caldarium* (hot bath) a few stucco friezes still look down on visitors as they would have on bathers.

Pompeii

19km (11 miles) SE of Herculaneum, 30km (18 miles) SE of Naples

Italy's most famous archeological site is the Disneyland of the ancient world. Not that there's anything shallow or ersatz about the extensive excavations of this town on the Bay of Naples where life stopped so abruptly on August 24, A.D. 79. It's just that no other ancient town has been brought to light so completely, providing an opportunity to step into a world locked in an ancient time. The 4 to 6 meters (13 to 20 feet) of volcanic ash with which Vesuvius buried the city preserved 44 hectares (109 acres) of shops, civic buildings, and private houses. Ever since 1748,, archaeologists have worked to painstakingly uncover the town, and the ruins provide the vicarious thrill of sharing space with residents of a lively, ancient Roman port.

How many people were living in Pompeii at the time of the eruption is not known. The city had been rocked by a major earthquake in A.D. 62 that, along with fires caused by toppled oil lamps, destroyed temples, houses, and public works. Repairs were still underway at the time Vesuvius erupted, though many of the city's 11,000 recorded inhabitants had probably resettled elsewhere. The unfortunate Pompeians who remained behind are the most haunting presence at the site. The decaying bodies of the deceased often left a mold inside the ash and lava that buried them. Excavators filled these empty spaces with plaster, and the eerie, lifelike casts lie in the Garden of the Fugitives and other places around town where the victims fell.

The entrance to the site is almost directly across the train station. Allow at least 4 hours for even a superficial visit.

Pompeii statue.

Pompeii

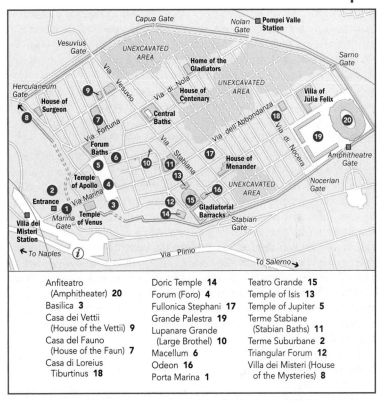

Anfiteatro (Amphitheater) **20**	Doric Temple **14**	Teatro Grande **15**
Basilica **3**	Forum (Foro) **4**	Temple of Isis **13**
Casa dei Vettii (House of the Vettii) **9**	Fullonica Stephani **17**	Temple of Jupiter **5**
	Grande Palestra **19**	Terme Stabiane (Stabian Baths) **11**
Casa del Fauno (House of the Faun) **7**	Lupanare Grande (Large Brothel) **10**	Terme Suburbane **2**
Casa di Loreius Tiburtinus **18**	Macellum **6**	Triangular Forum **12**
	Odeon **16**	Villa dei Misteri (House of the Mysteries) **8**
	Porta Marina **1**	

SCAVI DI POMPEII (POMPEII ARCHEOLOGICAL AREA) ★★★

Pompeii was a workaday town, and what stands out amid the ruins is a remarkable evocation of everyday life—streets, shops, bakeries, brothels, baths. The first thing you'll notice is the typical Roman plan of gridlike streets, on which stepping stones appear at every intersection. These were laid down to allow residents to cross the pavement even when the streets were being flushed with water, as they were at least once a day. Stones are spaced in just such a way to allow chariot wheels to roll past them. Raised sidewalks conceal water and sewage pipes, while glittering bits of marble mixed in with the volcanic pavement reflected light to make walking a little easier at night. Unlike Herculaneum, with its seafront district of lavish villas, in Pompeii the wealthy usually lived among the working classes. Houses are interspersed with shops (which were often combined with dwellings) all over town. All around town are remains of 25 street fountains, fed by a system of aqueducts and cisterns that supplied lead pipes to keep baths, businesses, and homes supplied with fresh water.

PORTA MARINA   The sight's main entrance is as busy now as it was back in the day, when this impressive gate, one of seven portals in the walls that surrounded the ancient city, opened to the seafront. Pompeii's docks did a brisk business importing and exporting goods that were often transported to and from Rome and around southern Italy on the nearby Appian Way. The shimmering sea that once washed against the shoreline in front of the gate is nowhere to be seen: the sprawl of modern Pompei (one "i" in the modern spelling) now stands between the excavations and the sea, which has receded by about ½ km (¼ mile) over the centuries. The Tempio de Venere (**Temple of Venus**), to the right of the entrance, has not fared as well as the gate, though a lone column still stands to attest to its onetime grandeur.

FORUM (FORO)   Pompeii's marketplace was severely damaged in an earthquake 16 years before the eruption of Vesuvius and hadn't been repaired when the final destruction rained down. Columns still line the portico that surrounded a large, rectangular open space on three sides and opened to a covered meat and fish market, the **Macellum.** Facing the forum are the **Basilica** (the city's largest single structure), a law court, exchange, and civic hall; early Christian churches adopted the floor plan of the main hall ending in a semicircle, along with the name. The Tempio di Apollo (**Temple of Apollo**), with its columned portico, was the city's most important religious building. The **Temple of Jupiter** (Tempio di Giove), with a triumphal arch, also faces the Forum. The **Granai del Foro** (Forum Granary) is now the repository for many of the plaster casts of victims made by 19th-century excavators (see above).

Pompeii's Porta Marina.

Pompeii's forum.

LUPANARE GRANDE (LARGE BROTHEL) Pompeii's most titter-inducing sight and prime photo op is a two-story brothel, just northeast of the forum off Via degli Augustali. Graphic wall paintings of varying degrees of artistic accomplishment reveal what certainly appears to be a libertine attitude toward sex. It's easy to see why, correctly or not, the city is often associated with easy virtue. In the basilica (above), where many travelers stopped on a visit to Pompeii, a bit of graffiti loosely read, "If anyone is looking for some tender love in this town, keep in mind that here all the girls are very friendly." A list of prices is inscribed on the wall nearby. It's believed that Pompeii may have had dozens of brothels and private sex clubs. Many of the graphic works that once covered the walls of this one, the city's largest and grandest pleasure palace, have been carted off to the Archeological Museum in Naples, though many remain in place in the ten small rooms equipped with stone beds.

VIA DELL'ABBONDANZA The town's main commercial street is rightfully named: The surrounding fields and vineyards kept Pompeii well supplied with an abundance of goods, as did a brisk trade with other Roman cities near and far. The street was the city's main commercial thoroughfare, lined with shops, including **Fullonica Stephani** (Stephen's Laundry), and little eateries where pots full of the daily offerings were kept on the counters that are still in place. In most of the houses along the street, a shop is on the ground floor and the owner's apartment is on the second level. Many of the painted signs for bars and shops are in place, and walls of many of the shops are still covered with red writing promoting candidates in local elections taking place at the time of the disaster. Signs have also revealed the world's first known bit of slick advertising punditry, advertising Vesuvinum—a clever combo of Vesuvius and "vinum," the word for wine.

TRIANGULAR FORUM This large open area was the heart of the theater district. The beautiful **Teatro Grande,** carved out of a hillside of volcanic rock in the 2nd century B.C., could seat an audience of 5,000, while the smaller, 1st-century B.C., 1,000-seat **Odeion,** or Small Theater, was used for music and mime shows. Audiences could step out between acts for a stroll along the columned **Quadriportico dei Teatri,** though the breezy walkway was later enclosed to serve as a barracks for gladiators. Nearby is the **Tempio di Iside** (Temple of Isis), one of the best-conserved temples to this goddess to survive from antiquity.

TERME STABIANE (STABIAN BATHS) One of the town's six public baths shows off the floor plan and arrangement of cold, tepid, and hot baths that was typical of these civic institutions, a mainstay of all Roman towns to provide a cleanse, relaxation, and socialization. The vaulted *apodyterium* (changing room) was the showpiece of this facility, with fanciful wall paintings of playful nymphs. Looking at them might have brightened the day of the slaves who accompanied their masters to the baths and waited for them in this vast chamber with orders to keep an eye on their belongings.

CASA DI LOREIUS TIBURTINUS Election placards painted on the facade gave this large house its name: "Vote for Loreius" and "Vote for Tiburnius." The name doesn't do justice to the owner, the well-off Octavius Quartio. He entertained his guests in a gardenlike *triclinium,* or dining room, where a delightful fresco depicts Pyramis and Thisbe. This lovely maiden and handsome youth of myth belonged to feuding families, and centuries later their doomed love inspired *Romeo and Juliet.*

GRANDE PALESTRA Sports events were held on this track and on the surrounding sports fields, while onlookers could escape the sun in the shade of an impressively long columned portico. A grandiose swimming pool was surrounded by plane trees (you can see the plaster casts of the stumps).

ANFITEATRO (AMPHITHEATRE) The oldest Roman amphitheater in the world, built in 80 B.C., could seat 1,000 people. It was the first Roman amphitheater to be built of stone, hence its longevity, and set a standard for architectural quality that only the Coliseum in Rome outdid a century later. Especially enlightened were the entrances, specially designed for crowd control, and the state-of-the-art latrines. The theater became known around the region for its gladiatorial contests, and the ancient counterparts of soccer hooligans packed in for events. Games were banned for 10 years after an A.D. 59 brawl between Pompeians and visitors from nearby Nuceria that left ten dead—the action on the field obviously just wasn't gory enough for the bloodthirsty fans.

Casts were made of the indentions victims' bodies left in the hardened ash.

TERME SUBURBANE The city's four bathhouses are among the finest to survive from antiquity. This one is unusual in that men and women shared the facilities. Vividly colored frescoes in the changing rooms depict graphic sex acts and are the subject of ongoing controversy: Were they meant to advertise sexual services available on the upper floors or were they simply amusing decorations? Since each scene appears above a box for storing belongings, perhaps the graphic scenes were intended to make such an impression on clients that they wouldn't forget where they'd stashed their togas and sandals. Whatever their intent, these scenes and other so-called pornography from Pompeii shocked Francis I, king of the Two Sicilies. Coming across erotic artifacts on an 1819 visit to Archeological Museum in Naples with his wife and daughter, he ordered many of them to be locked away in the museum's Gabinetto Segreto (Secret Cabinet) open only to "people of mature ages and respected morals."

CASA DEI VETTII (HOUSE OF THE VETTII) Pompeii's most elegant patrician villa was the ultimate bachelor pad, the home of wealthy merchants, the Vettii brothers. The huge phallus resting on a pair of scales at the entrance was not intended as a come-hither for female guests but was a sign of good fortune—which the black-and-red Pompeian dining room with its frescoes of delicate cupids and colonnaded garden show the brothers had plenty of. Strong boxes imbedded in the floor suggest that they might have made at least part of their fortune as money lenders.

CASA DEL FAUNO (HOUSE OF THE FAUN) The sumptuous decor is ancient proof that money and good taste can go together. Two of the great treasures of the Museo Archeologico Nazionale in Naples come from this huge spread, covering an entire city block, the biggest house in town. A bronze statue of a dancing faun decorated the *impluvium*, rain tank, used to collect water for the household. A much-celebrated "Battle of Alexander the Great" battle scene is one of many mosaics that decorated the lavish rooms.

VILLA DEI MISTERI (HOUSE OF THE MYSTERIES) A layer of ash ensured that this 90-room villa near the Porto Ercolano, just outside the walls (go along Viale alla Villa dei Misteri), retained its remarkable frescoes, the best still in place in Pompeii. Set against a background of a deep hue that's come to be known as Pompeian red, figures in the so-called Dionysiac Frieze are shown going through some sort of elaborate rituals that, scholars argue, might be preparations for a wedding or initiation into a sect of Dionysus (Bacchus), one of the many cults that flourished in Roman times.

Where to Eat

The decent Ciao cafeteria within the *scavi* in Pompeii provides a welcome snack break and saves time you might otherwise spend lingering over a meal. You'll also find cafes near the entrance to Herculaneum. In July, the region celebrates the feast of the Zandraglia, in honor of the namesake butterfly-shaped cookie. In Herculaneum, try one at Vaiano, near the excavations at Via Cirillo Emanuele 163 (© **081-537-4372**).

Il Principe ★★ NEAPOLITAN/ANCIENT ROMAN The talented chef here is an epicurean who would have been lauded at an ancient banquet. He claims to take inspiration from food depicted in the frescoes of Pompeii and

A WHOLE LOTTA shakin' GOING ON

In A.D 62, a major earthquake rocked Pompeii and Herculaneum, seriously damaging houses and public buildings and wreaking havoc on the waterworks in Pompeii. It's known that Pompeii, especially, never completely recovered from the quake. Many residents had resettled elsewhere, and repair was still ongoing 17 years later. Some records of the extent of the damage come from bas-reliefs found in the house of banker Lucius Caecilius Iucundus on Via Stabiae in Pompeii. Iucundus was an obsessive record keeper in all matters, and 153 wax tablets found in his house provide detailed records of loans and business transactions in ancient Pompeii.

It's believed that small quakes rattled the region with increasing frequency up to the time of the eruption of A.D. 79. Quakes that began to jolt residents on a hot summer day in August were nothing too far out of the ordinary, or so it seemed, until the sky darkened and ash began raining down on Pompeii at the rate of about 6 inches an hour. Some residents, obviously still not terribly alarmed, lingered to sweep the ash from their roofs. Less ash fell on nearby Herculaneum, but dark clouds and rumblings from the nearby mountain were enough to prompt many residents to flee. Shortly after midnight, a few survivors straggled into Pompeii from Herculaneum, telling of a catastrophic wall of volcanic mud that had completely buried their town. Pompeii didn't offer safety for long: Around 6:30am, clouds of superheated gases rush down the slopes of Vesuvius. Temperatures from the surge reached 250°C (482°F), instantly killing everyone in its path.

Both cities and their doomed residents lay covered beneath layers of mud and ash for 1,500 years. Architect Domenico Fontana came upon the first signs of the buried towns in 1599, when he uncovered frescoes while supervising crews digging a channel near Pompeii. Apparently he decided it was best to let the erotically charged panels lay where they were. Even an inscription mentioning the "town councilor of Pompeii" didn't tip him off to the presence of something big just beneath his feet. Full-scale excavations began in 1738, when Spanish military engineer Rocque Joaquin de Alcubierre (1702–80) stumbled upon some remains at Herculaneum while prospecting land to build an estate for King Charles VII of Naples. A decade later he began work at Pompeii. Excavations have continued almost ever since, revealing not just artifacts but a bounty of information about city planning, social customs, and the lives of poor and wealthy residents alike—some of our most extensive insights into the ancient world.

Herculaneum and described in the writings of Pliny and other ancient authors. That might be a wee bit of a stretch, since many of the delightful seafood pastas and fish dishes seem simply to be well-done takes on traditional Neapolitan fare. Should you be craving a taste of ancient Rome, try the pasta with anchovy sauce, a modern version of *garum*, the fish sauce that was a staple of every ancient household. You will enjoy your feast in deep-hued surroundings worthy of a Pompeian villa, or maybe a Bourbon palace.

Piazza Bartolo Longo, Pompeii. www.ilprincipe.com. ℭ **081-850-5566.** Main courses 12€–24€. Tues–Sat 12:30–3pm and 8–11pm; Sun 12:30–3pm.

Shopping

Well-dressed matrons of Pompeii and Herculaneum, archeologists have learned, spent some of their hard-earned *unciae* on coral jewelry. Picking up on the trend, jewelers in the region around the sites have specialized in crafting coral cameos since the 19th century. Time was, coral came from the sea just outside the workshop doors, though these days the raw material is likely to come from Thailand or somewhere else in Asia—where, in the absence of regulation, coral reefs are being depleted at an alarming rate. Shills offering visits to cameo workshops and showrooms often congregate around entrances to the sites. Should you be tempted to seek the handiwork out yourself, you'll find a cluster in the seaside suburb of Torre del Greco, midway between Herculaneum and Pompeii, on Via Enrico de Nicola. One of the town's most august and well-reputed dealers is **Basilio Liverino,** Via Montedoro 61 (www.liverino.it; © **081-881-1225**). You can pop in just to take a look at museum-quality cameos and other coral pieces.

OPLONTIS ★

5km (3 miles) W of Pompeii, 20km (12 miles) SE of Naples

Torre Annunziata, a coastal suburb best known for its flour mills, isn't the sort of place you'll want to spend much time. The best thing to be said for the drab expanse of highways, high rises, and factories is that the town produces some of Italy's tastiest pasta. It also happens to be built on top of a posh suburb of ancient Pompeii. It's a sign of the doomed town's onetime status that the name Oplontis comes from the Latin *opulentia,* meaning "opulence." Among the elite residents was Poppea Sabina, second wife of Nero, whose Villa di Poppea is still the height of luxury, even in ruin (see below).

Getting There

You can easily reach Oplontis on the **Circumvesuviana railway** (www.vesuviana.it; © **800-053939** toll-free in Italy) running between Naples and Sorrento; get off at **Torre Annunziata-Oplonti Villa di Poppea** (a few stops after Ercolano Scavi). The ride from Naples takes 20 to 35 minutes, depending on the number of stops.

By car, take the *autostrada* A3 Napoli-Salerno and exit at TORRE ANNUNZIATA SUD, then follow the brown signs for SCAVI DI OPLONTI.

Villa di Poppea ★★ RUIN   The largest ancient Roman suburban villa ever discovered was an imperial property, and was probably the retreat of Poppea Sabina (A.D. 30– A.D. 65), the second wife of Emperor Nero. Poppea was well accustomed to luxury, having schemed and plotted her way up the social ladder, and she was famous for taking a daily milk bath to preserve her legendary beauty. Here at Oplontis she bathed in a pool beneath a sumptuous fresco of Hercules in the Garden of the Hesperides, where the superhero undertook the almost impossible task of stealing apples belonging to Zeus as part of his Twelve Labors. Poppea's slaves labored in a primitive kitchen that's remarkably intact, and they slept in tiny cubicles arranged over two floors of an adjacent wing, providing a good look at life below stairs, Roman style. Most of the villa's statuary had been stashed in a storeroom, probably out of harm's way while renovations were underway—the villa may well have been damaged in the earthquake of A.D. 62. But most of the entertaining rooms are still floored in rich mosaics and beautifully painted, often with theater masks as well as trompe l'oeil windows and columns that make the entire villa seem like an elaborate stage set. As it turned out, the ambitious Poppea's life would soon become a tragedy. When she was about to give birth, Nero allegedly kicked her in the stomach, or jumped up and down on her repeatedly, and she died of complications. The repentant emperor found a beautiful boy who looked much like Poppea, had him castrated, married him, and called him by his late wife's name.

Nearby, but not open to the public, is the Villa of **L. Crassius Tertius,** a much more rustic, two-story house of rough, unadorned walls and earthen floors. In one of the storerooms, excavators came upon the skeletons of 55 poor souls, who took refuge while trying to escape by sea but were felled by hot vapors. Even in a crisis, the strict Roman social order took precedence. Clustered near the doorway were wealthy refugees carrying hordes of jewelry, gold, and currency, while the hoi-poloi huddled behind them.

Via Sepolcri 12, Torre Annunziata. www.pompeiisites.org. ☏ **081-862-1755.** Admission 5.50€ includes same-day entry to Boscoreale and Stabiae; cumulative ticket (22€) for Oplontis, Pompeii, Herculaneum, Boscoreale, and Stabiae good for 3 consecutive days. Nov–Mar daily 8:30am–5pm; Apr–Oct daily 8:30am–7:30pm. Last admission 90 min. earlier.

BOSCOREALE

5km (3 miles) N of Pompeii, 31km (19 miles) SE of Naples

The reputation of this outlying community near Pompeii precedes itself. You may have encountered coins, jewelry, silverware, and other treasures from Boscoreale in London's British Museum and the Louvre in Paris, or come across the rich and colorful Boscoreale fresco in New York's Metropolitan Museum of Art. These riches aside, Boscoreale was a farm town, as it still is, and the fertile soil on the slopes of Mt. Vesuvius yield wine, wheat, and olive oil. Nearby Boscotrecase is famous for the production of crisp, amber-colored Lacryma Christi, or Tears of Christ, probably the best of the D.O.C. Vesuvian wines. Treasure hunters plundered Boscoreale in the 19th century, selling off the treasures they found, though excavations are ongoing at more than 30 villas, most of them farmsteads. The most complete excavation is at Villa Regina, sadly closed for restoration with no reopening in sight. You can see the surrounding vineyards, planted as they were in Roman times, while the town museum, the Antiquarium, does a good job of explaining the way things were when Vesuvius blew its stack in A.D. 79.

Getting There

By train, take the **Circumvesuviana** (www.vesuviana.it; ✆ **800-053939**) from Naples or Sorrento to the Torre Annunziata stop. From the station, take a taxi or a local bus to the museum. By **car,** take the *autostrada* A3 and exit at TORRE ANNUNZIATA; follow the brown signs for COMUNI VESUVIANI and BOSCOREALE.

Antiquarium Nazionale Uomo e Ambiente nel Territorio Vesuviano (National Antiquarium: Man and Environment in the Territory of Vesuvius) ★ MUSEUM   Don't be put off by the highfalutin' name. What's here is an earnest and straightforward collection that shows what life in the region was like during the Roman era, with models and renderings depicting the setup of the surrounding farms and villas. On fleeting visits absentee landlords enjoyed lavish quarters (whose treasures have been carted off to museums around the world), while the laborers who tended to the livestock and took care of vineyards and grain fields lived in compounds that were like small villages in themselves. Residents didn't just live off the land, as you'll see from the ancient fish hooks, the fragment of a net, and an amphora that once contained *garum*, the fish sauce that was a staple on every Roman table. With so much else to see nearby you probably won't want to go out of your way to see this collection, but it's well worth a stop if you going to be spending some time around Pompeii and the surrounding sights.

Via Settetermini 15, Località Villaregina, Boscoreale. www.pompeiisites.org. ✆ **081-536-8796.** Admission 5.50€ includes same-day admission to Oplontis and Stabiae; cumulative ticket (22€) for Boscoreale, Pompeii, Herculaneum, Oplontis, and Stabiae good for 3 consecutive days. Nov–Mar daily 8:30am–5pm; Apr–Oct daily 8:30am–7:30pm. Last admission 90 min. earlier.

CASTELLAMMARE DI STABIA ★

5km (3 miles) SW of Pompei, 33km (20 miles) SE of Naples

Today, Castellammare di Stabia is a working class town, one of a long string of industrial suburbs along the western shores of the Bay of Naples. Shipyards and docks line the shores where, until the eruption of A.D. 79, the pleasure palaces of some of Rome's most powerful movers and shakers faced the sea. Ancient Stabiae began to come to light in the 18th century, though the Bourbon kings of Naples who sponsored the digs were much more interested in plundering for their private collections than in archeological posterity. Nearby Pompeii and Herculaneum have long since overshadowed the splendors of the ancient resort. Even so, the remains of villas that have been unearthed suggest the onetime grandeur of the place that was a summer retreat for some of the Roman Empire's most powerful men, Julius Caesar, the emperors Augustus and Tiberius, and the statesman-philosopher Cicero among them. Natural springs—28 of them, each with its own therapeutic characteristics—added to the allure of the resort. Pliny the Elder famously sailed into the eye of the storm when, seeing Vesuvius erupt from across the bay, he commandeered a navy vessel to rescue friends who were vacationing in Stabiae.

Essentials

GETTING THERE & AROUND   The **Circumvesuviana** (www.vesuviana.it; ✆ **800-053939**) railroad from Naples and nearby towns offers frequent service and makes four stops in town; get off at the main Castellammare/Via Nocera stop, then switch to bus no. 1 rosso, or walk to the ruins, following the signs to SCAVI; it takes about 20 minutes.

VISITOR INFORMATION   The tourist office, Piazza Matteotti 34, 80053 Castellammare di Stabia (www.stabiatourism.it; ✆ **081-871–1334**), provides local info.

Exploring the Town

It only takes a quick look over the bay, green headlands, and a backdrop of mountains to understand the allure of the location. The best way to take in the views is on a ride up the *funivia* (funicular) up **Monte Faito ★,** the 1,100m/3,609 ft. high summit behind the town. From April to October, cars leave every half-hour from a terminus in the center of town just outside the train station on Piazza Stazione Circumvesuviana; the round-trip fare is 7€. Residents once took refuge from Goth and Longobard raids in the 9th-century castle that gives the town its current name, while 18th-century Bourbon royals took in the sea air from **Villa Quisiana** (both are closed to the public). You'll get a bit of a sense of the good life for which the town was known well into the 19th century in the **Villa Comunale,** near the train station off Piazza Giovanni XXIII, a public garden that opens onto the Bay of Naples.

Scavi di Stabiae ★ ARCHEOLOGICAL PARK   While only a small part of Ancient Stabiae has been uncovered, the few excavated villas give a good idea of the over-the-top grandeur that was the norm here. Much of the **Villa di Arianna ★,** Via Piana di Varano, remains uncovered and parts have tumbled down a cliff into the sea. The staggeringly large villa is believed to have descended a seaside slope to cover 11,000 sq. meters (118,480 sq. ft.)—that's not too far short of being twice the size of its ostentatious American equivalent, Hearst Castle. Sumptuous rooms and atriums still have some of their intricate mosaic floors and lavish frescoes, including the scene from which the house takes its name. In one of many versions of this popular classical favorite of chicanery and revenge, Ariadne (Arianna in Italian), daughter of Cretan King Minos, helps the youth Theseus escape from the maze of the Minotaur and sails away with him. After a night of passion, he abandons her on Naxos; the god Dionysus rescues her, while the life of the lover who jilted her becomes a living hell. Two of the villa's particularly impressive amenities were a tunnel that burrowed beneath servants' quarters and stables to the beach below and a *palaestra,* exercise court, more than 100m (330 ft.) long and surrounded by a portico with 100 columns. **Villa di San Marco ★,** Via Passeggiata Archeologica, is similarly impressive, with porticos, halls, pools, a gym, and private thermal baths (in three temperatures: *calidarium, tepidarium,* and *frigidarium*), all decorated with stucco work, paintings, and frescoes.

A Bright Future for the Past

The splendors of Ancient Stabiae may one day re-emerge in a 61-hectare (150-acre) archeological park. Plans are underway to continue excavations at Villa di Arianna and Villa di San Marco and to uncover six or seven more identified ruins, unearthing the largest concentration of elite Roman villas in the Mediterranean. The Restoring Ancient Stabiae (RAS) Foundation oversees the project and aims to link the ruins via funicular to the Circumvesuviana railway, making the park easily accessible from Pompeii and other sites around the bay. Completion is probably years away; in the meantime, for updates visit www.vesuvianinstitute.it.

Even the kitchens, equipped to feed 125 guests at a sitting, are frescoed. Yet to be uncovered is a 108m (355 ft.) long colonnade that was well suited for an after-banquet stroll. Much of the tufta stone used on the construction of the Stabiae villas came from the **Grotta di San Biagio (St. Biagio's Grotto),** a quarry that was quite handily turned into a Christian oratory in the 5th to 6th centuries. The first bishops of Stabiae are buried beneath some primitive frescoes.

Via Passeggiata Archeologica (follow signs from station). www.pompeiisites.org. © **081-857-5347.** Admission 5.50€, includes same-day admission to Boscoreale and Oplontis; cumulative ticket (22€) for Stabiae, Pompeii, Herculaneum, Oplontis, and Boscoreale good for 3 consecutive days. Nov–Mar daily 8:30am–5pm; Apr–Oct daily 8:30am–7:30pm. Last admission 90 min. earlier.

SORRENTO & THE AMALFI COAST

The beautiful Sorrento Peninsula and the Amalfi Coast have been tempting travelers ever since Ulysses sailed by. He was forced to fill the ears of his sailors with wax and to tie himself to the mast of his ship to withstand the alluring call of the Sirens. Today, the pull of the sea and imposing rock-bound coast remain as compelling as they were in Homer's day. Even though it's besieged by tourists, graceful old Sorrento is a lovely place, perched high atop a cliff gazing across the sea toward the isle of Capri. The spectacular but nerve-racking Amalfi Drive (SS 163) heads vertiginously east, clinging to cliffs and rounding one bend after another until it comes to Positano, a tile-domed village hugging a near-vertical rock, and then to Amalfi, a little seaside town that was once the center of a powerful maritime republic.

As transporting as the green hillsides and azure seas are, as much as the scent of lemon and frangipani entices, the charms of Sorrento and the Amalfi Coast are no secret. You'll do yourself a favor if you schedule the pleasure of a visit for the early spring or fall, before or after the summer crowds, and even then accept the fact that you will not have this slice of paradise to yourself.

ESSENTIALS

Getting There

BY TRAIN Sorrento is connected to Naples' Stazione Centrale by the **Circumvesuviana** railway (www.vesuviana.it; ⓒ **800-053939**); the ride takes about an hour.

BY BUS SITA (www.sitabus.it; ⓒ **089-405145**) offers frequent bus service, more often in summer than in winter, from Naples to Sorrento, Amalfi, Positano, and Salerno. For Ravello, change buses in Amalfi. SITA buses run east along the coast from Sorrento to Positano and west along the coast from Salerno to Amalfi. If you're

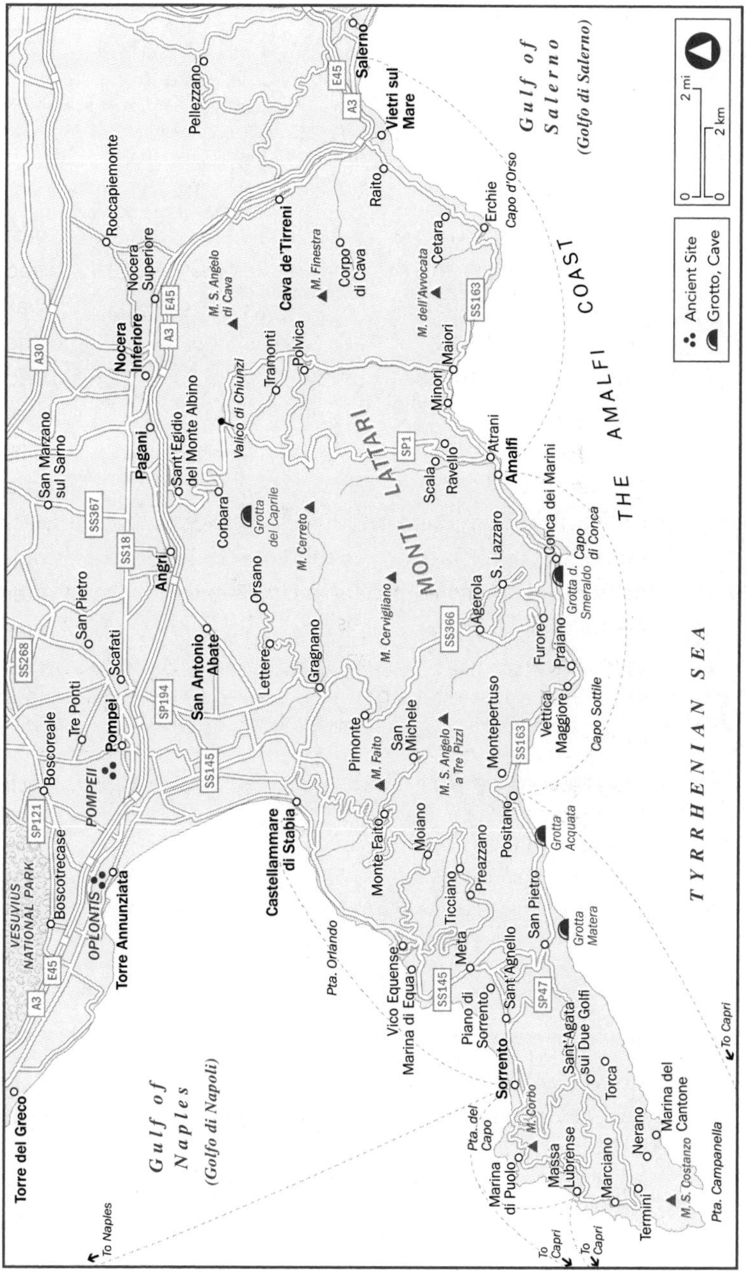
Salerno
Vietri sul Mare
Pellezzano
Raito
Erchie
Capo d'Orso
Gulf of Salerno
(Golfo di Salerno)
Roccapiemonte
Nocera Superiore
Nocera Inferiore
Cava de'Tirreni
Corpo di Cava
M. Finestra
M. S. Angelo di Cava
Cetara
M. dell'Avvocata
Maiori
Minori
Tramonti
Polvica
Valico di Chiunzi
Sant'Egidio del Monte Albino
Pagani
San Marzano sul Sarno
Corbara
Grotta del Caprile
M. Cerreto
LATTARI
MONTI
Scala
Ravello
Atrani
Amalfi
Conca dei Marini
Capo di Conca
Grotta d. Smeraldo
THE AMALFI COAST
S. Lazzaro
Agerola
M. Cervigliano
Orsano
Angri
San Pietro
Scafati
San Antonio Abate
Lettere
Gragnano
Furore
Praiano
Vettica Maggiore
Capo Sottile
Montepertuso
M. S. Angelo a Tre Pizzi
Pimonte
San Michele
M. Faito
Tre Ponti
Boscoreale
Pompei
POMPEII
Castellammare di Stabia
Monte Faito
Moiano
Positano
Grotta Acquata
Preazzano
Ticciano
TYRRHENIAN SEA
VESUVIUS NATIONAL PARK
Boscotrecase
OPLONTIS
Torre Annunziata
Pta. Orlando
Vico Equense
Marina di Equa
Meta
San Pietro
Grotta Matera
Sant'Agnello
Piano di Sorrento
Sorrento
Sant'Agata sui Due Golfi
To Capri
Torca
M. Corbo
Pta. del Capo
Marina di Puolo
Massa Lubrense
Marciano
Nerano
Marina del Cantone
M. S. Costanzo
Termini
Pta. Campanella
To Capri
To Capri
Torre del Greco
Gulf of Naples
(Golfo di Napoli)
To Naples
A3
E45
A30
SS18
SS367
SS268
SP121
SP194
SS145
SS163
SS366
SP1
SP47
Ancient Site
Grotto, Cave
0
2 mi
0
2 km

SOME how to's FOR ENJOYING THE AMALFI COAST

Choose Your Digs with Care: Some of the world's most legendary hotels are tucked into the cliff sides around Sorrento and along the Amalfi Coast. The price of one of their attractive and comfortable rooms often comes with sea views, a terrace, pool, often a private beach, and—a much-valued commodity on this coastline—a place to retreat from the crowds. Many moderate and lower-priced hotels are also loaded with character, and a room in any price range often comes with a balcony and a sea view. Wherever you stay, rates will almost always be substantially lower during winter and shoulder season, late spring and early fall, than they are in high season (but many hotels in this part of the world are closed from November through March).

Don't Rush Meals: You'll eat very well in Sorrento and along the Amalfi Coast, where the oft-quoted saying has it that residents keep one foot in a vineyard (or for that matter, garden plot) and one foot in a fishing boat. Seafood, of course, is plentiful, and that means fresh fish alla *griglia* (grilled), along with lots of *gamberone* (shrimp) and *aragosta* (lobster, more like crayfish here). These and other sea creatures often appear atop heaping piles of homemade pasta, maybe *scialatielli*, long and wide, like fettuccine. But that's just the beginning. This is the land of plenty, so fresh tomatoes, eggplants, artichokes, even figs

show up everywhere, as do lemons—in *risotto al limone, granita di limone* (lemon ice), sugary-sweet *delizie al limone* (a pastry), and the ubiquitous *SS* liqueur that any truly hospitable restaurant brings out at the end of a meal. Herbs grow on the mountainsides, and Agerola (see p. 146) and other farm towns turn out mozzarella and other cheeses. Residents of mountainous Tramonti (see p. 161) even claim to have invented the pizza, though you'd better not say that in front of a Neapolitan. Another sterling quality of life on the coast is that there's an unwritten rule that it's wrong to eat indoors unless it's really cold or really wet outside. That means you will enjoy many, many meals on a terrace, a pleasantly surprising number of which come with a sea view.

Take a Thrill Ride: Unless you're doing the driving, one of the most enjoyable experiences in these parts is riding along the two-lane road that clings to the coast between Sorrento and Amalfi. Steep forested mountainsides on one side, sheer, 150m (500-ft.) drops to the azure sea on the other—the thrills and views are of epic proportions. Provided you can get a seat, the trip along this coast on one of the SITA buses that ply the route is one of the cheapest scenic thrill rides anywhere. As you plod down the coast at safe speed, think of American writer John Steinbeck, who wrote about his trip along the coast, "Flaming like a meteor

trying to reach Sorrento or any of the towns along the coast between there and Amalfi, the quickest route from Naples is via the Circumvesuviana to Sorrento and the SITA bus down the coast from there. If your final destination is Amalfi, Ravello, or anywhere east along the coast from Amalfi, the quickest route from Naples is via the high-speed train to Salerno (about an hour) and the SITA bus east toward Amalfi from there. The Unico Costiera pass covers all the towns along around Sorrento and along the Amalfi Coast, from Meta we hit the coast, a road, high, high above the blue sea, that hooked and corkscrewed on the edge of nothing . . . . We didn't see much of the road. In the back seat my wife and I lay clutched in each other's arms, weeping hysterically."

Board a Boat: An easy and enjoyable way to get up and down the Amalfi Coast and out to Capri is by boat. Regular ferry services that operate between most towns are an especially welcome option in the height of high season, when traffic can be backed up for miles and the wait to get on a bus can be hours long. You might also want to consider setting out on a small boat and doing a little seafaring on your own, poking along the coast to find sheltered coves for a swim. Boats are available in marinas up and down the coast, where you can hire a boat and skipper for anywhere from about 200€ for a half-day excursion to about 25€ an hour for a navigate-yourself boat rental. Prices vary depending on demand and time of year, and you should never be shy about negotiating. Many hotels offer boat excursions, sometimes for free or for a reasonable fee.

Put on Your Walking Shoes: In your explorations you might spend days climbing staircases, inching down near-vertical inclines, and stepping over uneven stones—and that's just in your urban forays, even before you set out to *deliberately* hike along the footpaths that lace the region. Most towns are

closed to cars, not out of respect for pedestrians, but because the only possible way to navigate the *scalintelle* (staircases) and narrow *vicoli* (alleys) is on foot. The best advice is to wear comfortable shoes (*really* comfortable, as well as sturdy—forget about fashion, even if this is Italy) and take it slow and easy.

If you want to do some serious hiking, and don't mind some ascents and descents, you've come to the right part of the world. The paths that once linked coastal and mountain villages in the pre-road days are well maintained and well marked, though trails are steep and progress can be hampered by rocks and gravel. To tackle most of the paths you need to be moderately fit and have basic equipment: good shoes, a backpack, a sunhat, a good supply of water (especially in the summer), and a jacket for the rain and cold (all times of year).

You also need a head for heights. We've singled out some of the most scenic routes in our coverage of the towns they skirt; most trails pass through or close to towns or villages, making them accessible them by public transport when your legs give out and you just can't go another kilometer. You might want to arm yourself with the map published by the CAI (Club Alpino Italiano), *Monti Lattari Penisola Sorrentina, Costiera Amalfitana: Carta dei sentieri*, sold for 10€ at the best newsstands and bookstores in Ravello, Amalfi, Positano, and Tramonti.

di Sorrento to Salerno, and is available for 24 hours and for 3 days (7.60€ and 18€). The pass will allow you unlimited rides on SITA buses. To get the best views on the dramatic coastal drive, get a seat on the right side of the bus when you are traveling from Sorrento and the left side from Vietri, Amalfi, and Salerno. Curreri Viaggi (www.curreriviaggi.it; ✆ **081-801-5420**) runs a bus service from the Naples airport to Sorrento.

BY BOAT   In summer, ferries and hydrofoils operated by LMP-Linee Marittime Partenopee (www.consorziolmp.it; ☎ **081-551-3236**), NLG-Navigazione Libera del Golfo (www.navlib.it; ☎ **081-807-1812**), and Linee Lauro (www.alilauro.it; ☎ **081-497-2222**) make daily runs to and from Sorrento, Naples, Ischia, and Capri; and Volaviamare (www.volaviamare.it; ☎ **081-497-2291**) makes trips between Sorrento, Amalfi, and Positano. Boats not only provide a scenic ride, but also traveling by sea is a welcome alternative to the traffic-choked coast road in high season.

BY CAR   Taxis offer a flat rate of 100€ to Sorrento from Naples, or 130€ to Amalfi from the Naples Capodichino Airport. By **car** from Naples, take the A3 and exit at Castellammare di Stabia for the SS 145 to Sorrento. The SS 163 (the Amalfi Drive) branches off the SS 145 before you get to Sorrento and heads over the peninsula to Positano and Amalfi. To get to Ravello, take the SP1 off the A3. Allow about 1 hour and 10 minutes for the drive from Naples to Sorrento, 1 hour and 25 minutes to Positano or Amalfi, and an hour to Ravello.

SORRENTO ★★★

50km (31 miles) S of Naples

How does that old song, "Come Back to Sorrento," go? "*Vir 'o mare quant'è bello*" . . . or, "See the sea how beautiful it is." You'll be humming a few bars, because the sea, the scented gardens, and sun-drenched vistas that have been luring visitors to this cliff-top town for millennia really are exquisite. Monuments are few and far between, but views from the town center Piazza Tasso or a trek down to Marina Grande, a fisherman's port, show off the town's irrepressible appeal. Sorrento provides easy access to Naples as well as such fabled places as Capri, Positano, Amalfi, and the ruins at Pompeii, and is usually thronged with happy holiday-makers who, at their best, provide pleasant company.

VISITOR INFORMATION   The tourist office in Sorrento is at Via de Maio 35, off Piazza Tasso (www.sorrentotourism.com; ☎ **081-807-4033**); it's open Monday to Friday 9am to 4:15pm; in summer it's also open on Saturday mornings. You'll also find an information office in the green caboose just outside the train station; it's open daily 10am to 1pm and 3 to 7pm.

Exploring Sorrento

Sorrento is long and narrow, strung out along the top of seaside cliffs. Just about everything you want to see in town is an easy walk from the train station, with the exception of the town's two ports, which many residents opt to reach by bus. Marina Piccola, directly below Piazza Tasso (bus C or D, 1.20€), is the commercial port where ferries and hydrofoils dock; Marina Grande, below the western edge of town (bus D, 2.20€), is the old fishing port.

   The center of town is sunny **Piazza Tasso.** Amid the piazza's cafes, glossy shops, and crowds of promenaders stands a statue of the namesake poet,

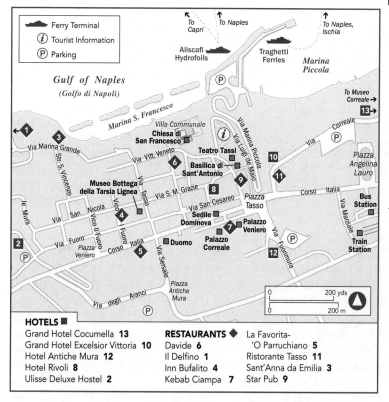

Ferry Terminal
(i) Tourist Information
(P) Parking

To Capri | To Naples | To Naples, Ischia

Aliscafi Hydrofoils | Traghetti Ferries | Marina Piccola

Gulf of Naples
(Golfo di Napoli)

Marina S. Francesco

To Museo Correale →

Villa Communale
Chiesa di San Francesco
Teatro Tassi
Basilica di Sant'Antonio
Museo Bottega della Tarsia Lignea
Piazza Tasso
Sedile Dominova
Palazzo Veniero
Duomo
Palazzo Correale
Piazza Antiche Mura
Piazza Angelina Lauro
Bus Station
Train Station

Corso Italia
Via Marina Grande
Via Vitt.-Veneto
Via Marina Piccola
Via Luigi de Maio
Via S.M.-Grazie
Via Tasso
Via San Cesareo
Via Fuoro
Via degli Aranci
Via Sersale
Via Correale
Via Marziale
Via Fuorimura
St. S.-Vincenzo
Via San Nicola

Piazza Veniero

0 — 200 yds
0 — 200 m

HOTELS ■
Grand Hotel Cocumella **13**
Grand Hotel Excelsior Vittoria **10**
Hotel Antiche Mura **12**
Hotel Rivoli **8**
Ulisse Deluxe Hostel **2**

RESTAURANTS ◆
Davide **6**
Il Delfino **1**
Inn Bufalito **4**
Kebab Ciampa **7**

La Favorita-
'O Parruchiano **5**
Ristorante Tasso **11**
Sant'Anna da Emilia **3**
Star Pub **9**

Tarquato Tasso, who was born in Sorrento into a noble family in 1544. The piazza dramatically spans a deep gorge; the north end overhangs a steep hillside that descends to Marina Piccola, while to the south you can follow a walkway and look far down into a verdant valley where a settlement flourished alongside a stream as early as the 5th century B.C.

The old town spreads out to the west, bisected by busy **Corso Italia** (closed to car traffic evenings in summer and weekend evenings in winter). Along the corso a few blocks west of the square, at Via Santa Maria della Pieta, is Sorrento's **cathedral** (www.cattedralesorrento.it; ✆ **081-878-2248;** admission free; open daily 7:30am–noon and 3–7pm). Frequent rebuilding has rendered the facade rather bland, except for an intriguing arcaded three-story campanile with embedded Roman columns; inside are doors inlaid with scenes of Sorrento life, a map of the town, and an enormous *presepe* (nativity scene), set on the streets of Naples with Mt. Vesuvius looming behind the manger. North of here are the quieter precincts around the gardens of the **Villa Communale.**

Just about everyone who visits Sorrento and the Amalfi Coast comes away with a favorite town to which they yearn to return. When choosing the place to put down your bags, it's hard to go too wrong in this beautiful part of the world, but you may want to take some practical considerations into account. **Sorrento** is the best situated as an exploring base, given its excellent train, bus, and boat connections to Capri, Naples, Pompeii, Herculaneum, and other towns along the coast. **Positano** is the most picturesque and resortlike, with the best (and most easily accessible) beaches, though getting in and out of town in high season on the traffic-choked coast road can be a nightmare (boats are a pleasant alternative). **Amalfi** provides small-town charm and gives you a two-fer—its beautiful and easy-to-reach neighbor **Ravello;** you can also avoid the worst of the coast traffic by approaching and leaving Amalfi from and to the east through Salerno, with its excellent train connections to Naples.

Chiesa di San Francisco ★ CHURCH Top choice for the most charming spot in Sorrento goes to the 14th-century Moorish cloisters of this church and convent, where an old pepper tree shades tufa-rock arches interspersed with elaborately capped columns. Inside the church, Francis is shown above the altar in a transcendent moment when, after weeks of fasting and praying, wounds opened on his hands, sides, and feet, he is brought close to the suffering Christ in body as well as in spirit.

Piazza San Francesco. Free admission. Daily 8am–1:30pm and 3:30–8pm.

Largo Dominova ★★ SQUARE For Sorrentines, this lovely little square tucked away in the old quarter at the intersections of Via San Cesareo and Via P. R. Giuliani is the real heart of town. At one time that was truly the case: The town council used to meet in the 16th-century Sedile Dominova, an arched loggia with a green-tile cupola. The richly frescoed interior of trompe l'oeil columns and rich scenes of aristocratic life is now a gathering spot for retired workers. The old gents are used to visitors popping in for a look at their opulent surroundings, so don't be shy about doing so.

Marina Grande ★★ NEIGHBORHOOD Walking past a row of narrow houses squeezed along the quays between the steep hillside and the sea, you'll get a sense of Sorrento as an old-time fishing port. Even so, you'll have to contend with shills trying to lure you into restaurants with multilanguage menus (a few restaurants down here are genuinely good; see "Where to Eat," p. 124). It's a nice walk from Sorrento down to the port (and remember, this is Marina Grande, as opposed to Marina Piccola, the commercial port where ferries disembark). Just follow the well-marked road from Piazza Vittoria; it eventually becomes a staircase and passes beneath a Greek gate—a reminder that Marina Grande was once a separate town that was vulnerable to pirate raids, a much riskier place to live than fortified Sorrento. You can take a dip here, but the small, pebbly beach is less than inviting (for better options, see "Beaches," below). The scene is quite romantic in the evening, with moonlight illuminating the harbor full of bobbing boats. Should you have one *limoncello* too many while taking in the spectacle, hop on the D bus to get back up the hill.

Museo Correale di Terranova ★ MUSEUM   A walk through these rather plain galleries carved out of an 18th-century villa introduces you to the good life as it's been enjoyed over the past few centuries in this part of the world. Counts Alfredo and Pompeo Correale donated to this museum the collectibles their family had amassed since 1500; the randomness of the assortment is its charm. Neapolitan paintings from the 17th through 19th centuries capture the scenic Sorrento views that have been inspiring travelers since the days of the Grand Tour. Inlaid intarsia furniture is from studios right here in Sorrento, and much of the porcelain was fired in kilns on the grounds of the Capodimonte palace in Naples (some especially delicate-looking pieces are from China and Japan, reflecting the 19th-century aristocratic craze for arts of the Far East). A lovely palm-shaded garden affords stunning views up and down the coast, a welcome spot in which to linger in relative solitude for a spell.

Piazza San Francesco. Free admission. Daily 8am–1:30pm and 3:30–8pm.

Piazza Tasso ★★★ PLAZA   This airy, cafe-filled space, with views of the sea to one side and mountains on the other, does justice to its namesake poet, Sorrento-born Tarquato Tasso (1544–95). Despite being a darling of royalty and authoring one of Europe's most popular poems, *Jerusalem Delivered,* Tasso spent much of his adult life in a madhouse and died at the age of 51, just before being crowned poet laureate. His epic dealt with the deliverance of Jerusalem from Saracens (the widely used word for Muslims) during the Crusades and was a bestseller of its time, largely because of its relevance—in the 16th century, Sorrento and other towns on the coast were still being attacked by Ottoman raiders from the east. The piazza is built over the foundations of one of the gates, Porta Catello, the main entryway in the walls that once enclosed the city. Piazza Tasso is still the gateway to old Sorrento, whose enticing lanes lead off the west side. Corso Italia is a busy shopping street, while narrower Via San Cesareo is far more atmospheric. On Via Santa Maria della Pieta, off the southwest corner, is the proud old Palazzo Correale (number 18); it's privately owned, but you can step into the magnificently tiled courtyard for a taste of aristocratic life as it once was.

Villa Communale ★★ PARK/GARDEN   Views from one side of this delightful, palm-studded patch of greenery take in the port far below and a broad sweep of the bay of Naples. From the far side of the gardens you can take an elevator down to Marina Piccola (1€) or follow a well-marked lane and stairway down. A statue of St. Francis stands amid the cliff-side gardens, looking as contented as the bench sitters around him in the pleasant surroundings.

Tours

You can spend a pleasant day exploring the coast on cruises with **Marine Club** (www.marineclub.it; ✆ **081-877-2621**). They operate from Marina Piccola daily and usually include stops in Capri for swimming and in Positano and Amalfi. This is an excellent way to see the coast in high season without contending with traffic, and supplies an affordable taste of *la dolce vita* along the coast. Tours begin at 45€ per person, and round-trips take a full day.

Beaches

You can swim from a pebbly patch at Marina Grande or rent a beach chair at one of the beach clubs there, but for real sand, take the A bus from Piazza Tasso east to **Meta,** where the beach is often jammed with Neapolitans out for a day in the sun. A more appealing option is west of town, also reachable on the A bus from Piazza Tasso, **Bagno della Regina Giovanna** (Queen Giovanna's Bath) at Punta del Capo, the northwestern tip of the Sorrento Peninsula. Here a small rock-sheltered pool of clear water, reached on a path through citrus and olive groves, was once the private harbor of the ancient Roman Villa of Pollio Felice. You can step through the ruins at the top of the cliff, where cultured man of letters Pollio Felice once entertained his guests with readings of Virgil and Horace. Just beyond, also reached by the A bus, is **Marina di Puolo,** a little fishing port where you can swim in a sheltered cove.

Where to Stay

EXPENSIVE

Grand Hotel Cocumella ★★★ Of all Sorrento's grand hotels, this magically converted monastery is the most beautiful, set amid lush gardens above the sea in elegant Sant'Agnello, a residential enclave at the eastern end of town. Rooms created from combined monks' cells are chic and sophisticated, mixing antiques with nice contemporary touches, offset with gleaming white tile floors. Some have sea-view terraces while others hang over the orange-scented gardens, where a pool is tucked into the greenery. An elevator descends to the sea and a swimming platform.

Via Cocumella 7, Sant'Agnello. www.hotelantichemura.com. ✆ **081-878-2933.** 48 units. 240€–380€ double; Rates include buffet breakfast. **Amenities:** Restaurant; bar; concierge; pool; beach; Wi-Fi (free).

Grand Hotel Excelsior Vittoria ★★★ The same family has been running Sorrento's most luxurious retreat since 1834, and their elegantly furnished lounges and vine-covered garden pergolas don't look much different than they did in the days of the Grand Tour. For that matter, Oscar Wilde, Richard Wagner, and many other notable guests of the past could walk into one of the elegantly appointed guest rooms and feel right at home, though the modern bathrooms and the elevator from Marina Piccola below the sea-facing gardens might make their heads spin. Choicest rooms have views overlooking the Gulf of Naples, others are hardly a step down in luxury and face a luxuriant garden, and most open to balconies or large terraces. A glittering pool set amid palms and flowers is a welcome hideaway from the busy lanes just outside the gate.

Piazza Tasso 34. www.exvitt.it. ✆ **081-877-7111.** 105 units. 250€–595€ double. Rates include buffet breakfast. Free parking. **Amenities:** 2 restaurants; bar; concierge; pool; room service; spa; Wi-Fi (free).

MODERATE

Hotel Antiche Mura ★★   An elegant Art Nouveau–style palazzo built on top of the town's former defensive walls reveals many surprises, including a huge, lovely garden filled with lemon trees surrounding a pool, while many rooms enjoy precipitous views into the deep gorge that runs through Sorrento. Gracious public lounges flow over a couple of floors and include a conservatory-like breakfast room. Guest quarters are bright and cheerful, with colorful Vietri-tile floors; many have balconies facing the gorge or town, while some are tucked into the garden. Service is as gracious and welcoming as the surroundings.

Via Fuorimura 7 (entrance on Piazza Tasso). www.hotelantichemura.com. ✆ **081-807-3523.** 46 units. 80€–250€ double. Rates include buffet breakfast. Parking 10€. **Amenities:** Bar; concierge; pool; Wi-Fi (free).

Hotel Rivoli ★   Convenience comes with high style at this strikingly revamped convent right in the center of town. A dramatic glass staircase floats up to the large, airy, and smartly decorated guest rooms and a rooftop breakfast room and terrace, while cozy, antiques-filled reading nooks open off the landings (there's also an elevator). You'll trade a pool and sea views for a center-of-town location—the pedestrian-only old town lanes are just outside the sound-proofed windows, and the train station, port, and bus stops are nearby, making this an especially handy base for exploring the coast.

Via Santa Maria delle Grazie 16. www.sorrentorivoli.com. ✆ **081-365-4089.** 8 units. 120€–140€ double. Rates include buffet breakfast. Substantial discounts for longer stays. **Amenities:** Wi-Fi (free).

INEXPENSIVE

Masseria Astapiana Villa Giusso ★★   An ancient monastery turned noble residence in the hills outside Vico Equense is surrounded by parkland, olive groves, and vineyards, all set on 14 hectares (35 acres) overlooking the sea and the coast. Monks' quarters in the atmospheric old house are charmingly and comfortably done with plump armchairs, family antiques, and wrought-iron beds, with a smattering of original frescoes and arched ceilings throughout. Breakfast is served a vast tiled kitchen, and the grounds are laced with woodland paths, sunny terraces, and other delightful getaways. Sorrento is 10km (6 miles) west.

Vico Equense, Via Camaldoli 51. www.astapiana.com. ✆ **081-802-4392.** 10 units. 90€–110€ double. Rates include buffet breakfast. Substantial discounts for longer stays. **Amenities:** Wi-Fi (free).

Masseria Astapiana Villa Giusso.

Ulisse Deluxe Hostel ★★　Hostel life takes on a glossy sheen in these sprawling, chic lounges and large, handsomely furnished guest rooms. A few quadruples remain true to the dormlike hostel image, but for the most part the emphasis is on quiet, hotel-standard comfort. Rooms lack a few thrills—no balconies or sweeping sea views—but white-tile floors shine, traditional wood furnishings are polished to a high gloss, beds are firm (many are king size) and extras include minibars and a luxury spa with steam room, sauna, and a large pool. The hillside perch is nicely located on the top of the road down to Marina Grande at the western edge of the historic center.

Via del Mar 22. www.ulissedeluxe.com. ✆ **081-877-4753.** 50 units. 90€–110€ double. Rates include buffet breakfast. Substantial discounts for longer stays. **Amenities:** Bar; spa; pool; Wi-Fi (free).

Where to Eat

For a quick meal and a meat fix, try the veal or chicken kebabs at **Kebab Ciampa,** Via Pieta 23 (www.kebabsorrento.com; ✆ 081-807-4595); they also serve falafel and meatballs. **Star Pub,** Via Luigi de Maio 17 (www.starpub.it; ✆ 081-877-3618) satisfies a craving for a hamburger, and also makes excellent meals-in-themselves salads, washed down with a thoughtful selection of wines and beers.

　The best gelato parlor in the area is at **Davide,** Via Padre Reginaldo Giuliani 39 (✆ **081-807-2092;** closed Wed in winter), where the 60 flavors include deliciously creamy *noci di Sorrento* (Sorrento walnuts), rich *cioccolato con canditi* (dark chocolate cream studded with candied oranges), and *delizia al limone* (a delectable lemon cream).

MODERATE

Il Delfino ★ SORRENTINE   A meal here comes with a perk, the chance to swim off the adjoining pier. That's a good incentive to eat lightly from the snack food menu, though the fresh fish and heaping platters of fresh seafood are tempting—and a popular Sunday afternoon lunch choice, when locals come down to take in the sun and indulge in excellent cooking and friendly service.

Western end of port off Via Marina Grande. ⓒ **081-878-2038.** Main courses 12€–24€. Daily 12:30–3:30pm and 6:30–11pm. Closed Nov–Mar.

Inn Bufalito ★ SORRENTINE   The approach here is to use only local products, especially buffalo meats and cheeses (buffalo-milk mozzarella is one of the region's most prized specialties). The brown-toned room is meant to give off a rustic vibe, even though the menu and service is decidedly polished. You can enjoy buffalo steaks or pasta with a heavy sauce of buffalo *ragu*, while a platter of cheeses and salamis provides a nice light meal and a taste of the house specialties.

Vico I Foro 21. www.innbufalito.com. ⓒ **081-365-6975.** Main courses 12€–24€. Wed–Mon noon–3:30pm and 6:30–11pm. Closed Nov–Feb.

La Favorita-'O Parruchiano ★★ SORRENTINE   This old-time Sorrento landmark goes back to 1868, when a former priest decided to get into the restaurant business (the name means "Priest's Place"). The vast, multi-level, greenhouse-like space opens to a vine-covered garden planted with potted citrus trees and is guaranteed to provide the grumpiest customer with a festive dining experience. Tour groups pour in, but there's room for everybody, and the food is consistently good as members of a third-generation of owners are on hand to ensure excellent service. Some dishes, such as baked

La Favorito-'O Parruchiano.

AN acquired TASTE?

Lunch and dinner in Sorrento and on the Amalfi Coast will often end with a *limoncello*, often complimentary and more often than not homemade. Almost every family in Campania has its own recipe for this potent and sweet liqueur, passed on for generations. True *limoncello* is made from *sfusato di Amalfi*, a particular lemon that has obtained D.O.P. recognition (the stamp of controlled origin for produce, similar to D.O.C. for wine). The Amalfi lemon is large, long, and light in color, with a sweet and very flavorful aroma and taste, almost no seeds, and a very thick skin. Many visitors are tempted to buy a few bottles to re-create an Amalfitana evening back home (easy enough to do); others would rather swallow mouthwash. You'll certainly have the chance to decide for yourself. You'll probably be introduced to other *rosoli* as well—sweet liqueurs made locally from fruits and herbs, of which *limoncello* is the best known. You might also be offered

finocchietto (wild fennel), *lauro* (bay leaf), *mirto* (myrtle), *nocello* (walnut), *nanassino* (prickly pear), *mandarino* (mandarin), or *fragolino* (wild strawberry).

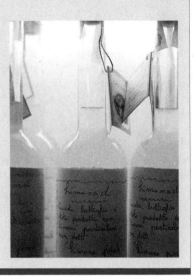

pasta crêpes stuffed with ricotta, mozzarella, and minced beef, have been on the menu since the beginning and get better with time; some wonderful seafood pastas are recent innovations and include shrimp ravioli in clam sauce.

Corso Italia 71. www.parrucchiano.com. ℭ **081-878-1321.** Main courses 10€–25€. Daily noon–3pm and 7–11:30pm (closed Wed mid-Nov–mid-Mar).

Ristorante Tasso ★★ SORRENTINE   Sorrento prides itself on fresh seafood, and the catch comes to the fore in this casually elegant room that resembles a garden pavilion (and there's also a large garden for al fresco dining). The choices change every day, with two reasonably priced set menus, though you can also dine lightly and a la carte. A little unexpectedly, given the classy surroundings, pizza is a specialty and is claimed by many regulars to be the best this side of Naples.

Via Correale 11d. www.ristorantetasso.com. ℭ **081-878-5809.** Main courses 12€–24€. Daily noon–4pm and 7–11:30pm.

INEXPENSIVE

Sant'Anna da Emilia ★ SORRENTINE   The simple pleasures of this old boat shed in Marina Grande are well known, so getting a table during the summer rush usually requires a long wait. Patience pays off with some old-time classics, such as *gnocchi alla Sorrentina* (Sorrento-style potato dumplings with cheese and tomato sauce), and *fritto misto* (deep-fried calamari and little fish). The best tables, of course, are on the pier outside. No credit cards are accepted.

Via Marina Grande 62. ℂ **081-807-2720.** Main courses 8.50€–14€. Daily noon–3:30pm and 7:30–11:30pm (closed Tues in winter). Closed Nov–Feb.

Shopping

On a walk along palazzo-lined **Via San Cesareo,** Sorrento's main shopping street, you can easily stock up on all sorts of things you don't need, mostly emblazoned with the town's signature lemons. If you decide to succumb to a purchase of the town's ubiquitous *limoncello* liqueur, head out to the charming **Giardini di Cataldo,** just off Corso Italia near the train station (www.igiardinidicataldo.it; ℂ **081-878-1888**); in a fragrant lemon and orange grove you can taste and buy *limoncello*, marmalade, and other products made on the premises.

Sorrento craftspeople are known for producing the beautiful inlaid wood designs known as intarsia, as they have for centuries. You can see fine examples at the **Museobottega della Tarisalignea,** Via San Nicola 28 (www.alessandrofiorentinocollection.it), and can even order a custom-made piece of furniture if you're tempted. The 19th-century prints of old Sorrento are equally enticing (admission 8€; April to October daily 9:30am to 1pm and 4 to 8pm, November to March daily 9:30am to 1pm and 3 to 7pm). **Gargiulo & Jannuzzi,** Piazza Tasso 1 (ℂ **081-878-1041**) sells fine pieces with wood intarsia, and you can visit the workshops for a demonstration.

Libreria Tasso, Via San Caesaro 96 (www.libreriatasso.com, ℂ **081-807-1639**) stocks a good selection of English-language titles, from the latest thrillers to guidebooks. Should the shimmering sea instill thoughts of sailing away, begin with a stop in **Nautica Palomba,** Piazza A. Lauro (ℂ **081-807-2185**), where clothing, bric-a-brac, and prints all bear a nautical theme.

Nightlife

Epicenter of nightlife in Sorrento is the lively terrace of the **Fauno Bar,** Piazza Tasso 13 (www.faunobar.it; ℂ **081-878-1135**), popular for an *aperitivo* (aperitif) and people-watching throughout the day till late into the evening. The adjoining nightclub caters to a mature crowd willing to fork over the 25€ cover charge. Some popular casual bars, usually packed with an international crowd, are **Chantecler,** Via Santa Maria della Pietà 38 (www.chanteclers.com; ℂ **081-807-5868**) and the **English Inn,** Corso Italia 55 (ℂ **081-807-4357**).

The **cloister of San Francesco,** Piazza Francesco Saverio Gargiulo, is the evocative setting for summertime concerts. Contact the Sorrento tourist office (see p. 118) for a schedule of events, including others staged at many restaurants and taverns in town. *Sorrento Musical* is a perennially popular revue of Neapolitan songs hosted by **Teatro Tasso,** Piazza Sant'Antonino (www.teatrotasso.com; ℂ **081-807-5525;** tickets cost about 25€ depending on show; 50€ including dinner).

6 THE SORRENTO PENINSULA

When Sorrento seems a little too crowded, it's easy to get away. For terrain that's a little wilder and a lot more peaceful, you need only travel south to the southwestern stretches of the Sorrento Peninsula, where the ruggedly beautiful landscapes come with soul-soothing sea views.

Essentials

GETTING THERE SITA buses (www.sitabus.it; ☎ **089-405145**) serve towns on the Sorrento Peninsula. By car, SS 145 leads west then south for access to the *limoncello*.

VISITOR INFORMATION The tourist office in Sorrento (see p. 118) has information on towns and activities, including hiking, on the Sorrento Peninsula. Another source for local information is the small tourist office in **Massa Lubrense,** Viale Filangeri 11 (☎ **081-533-9021**).

Sant'Agata sui Due Golfi ★★

7km (4 ½ miles) S of Sorrento

It won't take you too long to figure out where this hilltop village (at 300 meters, or 990 feet, you could almost say mountaintop) got the "two gulfs" part of its name. Look to the south, and you'll see the Gulf of Sorrento, Turn your head to the north, and there's the Gulf of Naples. It's also easy to see why the town was already famous in the days of the Roman Empire as the junction of trading routes across the peninsula. Artisans working on the 17th-century church of **Santa Maria delle Grazie** decided to try to outdo these views and created a ridiculously sumptuous altar with lots of marble, mother of pearl, and lapis lazuli (usually open from about 9am to 1pm and 4pm to 7pm). Nuns desiring less ostentatious surroundings settled in the **Convento del Deserto,** on a hillside about a kilometer (half a mile) outside town; follow Corso Sant'Agata from the center. You'll only rarely be invited inside, but you're not missing much—the attraction is the view from the terrace, all the way to Ischia in the northwest down the coast to Paestum in the east. In the 19th century, especially before the road to Positano and Amalfi opened in the late 1830s, this was a major stop on the Grand Tour, as far along the coast as view-seekers could get. The terrace is generally open from April through September, daily 8am to noon and 5 to 7pm and October through March, daily 10am to noon and 3 to 5pm.

Marina del Cantone ★★

5km (3 miles) S of Sant'Agata sui Due Golfi

This lovely cove cut into the cliffs was known to the ancient Greeks as Hyeros Anthos, meaning "Sacred Flower." From Sant'Agata, follow the road down through Metrano then on to Nerano–Marina del Cantone; SITA buses from Sorrento (see above) make the run to and from Marina del Cantone throughout the day. The beach (mostly pebbles) is the longest for miles around, backed by houses and a few restaurants and shops. You'll be part of a crowd here, especially on summer weekends when the beach attracts festive sun seekers from as far away as Naples. Looming just off-shore are Li Galli, an archipelago of tiny islets once owned by dancer Rudolf Nureyev. Legend has it that they were home to the Sirens of *Odyssey* fame whose song lured sailors to their deaths and are known also as the *Isole Sirenuse*.

Massa Lubrense ★★

5km (3 miles) W of Sant'Agata sui Due Golfi

Marina del Cantone.

Quiet little Massa Lubrense was once a powerful rival to Sorrento for dominance over this coast. These days, a position off the beaten track and firmly out of the limelight, along with considerable natural beauty, are its greatest assets. You'll want to pause long enough on Largo Vescovado to take in the dead-on view of the shimmering profile of Capri, just across the bay at this point, then step into the church of **Santa Maria delle Grazie** for a look at the colorful majolica floor; it's open daily 8am to noon and 4 to 8pm. Sparkling just below is the sea at Marina della Lobra, a steep 2-km (1 mile) descent that deposits you on a quiet little beach.

Punta Campanella ★★

9km (6 miles) S of Massa Lubrense

Land's end on the Sorrento Peninsula is this rocky point where a lighthouse guides ships through the treacherous Capri Narrows, the 3km (2 miles) of swift-moving waters between the peninsula and the famous island. Punta Campanella takes its name from the bell on **Torre Minerva,** a 14th-century watchtower that once warned of pirate incursions (*campanella* means "small bell"). That, in turn, was built next to the ruins of a temple dedicated to Athena (called Minerva by the Romans). With some luck and divine guidance from the goddess of wisdom, ancient sailors could possibly make it through the rock-strewn narrows. The goddess might have been kindly disposed to mortals, who surrounded her temple with olive groves that supplied plenty of oil that they could present as offerings.

Tours

Due Golfi Train Tour ★ (www.duegolfitraintour.com; ✆ **081-350-5983**) provides a slow, laid-back ride on a small train from Sant'Agata sui Due Golfi through the countryside to scenic hamlets around Massa Lubrense, stopping at local farms for tastings of mozzarella, jams, and other local specialties. Sitting back and chugging through the sunny landscapes is a nice way to spend a few hours, maybe followed by lunch in one of the nearby towns, then a swim. The train departs from the Agip service station in Sant'Agata sui Due Golfi. Departures are from May through October daily at 10am. The cost is 20€ for adults and 10€ for children.

Getting Active

The peninsula is riddled with a network of 22 well-maintained **hiking** paths that crisscross valleys, meander atop seaside cliffs, and descend hillsides to secret coves for a total length of 110km (68 miles). The tourist office in Sorrento (see p. 118) can provide you with maps.

One of the most scenic walks is from the village of Torca (2km/1 mile southeast of Sant'Agata sui Due Golfi), where Via Pedara becomes a dirt path that descends a cliff face past the ruins of the 12th-century abbey of San Pietro to a delightful cove. Just offshore are Li Galli islands, the very rocks where it's said the Sirens lured innocent mariners into wrecking their ships on the rocks.

Another walk descends from the village of Termini (5km/3 miles southwest of Sant'Agata sui Due Golfi) into the Vallone della Cala di Mitigliano, carpeted with olive groves and *macchia mediterranea*, typical Mediterranean vegetation that includes the beautifully scented *mirto*. The trail then crosses a plateau with large boulders and the ruins of Torre di Namonte, a medieval watchtower, before beginning a steep descent toward the sea, with the profile of Capri looming ahead.

On the southern side of the peninsula, the seashore and offshore waters are protected as a marine park, **Area Marina Protetta di Punta Campanella** (www.puntacampanella.org; ✆ **081-808-9877**). The most scenic way to see the unspoiled coast is to rent a **boat,** hugging the rocky shoreline as you pass hidden coves and stopping now and then for a swim. Marina del Cantone (see above) is the port of departure. Skipper Peppe takes day sailors out on his beautiful boat, *La Granseola* (www.lagranseola.com; ✆ **081-808-1027**). Other seaworthy providers are **Cooperativa S. Antonio** (✆ **081-808-1638**) and **Nautica 'O Masticiello** (www.masticiello.com; ✆ **081-808-1443**).

Where to Stay & Eat

Locando del Capitano ★★   The best lodgings in Marina del Cantone are nestled above the seashore fishermen's houses and are airy and atmospheric, with colorful Vietri-tile floors, beamed ceilings, and wrought-iron beds. They come with two big perks—sparkling sea views outside the large windows and from the terraces, and an excellent restaurant downstairs. Delicious and rather extravagant dishes are based on old local recipes with some Moorish touches and include some wonderful pastas stuffed with seafood and *pesce alla salsa di agrumi* (fish in citrus sauce); tasting menus and a la carte choices are available, with main courses from 15€.

Piazza delle Sirene 10, Marina del Cantone. www.tavernadelcapitano.it. ✆ **081-808-1028.** 15 units. 120€–280€ double. Rates include buffet breakfast. Closed 6 weeks Jan–Feb. **Amenities:** Restaurant; bar; beach; Wi-Fi (free).

Antico Francischiello ★★ SORRENTINE   The third generation of Gargiulos welcome diners to two wood-beamed, brick-arched rooms filled with antiques and ceramics. The food is as traditional and satisfying as the surroundings—no skimpy portions here, which you'll appreciate as platters of *gnocchetti verdi all'astice* (green potato dumplings with lobster) and baccalà (slated cod) in olive oil with a sweet-and-sour sauce start to arrive. A meal should begin with an *apertivo* on the terrace overlooking the olive groves and end with a selection from the overladen dessert trolley.

Via Partenope 27, 80061 Massa Lubrense. www.franischiello.com. ✆ **081-533-9780.** Main courses 18€–38€. Daily noon–3pm and 7–11:30pm (closed Wed in winter).

Don Alfonso 1890 ★★★ CREATIVE SORRENTINE   The Iaccarino family has elevated their charming and elegant dining rooms into international fame, and the secret to their success soon becomes clear. A team of excellent chefs makes the most of local produce, with breads and pasta made in-house and almost everything else coming from the family plot or from a tight network of local suppliers, with owner and former chef Alfonso Iaccarino growing the vegetables, shopping, and ordering (his wife, Livia, oversees the dining room). Even the homegrown tomatoes here seem like exotic fruits, and they infuse dishes as simple yet transporting as ravioli filled with farmhouse cheese and served with tomato sauce and basil or a bouillabaisse with freshly caught fish. Tasting menus and a la carte choices are available, and an informal lunch is served in a beautiful garden next to a swimming pool in summer. For many travelers, a meal here is reason enough to come to Sorrento, and if you wish to prolong the experience, Don Alfonso 1890 Relais houses guests in nine elegant rooms, many with a glimpse of the sea and furnished with antiques (from 400€).

Corso Sant'Agata 11, Sant'Agata sui Due Golfi. www.donalfonso.com. ✆ **081-878-0026.** Main courses 35€–45€; tasting menu 140€–155€. Wed–Sun 12:30–2:30pm and 8–10:30pm (June–Sept also Tues 8–10:30pm). Closed Nov–Mar.

Maria Grazia ★★ SORRENTINE/SEAFOOD   Diners have relished the sea views and simple dishes at this waterfront institution for more than 50 years. The barebones room right across from the boats moored along the pebbly beach lets you know what you can expect—fresh grilled octopus and grilled fish of any kind that's just been caught, along with some basic pastas that include the house specialty, *pasta con i cucuzzielli,* spaghetti in a light tomato sauce with baby eggplant, basil, and *caciocavallo* cheese. It's all delicious, washed down with jugs of the house white wine, and followed up with a *limoncello* or other homemade *digestivo*.

Marina del Cantone. massalubrense.it/mariagrazia.htm. ✆ **081-808-1011.** Main courses 10€–18€. Mar–Dec daily noon–3pm and 7–10pm.

VICO EQUENSE ★

11km (7 miles) NE of Sorrento, 42km (26 miles) SE of Naples

Another excursion from Sorrento heads back east toward Naples, to this gracious old bayside town perched quite picturesquely on a ledge above the sea. Vico Equense is off the typical sightseeing circuit, but that's not for lack of beauty or charm. Or fame, at least in pop-culture circles—eternally popular Bruce Springsteen's great *nonna* sailed from Vico Equense for Ellis Island with her five children in 1900.

Essentials

GETTING THERE You can easily reach Vico Equense by **train,** from Sorrento via the **Circumvesuviana** railway (www.vesuviana.it; ℂ **800-053939**), or by **bus,** via **SITA** (www.sitabus.it; ℂ **089-405145**). By **car,** SS 145 leads east from Sorrento toward Vico Equense.

VISITOR INFORMATION The tourist office in Vico Equense (www.vicoturismo.it; ℂ **081-801-5752**) is at Via San Ciro 16 and maintains an information stand at Piazza Umberto I 19.

Exploring Vico Equense

A walk down lanes from Piazza Umberto shows off medieval palaces from the time when King Charles II of Naples (reigned 1284–1309) used to spend summers here and liked the place so much he built a castle. Atmospheric Via Monsignor Natale ends at **Largo dei Tigli,** a balcony hanging high above the sea. Facing the sea from a 90-m (300-ft.) perch on nearby Via Vescovada is the pink and white facade of the **Chiesa dell'Annunziata,** with roots in the 14th-century Gothic style but redone in 18th-century baroque (Sunday and holidays 10am to noon; ℂ **081-879-8004**). Portraits show off the town's bishops, minus one. Michele Natale was executed for his support of the Pathenopean Republic, the short-lived 1799 rebellion that attempted to establish French republican rule in Naples and its holdings. In his place is an angel with its finger to its lips, a warning to any citizens with forward-thinking ideals that it pays to keep your mouth shut. Vico has been kinder to Gaetano Filangieri (1752–88), who lies in a magnificent tomb. The nobleman wrote tirelessly on his favorite subject, criminal justice, attracting the notice of Benjamin Franklin. The two corresponded frequently up to the time of Filangieri's death from tuberculosis at a villa outside of town.

Scrajo Terme ★ SPA   When in Vico Equense, do as the Equense do, and step into this cliff-side thermal establishment and soak in the waters. Treatments aren't inexpensive, and some address ailments you can count your lucky stars you don't have, but you can come just to soak, too, and a session comes with the use of pools, seaside terraces, and a private beach where the water is warmed here and there with hot springs.

Via Luigi Serio 10 (SS 145),. www.scrajoterme.it. ℂ **081-801-5731.** Booking required. Closed Dec–Apr.

Getting Active

From the municipio in the center of town, follow **Via Castello Marina,** a steep footpath, through olive groves down to **Vico Marina;** the cove-laced shoreline down here shelters many fine, small beaches. One of the nicest is **Marina di Equa,** just west of a defense tower built in the 17th century.

If the prospect of squeezing onto a bus for the trip down the coast from Sorrento to Positano seems unappealing, here's an alternative: a **hike** along a network of trails that, provided you're moderately fit, will take you from Vico Equense to Positano in about 3½ hours (in heavy summer traffic, the trip by bus can take almost that long, or at least seem to). You'll need a good trail map (available from the tourist office in Sorrento or Vico Equense) and you'll have to follow it carefully, as trails intersect and shoot off in many directions. Roughly, the route first takes you south toward Ticciano until you reach the bridge over the Milo, then across and the western spur of Monte Comune (altitude 877m/2,877 ft.), and finally the descent to Positano.

Where to Eat

Da Gigino Pizza a Metro ★★★ PIZZA   Back in the 1950s, local pizza maker Gigino Dell'Amura decided to buck tradition and started baking pies that were long rather than round. His delicious creations came to be known as "pizza a metro" (by the meter), and appreciative customers have been packing into the large, simply-furnished pizzeria ever since. His five sons now manage the three large ovens and handle the crowds that arrive by the busload. A wait is likely but worth it (no reservations accepted), and a meter (about 3 ft.) feeds a family and comes with a huge choice of toppings.

Via Giovanni Nicotera 15, www.pizzametro.it. ✆ **081-879-8426** or 081-879-8309. Pizza from 7€. No credit cards. Daily noon–1am.

POSITANO ★★

16km (10 miles) E of Sorrento

Hugging a semivertical rock formation, Positano is the very essence of picturesque, an enticing collection of pastel-colored houses and majolica domes that spill down a ravine to the sea. Novelist John Steinbeck, who was much taken with Positano during a visit in 1953, described it in words that still ring true: "It is a dream place that isn't quite real when you are there and becomes beckoningly real after you have gone. . . ."

It's not surprising that in the 1960s and 1970s Positano was the retreat for *la dolce vita* set. In mid-summer, its throngs of admirers can seem like an invading horde, much like those that attacked the little seaside kingdom back in the 9th to 11th centuries, when it was part of the powerful Republic of the Amalfis, rival to Venice as a sea power.

VISITOR INFORMATION   The tourist office at Via del Saracino 4 (www.aziendaturismopositano.it; ✆ **089-875067)** is open Monday to Saturday 8:30am to 2pm, with additional hours (3:30–8pm) in July and August.

Exploring Positano

Whether you arrive by boat or bus, you're in for an uphill or downhill climb along narrow lanes and steep lanes (wear comfortable walking shoes). At some point you'll want to stay put, probably along the sea at **Marina Grande,** where the town's few fishermen still haul up their boats and ferries arrive and depart. Most of the pebbly shoreline is taken up with a beach, backed by restaurants and bars in what were once shipyards and storehouses when Positano was a naval power. From Marina Grande, **Via Positanesi d'America,** a cliff-side pedestrian promenade, stretches along the shore past the cape of **Torre Trasita** and a 13th-cenury lookout to the smaller and slightly more relaxing beach of **Fornillo.**

Positano at night.

If you wander up the steps from Marina Grande you'll soon find yourself amid a souk-like sprawl of shops shaded by bougainvillea-laced trellises. The majolica-domed **Collegiata di Santa Maria Assunta ★★,** Piazza Flavio Gioia (© **089-875480;** daily 8am–noon and 4–7pm), is Positano's main church, founded as a Benedictine monastery in the 13th century. The "Madonna Nera" (Black Madonna), a Byzantine-style icon above the altar, allegedly gave the town its name when a 12th-century pirate ship carrying the icon sailed into a violent storm. Sailors heard the Madonna on the icon saying *"Posa, Posa"* ("Put me down") and they took their ship to safety in what would become the harbor of Positano. A relief on the campanile outside curiously shows a wolf nursing seven fish, a clue to how the town once made its living. If you're waiting for a bus at the western bus stop (on the Sorrento side of town) step into the small **Chiesa di Nuova,** Via Chiesa Nuova, for a look at the lovely majolica tile floor.

Beaches

Positano has two in-town beaches, **Spiaggia Grande** and the slightly quieter **Fornillo.** You can swim for free at both, or rent a lounger and umbrella for about 10€. To reach slightly more idyllic settings, step aboard any of the tour boats that set off from Spiaggia Grande for stops at coves along the coast, or rent a rowboat and poke along the rocky shoreline at your own pace.

You can explore the cove-laced shoreline in a rental boat from **Lucibella** (© **089-875032**), between 35€ and 60€ per hour, without skipper, depending on the kind of boat and the duration of the rental. Many day sailors set their sights on **Li Galli (The Roosters) ★★,** the four small islands visible to the

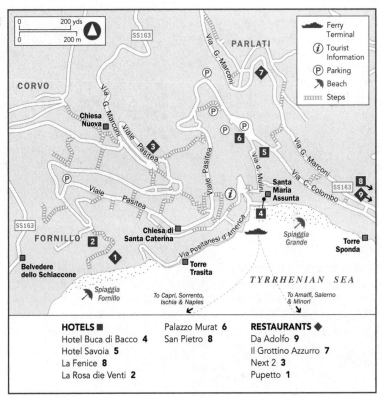

	Ferry Terminal
(i)	Tourist Information
(P)	Parking
	Beach
	Steps

HOTELS ■
Hotel Buca di Bacco **4**
Hotel Savoia **5**
La Fenice **8**
La Rosa die Venti **2**

Palazzo Murat **6**
San Pietro **8**

RESTAURANTS ◆
Da Adolfo **9**
Il Grottino Azzurro **7**
Next 2 **3**
Pupetto **1**

west of Marina Grande. According to Homer, the Sirens lived on the rocky outcroppings and lured mariners to their deaths on the rocky shoals with their enchanting songs. Sirens themselves were less than enchanting in the flesh, birdlike creatures (hence the name, Li Galli, "The Roosters") with human faces and the bodies of fish. If the light is right and you've had some wine on the voyage, it's easy to see how the rooster-shaped islets might have appeared to be Sirens rising out the sea mist. The island to head for is Gallo Lungo, where a medieval watchtower rises above a little beach.

Getting Active

Should you wish to explore the coast on foot, you can follow the **Via degli Incanti (Trail of Charms)**, a 25-km (15-mile) long path between Positano and Amalfi. You'll wend your way through cultivated terraces and citrus groves, enjoying spectacular views. If you don't want to do the entire trail, you can catch the coast-road bus at any of the towns and settlements along the route.

A view of Positano's beach and town.

Where to Stay

Small, guesthouse-style rooms offer a way to beat Positano's sky-high lodging prices. The tourist office (see p. 133) has a full list of bed-and-breakfasts, home stays, and other moderately priced accommodations.

EXPENSIVE

San Pietro ★★★ One of the world's most fabled getaways is luxurious and enchanting, perched on its own promontory above the sea and the discrete retreat of royalty, movie stars, and plain folks who want the vacation experience of a lifetime. Opulently tiled terraces cascade down the cliff face and are laced with shaded nooks and crannies, perfectly poised for hours of relaxation (and the best setting in Positano for a cocktail, expensive but memorable, and a sound investment for anyone trying to infuse an evening with romance). Large accommodations face the sea through huge windows and from private terraces and are a gracious mix of antiques, stylishly informal and comfortable pieces, and elaborate tiles and artwork. The piece de resistance is the private beach, reached by an elevator that descends through the cliff. For those who might want to venture farther, the hotel's private yacht takes guests on complimentary coast cruises, and a free shuttle plies the 2km (1 mile) to town. Many guests choose to stay put amid the hedonistic surroundings, with the glorious, view-filled terrace of Il San Pietro restaurant providing exceptional sustenance.

Via Laurito 2. www.ilsanpietro.it. ⓒ **089-875455.** 60 units. 550€–680€ double. Rates include lavish breakfast. 3 nights minimum stay in high season. Free parking. Closed Nov–Mar. **Amenities:** Restaurants; bar; concierge; health club; pool; room service; sauna; spa; tennis court; Wi-Fi (free).

MODERATE

Hotel Buca di Bacco ★ The closest Positano comes to a beach hotel is this former fisherman's hut, much expanded and glorified over the years, that's right on Marina Grande. The beachfront perch puts you in the center of the action, so convenience comes with a bit of noise, along with endless sea views from colorfully tiled balconies and terraces. Even the rooms with only partial sea views or no sea views are a bit of a treat, with handsome antiques and comfy upholstered pieces set on tile floors to create a casual, gracious elegance that's typical of the Amalfi Coast. Three generations of the Rispoli family look after guests with care that extends to excellent meals in a sea-facing dining room and an informal snack bar.

Via Rampa Teglia 4. www.bucadibacco.it. ⓒ **089-875699.** 54 units. 245€–450€ double. Rates include buffet breakfast. No parking. Closed 2 weeks in winter. **Amenities:** Restaurant; bar; beach (public); babysitting; concierge; room service; Wi-Fi (free).

Palazzo Murat ★★ Gioacchino Murat, Napoleon's brother-in-law and king of Naples, built this enticing and vaguely exotic 18th-century baroque palace near Positano's small port as a summer getaway. It's still a retreat of royal magnitude, set amid a vast garden and orchard dripping with flowering vines and scented with lemons and jasmine. Five especially large rooms, filled with handsome antiques, are in the original palace, and others are in a new yet extremely tasteful addition, where tile floors and traditional furnishings adhere to the historical ambience. Most rooms have balconies, some with sea views; others overlook the surrounding greenery, the tile-domed church of Santa Maria Assunta, or the town. Buffet breakfast is served in the garden in good weather.

Via dei Mulini 23. www.palazzomurat.it. ⓒ **089-875177.** 31 units. 220€–450€ double. Rates include buffet breakfast. Parking 25€ nearby. Closed Jan to week before Easter. **Amenities:** Restaurant; concierge; pool; room service; Wi-Fi (free).

INEXPENSIVE

Hotel Savoia ★★ You won't find a lot of luxurious amenities, but this hotel's great location right in the heart of Positano, steps from the beach, is coupled with pleasant decor—bright tile floors, comfortable beds, and attractive traditional furnishings. Some rooms have sea views, and others take in the sweep of the old town climbing the hillside. The old-fashioned ambience comes with a provenance: The D'Aiello family has been running this place since 1936, when Positano was a getaway for a select few, and that's still how they treat their guests.

Via Cristoforo Colombo 73. www.savoiapositano.it. ⓒ **089-875003.** 42 units. 120€–190€ double. Rates include buffet breakfast. Parking 25€ nearby. **Amenities:** Bar; babysitting; concierge; room service; Wi-Fi (free).

La Fenice ★★★ All the charm and beauty of Positano comes to the fore in this little parcel of heaven clinging to a cliff on the outskirts of town. A stay requires a bit of walking and climbing, to and from the town center (about a 10-minute stroll), as well as on the gorgeous property itself, along shaded walkways and stone stairways through gardens and groves to the pool and private beach below—an amenity that's the pride of only a few other much more expensive retreats along the coast. Charming and simple rooms, most with tiled terraces overlooking the sea, are tucked into a couple of villas and several cottages that descend the hillside amid lemon groves and grape vines. Owner Constantino Marino and his family live on the property and go out of their way to make guests feel at home, and that includes carting bags up and down the stairs and serving informal meals made with produce from the garden (meals served on request).

Via Giuglielmo Marconi 4. lafenicepositano.com. ℰ **089-875513.** 14 units. 120€–160€. Rates include breakfast. Cash only. **Amenities:** Pool; beach; Wi-Fi (free).

La Rosa dei Venti ★★   Each of the homily furnished, tile-floored rooms in this house high on a hillside in the quieter part of Positano comes with a big perk—a large planted terrace with a sea view. It's tempting to settle in and stay put here, but moving around town and the coast is easy to do: The beach at Fornillo is at the bottom of the hill, shops and restaurants are nearby, and it's an easy climb up to the bus stop on the coast road or down to the harbor.

Via Fornillo 40. www.larosadeiventi.net. ℰ **089-875252.** From 130€ double. Rates include breakfast. **Amenities:** Wi-Fi (free).

Where to Eat
EXPENSIVE

Next 2 ★★ AMALFITAN   Step through the iron gates into one of Positano's most sophisticated lairs. A softly lit courtyard with knockout sea views and a contemporarily styled room of dazzling white linens and bright cushions are the setting for refined takes on local favorites made with fresh ingredients, many from the restaurant garden. Fried ravioli stuffed with ricotta and mozzarella is set on a bed of tomatoes plucked from the vine minutes before, while *fiori di zucchini* (zucchini flowers) are filled with ricotta, mozzarella, and basil and served with pesto sauce. Fresh fish is a speciality, of course, and paired with the same homegrown ingredients.

Via Pasitea 242. www.next2.it. ℰ **089-812-3516.** Reservations recommended in high season. Main courses 16€–25€. Daily 7–11pm. Closed Nov–Mar and Mon off season.

MODERATE

Da Adolfo ★ AMALFITAN/SEAFOOD   One of Positano's old-time favorites makes the most of its beachside location with a laid-back ambience and an emphasis on fresh seafood and water views. You can venture into some local specialties here, including mozzarella *alla brace* (grilled on fresh lemon leaves) followed by a beautifully seasoned *zuppa di cozze* (mussel stew). Come for lunch and spend the afternoon, making use of the adjacent changing rooms, showers, and chair-and-umbrella rentals. Sooner or later, though, you'll have to face the 450 rugged steps that climb the hillside up to the road—better yet, take the free water-shuttle service to Marina Grande.

Via Spiaggia di Laurito 40. www.daadolfo.com. ℰ **089-875022.** Main courses 10€–18€. Daily 1–4pm. Closed mid-Oct–early May.

Il Ritrovo ★★ AMALFITAN/PIZZA   Just being in this mountainside village above Positano is a treat, far removed from all the crowds and frenzy on the coast 450m (1,500 ft.) below. The airy terrace makes the most of the sea and mountain views, and the menu is inspired by both. *Grigliata mista* (grilled meat medley), and the chicken roasted with mountain herbs, are hearty and excellent, as are the excellent pastas laden with fresh seafood. Chef Salvatore might come out and insist you follow up a meal with one of his homemade liqueurs. He shares his considerable skills in year-round cooking classes. You can take the SITA bus up from town, or the restaurant will send a car down for a free pickup.

Via Montepertuso 77, Montepertuso. www.ilritrovo.com. ℭ **089-812005.** Main courses 10€–20€; set-price menu 30€–40€. Thurs–Tues noon–3:30pm and 7pm–12:30am; open daily Apr–mid-Oct. Closed Jan.

INEXPENSIVE
Il Grottino Azzurro ★ AMALFITAN/WINERY   A modest little wine cellar opening onto the street near the top of the town is a favorite with locals, who count on the kitchen for delicious renditions of simple recipes. *Manicaretti* (large ravioli) and cannelloni are filled with meat and baked with cheese and homemade tomato sauce, with extra sauce served on the side, while *spaghetti alla vongole* is piled high with sweet, tender clams from local waters. A good choice of regional wines is on hand.

Via Guglielmo Marconi 158 (SS 163). ℭ **089-875466.** Main courses 8€–16€. Thurs–Tues 12:30–3pm and 7:30–11pm (also Wed in summer).

Pupetto ★ AMALFITAN/PIZZA   You can reach this lovely spot by elevator off the coast road above, but it's hard to beat the approach by the seaside footpath from Marina Grande. Once here, the lovely, lemon-scented terrace stretching above Fornillo beach is the setting for a simple meal of grilled fresh fish or one of the many seafood pastas. Pizzas are served in the evening, and light snacks during the day, when a seat beneath the bamboo awnings is a prime spot for a drink after a swim on the beach below.

Via Fornillo 37. www.hotelpupetto.it. ℭ **089-875087.** Main courses 12€–22€; pizza 7€–10€. Daily 12:30–3pm and 7:30–10pm. Closed Nov–Mar.

Shopping
Though Positano appears to have sold its soul to the devils of commerce, the endless rows of shops are curiously unenticing. If you must spend money, consider some loungewear, a throwback to the 1970s when Moda Positano was all the rage. A holdover from those days is the excellent **Sartoria Maria Lampo,** Viale Pasitea 12 (www.marialampo.it; ℭ **089-875021**). The town is also famous for hand-crafted sandals, often made while you wait. Among the best shoemakers are **D'Antonio,** Via Trara Genoino 13 (ℭ **089-811824**); **Dattilo,** Via Rampa Teglia 19 (ℭ **089-811440**); or **Safari,** Via della Taratana 2 (www.safaripositano.com; ℭ **089-811440**).

Photo Op

If you're traveling by car or taxi just west of Positano on SS 163, keep an eye out for the renowned **Belvedere dello Schiaccone.** This is the best lookout point on the Amalfi Drive, 200m (656 ft.) above sea level. The view extends across palm and citrus groves to the archipelago of Li Galli and Capo Sottile, with the splendid summit of Monte Sant'Angelo a Tre Pizzi in the background. If you catch the profile of Monte Sant'Angelo in a shot, you'll have a good story to tell when showing off your photos. According to legend, the devil challenged the Virgin Mary to see who could manage to pierce the rock face. The devil could only scratch the surface, but at the Virgin's touch the rock crumbled and the large opening that you see in one side of the peak appeared.

Nightlife

You can still get a whiff of Positano's jet-set days at **Music on the Rocks,** Via Grotto dell'Incanto 51 (www.musicontherocks.it; ℂ **089-875874**), a two-level dance club carved into the rocks above Spiaggia Grande; the upstairs terrace provides nice views and mellow piano music, while dancing is in the cavelike disco beneath. Right on the beach, **La Buca di Bacco,** Via del Brigantino 35 (www.bucapositano.it; ℂ **089-811461**) has been Positano's prime stop for an after-dinner drink for half a century.

Around Positano: Montepertuso ★ & Nocelle ★

An easy way to escape the summertime crowds in Positano is to head up to these two villages high in the Lattari Mountains. Montepertuso is only 3km (2 miles) from Positano, but the distance, via SITA bus, seems to be entirely vertical. The perch is 450m (1,500 ft.) above sea level and, while the collection of houses and shops is pretty enough, the draws are the eagle's-nest views up and down the coast. Actually, "falcon's nest" is more historically accurate, as this is where Frederico II of Sicily bred his sporting birds in the 13th century. The bus continues another 2.5km (1^1/$_2$ miles) to tiny little Nocelle, but the preferred approached is by footpath. Since you've already gained the altitude on the ride up to Montepertuso, the 30-minute walk is not too strenuous, above pine-scented ravines and up and down ages-old staircases. This is how residents once got from one village to another, and they, too, must have relished the views, the sublime light, and the spectacle of towering cliffs.

PRAIANO & VETTICA MAGGIORE ★★

6.5km (4 miles) E of Positano

With a graceful profusion of porticos and domes, medieval Praiano sits 120m (394 ft.) above sea level on the slopes of Monte Sant'Angelo as they drape seaward over the promontory known as Capo Sottile. The little town was the

Praiano.

preferred summer residence of the Amalfi doges, who loved the beautiful views over Positano, Amalfi, and the Faraglioni of Capri. These enchanting outlooks are still the main draw, as are twin coves on either side of town where you can dip your toes in the sea and watch fishermen bring in the haul that will appear on your table that evening.

VISITOR INFORMATION Praiano's **tourist office** (www.praiano.org; ✆ **089-874557**) is at Via G. Capriglione. **La Sibilla,** Via Marina di Praia 1, Praiano (www.lasibilla.org; ✆ **089-874365**) offers **water taxi** service to and from Marina di Praia from Amalfi, Atrani, Capri, and Positano (about 65€ per hr.); it also offers boat rentals and daily excursions to Capri, the Emerald Grotto (p. 145), and Furore.

Exploring Praiano

You'll soon catch on that Praiano is actually one part of a set of twins—the steep lanes of Praiano hug the east side of the promontory, while Vettica Maggiore is on the west side. Little matter, since the pretty streets of one blend seamlessly into those of the other. They eventually merge into a sea-facing, majolica-paved piazza that seems more like the deck of ship than it does a shelf of terra firma carved out of the hillside. Each town has its own tile-domed, tile-floored church—**San Luca** in Praiano and **San Gennaro** in Vettica Maggiore. For that matter, twin towns, twin harbors: East of Praiano is tiny, picturesque **Marina di Praia ★★**, at the bottom of a deep chasm with its small pebbly beach and clear waters; the path starts from the tourist office. To the west is a tiny slip of pebbles at **Marina Piccola,** tucked into a cove beneath olive groves (follow the signs for SPIAGGIA from the piazza). It's said that "Whoever wants to live a healthy life spends the morning in Vettica and the evening in Praiano," which is probably just supposed to mean that life is good enough in the twin villages that it's really not necessary for residents, or their visitors, to venture too much farther afield.

Praiano's other landmark is the **Torre Asciola** (also known as Torre a Mare, or Tower by the Sea), reached on a vertigo-inducing footpath toward Marina di Praia from the center of town. The origins of this limestone lookout are the subject of ongoing debate as to whether it was erected in 1278 or 1558. Whatever the tower's age, it's the best preserved of 34 such defenses that were built along this stretch of coast in more perilous times to keep watch for pirates. The squat round tower must have also provided anyone holed up inside with a great sense of security, as they could hide behind walls 3m (10 ft.) thick with a tank full of fresh water in the cellar. These days the tower houses the studios of painter and sculptor **Paolo Sandulli,** whose plump maidens ride sea creatures that are only a bit more fantastical than those fishermen haul up in nets from the sea just below. The studio (www.paolosandulli.com; ✆ **089–874149**) is open daily, with varying hours, often from 10am to 7pm in the summer.

Where to Stay & Eat

Praiano lacks the buzz and sophistication of Positano, but for many travelers the quiet and the down-to-earth atmosphere are a big plus.

Hotel Margherita ★ Vaulted ceilings and colorful tiles everywhere—floors, terraces, bathrooms—add a note of charm to these large, straightforward, traditional accommodations in a sparkling white villa set amid hillside lemon groves. A swimming pool and panoramic terraces overlook the sea, as do many of the private balconies, while a nearby path winds down through town to the beach at Marina Piccola.

Via Umberto I 70 (off Via Roma [SS 163]). www.hotelmargherita.it. ✆ **089-874628.** 28 units. 110€–150€ double. Rates include breakfast. Free parking. **Amenities:** Restaurant; bar; pool; room service; Wi-Fi (free).

Hotel Onda Verde ★★ You can connect with the mariner deep within you at this seaside perch, where the sumptuous blue sea takes center stage—from endless terraces, swimming platforms, and a pebbly cove. Spacious, tile-floored accommodations in five cliff-side villas are a wee bit fussy and formal for the beach locale, but they all open to terraces hanging just above the waves, have nice little sitting areas, and provide comfort and views at a fraction of the cost of other luxe seaside resorts along the coast. If you wish to head out to sea and explore the coast and islands, boats depart from a jetty just below the hotel.

Via Terramare 3, Marina di Praia. www.ondaverde.it. ✆ **089-874143.** 24 units. 210€–230€ double. Rates include buffet breakfast. Free parking. Closed Nov–Mar. **Amenities:** Restaurant; bar; beach; Wi-Fi (free).

La Brace ★★ AMALFITAN/PIZZA Nothing about this second-floor indoor/outdoor room alongside the coast highway is fancy, but the food is excellent, service is friendly, and, provided you sit on the terrace, you'll take in some nice views of the coastline along with your meal. Pastas are the hit here—fusilli *con provola, melanzane, e basilico* (with provola cheese, sautéed eggplant, and fresh basil) is a meal in itself, or a satisfying follow-up to an antipasto of local salamis and cheeses or prelude to grilled fresh fish. Pizzas bring in a big evening crowd.

Via Gennaro Capriglione 146 (SS 163). ✆ **089-874226.** Main courses 9€–20€. Thurs–Tues 12:30–3pm and 7:30–11:30pm (also Wed Apr–Sept).

Shopping

At **Bottega Scala** ★★, Via Umberto I 68A (www.liuteriascala.com; ✆ **089-874894**), the *liutai* (stringed instruments makers) Pasquale and Leonardo Scala create instruments using traditional techniques. They specialize in classical guitars, but also make reproductions of early stringed instruments that date from medieval and baroque times, and their famous clients include Pino Daniele.

Nightlife

Back in the *anni ruggenti* (roaring years) of the 1960s, anyone who was anyone found the way to **L'Africana** ★★ (www.africanafamousclub.com; © **339-202-5267**), and it's not that easy to do so—it's off SS 163 between Praiano and Marina di Praia; take the elevator down from the highway to the seashore or follow the footpath from Praiano. The mythical hangout is still a pretty enchanting place, and still a bit hedonistic, set in a grotto just above the lapping waves, with a sea cave for a dance floor. The club is open Tuesday to Sunday from 9pm (closed Oct–Apr); on weekends in season a shuttle imports clubbers from Positano and other places along the coast.

FURORE ★

10km (6½ miles) SE of Positano

Residents of this gravity-defying little settlement might have the strongest legs in Italy, since it's a climb of more than 500m (1,600 ft.) from one end of the town to the other, from the sea to a sky-high perch above. Down at sea level is the fjord of Furore, a deep cleft in the cliffs that provides a natural harbor. Meanwhile, the top of the village is perched high in the mountains above, safely out of reach of pirates who once raided the coast. Wherever you go, you'll do some climbing: It's 944 steps down to the harbor, and 3,000 steps from there up to the top of town along the Sentiero della Volpe Pescatrice (The Fox-Fish's Path) and the Sentiero dei Pipistrelli Impazziti (The Mad Bats' Path).

VISITOR INFORMATION   It's easier to approach Furore by the bus that runs along the coast road between Sorrento and Amalfi than to try to find a place to park. Even if you don't alight here, you'll see the fjord and harbor far below as you zip across the viaduct. If driving, you'll have to stash your car (6.50€) in a turnoff past the viaduct toward Amalfi, near the service station. From there you set off walking and climbing, down to the harbor and up to the rest of town.

Exploring Furore

In your climbs around town, you'll notice murals painted on the sides of many houses. That's part of a local effort to give the town an identity as the *paese dipinto,* or "painted town," and overcome its age-old reputation as the *paese che non c'è,* or "town that doesn't exist." That name came from the fact that much of the town is strung out for many miles along roads leading into the mountains, thereby lacking a real center.

When a storm rolls in and water roars though the fjord with a fury, it's easy to see how the town got its formal name. You can sit in one of the little waterside bars and consider the perils of life on the coast as you sip one of the delicious wines from the town's highly acclaimed winery, **Cantine Marisa Cuomo,** Via Lama 14 (www.marisacuomo.com; ℰ **089-830348**); open for tastings from noon to 6:30pm by appointment for two or more. The standout is Gran Furor Divina Costiera Bianco, an aromatic white quite accurately promoted by the vineyard as "a passionate wine filled with the essence of rock and sea, without even the slightest hint of sweetness." A tour introduces you to the rigors of growing vines in rocky soil in nearly vertical landscapes. Vineyards in Furore cling to walls and terraces among the houses that are scattered across the hillsides all around town, and townsfolk like to claim they originated the phrase used up and down the Amalfi Coast that they have one foot in their boats and the other in their vineyards.

Where to Stay & Eat

Antica Hostaria di Bacco ★★ AMALFITAN   An 85-year-old institution is a throwback to life on the Amalfi Coast as it once was, serving deliciously simple meals on a shady terrace surrounded by vineyards and filled with sea views. The signature dish is a meal in itself: *ferrazzuoli alla nannarella,* fresh pasta handmade using a small iron tool and topped with a mix of grape tomatoes, smoked swordfish, raisins, red pepper, and arugula. Namesake "Nannarella" is the late, great actress Anna Magnani, one of many Italian celebs who have been dazzled by the Cuomo family's cooking and hospitality. Owner Rafaella, Furore's lifetime mayor, and his clan are part of the town's wine-making dynasty, so you can count on an excellent house white to accompany your meal. Guests who are totally smitten with the surroundings can settle into one of the six simple, bright guest rooms, all with private terraces (100€ double).

Via G.B. Lama 9. www.baccofurore.it. ℰ **089-830360.** Main courses 12€–20€. Sat–Thurs 12:30–3pm and 7:30–11pm (also Fri June–Sept).

CONCA DEI MARINI ★★

12km (7 1/2 miles) E of Positano, 2km (1 mile) E of Furore

Rambling little Conca is really just a hamlet of hillside-perched houses strung out along the coast road between Positano and Amalfi. It's hard to believe that the little harbor in the picturesque cove once bustled with enough boat-building to make the town richer than Amalfi. The name, though, is a giveaway—it means "Seafarer's Basin," and at one time 27 galleons were moored in the tiny harbor beneath a fortified tower on the Capo di Conca.

VISITOR INFORMATION   You can get tourist information at the municipal office: Casa Comunale (ℰ **089-831301**).

Exploring Conca dei Marini

Conca is best known as the jumping-off point for the **Emerald Grotto** (see below). But stick around long enough to try some *sfogliatella* di Santa Rosa, a delicious pastry invented by nuns at the local **Convento di Santa Rosa** in

Conca dei Marini.

the 17th century. The enterprising, sweet-toothed sisters decided to replace the traditional ricotta cheese filling of the popular Neapolitan *sfogliatella* with cream and a dash of *amarene,* candied sour cherries in syrup. And mama mia—their creation was a surefire hit that you can still taste in pastry shops up and down the coast. Little wonder such a delicious delight came out of surroundings like these, where white houses tumble down the emerald-green hillsides and meet the blue sea in almost ridiculous explosion of color. These views and Conca's out-of-the-way quiet have been a lure for a long line of privacy-seeking celebs, among them Jacqueline Onassis, Carlo Ponti, Princess Margaret of England, and the Queen of Holland.

You'll soon see the allure as you slip down the staircase to the little harbor, overseen by the appropriately small **Chapel of Santa Maria della Neve.** On some feast days mass is celebrated on the beach in front, since the congregation can't squeeze inside. At other times, this might be the most picturesque spot on the entire coast for a swim, with the chance to float in the warm, azure water while admiring the dazzling white houses climbing the hillside—quite Moorish-looking, with their arches, terraces, and outdoor staircases. A short climb up the hillside, on a steep road and staircase, brings you to the **Church of San Pancrazio,** where views from the palm-shaded courtyard will convince you that all the huffing and puffing was worth it.

Grotta dello Smeraldo (Emerald Grotto) ★★ NATURAL WONDER
This enchanting sea cave, discovered in 1932, gives Capri's Blue Grotto (see p. 179) a run for its money. The chamber of stalactites and stalagmites produces transcendent light effects, most stunningly the namesake blue-green light that envelops the grotto in otherworldliness when the sun is high (best between noon and 3pm) and the sea is calm. The underwater ceramic nativity scene is a 1950s addition, a bit of schmaltz that nonetheless makes a trip through the grotto a popular Christmastime pilgrimage. The stalagmites (those are the ones rising out of the sea) are telltale signs that the cave was once on dry land, or these rock formations could never have come to be. You can reach the cave from Conca dei Marini by taking an elevator from SS 163, or a long series of steps, then climbing into a rowboat. You can also take a boat from Amalfi, just 5km (3 miles) down the coast (trips are usually 15€, with admission to the grotto).

Below SITA bus stop on SS 163, near Conca Azzura Hotel. Admission 6€, includes the rowboat ride. Mar–Oct daily 9am–7pm, Nov–Feb daily 9am–4pm.

Where to Stay & Eat

Hotel Il Belvedere ★★★ Generations of travelers have found their parcel of paradise at this beautiful seaside perch, and many guests return year after year. Welcoming salons filled with overstuffed armchairs and oil paintings suggest old-world refinement, and polished service lives up to the surroundings. Airy and spacious guest rooms strike just the right note between elegance and comfort, with colorful tile floors and plenty of homey touches that make them seem like bedrooms in a private villa; all open to small sea-facing terraces, while the glorious pool, tucked into cliff-side greenery, and a private beach are reached by elevator.

Via Smeraldo 19 (off the SS 163). www.belvederehotel.it. © **089-831282.** 36 units. 220€–240€ double. Rates include buffet breakfast. Free parking. Closed Nov–Mar. **Amenities:** Restaurant; bar; pool; beach; Wi-Fi (free).

La Tonnarella ★★ AMALFITAN A boat shed on the beach at Marina di Conca hails to the days when tuna fishing was big business. Most of the ingredients of a delicious meal still come off the fishing boats and appear in traditional favorites such as *scialatielli ai frutti di mare* (fresh pasta with seafood and tomatoes) and *totani alle patate* (flying squid and potatoes). Many guests arrive by sea as well and they enjoy these simple and near perfect preparations served on a terrace just feet away from the lapping waves.

Via Marina 1, Borgo Marinaro. © **089-831939.** Main courses 15€–30€. Tues–Sat 12:30–3pm and 7:30–11pm; Sun–Mon 12:30–3pm. Closed Nov–Mar.

Around Conca dei Marini: Agerola ★

13km (8 miles) NW of Conca dei Marini

Views and cheese are what draw visitors up to this high plateau above the coast in the Monti Lattari range (by car from Conca dei Marini, follow SS 366). For the views, head to Agerola, then to the outlying hamlet of **San Lazzaro,** where, past the church to the left, the **Punta** is a natural terrace hanging over the sea far below. Shops in Agerola sell the output of local farms, said by many to be the tastiest cheese in all of Italy. Specialties up here are *fiordilatte,* a form of mozzarella; *caciocavallo,* a stringy, tangy cow's-milk cheese (the name means "cheese on horseback," because it's usually tied with a rope and hung to dry and age); and *scamorze,* another cow's-milk cheese similar to mozzarella. Among the best sources are **Caseificio Agrisole,** Via Case Sparse 81 (© **081-873-1022**); **Caseificio Belfiore di Cioffi,** Via Belvedere 35 (© **081-879-1338**); and **La Montanina,** Piazza Avitabile Gennaro 3 (© **081-802-5272**).

AMALFI ★★

19km (12 miles) E of Positano

From the 9th to the 11th centuries, the seafaring Republic of Amalfi rivaled the great maritime powers of Genoa and Venice, and its capital, Amalfi, still enjoys some prominence today as a major resort on the Amalfi Drive. Set

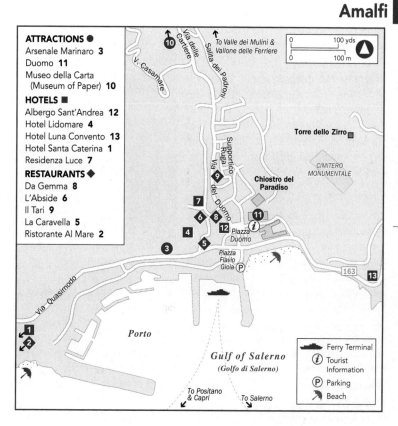

ATTRACTIONS ●
Arsenale Marinaro **3**
Duomo **11**
Museo della Carta
  (Museum of Paper) **10**

HOTELS ■
Albergo Sant'Andrea **12**
Hotel Lidomare **4**
Hotel Luna Convento **13**
Hotel Santa Caterina **1**
Residenza Luce **7**

RESTAURANTS ◆
Da Gemma **8**
L'Abside **6**
Il Tari **9**
La Caravella **5**
Ristorante Al Mare **2**

To Valle dei Mulini &
Vallone delle Ferriere

0 ____ 100 yds
0 ____ 100 m

Torre dello Zirro ■

CIMITERO
MONUMENTALE

Chiostro del
Paradiso

Piazza
Duomo

Piazza
Flavio
Gioia ℗

163

Via Quasimodo

Porto

Gulf of Salerno
(Golfo di Salerno)

To Positano
& Capri

To Salerno

🚢 Ferry Terminal
ⓘ Tourist
   Information
℗ Parking
🏖 Beach

among terraces of lemon groves and olive trees on the slopes of the steep Lattari mountains and the Bay of Salerno, where narrow public beaches flank the harbor, Amalfi is a lovely town. Despite its popularity, Amalfi doesn't seem crushed by tourism as Positano does—at least not in the early morning and evening hours after the tour buses and boats depart. With its porticos, little squares, stepped medieval streets, and green mountainsides on one side and blue sea on the other, it's a pleasant place to spend some time.

GETTING THERE If you're coming to Amalfi from Positano by land, you'll take the famous Amalfi Drive. But if you're going right to Amalfi from Naples or somewhere else in Italy, you're better off taking the high-speed train to Salerno from Naples and from there heading west up the coast on the SITA bus (www.sitabus.it; ☏ **089-405145**). This is a convenient time saver that eliminates the trip by train to Sorrento and the transfer to the bus for the long trip down the coast road. You can also take the SITA express bus that operates between Naples and Amalfi, though schedules are geared to workers rather than leisurely vacationers. Buses to Amalfi operates mornings and late afternoons on some days, but the return bus to Naples from Amalfi is in the wee hours of the morning.

VISITOR INFORMATION The tourist office (www.amalfitouristoffice.it; © **089-871107**) is in Palazzo di Città, Corso delle Repubbliche Marinare 19. It's open Monday to Friday 9am to 1pm and 2 to 6pm, Saturday 9am to noon. In winter, it is only open in the morning.

Exploring Amalfi

Just outside the old town walls, **Piazza Flavio Gioia** opens onto the harbor: It commemorates the local navigator who some say invented the compass around 1300 (a dubious claim, since sailors were

Amalfi street scene.

using rudimentary compasses, probably introduced by Arab navigators, long before then). Let's just say he might have perfected the compass for marine use, and it is bona fide fact that sailors returning to Amalfi provided material for some of the first nautical charts of the Middle Ages. They also came up with a maritime code, the Tavole Amalfitane, which was followed in the Mediterranean for centuries, with guidelines for everything from terms for haulage to conditions for the crew. This document is on view in the **Arsenale Marinaro** (see below).

Should your imagination not allow you to make the leap to the days when Amalfi was one of the most important ports and maritime powers in the world, a tile panel in the Porta Marina, created by the artist Renato Rossi in the 1950s, depicts Amalfi's commercial empire in the Middle Ages. Another ceramic piece, just up the Corso delle Repubbliche Marinare, this one from the 1970s, tells more of Amalfi's history, from its founding by Romans to the arrival of St. Andrew's body from Constantinople.

The medieval heart of Amalfi, a maze of covered porticos and little streets, stretches from **Piazza Duomo,** a lovely cathedral square near the sea, into an increasingly narrow ravine. You can easily walk the length of town in 10 minutes or so, following Via Amalfi from Piazza Duomo up to the **Museo della Carta** (see below). For much of the town's history, Via Amalfi was a rushing stream, and you can still hear water gurgling beneath the pavement. To navigate the town as medieval residents once did, follow the **Rua Nova Mercatorum,** a narrow, tunnel-like alley that ends in a little piazza with a fountain, Capo di Ciuccio (Donkey's Head). It's so called because the hard-working beasts could pause here and dip their muzzles into the cool water.

Arsenale Marinaro ★ HISTORIC SITE In this medieval shipyard, beneath pointed arches and cross vaults resting on stone pillars, the Republic of Amalfi built galleys up to 40m (131 ft.) and powered by 120 oarsmen that enabled sailors to maintain power over the Mediterranean. Stone-vaulted boat sheds now house the solid-looking gold coins (*tari*) that Amalfi once minted and the documents with which the republic wielded its considerable legal clout. The spotlight is on the 66-chapter Tavole Amalfitane, a code that more or less established the laws of the high seas from the 13th through 16th centuries. Storms have erased much of the complex, but 10 of 22 piers retain some semblance of their former appearance.

Via Matteo Camera (off Piazza Flavio Gioia). Admission 2€. Easter–Sept daily 9am–8pm.

Duomo ★★ CHURCH This monument to Amalfi's rich past, covered in black-and-white marble and rich mosaics, sits atop a monumental staircase just inland from the sea. The **Chiostro del Paradiso** (Cloister of Paradise), to the left of the entrance, is decidedly Moorish, with a whitewashed quadrangle of interlaced arches and brightly colored geometric mosaics. Amalfi's medieval nobles are entombed in the sarcophagi littered around this exotic enclosure. The **Crypt** houses the remains of St. Andrew, Amalfi's protector saint, one of the Apostles who forsook fishing to join Christ. It was important for Amalfi to have a famous patron, just as Venice had St. Mark, so soldiers brought the remains of Andrew back from Constantinople at the end of the 4th Crusade, in 1206. Legend has it that Andrew has been working miracles ever since. After the pirate Ariadeno Barbarossa attacked Amalfi in 1544, his fleet was suddenly sunk in a giant sea surge. Andrew's other miraculous presence is in the form of a thick ooze, reverentially called "manna," that appears on

Amalfi's Duomo as seen from the piazza.

this tomb every once in a while. A painting in the main part of the cathedral dramatically depicts the saint's crucifixion on an X-shaped cross, though the surroundings are disappointingly mundane—the 18th-century baroque restoration with rich marbles and mundane frescoes is no match for the wonderfully fanciful facade and cloisters or the medieval austerity of an adjacent basilica, now housing a museum of gold chalices and other treasures. You'll encounter Andrew again on the square below the cathedral, standing amidst the gurgling waters of a fountain.

Piazza del Duomo. Duomo: ✆ **089-871059.** Free admission. Nov–Feb daily 10am–5pm; Mar–Oct 9am–9pm. Museum and cloister: ✆ **089-871324.** Admission 3€.

Looking at pleasant little Amalfi, it might be hard to believe that the town was once one of the most important cities in the western world, with as many as 100,000 citizens and a fleet that more or less controlled Mediterranean trade. Then again, look hard enough, and the clues are everywhere. The magnificent facade and exotic cloisters of the cathedral show influences from Constantinople and the Near East. Enough is left of the Arsenal to suggest how the vaulted halls could have once turned out sleek ships manned by 120 oarsmen. The town's narrow alleyways and tunnel-like passageways are obviously the creation of someone who had wandered through the souks of North Africa.

By around the year 600 Amalfi was already doing a brisk trade in Byzantine silks. The heyday was from the 9th century until well into the 13th century. The republic was powerful and prosperous, with churches, monasteries, its own currency, a ruling body of doges, and extensive trading links. Amalfi was a sea power with the clout to lay down the law with the Tavole Amalfitane, a code that ruled maritime conduct well into the 16th century. Soon enough, constant invasions and a shift in world trading power had reduced once-mighty Amalfi to just another seaside town. Even so, these days the remnants of this long history, plenty of charm, and a prime setting on one of the most beautiful sea coasts in the world ensure that Amalfi is anything but a backwater. The town celebrates its past glory days every four years when it hosts the Regatta of the Ancient Maritime Republics in early June. Amid much pageantry, the town is pitted in boat races against Genoa, Venice, and Pisa, much larger cities that were at one time dwarfed by Amalfi's might (2017 is one of those years).

Museo della Carta (Museum of Paper) ★ HISTORIC SITE   Among the many goods Amalfi's sailors and merchants brought back from their voyages was paper, a popular commodity throughout the Middle East that Arab traders had come across in China. From the 13th through the mid-19th centuries, Amalfi was one of Europe's largest exporters of paper, produced in factories whose ruins now litter the Valle dei Mulini (Valley of the Mills) at the inland end of town. Waterwheels once powered machines that beat linen, cotton, and hemp into fine parchment. In the remains of one of the once-thriving enterprises, a guide shows off vintage machinery and the product that is still sold in Amalfi shops. Neighboring factories are evocative ruins that you can view from a path through the valley.

Palazzo Pagliara, Via delle Cartiere 24. www.museodellacarta.it. ℂ **089-830-4561.** Admission 4€. Nov–Mar Tues–Sun 10am–3pm; Apr–Nov daily 10am–6:30pm.

Getting Active

A popular hike from Amalfi is the easy walk along **Valle dei Mulini (Valley of the Mills).** Follow Via Genova from Piazza del Cuomo until it turns into a picturesque trail that leads through lush countryside to the **Mulino Rovinato (Ruined Mill),** about 1 hour away. A number of flour mills once thrived here, as did paper mills. If you continue to ascend the hillside, you'll come to the

Vallone delle Ferriere, where now-ruined *ferriere* (iron mills) operated into the 19th century. At the top of the valley is a delightful waterfall; allow about 2 hours to reach the falls from Amalfi. If you're really ambitious and have another 2 hours, you can continue from here up to Ravello (see below).

Amalfi's **beaches** are two pebbly strips on either side of the harbor. For a large stretch of sand, take the footpath to **Atrani,** a pretty village 1km (half a mile) along the coast, an easy 15-minute stroll eastward. From the harbor at Amalfi's **Marina Grande** you can rent **boats**—with or without a skipper—to explore the nooks and crannies of the coast. **Cooperativa Sant'Andrea** (www.coopsantandrea.it; ℂ **089-873190**) offers regular service to the beaches of Duoglio and Santa Croce, only a few minutes away; in summer, boats leave every 30 minutes between 9am and 5pm.

Where to Stay
EXPENSIVE

Hotel Luna Convento ★★ St. Francis himself founded this seaside monastery in 1222. The beautiful cloisters and transformed monks' cells and chapel also have a venerable history of hospitality as one of the first grand hotels on the Amalfi Coast, receiving guests since 1822. Among the famous guests were Norwegian playwright Henrik Ibsen, who wrote *A Doll's House* here in 1879. American playwright Tennessee Williams also spent time here, as did heads of state Otto von Bismarck and Benito Mussolini. Adding even more luster to the storied and atmospheric surroundings are a 15th-century Saracen watchtower, these days housing a bar and standing guard over a little strip of private beach and a large seawater pool. Most of the delightful guest rooms have sea views, some have terraces, and all are embellished with some nice art and antiques to enhance the historic provenance. Lounging in the sunny gardens that once supplied the monks' kitchens is yet another experience to savor at this unusual retreat.

Via Pantaleone Comite 33. www.lunahotel.it. ℂ **089-871002.** 48 units. 250€–340€ double. Rates include buffet breakfast. Parking 18€. **Amenities:** 2 restaurants; bar; babysitting; concierge; outdoor pool; room service; Wi-Fi (free).

Hotel Santa Caterina ★★★ One of the world's great getaways provides a stay of a lifetime while making guests feel right at home. Its comfortable yet unpretentious rooms and suites are set in gardens and citrus groves hovering above the water. Colorful Vietri tiles and handsome antiques add notes of elegance, while balconies and terraces make the most of the cliff-side location. Glassed-in elevators and a winding garden path descend to a private beach and saltwater swimming pool, and memorable meals are served in a vine-covered, glassed-in dining room and on a seaside terrace in good weather. Several private bungalows with private pools tucked into citrus groves provide the ultimate hideouts.

Via Nazionale 9. www.hotelsantacaterina.it. ℂ **089-871012.** 49 units. 315€–770€ double. Rates include lavish buffet breakfast. Parking 15€. Closed Nov.–Mar. **Amenities:** 2 restaurants; bar; beach; concierge; gym; pool; room service; spa; Wi-Fi (free).

The Hotel Santa Caterina.

MODERATE

Residenza Luce ★★★   These lovely rooms near the town center are at the top of the list for an affordable stay in Amalfi. Half of the handsomely decorated, tile-floored units are bilevel, with sleeping lofts tucked above living areas; many have balconies and all have large windows overlooking medieval lanes and squares. A sunny rooftop breakfast room overlooks the surrounding hills, while the beach and port are just steps away.

Via Fra Gerardo Sasso. www.residenzaluce.it. ✆ **089-871537.** 8 units. 90€–140€ double. Rates include buffet breakfast. **Amenities:** Wi-Fi (free).

INEXPENSIVE

Albergo Sant'Andrea ★★   One of the most authentic ways to experience old Amalfi is from these tidy rooms smack-dab in the center of town, directly across from the Duomo. Views of that magnificent facade are the focal point of some of the guest rooms, while others look out to sea and, some, alas, into alleyways. For guests not looking for luxury, the location, the warm hospitality, immaculate surroundings, and some of the lowest rates on the Amalfi Coast might compensate for old-fashioned rooms that are well-maintained and good-sized but decidedly barebones.

Piazza Duomo. www.albergosantandrea.it. ✆ **089-871145.** 8 units. 70€–90€ double. Rates include buffet breakfast. **Amenities:** Wi-Fi (free).

Hotel Lidomare ★   One of Amalfi's few bargains is set on a small square just beyond the main street fray, and provides a lot of pleasant, old-fashioned ambience in a 13th-century palazzo. You might find the enormous, high-ceilinged, tile-floored guest rooms to be charmingly old-fashioned or a bit ramshackle, but many have sea views, and all are furnished with a scattering of antiques and comfy old furnishings. Amalfi's beach is just steps away.

Largo Piccolomini 9. ✆ **089-871332.** 15 units. 103€–145€ double. Rates include continental breakfast. Parking 18€. **Amenities:** Wi-Fi (free).

Where to Eat

Amafi is well suited to cafe-sitting. On Piazza Duomo, the elegant **Bar Francese** (✆ **089-871049**) serves excellent pastries. Another stop on the piazza for a sweet is **Pasticceria Pansa** (✆ **089-871065;** closed Tues), concocting delicious pastries since 1830; try their *torta caprese* or sticky, lemon-flavored *delizia al limone*. **Gelateria Porto Salvo,** Piazza Duomo 22 (✆ **089-871636;** closed Jan–Mar), is one of the best *gelaterie* on this part of the coast—try the *mandorla candita* (candied almond) flavor. **Gran Caffè di Amalfi,** Corso Repubbliche Marinare (✆ **089-871047**) overlooks the sea, making it a prime spot for an *aperitivo*.

EXPENSIVE

Da Gemma ★ SEAFOOD/AMALFITAN Amalfi's old-time classic, in warm-hued rooms tucked behind the cathedral and in the hands of the Grimaldi family for several generations, holds high standards for the seafood it serves to a loyal and discerning clientele. The house *zuppa di pesce* is a meal in itself, prepared only for two, and equally memorable is a special pasta, *paccheri all'acquapazza,* made with shrimp and monkfish. The dessert of choice is *crostata* (pie with jam), made with pine nuts and homemade marmalades of lemon, orange, and tangerine. Reservations, especially on weekends, are a must.

Via Frà Gerardo Sasso 11. www.trattoriadagemma.com. ✆ **089-871345.** Main courses 16€–26€. Daily 12:30–2:45pm and 7:30–11pm (closed Wed Nov to mid-Apr). Closed 6 weeks Jan to early Mar.

La Caravella ★★★ MODERN AMALFITAN You'll leave today's world (along with sea views) behind when you step into this 12th-century palazzo in medieval Amalfi. Decidedly romantic dining rooms where candlelight plays off stucco walls adorned with patches of colorful frescoes and terrazzo floors are the stagelike setting for some of the best food on the coast, recognized when the restaurant became the first in Italy to win a Michelin star way back in 1967. Ever since then, the dolce vita set has made a beeline to the linen-covered tables, where the Amalfi classics that appear are as simple as *scialatelli alla caravella* (handmade pasta in a tomato-seafood sauce) or *pezzogna* (fresh local fish) enlivened with local lemons and mountain herbs. Reservations are a good idea, especially in summer, and refined as the food and the surroundings are, smart informal attire is acceptable; after all, this place is playful enough to embellish its tables with ceramic donkeys.

Via Matteo Camera 12. www.ristorantelacaravella.it. ✆ **089-871029.** Main courses 25€–35€; tasting menu 90€. Wed–Mon noon–2pm and 7:30–11pm. Closed Nov and Jan.

Ristorante Al Mare ★ PIZZA/AMALFITAN The bamboo-roofed, al fresco dining terrace just above the beach at the Hotel Santa Caterina (see above) is an alluring spot for a seaside lunch. The menu offers a nice choice of pizzas, grilled fish, and pastas that include the hotel specialty, *tagilolini limone,* homemade noodles with a lemon cream sauce. Prices aren't exactly in the beach-shack category, but it's hard to beat the magnificent surroundings for a dash of informal glamour.

Via Nazionale 9. www.hotelsantacaterina.it. © **089-871012.** Main courses 20€–35€, pizzas from 20€. May–Oct daily 12:30–3:30pm.

MODERATE

L'Abside ★★ SEAFOOD/AMALFITAN   If this charming small place were more formal you could call it a temple of gastronomy, as it occupies part of a former church. As is, the delightful, whitewashed and arched room adds even more charm to a delicious meal (also served on a terrace out front in good weather). Seafood and vegetables are so fresh that even a simple bruschetta with anchovies is memorable, and a bounty of sea creatures also makes a showing atop several homemade pastas and in garden fresh salads.

Piazza dei Dogi. www.ristorantelabside.it. © **089-873586.** Main courses 9€–20€. Daily 12:30–2:45pm and 7:30–11pm.

Il Tari ★ AMALFITAN/PIZZA   The name (after the coin used in the days of the Amalfi Republic) and the setting (an old stable that's nicely done with white walls and colorful artwork) hark back to older times in Amalfi, as does the straightforward menu of traditional favorites. *Scialatielli* (long, fettuccine-like noodles) and other pasta come laden with mussels and other seafood (a trio of pastas with various sauces is served as a starter) and the fish soup with pasta and beans is an old Amalfi recipe. Excellent pizzas are served at lunch and dinner, and the set menus are an especially good value.

Via P. Capuano 9. www.amalfiristorantetari.it. © **089-871832.** Main courses 8€–19€. Wed–Mon noon–2:30pm and 7:30–10:30pm.

Around Amalfi: Atrani ★★

Pretty little Atrani is just 1km (half a mile) along the coast, an easy 15-minute stroll eastward. Leaving town, follow the sidewalk along the main road until you come to a staircase (signposted for ATRANI) up to a path that is really a series of alleyways between hillside houses; it soon drops down to the sea again. From the beach, a maze of arched and vaulted alleys and stepped streets leads through a labyrinth of white houses to Piazza Umberto I, where more than a few window boxes put the final flourishes on the charming scene. M. C. Escher (1898–1972), the Dutch artist who depicted scenes filled with intricate geometric patterns and complex perspective, loved Atrani and sketched it often; looking at the layer upon layer of connected, whitewashed houses it's easy to see why.

The Roman aristocracy who settled in Atrani had a rough time of it. The eruption of Mt. Vesuvius in A.D. 79 buried their villas in ash and debris, and in the later years of the empire, seafaring barbarians repeatedly sacked the settlement. By the 12th century, Atrani was doing a lot better as the preferred residence of the aristocrats of Amalfi. In fact, Amalfi doges were crowned and buried in the 10th-century **church of San Salvatore de Bireto.** Inside, beyond the elegant portico and the bronze doors pillaged from Constantinople, a marble plaque shows off two peacocks, signs of vanity and pride, something the rich little town once had plenty of. The church's sweeping staircase is a baroque flourish that's perfectly in keeping with the picturesque surroundings.

Where to Eat

'A Paranza ★★ AMALFITAN/SEAFOOD   The walk between Amalfi and Atrani is an excellent way to begin and end a meal, especially when the feast is as memorable as the one you'll have in this old-fashioned room just off Atrani's main piazza. The seafood-based menu changes daily, and the antipasti should be part of any meal—in fact, you can dine very well on one small dish after another, from heavenly slices of fresh tuna to small portions of stewed octopus and seafood risotto to grilled razor clams and fried anchovies. Not everything is from the sea, and some local favorites include *sarchiapone,* a long gourd stuffed with ground meat, or *melanzane con la cioccolata*—yes, that's right, eggplant with chocolate, deep-fried and topped with walnuts and dried fruit. The pear and ricotta tart is more traditional but no less delicious. The wine list is short but includes excellent local labels.

Via Dragone 1–2. www.ristoranteparanza.com. © **089-871840.** Main courses 12€–23€. Wed–Mon 12:30–3pm and 7:30–11:30pm (also Tues in summer). Closed 2 weeks in Dec.

RAVELLO ★★★

7km (4 miles) N of Amalfi

Clinging to a mountainside overlooking the sea, Ravello can seem like a world removed from the clamor down on the coast. This sense of escape, along with

Relaxing in Ravello.

views and some of the world's most splendid gardens, has long made this aerie 1,000 feet above the coast a refuge for the rich and famous. Its eclectic group of admirers has included composer Richard Wagner, writers D. H. Lawrence and Gore Vidal, and actress Greta Garbo. Like they did, you'll come up here not to do too much but stroll in the gardens, gaze up and down the coastline, and maybe relax for a few days in one of many villas converted into luxury hotels. Above all, which the town actually is, Ravello is simply a beautiful, beautiful place, maybe more so than any other town in Italy.

GETTING THERE   The most convenient way up to Ravello from Amafi is the SITA bus from Amalfi (www.sitabus.it;

Wine Tasting

The wines produced in the harsh, hot landscapes of Campania seem stronger, rougher, and, in many cases, more powerful than those grown in gentler climes. You'll encounter them in shops and on restaurant tables. Ones to try are Lacryma Christi (Tears of Christ), a white that grows in the volcanic soil near Naples, Herculaneum, and Pompeii; Taurasi, a potent, full-bodied red also known as Aglianico; and Greco di Tufo, a pungent white laden with the odors of apricots and apples. *Falanghina*, one of the most popular white wine varieties, is produced from the famed Falernian grapes so favored by the ancient Romans, but the grape is probably of ancient Greek origin. Other grape varieties of special interest include the light-white *Greco di Tufo*, another grape of possible Greek origin, and fruity *Piedirosso*, a dark red grape that is famously grown on the slopes of Vesuvius and the isle of Capri.

🕾 **089-405145**), running about every half-hour. If you're driving from Naples or other places off the coast, you can avoid the traffic-choked coast road by taking the A3, then climbing over the mountains from the north and dropping into Ravello on the Valico di Chiunsi. When arriving by car, you can't go any farther than the large, well-marked public parking lot not far from the Duomo.

VISITOR INFORMATION Ravello's **tourist office,** Via Roma 18 (www.ravellotime.it), is open daily from 9am to 7pm; November to May it closes at 6pm. The town is largely pedestrian, with steep, narrow lanes and many flights of stairs.

Exploring Ravello

The heart of town is **Piazza del Vescovado,** a terrace overlooking the valley of the Dragone, and the adjacent **Piazza del Duomo.** Climb up steep, stepped Via Richard Wagner (behind the tourist office) to reach **Via San Giovanni del Toro,** which is lined with some of Ravello's grandest medieval palaces, built as hilltop retreats for wealthy merchant families of the Amalfi Republic and now housing some of Italy's most distinguished hotels.

Auditorium Niemeyer ★★ LANDMARK Ravello's most controversial landmark is also its newest, inaugurated in 2010 to critical architectural acclaim but to the disdain of many residents and their visitors. Naysayers find the sweeping, curved, dazzling-white canopied white roof of Brazilian architect Oscar Niemeyer's auditorium to be sorely out of keeping with Ravello's medieval ambience. It's hard, though, not to admire the way the sinuous curves tuck so naturally into the hillside. And no one can complain about the pleasure of enjoying a concert while viewing the spectacle of sea and sky through the huge eye-shaped window.

Via della Repubblica 12. www.auditoriumoscarniemeyer.it. 🕾 **346-737-8561.** Open for concerts and film screenings (check the tourist office for events).

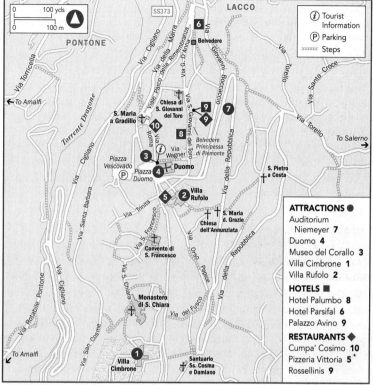

LACCO

| 0 | 100 yds |
| 0 | 100 m |

SS373

PONTONE

To Amalfi →

(i) Tourist
Information
(P) Parking
Steps

ATTRACTIONS ●
Auditorium
  Niemeyer **7**
Duomo **4**
Museo del Corallo **3**
Villa Cimbrone **1**
Villa Rufolo **2**

HOTELS ■
Hotel Palumbo **8**
Hotel Parsifal **6**
Palazzo Avino **9**

RESTAURANTS ◆
Cumpa' Cosimo **10**
Pizzeria Vittoria **5**
Rossellinis **9**

Duomo ★★★ CHURCH   All the glories of Ravello's past seem to come to the fore in the beautiful cathedral that Orso Papiro, first bishop of Ravello, founded in 1086. The 54 embossed panels of the 12th-century bronze doors, cast in Constantinople, were intended to delight the faithful with stories of Christ's miracles and other familiar Bible stories. Another piece of scripture comes to life in the beautiful mosaics of the **Ambone dell'Epistola** ★★★, a pulpit dating from 1130 that depicts the story of Jonah being swallowed by the whale. Opposite is another pulpit resting atop twisting columns that in turn rise out of the backs of two regal-looking lions, with a mighty eagle perched on top of the whole affair. Surrounding them is a wonderfully eclectic collection of Roman sarcophagi and columns, bits of medieval frescoes, and a tiled floor that tilts gently toward the entrance, an artful attempt to enhance the perspective and visually enlarge the space. The cathedral's patron is honored in the **Cappella di San Pantaleone.** The physician saint was beheaded in Nicomedia (in present-day Turkey) on July 27, 305, and the blood housed in

157

his reliquary is said to liquefy and come to a boil every year on the anniversary of his death.

Piazza del Vescovado. ℂ **089-85831.** Duomo: Free admission. Daily 9am–noon and 5:30–7pm. Museum: Admission 2€. Summer daily 9am–7pm; winter daily 9am–6pm. Guided tours available.

Museo del Corallo ★ MUSEUM/SHOP   For centuries, craftspeople around the Bay of Naples carved precious cameos and other objects out of coral. In fact, the earliest object in this stunning private collection is a 3rd-century-A.D. Roman amphora with a coral formation inside it. The 600 pieces are the possessions of cameo craftsman Giorgio Filocamo, whose Camo workshops are attached to the museum. That he still toils is a tribute to his love for the art, since his antique pieces, such as a 17th-century coral figure of Christ on the Cross, are coveted by museums and auctioneers around the world. Filocamo has carved cameos for Hilary Clinton, Pope John Paul II, and Princess Caroline of Monaco, and you can pick up one of his creations for yourself in the adjoining shop.

Piazza Duomo 9. www.museodelcorallo.com. ℂ **089-857461.** Free admission. Mon–Sat 9:30am–noon and 3–5:30pm.

Villa Cimbrone ★★★ GARDEN   The Englishman Lord Grimthorpe, a dilettante, gardener, and erstwhile banker, created this grand villa in 1904, embellishing a crumbling 14th-century farmhouse with towers, turrets, and many exotic Arabesque details (the villa is now a hotel). The lavish salons and gardens soon became associated with the 20th-century elite, few more elusive than Swedish actress Greta Garbo, who hid out here in 1937—not to answer her famous siren call, "I want to be alone," but to be with her lover, the conductor Leopold Stokowski. The high point of the lavish gardens, quite literally, is the **Belvedere Cimbrone,** where you'll have the dizzying sensation of being suspended between sea and sky. The writer and long-time Ravello resident Gore Vidal, who never really had anything very nice to say about anything, called the outlook "the most beautiful view in the world."

Villa Rufolo.

Via Santa Chiara 26. www.villacimbrone.it. ℂ **089-857459** for hotel reservations. Admission 6€ adults, 4€ children. Daily 9am–sunset. Last admission 30 min. before close.

Villa Rufolo ★★ GARDEN   The 14th-century poet Boccaccio was so moved by this onetime residence of 13th-century merchant prince Landolfo Rufolo that he included it as background in one of his tales. In the mid–19th century, Scotsman Sir Francis Reid transformed the house into an exotic fantasy, with

Moorish cloisters surrounded by interlacing arcs. The most famous visitor to the palace was Richard Wagner, who composed an act of *Parsifal* here in 1880 and used the surroundings for his *Garden of Klingsor,* home of the Flower Maidens. The 14th-century Norman tower was renamed Klingsor's Tower in his honor. Paths wind through beds of rare plantings to lookout points high above the coastline, where the surreal scene of sea meeting sky in a wash of blue are as transporting as the house and gardens. The lower garden, known as the Wagner Terrace, is the setting for the Concerti Wagneriani during the summertime Ravello festival.

Piazza Duomo. www.villarufolo.it. ✆ **089-857621.** Admission 5€. Summer daily 9am–8pm; winter daily 9am–sunset. Last admission 15 min. earlier.

Getting Active

Hikers can take heart in the fact that from Ravello it's all downhill—or mostly, since a popular hike is up the **Monastery of Saint Nicholas** at an altitude of 486m (1,594 ft.). From the center of Ravello, take the road to Sambuco for 1km (half a mile), and from there the trail that climbs to the monastery. Plan on about 2 hours for the 9-km (6-mile) round-trip. Now, the downhill stretch: From the center of town, take another footpath—actually, a series of steps and hidden alleys—that descends all the way down to seaside **Minori** (see p. 163). Start from the alley to the left of Villa Rufolo, next to the small fountain. It will take you past the small 13th-century Annunziata church, and then the church of San Pietro, before reaching the hamlet of Torello. From there the picturesque path descends through olive trees down to Minori. The hike down takes a half-hour; double that for the ascent.

Where to Stay
EXPENSIVE

Palazzo Avino ★★★ A 12th-century patrician palace strikes just the right balance between comfort and opulence, with enough antiques, Vietri ceramic floors, and fine linens to satisfy the most discerning guests. Especially winning are the views that, making the most of Ravello's aerielike position, extend for miles up and down the coast. They're enjoyed through the huge windows in just about every room, on the rooftop terrace with two Jacuzzis, from the sumptuous gardens and pool that cascade partway down the cliff, and from the hotel's double-Michelin-starred, dinner-only **Rossellinis** (see below). A free shuttle takes guests down to the **Clubhouse by the Sea** (open May–Sept), the hotel's beach club where there is a small outdoor pool, a waterside terrace with lounge chairs and umbrellas, and a casual restaurant.

Via San Giovanni del Toro 28, Ravello. www.palazzoavino.com. ✆ **089-818181.** 44 units. 350€–710€ double. Rates include lavish buffet breakfast. Parking 34€. Closed mid-Oct to Mar. **Amenities:** Restaurant; bar; concierge; gym; Jacuzzi; pool; room service; spa; Wi-Fi (free).

MODERATE

Hotel Palumbo ★★★ A popular stop on the 19th-century Grand Tour circuit (and a favorite of many 20th-century celebs, too), Hotel Palumbo only seems to get better with age, holding its own against much glitzier competitors as a mainstay of old-world refinement. Beyond the bougainvillea-covered entryway is an exotic and rarefied world of columns, arches, exquisitely tiled floors, fine art, and finely upholstered, highly buffed furnishings. The wonderful old-fashioned ambience extends throughout the 12th-century palazzo and an adjacent annex, and many of the antique-filled guest rooms in both open to terraces overlooking the coastline and the hotel's multilevel gardens and lemon groves. This isn't a place to pad around in your beach togs, but the nooks and crannies and citrus-scented walkways are such a romantic throwback you'll be happy to dress for the part.

Via San Giovanni del Toro 16. www.hotelpalumbo.it. ✆ **089-857244.** 21 units. 190€–480€ double. Rates include breakfast. Parking 11€. **Amenities:** Restaurant; bar; pool; Wi-Fi (free).

INEXPENSIVE

Hotel Parsifal ★★ A convent-turned-luxury-getaway is hardly a rarity on the Amalfi Coast, but very few offer good-value accommodations like these in such charming architectural surroundings. The cloisters, tiled hallways, fishpond, and flower-filled patios still exude a peaceful monastic air, just as the original 13th-century residents intended. Whitewashed rooms fashioned from the former monks' cells are still basic enough to suit their former inhabitants, but they're embellished with colorful tile floors and, in some, sensational sea views.

Via Gioacchino D'Anna. www.hotelparsifal.com. ✆ **089-857144.** 17 units. 135€–210€ double. Rates include buffet breakfast. Parking 15€. **Amenities:** Restaurant; bar; concierge; Wi-Fi (free).

Where to Eat

EXPENSIVE

Rossellinis ★★★ CREATIVE AMALFITAN Meals in this elegant dining room and view-filled terrace come with credentials—two Michelin stars and a reputation as one of Italy's best. What might come as a surprise is an ambience that's not informal but far from stuffy—a sense that with food this good, and prices this high, no one needs to be anything other than comfortable. Service is impeccable, and the staff will gladly lead diners through chef Mario Deleo's creative takes on local cuisine, infused with extra passion since he's from the region. Even the bread, with ham baked into it, is exceptional, as are such sublime creations as ravioli stuffed with squid and cod in an olive crust. Meals are paired with local wines and followed with mountain cheeses and sweets that, like everything else here, are satisfying without being overwhelming.

Via San Giovanni del Toro 28 (in the Palazzo Avino, see above). www.palazzosasso.com. ✆ **089-818181.** Main courses 28€–32€; tasting menus from 120€. Daily 7:30–11pm. Closed Nov–Mar.

Moderate

Cumpa' Cosimo ★★ AMALFITAN   Netta Bottone runs the restaurant her family started back in 1929, serving generous portions of pastas (including an extravaganza with seven types of noodles topped with seven different sauces), big platters of *frittura di pesce* (fish fry), and some very well done lamb and veal dishes (Netta also runs the butcher shop next door). Artichokes and other vegetables are right out of the nearby garden plots. Whatever you order, Netta herself may well serve it with a flourish and a kiss on the cheek.

Via Roma 44. ✆ **089-857156.** Main courses 11€–18€; pizza 6€–10€. Daily 12:30–3pm and 7:30–11pm. Closed Mon Nov–Feb.

INEXPENSIVE

Pizzeria Vittoria ★★ PIZZA/AMALFITAN   It's refreshing to know that life in Ravello can come down to earth, too, as it does in this friendly pizzeria near the Duomo. Thin-crust pies with a huge variety of toppings are the draw, and even the simple classic Margherita seems like perfection, given that everything is fresh—tomatoes and basil from the garden, mozzarella from nearby farms, herbs from the mountains. Some simple pasta dishes are similarly delicious. The tile-floored rooms can be packed, even at lunch, so plan on eating early or late.

Via dei Rufolo 3. www.ristorantepizzeriavittoria.it ✆ **089-857947.** Main courses 10€–15€. Daily 12:30–3pm and 7:30–10pm. Closed Nov–Mar.

Shopping

In addition to the cameo handiwork that might tempt you at the **Camo** workshops at the Museo del Corallo (see above), you'll encounter some beautiful ceramics at **Ceramiche d'Arte Carmella,** Via dei Rufolo 16 (www.ceramiche dartecarmela.com; ✆ **089-857303**). Many of the pieces are from Vietri down the coast (see p. 216), though works by other local ceramicists are on display, too. **Profumi della Costiera,** Via Trinita 37 (www.profumidellacostiera.it; ✆ **089-858167**) carries a remarkable selection of *limoncello* and other sweet liqueurs, while the in-town outlet of 150-year-old **Episcopio Winery,** operated by the Palumbo family, is in the Hotel Palumbo at Via Giovanni a Toro 16 (✆ **089-857244**).

Nightlife

Ravello's otherwise staid entertainment scene ramps up considerably in the summer, when the town hosts the internationally famous **Festival di Ravello** (www.ravellofestival.com; ✆ **089-858422**) from July through September. The focus is on classical music and includes the concerts of the **Festival Musicale Wagneriano,** held in July in the garden of **Villa Rufolo** ★★. Tickets run from 15€ to 130€.

Around Ravello: Scala ★ & Tramonti ★

Only 2.5km (1½ miles) from Ravello, and even higher, Scala commands a perch 400m (1,200 ft.) above the coast. This aerie apparently provided a lookout and sense of security to the 4th-century Roman sailors and their passengers who settled up here after being shipwrecked on the shores below while making their way to Constantinople. The heights and remarkable views up and down the coast made Scala a handy strategic stronghold of the Amalfi Republic, and the town was important enough to be sacked by the Pisans and the Sicilians. Two castles—one guarding inland approaches, the other overlooking the sea—were connected by walls that once enclosed the town completely, but all are now in ruins. Centuries of warfare aside, Scala has an almost spiritual air to it, as the whole town seems to float between the sea far below and the wild Lattari mountains behind. This sense of otherworldliness might explain why Scala and its surroundings once had 130 churches. Among the few remaining is the 12th-century **Duomo,** Piazza Municipio 5 (© **089-857397;** daily 8am–1pm and 6–7pm). This is a favorite spot for weddings next to the sumptuous 14th-century **funerary monument** that nobleman Antonio Coppola erected for his young wife, Marinella Rufolo. **Minuto,** 1km (half a mile) south, is similarly picturesque, and in addition to views, it's graced with the beautiful 11th-century **Chiesa della Santissima Annunziata,** where primitive Byzantine frescoes enliven the crypt. You might have to settle for the views up and down the coast from the front porch, since the church is usually only open for mass on Sunday morning.

   Tramonti, about 10km (6 miles) inland from Scala, is a world apart from the coast—a fertile agricultural plateau *intra montes,* or "between the mountains." Lemon groves and vineyards kept some of the residents busy while others went to sea as sailors of the Amalfi Republic. It's said that those who remained behind invented pizza—a claim that's shared by many others, for sure. But the pizzas here, once baked in communal bread ovens, are undeniably delicious, and make the little village a bit of a culinary outpost. Local nuns added to the offerings when they came up with *concierto,* a bittersweet digestive liquor concocted from nine different mountain herbs and spices. You can try some at their convent, **Regio Conservatorio dei Santi Giuseppe e Teresa.** Keep climbing from Tramonti and you'll come to **Valico di Chiunzi,** a high pass in the mountains once guarded by a powerful castle that's now reduced to a single tower. At 656m (2,152 ft.), the viewpoint affords a spectacular **panorama** across the plain to Pompeii and Mt. Vesuvius.

GETTING ACTIVE

One of the best **hikes** in the area is from **Campidoglio di Scala,** just outside Scala, a high perch at an altitude of 470m (1,542 ft.). The first part of the route is a ridge trail, extremely scenic and not very arduous. From there, you can descend all the way to Amalfi. You'll pass the ruins of the 12th-century **church of Sant'Eustachio,** then continue through a natural rock formation called Castello that creates an amphitheater and is littered with the ruins of ancient fortifications. About 2 hours into the hike you will reach waterfalls at the top of the Vallone delle Ferrier. You can follow the Vallone into the Valle dei Mulini, and follow that into Amalfi. Allow about 2 hours to get to the waterfall and an additional 2 hours to get to Amalfi. Tourist offices in Ravello and Amalfi (see p. 156 and 148) can provide maps.

WHERE TO EAT

Da Lorenzo ★★ AMALFITAN/SEAFOOD   A lot of diners come out to Scala from Ravello for a meal on the terrace of this delightful countryside restaurant, often for a weekend lunch—a walk out and back is a good way to work up an appetite or undo the indulgence of a meal. The chef is partial to ingredients from the sea, and waiters will bring around the fresh catch and propose a preparation; seafood also appears in *pappardelle con il coccio* (wide noodles with fish) and some other unusual pastas. First, though, begin with the antipasto: After working your way through plate after plate—tiny, lightly fried fish, marinated anchovies, croquettes filled with shrimp and anchovies—you may want nothing more than a garden-fresh salad.

Via Frà G. Sasso, Santa Maria, Scala. www.trattoriadalorenzo.com. ℰ **089-858290.** Main courses 15€–25€. Winter Sat–Sun noon–2:30pm and 7:30–10:30pm; summer daily noon–2:30pm and 7:30–10:30pm; July and Aug open until midnight.

Da Nino ★★ AMALFITAN/PIZZA   You can't come to Tramonti without trying the town's famous pizza, and the way to do it is to join the locals at the place they call "Ninuccio" (little Nino). Whole-wheat crusts are topped for the most part with ingredients from the owners' farm, or at least come from their neighbors—the salami and mozzarella are homemade, the vegetables are homegrown, olive oil is from the surrounding groves, and bread is fresh out the oven.

Via Pucara 39, Tramonti. ℰ **089-855407.** Main courses 8€–15€; pizza from 7€. No credit cards. Wed–Mon noon–3.30pm and 7:30–11 pm (also Tues in summer).

MINORI ★

3km (2 miles) E of Amalfi

This pretty little workaday town at the mouth of a small stream, the Reginna Minor, is not nearly as famous as some of its glitzier neighbors, and it's even overshadowed by adjoining Maiori. Little matter—Minori has an asset that's the envy of almost every other town on the Amalfi Coast: a long, sandy beach. In fact, only the one in Maiori is longer, and Minori's seafront is a lively, festive place that's the choice of many Italian families for a holiday or a day in the sun.

GETTING THERE   SITA buses (www.sitabus.it; ℰ **089-405145**) run regularly to and from Salerno and Amalfi.

VISITOR INFORMATION   The tourist office (www.proloco.minori.sa.it; ℰ **089-877087**) is on Piazza Cantilena.

Exploring Minori

Nestled picturesquely between the blue sea and citrus groves, Minori doesn't really suggest its onetime importance. Its perfect cove once provided safe harbor for Roman ships and later the fleet of the Amalfi Republic. The Romans left behind a fancy villa (Villa Romana, see below) and Minori is the final resting place of Amalfi's patron, Saint Trofimena. She's grandly entombed in the **Basilica of Santa Trofimena,** with origins in a Roman temple within which a small Christian church was carved out in the 7th century. A grander 12th-century replacement was more or less obliterated by a 19th-century redo. Trofimena's presence is quite an honor for the little town, especially since she's here by choice. According to legend, Trofimena was engaged to be married at the age of 12 when an angel told her instead to embrace Christianity and devote her life to Christ. Her father was so upset by the idea that he killed the young woman and put her remains in an urn that he cast into the sea. It washed up in Minori, where townspeople placed it on the backs of two white calves. The beasts carried the urn only so far then refused to budge, and that's where Trofimena is buried. Trofimena made it clear this is where she wishes to remain when a 9th-century bishop of Amalfi decided to remove her up the coast to his cathedral for safekeeping from pirate raids. Though Trofimena told the bishop in a vision that he would meet a terrible fate if he disturbed her, he carried off her remains nonetheless. Sure enough, the bishop soon died, his tomb was destroyed, and wild dogs devoured his corpse. Trofimena, a little the worse for wear, was brought back to Minori and stashed away in the church, where she's remained ever since. The 12th-century **Campanile** that rises above Minori from a green hillside is all that remains of another church, Santa Annunziata.

Villa Romana ★ ARCHEOLOGICAL SITE   Ancient Romans enjoyed the good life along the Amalfi Coast in luxurious spreads like this one, built for an unknown patrician in the 1st century A.D. The centerpiece was a vast courtyard that faced the sea and had a large pool surrounded by porticos and two floors of rooms on three sides. Indoor entertaining took place in a vaulted hall that was richly decorated with frescoes and stuccos and led to a hedonistic spa. In the centuries before the villa was discovered in 1932 and excavated in the 1950s, its ground-level chambers came in handy for local farmers, who stored equipment in the vast, well-preserved spaces. The adjoining **Antiquarium** shows off bits of frescoes and many rows of amphorae that once stored oil and wine.

Minori's splendid beach.

Via Santa Lucia. (℉ **089-852893.** Free admission. Mon–Sat 9am to 1 hr. before sunset.

Where to Eat

Minori is an unsung culinary heaven with some distinctive specialties. Among them are *sarchiapone* (squash filled with ground meat and ricotta and cooked in a tomato sauce) and *'ndunderi* (fresh homemade dumplings made of spelt flour and fresh cheese, served with olive oil, cheese, local herbs, and often chopped walnuts). The town's favorite mouth-watering dessert is *sospiri* (sighs), also known less politely as *Zizz'e monache,* or "nuns' breasts." Whatever you call them, the dome-shaped pastries filled with lemon cream are delicious. You can taste them at **Pasticceria De Riso,** Piazza Cantilena 1 (✆ **089-877396**), one of the best pastry shops in Italy.

Il Giardiniello ★ AMALFITAN/PIZZA A Minori institution is just up the street from the beach, and the lemon-scented terrace is especially popular when the pizza oven fires up in the evening. Good as the pies are, it would be shame to stop there. *Alici impanate con la provola* (fresh anchovies deep-fried with cheese) is a good start to any meal, and among the many excellent seafood dishes is *laganelle alla marinara* (fresh eggless pasta with squid, shrimp, arugula, and cherry tomatoes).

Corso Vittorio Emanuele 17. www.ristorantegiardiniello.com. ✆ **089-877050.** Main courses 14€–22€; pizza 5€–11€. Thurs–Tues noon–3pm and 7–11:30pm (also Wed June–Sept).

MAIORI ★

6km (4 miles) E of Amalfi on SS 163

This ungainly and overbuilt town may not be nearly as picturesque as Positano or Amalfi, but its beach, albeit jammed with umbrellas and lounges, is the best on the coast. An inland excursion from the long stretch of sand and pebbles leads up flower-bordered walkways along the Reginna, the river that flows right through the center of town and is a curse or a blessing, depending on the mood of the usually gentle stream. During floods in 1954, the river picked up such force that it wiped out most of the medieval town—gates, palaces, and all—leaving only a few remnants of what was once an important and beautiful city.

Essentials

GETTING THERE SITA buses (www.sitabus.it; ✆ **089-405145**) run regularly to and from Salerno and Amalfi.

VISITOR INFORMATION **Azienda Autonoma di Soggiorno e Turismo** (www.aziendaturismo-maiori.it; ✆ **089-877452**) provides tourist information at Corso Reginna 73.

Exploring Maiori

In the days of the Amalfi Republic, Maiori was an important port, with vast warehouses for salt. In the Middle Ages, paper mills made the town rich enough to be a prize for French and Spanish rulers. These days the action centers on the pleasant seaside promenade that stretches from the rocky

It's easy to see where the beautiful scenery of Sorrento and the Amalfi Coast would dazzle filmmakers. The only danger is that the backdrops can outshine what's happening on-screen. That's certainly the case with *Beat the Devil*, a 1953 box-office flop that's become a cult classic, partly because the gardens of Ravello (see p. 155) look as ravishing as sultry Italian actress Gina Lollobrigida. The action in *Under the Tuscan Sun* (2003) shifts from beautiful Tuscany down to Positano (see p. 133), creating the same dilemma many travelers face: Which is the more beautiful? Italian neorealist director Roberto Rossellini filmed five films in Maiori. They provide a fascinating look at Maiori before the floods of 1954 swept much of the old town away, and the sunny, romantic settings seem to have had an effect on the director. He had steamy and much publicized affairs with two of this leading actresses. Rossellini and the earthy Anna Magnani, who starred in his two-part *Amore* (1948), lived in a simple fisherman's hut overlooking the fjord of Furore (see p. 143). Their home life could be as choppy as the sea just outside the door—she once famously threw a plate of spaghetti in his face. Rossellini later married Swedish actress Ingrid Bergman, who starred in *Viaggio in Italia* (*Journey in Italy*, 1953), and she preferred the laid-back seclusion of Conca dei Marini (see p. 144).

outcropping that separates Maiori from Minori to a Norman tower in the east. Above town, at the top of a flight of 108 steps, is the **Collegiata di Santa Maria a Mare,** off Corso Reginna. Beneath a large majolica cupola and a richly carved wooden ceiling is a miraculous statue of the church's namesake. Not long after the Pisans raided the town in 1137 and destroyed a fortress and chapel on this spot, a wooden statue of the Virgin, wrapped in a bale of cotton, washed up on shore—a good incentive to create this church in her honor. The church is open from May through October, Tuesday through Saturday, 5pm to 8pm, and Sunday 10am to noon and 5pm to 8pm; November through April, Thursday and Saturday, 4pm to 7pm, and Sunday, 10am to noon and 4pm to 7pm.

Abbazia di Santa Maria de Olearia ★★ RELIGIOUS SITE   In the 10th century, a hermit built a primitive shrine to Santa Maria de Olearia, carving it out of a solid rock face. Soon a monastery, more or less a cluster of cliff dwellings, grew up around it. The monks and their followers also hewed three chapels, one on top of the other, out of the rock, and richly decorated them with 11th-century frescoes. Best preserved are those in the lower chapel, the so-called crypt, where Mary is surrounded by bearded saints and Christ is flanked by St. John the Baptist and St. John the Evangelist. In the main chapel frescoes follow the life of Jesus, and still-colorful panels in the top chapel depict St. Nicholas saving three innocent men from the executioner's sword. This "humility trumps power" tale, a favorite of medieval religious storytellers, seems especially poignant in such humble surroundings.

Via Diego Tajan, off SS 163 east of town. ℭ **089-814209.** Free admission. Wed 2:30–6:30pm, weekends 9am–1pm (hrs. vary; check with tourist office).

Where to Eat

Torre Normanna ★★ CREATIVE AMALFITAN The four Proto brothers are well-known Maiori restaurateurs, and they've set up shop in the most distinctive landmark in town, a 16th-century coastal lookout tower. For diners that means lots of atmosphere, endless views, a waterside terrace, and even a little beach at the foot of the stairs. Ironically, given the location, the menu strikes an even balance between land and sea dishes, with braised lamb and meat-stuffed ravioli getting equal time with fish stew and a wonderful starter of mixed fish.

Via Diego Taini 4. www.torrenormanna.net. ℂ **089-851418.** Main courses 15€–45€. Daily 12:30–3pm and 7:30–11pm (closed Mon Nov–Mar). Closed 3 weeks in Nov and 3 weeks in Jan.

Around Maiori: Capo d'Orso ★★

The coast east of Maiori is quite picturesque, especially around the Capo d'Orso, 6km (4 miles) east. The wild, 500-hectare (1,235-acre) headland is some 70m (230 ft.) above the sea. Limestone has been eroded to create a strange landscape where boulders rise above wild Mediterranean vegetation. The way to immerse yourself in the spectacle is on the well-marked scenic trail that leads from the main coast road, SS 163, to the lighthouse. The little fishing village of Erchie is nestled into the eastern flanks of the promontory. Legend has it that Hercules himself founded the settlement, though by the Middle Ages a powerful community of Benedictine monks had wrestled control of the nearby coast. In an unenlightened arrangement known as Ius Piscariae, fishermen were allowed to keep one-tenth of their catch, while the rest went to the monastery kitchens to ensure the good graces of the holy benefactors. Violent storms washed the monastery away long ago, and the elegant little church of Santa Maria Assunta stands on the site. All around it, tidy white houses climb the hillsides on lemon-scented terraces above a pebbly beach.

THE ISLANDS: CAPRI, ISCHIA & PROCIDA

Just about the only thing these three islands floating in the Bay of Naples have in common is their proximity to one another. While travelers might rightfully lump the three together as idyllic Mediterranean getaways lapped by warm turquoise waters, each has a character so much its own that it can be hard to believe how easy it is to float from one to the other. It's hard to try to sum up these fabled islands in a few words, but Capri has long been a glamorous getaway, still as popular with tabloid celebrities and day-trader zillion-aires as it was with Roman emperors and 1950s movie stars. Ischia is all about laid-back relaxation, on long beaches, in hot springs, and in the pools of dozens of quirkily charming thermal bathing establishments. Procida is just plain pretty, so picturesque that it's hard to remember the real world is just a short hop away.

It's easy to reach any one of the islands on a day trip, but here's some advice you'd be wise to listen to: Don't. You will want to spend some time on any of them. Do so and each will soon become your own. On Capri, the sound of birdsong in the morning and the cliff-side views of the Faraglioni, the three rock formations rising out of the sea, are pleasures that far outweigh the island's sophisti-cation and really can make you think you're in heaven. On Ischia, sitting back in one of the island's hundreds of thermal pools, many of them surrounded by umbrella pines and luxuriant foliage, might easily make you into a sybarite. On Procida, leave time to lounge on one of the spectacular lava beaches and wander through the labyrinth of lanes that spread across the tiny island.

CAPRI ★★★

5km (3 miles) off the tip of the Sorrentine Peninsula

Rugged, mountainous Capri (pronounced *Cap*-ry, not Ca-*pree*), lying just off the tip of the Sorrentine Peninsula, is one of the most

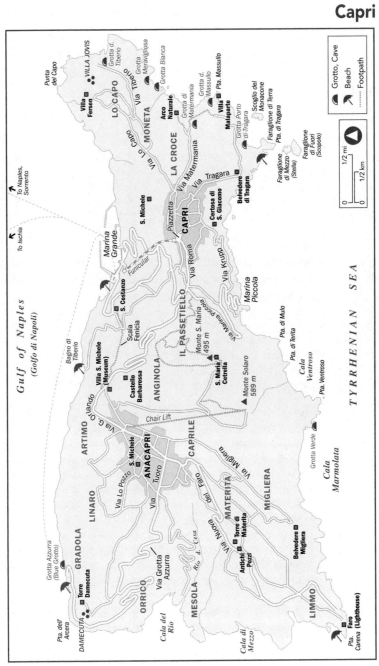

Map labels:

Gulf of Naples
(Golfo di Napoli)

TYRRHENIAN SEA

Grotto, Cave
Beach
Footpath

½ mi
½ km

To Naples, Sorrento

To Ischia

Punta del Capo
VILLA JOVIS
Grotta d. Tiberio
Grotta Meravigliosa
Grotta Bianca
Villa Fersen
LO CAPO
MONETA
Via Tiberio
Via Lo Capo
Arco Naturale
Grotta di Matermania
Grotta d. Massullo
Pta. Massullo
Villa Malaparte
Scoglio del Monacone
Faraglione di Terra
Grotta Porto di Tragara
Pta. di Tragara
Faraglione di Mezzo
Faraglione di Fuori (Scopolo)
Faraglione di Fuori (Stella)
LA CROCE
Via Matermania
Via Tragara
S. Michele
Piazzetta
CAPRI
Certosa di S. Giacomo
Belvedere di Tragara
Via Roma
Via Krupp
Marina Grande
Funicular
Marina Piccola
Via Marina Piccola
S. Costanzo
Scala Fenicia
IL PASSETIELLO
Monte S. Maria 495 m
S. Maria Cetrella
Monte Solaro 589 m
Pta. di Mulo
Pta. di Terita
Cala Ventroso
Pta. Ventroso
Bagno di Tiberio
Villa S. Michele (Museum)
Castello Barbarossa
ANGINOLA
ARTIMO
Via G. Orlando
Chair Lift
CAPRILE
Grotta Verde
Cala Marmolata
Grotta Azzurra (Blue Grotto)
GRADOLA
LINARO
Via Lo Pozzo
S. Michele
ANACAPRI
Via Tuoro
Via del Faro
Via Migliera
MATERITA
MIGLIERA
Torre di Materita
Antichi Pozzi
Belvedere Migliera
ORRICO
Via Grotta Azzurra
Rio d. Cesa
Via Nuova
MESOLA
DAMECUTA
Torre Damecuta
Pta. dell'Arcera
Cala del Rio
Cala di Mezzo
LIMMO
Faro (Lighthouse)
Pta. Carena

169

glamorous and beautiful islands in the world. The legend-steeped, gossip-soaked outcropping of limestone, a mere 4 square miles in size, has beguiled a long, long list of admirers. Emperor Tiberius tucked himself away on the pine- and rosemary-scented cliffs and ruled the Roman Empire from here. Russian novelist Maxim Gorky exiled himself to the island from 1906 to 1913. British music hall star Gracie Fields used to belt out tunes for the likes of Maria Callas and Liz Taylor at her seaside hideaway on Marina Piccola. Poets Pablo Neruda and Rainer Maria Rilke took inspiration from the magical landscapes. The island is still a magnet for the very wealthy, celebrities, artists, eccentrics, and mostly, just plain folks. We all delight in the same pleasures: stark-white, Moorish-style villas; garden walls that drip with bougainvillea, olean-

Capri as seen from the water.

der, and hibiscus; azure seas that surround the rugged coasts; a chorus of birdsong; and a heady taste of the easy-going good life. The emperor Augustus was on to something when he called the island Apragopolis, or City of Sweet Idleness.

Crowd Control

Most visitors come on day trips from Naples and Sorrento, but the longer you stay, the more charms this enchanting beauty reveals. Ah, but be forewarned—you might well find the island to be a charmless tourist trap. If you're visiting on a summertime day trip and disembark any time between 10am and 5pm, your impressions will probably be of crowds and long lines—you might wait hours to get on the bus or funicular up to Capri Town from the port, hours to get on the chairlift from Anacapri up Monte Solaro, hours to board a boat to be rowed through the Grotta Azzurra. Whether or not Capri's beauty will transcend the tourist crowds for you depends on your tolerance levels and when you come. To avoid the greatest crush, arrive as early as you can or plan on staying over at least one night to enjoy an evening passeggiata along moon-lit paths and the chance to begin a day with a dip in the cool, silky sea. Avoid summer weekends especially, when Neapolitans come over for the day and bronzed sun worshippers come from as far away as Rome. Actually, to enjoy the island at its best, you might want to forgo a summertime visit altogether and visit in the spring or early fall. And take heart: Once you've sipped a coffee in the Piazzetta in Capri Town and been rowed through the Blue Grotto, you'll be able to find plenty of tranquil spots on the island.

Essentials

GETTING THERE   You can easily reach Capri from either Naples or Sorrento, and in summer there's also regular service from Amalfi and Positano. Don't let the profusion of companies confuse you: At tourist offices, docks, and most hotels on the islands and along the Amalfi Coast you'll find simplified listings of ferry schedules. From Naples's Molo Beverello dock (take bus or taxi from the train station), the **hydrofoil** (*aliscafo*) takes just 45 minutes and departs several times daily (some stop at Sorrento). Regularly scheduled **ferry** (*traghetto*) service, departing from Porta di Massa, is cheaper but takes longer (about 1½ hrs. each way). **Caremar** (www.caremar.it; ℂ **199-116655** in Italy) runs ferries to Capri from Naples and Sorrento. **NLG-Navigazione Libera del Golfo** (www.navlib.it; ℂ **081-552-0763**) runs to Capri from Naples, Sorrento, and Castellammare di Stabia. **Alicost** (www.lauroweb.com/alicost.htm; ℂ **089/234892**) and **Alilauro** (www.alilauro.it; ℂ **081-497-2222**) connect Capri and Salerno, Positano, Amalfi, and Ischia. **SNAV** (www.snav.it; ℂ **081-428-5555**) runs hydrofoils and catamarans to Capri from Mergellina and Naples (Molo Beverello). **Travelmar** (www.travelmar.it; ℂ **081-704-1911**) maintains regular service between Capri and Salerno. **LMP** (www.consorziolmp.it; ℂ **081-551-3236**) has regular hydrofoil and boat service from Positano and Sorrento. **Volaviamare** (www.volaviamare.it; ℂ **081-497-2211**) runs fast boats between Naples, Sorrento, Amalfi, Positano, Salerno, Ischia, and Capri. During the summer, Amalfi-based **Cooperativa Sant'Andrea** (www.coopsantandrea.it; ℂ **089-873190**) offers scheduled service from Amalfi, Capri, Minori, Salerno, and Sorrento; Positano-based **Lucibello** (www.lucibello.it; ℂ **089-875032**) also makes runs to and from Capri.

From the harbor, you can take a **taxi, bus,** or the **funicular** up to Capri Town and bus or taxi to Anacapri (see "Getting Around," below). Porters will approach you at the dock, and if you're taking a bus or funicular don't be in a hurry to shoo them away. Turn over your bags and they will soon appear in your hotel lobby, saving you the trouble of lugging them onto tightly packed conveyances and dragging them along the island's pedestrian-only lanes. These fellows are trustworthy, and the charge is well worth the 6€ to 8€ per piece of luggage (depending on size).

GETTING AROUND   The island is serviced by funiculars, taxis, and buses. From the ferry dock in Marina Grande, take the funicular or a bus to **Capri Town** (1.80€ for either, buy tickets at the office near the funicular terminal, from newsstands or tobacco shops, or from the driver). A day pass for 6.90€ is valid for two funicular rides and unlimited bus service on the island. Buses also run between Capri and **Anacapri** about every 15 minutes throughout the day.

If you wish to explore farther, there's a chairlift from Anacapri to the top of Monte Solaro, and buses run between Anacapri and the Faro (lighthouse) at the far southwestern tip of the island or the Grotta Azzurra, on the northwestern coast.

Tourists ride the chairlift to Anacapri.

The funicolare, run by SIPPIC (℗ **081-837-0420**), is the picturesque means of transportation between Marina Grande—where the ferry and hydrofoil landings are—and the town of Capri, where it arrives in the heart of town, off Piazza Umberto I. Funiculars leave about every 15 minutes for the 5-minute ride.

The public **bus** system is excellent, but in high season, a ride in one of these diminutive vehicles can feel like being in the proverbial sardine can. **ATC** (part of SIPPIC, above) offers service between Marina Grande, Capri, Marina Piccola, and Anacapri, while **Staiano Autotrasporti** (www.staianogroup.it; ℗ **081-837-2422**) offers service between Anacapri, the Faro (lighthouse), and the Grotta Azzurra.

Taxis, usually readily available and eager at the port and at taxi stands outside the towns, are expensive but a welcome alternative when you encounter long lines to board buses and the funicular. Fares are about 15€ for the short ride from the port up to Capri, 15€ between Capri and Anacapri, and 20€ between the harbor at Marina Grande and Anacapri. There are supplements for baggage (2€ per piece), and nighttime services.

Even when traveling by bus or the funicolare (funicular), wear comfortable shoes, as you'll do a lot of walking on Capri, where all but a few main roads are closed to cars. You can be environmentally friendly and patronize **Rent an Electric Scooter,** Via Roma 68 (℗ **081-837-5863**), while gas-powered scooters are available from such outlets as **Antonio Alfano,** with two locations: Via Marina Grande 280 (℗ **081-837-7941**) and Piazza Barile 26, Anacapri (℗ **081-837-3888**).

VISITOR INFORMATION The **tourist office** is in Capri Town on Piazzetta Italo Cerio (www.capritourism.com; ℰ **081-837-5308**). From April to October, it's open Monday to Saturday 8:30am to 8:30pm, Sunday 8:30am to 2:30pm; November to March, hours are Monday to Saturday 9am to 1pm and 3:30 to 6:30pm.

Exploring Capri

You'll soon discover that life on the island, quite literally, has its ups and downs. From Marina Grande, the main harbor, you'll go up, via road or funicular, to Capri Town. The white houses of the island's main settlement rise and dip across hilly terrain on a saddle between the twin peaks of Monte Tibero and Monte Solaro. Anacapri, the island's other town, is even higher, tucked onto the slopes of Monte Solaro. Getting down to the sea from these towns, and elsewhere on the island, often means descending the formidable, grotto-laced cliffs that ring the shoreline. More often than not you'll do so via paths and steps, hundreds of them, that often lead to viewpoints where you can catch your breath and take in the scenery. The easiest, and often only, way to get around is on foot, and it would be hard to find a more inviting place on the planet to walk.

Marina Grande ★

Most visitors arrive at the largest harbor on the island and hurry on to Capri or Anacapri. If you're eager to start sightseeing as soon as you step off the boat, pop into the island's oldest church, **San Costanzo,** near the waterfront on Via Provinciale Marina Grande. Despite a venerable history that dates back to the 5th century with origins as a Roman bath before that, the church has suffered a bit over the centuries. In 1776, ham-handed engineers removed some columns to use for the marble flooring at the palace of Caserta, creating a bit of a structural sag, and the follow-up repairs, and some 20th-century additions, are less than graceful. The **Palazzo a Mare,** one of the 12 palaces that Emperor Tiberius built around the island, has fared even worse, and part of the ruined complex lies underwater. Even so, as you take a look at the rubble from the end of Via Palazzo a Mare, it's easy to imagine just what a delightful summer retreat this complex must have once been.

Capri Town ★★

Most visitors approach Capri's mountainside main town, tucked into a high saddle between Monte Tiberio and Monte Solaro, on the funicular railway that climbs steep slopes just behind the harbor. A traffic-choked road also makes the ascent, as does a footpath for the hearty. However you make the climb, as soon as you step into the enticing warren of narrow lanes lined with walled villa gardens, you'll realize you're in a rather exotic place that's lofty in more ways than one. Town life radiates from the Piazzetta, a small square that at times is so full of visitors it's called the "world's living room." While the crowd of Gucci-dressed beauties and swarthy Lotharios suggests a certain "see and be seen" glamour, the little square's **Palazzo Cerio** is sturdily medieval and the **Museo Caprense Ignazio Cerio** inside is decidedly down to earth, housing the island's repository of archaeological and geological finds (see below). Overlooking the scene is the pleasantly plain **Torre dell'Orologio,** rising above the old city gateway, and tucked next to it is the homey **church of Santo Stefano.**

Capri Town's Piazzetta.

If the square's collection of celebrities, jetsetters, obscure royals, and many pretenders starts to get on your nerves, remember that the island has attracted a jaded set for centuries. Early 20th-century novelist D. H. Lawrence grumpily referred to Capri as "a gossipy, villa-stricken, two-humped chunk of limestone, a microcosm that does heaven much credit, but mankind none at all." You might also want to remember that not too many centuries ago the hilly uplands that cradle the pretty white town were grazing land for the goats, *caprerae,* that gave the island its name.

It's easy to escape the fray, even in busy Capri Town. From the Piazzetta, the old town's narrow streets lead west past glittering shops along vista-filled, pine-scented walkways to the more sedate **Certosa di San Giacomo** (see below). Just beyond are the **Giardini di Augusto ★★,** terraced pine-shaded public gardens that overlook the sea with panoramic views toward Monte Solaro, the Faraglioni, and Marina Piccola. German steel manufacturer and longtime Capri visitor Friedrich Alfred Krupp (1854–1902) laid out the gardens to show off the island's rich flora. An unexpected presence amid the shaded flowerbeds and viewpoints is that of Vladimir Lenin (1870–1924), the first leader of the Soviet Union. In 1908, the great revolutionary stayed on Capri as a guest of Russian writer Maxim Gorky, who lived on the island from 1906 to 1913. At the time of Lenin's visit, the novelist and political activist, who began his *Encyclopedia of Russian History* on the island, was living in the villa opposite the gardens, now the Villa Krupp hotel.

Certosa di San Giacomo ★ RELIGIOUS SITE   The island's most imposing architectural landmark is this monastery that Count Giacomo Arcucci built in the 14th century as a place to retire from the world. Arcucci's former employer, Queen Joanna I of Naples, provided the prime parcel of land and the funds. The count obviously managed to remain on the good side of the queen, who was adept at political intrigue and whose husbands and lovers had a way of meeting grizzly ends. Arcucci became a Carthusian monk, ending his days in solitary contemplation. If you've visited the Carthusian Certosa di San Lorenzo on the mainland south of Salerno (see p. 224), you will have noticed that the order created fairly sumptuous surroundings for themselves. The monks were not popular with the islanders, whose hunting and grazing lands the community confiscated, then added insult to injury by taxing them for ongoing improvements to the monastery. Things came to nasty head when the brothers locked out islanders who showed up at their gates seeking refuge from the plague of 1653. The suffering populace retaliated by throwing the corpses of the victims over the monastery walls. It's rather ironic that the complex, perched poetically above the sea, is quite community oriented these days, housing the island's public library and a high school. The cloisters are the evocative settings for concerts, and the garden with a viewpoint that looks out into azure infinity is a favorite spot for romantic tête-à-têtes. The quirky **Museo Diefenbach** shows off the works of painter Karl Wilhelm Diefenbach, an outspoken advocate of peace, free love, and nudism who lived and worked on Capri from 1900 to 1913. Many of his large canvases capture moodily lit, iconic island scenes, and he was a bit of an attraction himself, walking the paths barefoot, wearing a white robe, his long gray hair flowing behind him.

Via Certosa. ✆ **081-837-6218.** Admission 4€. Tues–Sun 9am–2pm (and 5–8pm in summer).

Museo Caprense Ignazio Cerio ★ MUSEUM   Shelves are piled high with fossils, minerals, and archeological tidbits that local paleontologist, engineer, historian, and architect Edwin Cerio (1875–1960) and other naturalists and scholars have unearthed over the years. Some of the stone amulets and flint daggers are from the Grotto delle Felci (Cave of the Ferns), a slit in the cliff face above Marina Piccola on the south side of the island. Findings prove that early islanders were living in the tall, 26-m (85-ft.) high cave as early as 5,500 years ago, no doubt enjoying the same timeless sea views that heights around the island still supply.

Piazzetta. centrocaprense.org. ✆ **081-837-6681.** Admission 2.50€. Tues–Sat 10am–1pm.

Villa Jovis ★★ ARCHEOLOGICAL SITE   From Capri Town, a comfortable 45-minute stroll of about 2.4km (1½ miles) ends with a steep climb to the northeastern tip of the island and the most sumptuous and best-preserved of the 12 villas the Roman emperor Tiberius (ruled A.D. 14 to 37) built on Capri. The emperor spent the final 10 years of his reign on the island, partly because he was fond of the scenery and the views, but also because the sheer waterside cliffs and the few closely guarded harbors made the island unassailable to assassins—an antidote to his increasing paranoia. Even then, the emperor had his bread imported from Positano, afraid the islanders would poison him. He installed elaborate baths, forcing his architects to adapt to the mountaintop location by devising an ingenious system of canals and cisterns to collect rainwater. Eight levels of walls and many staircases remain to suggest the enormous size of the villa, probably covering about 1½ acres, with vast terraces and many floors of reception halls and living quarters clinging to the craggy summit of Monte Tiberio. The covered Loggia Imperiale follows the cliff edge to the Salto di Tiberio, a 330m-high (1,083-ft.) precipice from which it's long been said that Tiberius used to hurl lovers of whom he had grown tired and others who did not please him. Even his contemporaries fueled what's believed to have been anecdotal gossip. The historian and biographer Seutonius added some salacious details along the lines of "A party of mariners were stationed below, and when the bodies came hurtling down, they whacked at them with oars and boat-hooks, to make sure they were completely dead." Take your mind off the grisly speculation to enjoy the stunning views across the island and over the straits to the Sorrentine Peninsula.

Via Tiberio. www.capri.net. Admission 2€. April–Oct, Wed–Mon 9am–6pm and Nov–Mar, Wed-Mon 10am–2pm.

Villa Lysis ★ ARCHITECTURAL SITE   Of the many eccentric foreigners who have sought refuge on Capri, Baron Jacques d'Adelsward-Fersen (1880–1923) might be the most colorful character of all. When a scandal involving French schoolboys, and a subsequent prison stint, forced the dissolute baron to leave France in 1905, he came to Capri with his lover, the famous young Roman model of erotic photographers, Nino Cesarini. The house Fersen built on the heights just below Villa Jovis is a neoclassic fantasy of marble, columns, tile work, and gilt mosaics, with a motto etched in stone above the entrance proclaiming the premises to be a "shrine to love and sorrow." Lysis, from the Socratic dialogues, is a reference to homosexual love. The furnishings have long since been removed, but the blue-and-white majolica-tile lounge, the huge bedroom with three windows facing the Bay of Naples and three facing Monte Tiberio, and the lovely terraces all suggest that Fersen drowned his sorrows in the good life. And more than that: In the Chinese room in the basement, specially built for smoking opium, he succumbed to an overdose of cocaine while sipping champagne.

Via Lo Capo. www.cittadicapri.it. ⓒ **081-838-6111.** Free admission. May, Sept, and Oct, Thurs–Tues 10am–6pm; June–Aug, Thurs–Tues 10am–7pm; Nov–Dec, Thurs–Tues 10am–4pm.

Marina Piccola ★★
The island's largest beach, on the southern shore, is nothing much, just a pebbly strip tucked picturesquely amid the rocky shorelines, but the water is clean and crystal clear. The pretty cove has been a focus of island life since the Romans harbored their boats here. In recent centuries fishermen have been sharing the space with visiting glitterati, who frequent the many little bathing establishments perched on the rocks to swim and lounge in the sun, but mostly just to be part of the island's social scene. Even the most jaded beachgoers can't help but admire the views of the famous **Faraglioni,** three rock stacks that jut out of the sea nearby (see below). It's said that the outcropping that divides Marina Piccola neatly into halves is the very rock from which the Sirens tried to lure Ulysses and his crew onto the shoals and wreck their ships. That's a lot of mumble jumble, of course, but the story adds even more romance to an already idyllic setting.

The Via Krupp leading to the Marina Piccola.

While buses make frequent runs between Capri Town and Marina Piccola, the classic approach is on the Via Krupp, a steep path that descends the cliffs in a series of giddily tight switchbacks from the Gardens of Augustus at the edge of Capri Town. Capri aficionado Friedrich Alfred Krupp had the walkway built at the turn of the 20th century so he could easily get back and forth between his two yachts moored at Marina Piccola and his suite at the Quisisana Hotel in Capri Town. Word soon leaked out that Krupp also used the path to access the notorious Grotta di Fra Felice, a cave at the base of the cliff where gentlemen gathered to enjoy the sexual favors of island youth. Krupp was forced to leave Italy, and he committed suicide soon after. Falling rocks can render passage unsafe and the path is often closed for repairs.

Faraglioni ★★★ NATURAL WONDER Among Italy's most famous natural sights are these three rock stacks that rise as high as 100m (330 ft.) from the sea off the southeastern coast of the island. The outermost rock is home to a particular type of bright blue lizard, the *Podarcis sicula coerulea*, which is found nowhere else on the planet. It's believed that the blue color serves as camouflage that allows the little reptiles to blend in with the surrounding sky and water. Whether or not Capri can claim the lizard as its own is a matter of debate, as records suggest that ancient Roman aristocrats imported the colorful creatures from Greece to brighten up their island gardens. The middle stack, Faraglione di Mezzo, is punctured with a poetic little archway where waves have worn away part of the base. It's a popular game for anyone at the helm of a boat to navigate the opening. A shale ledge connects the rock closest to shore, Stella, to the island, and the base shelters two famous beaches with bathing establishments, La Fontelina and Da Luigi. Boats ferry customers to and from Marina Piccola, but a far more sporting way to reach the base of the rocks is on the hundreds of stone steps that descend the cliff from the viewpoint at Punta Tragara.

PUNTA TRAGARA ★★★

Just 10 minutes beyond the Piazzetta, on pine-shaded paths, is a world far removed from the clamor and bling. Ostentation is discretely hidden behind villa walls, the island's natural beauty comes to the fore, and the enticing, azure sea is never far from sight. The island's most dazzling walks are along this stretch of coastline on Via Tragara and its eastward continuation, Via Pizzolungo, skirting lush vegetation on the top of the cliffs and affording glimpses of spectacular seascapes through the trees. The enchanting paths intersect at the Punta Tragara lookout, a perch high above the sea and the Faraglioni. Among those who have admired the views is the Chilean poet-in-exile Pablo Neruda, who in 1953 stayed in a villa on Via Tragara as a guest of Edwin Cerio (see the listing for "Museo Caprense Ignazio Cerio," above). Steps leading down to the Faraglioni from the viewpoint are informally known as the Neruda path and a plaque honoring the poet is at the top.

Aptly named Via Pizzolungo (High Point) continues northeast along the coast, with admirable sights along the way. One of the most arresting is man-made **Casa Malaparte,** a modernist creation that architect Adalberto Libera designed for journalist, novelist, and diplomat Curzio Malaparte in 1937. You'll only see it from afar, looking down on its dramatic cliff-top perch from the path. A bit farther along, steps lead to the Grotta di Matermania, a cave in the flanks of Monte Tuoro. Stepping into the bare, ordinary-looking cavern doesn't begin to suggest its onetime importance as a place to honor the dawn (the first rays of sun ignite the entrance) and engage in rituals and sacrifices honoring Cybele, the mother god. Only a few scant frescoes remain to suggest the sacred nature of the cave. Another viewpoint overlooks Arco Naturale, where two rock pillars that were millennia ago parts of a cave nicely frame sea views.

Casa Malaparte ★ ARCHITECTURAL SITE Ever since the low-slung red-sandstone structure took shape on the top of Punta Massullo, its presence has been mired in controversy, with owner Curzio Malaparte and his house equally vilified. The free-thinking, outspoken Malaparte curried favor with Fascists, communists, and even Italy's Allied liberators during the 1930s and World War II years. His connections with Mussolini (of whom he later ran afoul) saved his neck when he published mocking criticism of Hitler and also garnered him the permits required to override rules and build on the protected cliffs, to the ire of islanders. He threw out architect Adalberto Libera's designs and did the work himself with a local stone mason, calling the sturdy yet whimsical form that resulted "a house like me." Many critics still fail to see the enchantment of the boxlike structure that seems to grow out of the rock, with distinctive steps in the shape of an inverted pyramid leading to a rooftop terrace. One observer said the isolated dwelling "makes you think of Greta Garbo's famous line, 'I want to be alone.'" The house is the star of Jean-Luc Goddard's 1963 film *Contempt.* Its cold, vast spaces and vertigo-inducing perch high above the sea perfectly reflect the estrangement and sense of looming disaster between a couple, played by Brigitte Bardot and Michele Piccoli. The film might afford your only look at the interior, as the house is now owned by the Ronchi Foundation and open only occasionally for cultural events. You can get glimpses from the path above, but the best views are from a boat.

Giro dell'Arco Naturale.

Blue Grotto (Grotta Azzurra) ★★★

Italy's tourist trap extraordinaire can be beguiling, despite all the hassle a visit entails—the frenzy of climbing off a motorboat into a small rowboat, waiting for your turn to be rowed in, lying back, squeezing through a narrow opening, and being rowed out again just as you are beginning to enjoy the experience. The magical colors of the water and walls of this huge grotto are extraordinary, even more so than they appear in countless photographs. Little wonder postcard writers have rhapsodized about the cave since it became part of the tourist circuit in the 19th century. (Actually, a small, ancient Roman dock and some statues retrieved from seafloor suggest this outlet of a vast system of shoreline caverns was known long before then.) It's open daily 9am to 5pm. In summer, boats leave frequently from the harbor at Marina Grande, transporting passengers to the grotto's entrance for 17€ round-trip (and that includes the fee for the rowboat that takes you inside). If you get to the entrance to the Blue Grotto under your own steam (via bus from Anacapri), you'll still pay 13.50€ to be rowed in. The boat trip out from Marina Grande is well worth the few extra euros, as it delivers sea-level views of the island's spectacular cliffs and rugged shoreline. Better yet, consider swimming in. You can do so from the nearby beach once the last boat rows out shortly after 5pm. The memorable exercise requires some moderate competence and comfort being in deep water for the half-hour or so you'll be splashing around in the magic cave.

The entrance to the Blue Grotto.

Anacapri ★★★

Capri's second town, perched on heights surrounded by vineyards, is a pleasant place where, once away from the main square, life transpires like you might have hoped it would on a small island in the Mediterranean. Your impression as you arrive at the main squares, Piazza Monumentale and adjacent Piazza Vittoria, might be otherwise. This is where crowds gather to board buses down to the Blue Grotto, get onto the chairlift to be whisked up Monte Solaro, and make the short walk out to Villa San Michele.

Actually, you might be a bit shell-shocked by the time you squeeze out of the little orange bus that makes the trip

His Heart Was on the Isle of Capri . . .

Swedish-born Axel Munthe came to Capri for the first time in 1875 as an 18-year-old medical student. He stumbled upon a house and ruined chapel that he vowed he would one day make into his home, and he did. Long after Munthe's death in 1947 at the age of 91, he continues to be a goodwill ambassador for the island. The home he converted from ruins at the top of the Scala Fenicia, Villa San Michele, is one of the island's great landmarks. His anecdotal book about life on the island, *The Story of San Michele*, is a perennial bestseller and a great read while you're enjoying Capri. Not many foreigners who at one time or another called the island home enjoyed a life as rich and colorful as Munthe's. A physician, psychiatrist, and man of the world, Munthe studied medicine and practiced in Paris, offered his services for free during the 1884 cholera epidemic in Naples, and drove a British ambulance during World War I. He had a famous affair with British aristocrat and socialite Lady Ottoline Morrell, and eventually married another British aristocrat, Hilda Pennington-Mellor. During his many years on Capri he indulged in his love of animals, establishing a bird sanctuary behind his home, and walking his beloved pet baboon around the island. His human companions included the Swedish Queen consort, Victoria, who spent winters on Capri for 35 years, and Norman Douglas, whose 1917 novel *Southwind* is a thinly disguised expose of life on the island and another good Capri-vacation read.

along the island's narrow main road from Capri Town. The noisy vehicle zips along straightaways 1,000 feet above the sea, then grinds around switchbacks in first gear. You may well wonder where all those glamorous habituees of the Piazzetta cafes have gone as elderly housewives jab you with sharp elbows and knock you around a bit with huge bags full of mysterious foodstuffs. Time was, the only way to get between Capri's two towns was on the *Scala Fenicia* (**Phoenician Staircase**), a steep path (with no authenticated connection to the ancient peoples of its name) that's basically a long staircase with 881 steps—and many superb views.

Wander off the square onto Via Orlandini and you'll soon be passing tailor shops and shoemakers. Villagers sit on the ceramic benches in front of the **church of Santa Sofia,** and from the lively church square streets meander off into narrow lanes lined with vineyards, lemon groves, and gardens brimming with fragrant flowers. With a bit of careful navigating you can walk as far as Punta Carena, about 2km (1 mile) beyond Anacapri at the southwestern tip of the island (the most scenic route takes you along Via Migliara to a coastal path, the **Sentiero die Forini,** or Path of the Forts; see "Getting Active," below). The little cove beneath the Faro (lighthouse) is one of the nicest places on the island for a swim. From there, a bus takes you back to Anacapri.

Casa Rosa ★ HISTORIC HOME   By the time John Clay MacKowen (1842–1901) came to Capri from Louisiana in the 1870s, he had fought in the Civil War, studied medicine at Dartmouth, and earned fame for his work battling yellow fever. He bought up properties that included the ruined Roman Villa of Gradola and, quite amazingly, the Blue Grotto—what a cash cow that attraction could have been for his descendants! He also purchased a crumbling 14th-century defensive tower that he converted into this Pompeiian-red, Moorish–medieval castle fantasy, with crenulations, mullioned windows, and towers. Among the colonel's eclectic collections filling the rooms are a Roman column found beneath the waves in the Blue Grotto, leading to speculation that the cavern may at one time have been used as a sanctuary to the nymphs. Walls are hung with delightful paintings by artists who have been captivated by Capri, including some nostalgic scenes of barefoot islanders by Edouard Alexandre Sain (1830–1910), a French master of rustic scenes.

Via Giuseppe Orlandi. www.comunedianacapri.it. © **081-838-7111.** Admission 3€. April–May, Tues–Sun 10am–5pm; June–Sept, Tues–Sun 10am–1:30 and 5:30–8pm; Oct, Tues–Sun 10am–4pm.

Castello Barbarosa ★ LANDMARK Among the many foreigners who set their sights on Capri was Barbarossa (Red Beard), or Khair Edden, a 16th-cenutry admiral of the Turkish fleet. He lent his name to the 10th-century fortress he destroyed when he sacked Capri in 1544, kidnapping the terrified islanders who had holed up inside. Axel Munthe (see the listing for "Villa San Michele," below) bought the ruins to set aside as a bird sanctuary, offering safe refuge to the many species that alight in Capri on annual migrations between northern Europe and Africa. The purchase was one of Munthe's many efforts on behalf of animals, and he also successfully lobbied Italian dictator Benito Mussolini to ban hunting on the island. The castle is these days an ornithological institute run by the Axel Munthe Institute, which organizes free guided visits on Thursdays. You may visit the tower at other times on request.

Viale Axel Munthe 34.

The exquisite floor of the Chiesa di San Michele.

Chiesa di San Michele ★★ CHURCH The 18th-century builders of this octagonal church made a wise decision when they decided to install a delightful **majolica floor,** now one of the island's most colorful manmade sights. Francesco Solimena (1657–1747), the undisputed master of Neapolitan baroque painting, did the design, full of his typical flamboyance and swirls; and Naples' finest ceramics master, Leonardo Chiaiese, executed the hand-painted tile work. Their minutely detailed assemblage recreates the drama-filled moment when Adam and Eve are expelled from the

Garden of Eden, as a unicorn, goat, and other unlikely creatures look on. The final effect of the piece is so pleasing that no one's ever felt comfortable treading on the floor, creating some logistical problems. Pews were never installed, and worshippers and visitors are relegated to a wooden-planked walkway around the perimeter. Those in the known head up the spiral staircase for a bird's-eye view of the multicolor scene.

Piazza San Nicola. ℂ **081-837-2396.** Admission 2€. Apr–Oct daily 9am–7pm, Nov–Mar 10am–2pm; closed the first 2 weeks of Dec.

Monte Solaro ★★★ NATURAL WONDER   Capri's highest peak soars to 590m (1,932 ft.), a magnet for view seekers who "ooh" and "ahh" at the spectacle of the island and the Bay of Naples unfolding at their feet. You can hike up along some fairly easy paths in about an hour (the easiest is the well-marked route that begins next to Villa San Michele). The chairlift **Seggiovia Monte Solaro** (capriseggiovia.it; ℂ **081-837-1428**) departs from Piazza Vittorria and whisks you to the top in just 12 minutes. Tickets cost 7.50€ one-way, 10€ round-trip, free for children 8 and under; hours of operation are March and April, daily 9:30am to 4pm; May through October, daily 9:30am to 5.30pm; and November through February, daily 9:30am to 3:30pm. Emperor Augustus greets you at the top, his right arm outstretched as if he's claiming everything in the vast panorama in the name of the Roman Empire.

Philosophers Park ★ PARK/GARDEN   Should the landscapes of Capri inspire deep thoughts, Swedish philosophy professor Gunnar Adler-Karlsson has provided a place to ponder them while strolling, thinking, and meditating. Paths through a sunny parcel of hillside carpeted in scrub and broom are lined with 60 ceramic plaques bearing inscriptions from the great philosophers. As you listen to the birdsong and take in the views, you can ponder such questions as "I think, therefore I am." The easy, 20-minute walk out from Anacapri is along flat Via Migliara, flanked with gardens and vineyards. Just beyond the garden is the Belvedere Migliara, overlooking the southern coast.

The view from Monte Solaro.

Via Migliara. www.philosophicalpark.org. Free admission. Dawn–dusk.

Villa San Michele ★★★ HISTORIC HOUSE   Swedish doctor and writer Axel Munthe built this lovely house in the 19th century on the ruins of one of Tiberius's villas. He had the funds and inspiration to fulfill his wish that "My home shall be open for the sun and the wind and the voices of the sea—like a Greek temple—and light, light, light everywhere!"

Villa San Michele.

Perched on a lofty ledge at the top of the Scala Fenicia (see above) entrance to Anacapri, the spacious, airy rooms are still filled with Munthe's art and antiques. They surround peaceful, flower-filled gardens and an arbor-lined path that leads to a parapet with panoramic views across the Bay of Naples. A sphinx looks out to sea, and touching its well-worn hindquarters is said to bring good luck.

Munthe preferred San Michele to his residences in England and Sweden, though a devastating eye condition forced him to forgo the bright light of Capri for a time in the 1920s. In his absence he rented San Michele to the eccentric heiress Luisa Casati (1881–1957). The socialite and patroness of the Ballet Russes famously said "I want to be a living work of art," and she shocked islanders by doing so—walking around the island with leashed cheetahs and wearing live snakes as jewelry. Her lavish lifestyle at Villa San Michele and elsewhere left her $25 million in debt, and she lived out her days in relative poverty in London. After a successful eye surgery, Munthe came home to Capri, where he spent many happy years before returning to Stockholm during World War II as a guest of the royal family.

Viale Axel Munthe 34. www.sanmichele.eu. ℂ 081-8371401. Admission 6€; Nov–Feb 9am–3:30pm, Mar 9am–4:30pm, Apr and Oct 9am–5pm, May–Sept 9am–6pm.

Beaches

Inviting as Capri's crystalline waters are, getting into them can be bit of a challenge. The most convenient place to get wet is **Marina Piccola,** where the pebbly beaches are accessible by bus from Capri Town. Also near Capri Town is **Bagni di Tiberio,** a nice sandy stretch on the north side of the island about 1km (a half-mile) east of Marina Grande. Getting down from the cliff path and, especially, back up, requires a bit of a climb, though you can also get there and back in one of the little boats that makes the run from Marina Grande for about 3€ each way. Other beaches are next to the Blue Grotto (Via Grotta Azzurra), accessible by bus from Anacapri; below the Faro (lighthouse) at **Punta Carena,** at the southwestern tip of the island, also reached by bus from Anacapri; and at the base of the **Faraglioni,** reached by hundreds of steps from the Via Tragara or by boat from Marina Piccola.

You can bring a towel and lounge on the beach and rocks at any of these places. Most are lined with beach clubs (*stabilimenti balneari*) that usually open mid-March to mid-November, 9am to sunset, and charge about 20€ a day for use of a changing room, chair or lounge, and towels; you'll find snack bars at most, excellent restaurants at some (see "Where to Eat," below) and pools at a few.

Getting Active

Capri is heaven for walkers. The island is laced with enchanting paths that should beckon anyone with a good pair of walking shoes, a sun hat, and a bottle of water. Some especially enticing routes just outside Capri Town take you across handsome, view-filled landscapes around Punta Tragara and to some of the island's most famous sights, including the Faraglioni and Villa Jovis (see above). A lesser traveled but no less exhilarating route is on the western side of the island, the **Sentiero die Forini (Path of the Forts).** The 5km (3-mile) walk between the Blue Grotto and Faro (lighthouse) at Punta Carena passes four small coastal fortresses erected over the centuries to keep pirates and foreign powers at bay. However busy the rest of the island might be, here you'll find yourself in generous sweeps of Mediterranean country-side, treated to an almost inexhaustible supply of sparkling sea views.

A pleasant (and mostly downhill) walk is from the summit of Monte Solaro (see above) into the **valley of Cetrella.** You may opt to take the chairlift to the mountain's summit, saving your energy for the descent through wooded coun-tryside along mule paths once used by the Carthusian monks of the Certosa di San Giacomo (see above), who came out here to check their herds. The path passes the aptly named **Villa Solitaria,** the onetime home of British novelist Compton Mackenzie (1883–1972). Mackenzie and his wife, Faith, lived on Capri from 1913 to 1920 and intermittently thereafter. The island's famous tolerance of homosexual foreigners, along with Faith's affair with the classical pianist Renata Borgatti, inspired Mackenzie's lesbian-themed 1928 *Extraor-dinary Women.* The novel was so obviously a *roman a clef* that many residents blushed and the general public back home in England was shocked. A less secular landmark is just down the path, where the lovely little **hermitage of Cetrella** and its **church of Santa Maria** nestle in a verdant copse. A shrine to the Virgin Mary is especially popular with sailors, who trek out on the rare Sundays when mass is celebrated; the church is not often open, so check with the tourist office before setting out if a look inside at the double nave is high on your list of must-sees. The path then descends back into Anacapri, ending at the Villa San Michele.

Where to Stay
EXPENSIVE

Capri Palace ★★★　If you find it hard to leave the island, a perfect place to give into temptation is this delightful getaway in Anacapri on the slopes of Monte Solaro. Everything here seems geared to soothing relaxation: An expanse of green lawn surrounds the swimming pool, chic lounges are quiet and welcoming, and guest rooms are done in restful creams with rose-colored tile floors and white linens and upholstery. Some suites have private pools, and some rooms look across the sea all the way to Vesuvius, but even the outlooks from rear rooms over the green flanks of Monte Solaro are relaxing. A shuttle bus runs to the port, Capri Town, and a delightful beach club where platforms make it easy to dip into the Mediterranean.

Via Capodimonte 2, Anacapri. www.capri-palace.com. ✆ **081-978-0111.** 79 units. 340€–1,250€ double. Rates include buffet breakfast. Closed Oct 17–Mar 31. No children under 10 June–Aug. **Amenities:** 2 restaurants; bar; beach club; heated pool; room service; spa; Wi-Fi (free).

Hotel Punta Tragara ★★ French architect Le Courbusier designed the multilevel villa in the 1920s, and Winston Churchill and Dwight Eisenhower are among those who have enjoyed falling asleep to waves lapping on the shore far below and waking up to birdsong. The stylish quarters are all different, some strikingly contemporary, others comfortingly traditional, though all are luxurious without being pretentious, and open to terraces. Most come with views of the Faraglioni. You can make the descent to the sea on the hundreds of steps just outside the gate, or enjoy a swim in the two pools tucked into gardens.

Via Tragara 57, Capri Town. www.hoteltragara.com. ✆ **081-837-0844.** 45 units. 450€–850€ double. Rates include buffet breakfast. Closed Nov–Easter. **Amenities:** Restaurant; bar; concierge; gym; 2 pools; room service; spa; Wi-Fi (free).

MODERATE

Casa Mariantonia ★★ A gracious old villa near the Church of San Michele commands some of the best real estate in Anacapri—a shady lemon grove, lawns, gardens, and a big swimming pool are all right in the center of town. Four generations have been welcoming guests to the family home, which in its current guise mixes traditional island architecture with contemporary touches for a relaxed-though-luxurious ambience. The family claims that great-grandmother Mariantonia invented *limoncello*, which may be a bit of a stretch—even so, sipping some of the homemade elixir on a terrace next to the trees from whence it comes is a great Capri experience.

Via G. Orlandi 180, Anacapri. www.casamariantonia.com. ✆ **081-8372923.** 10 units. From 120€–190€ double. Rates include buffet breakfast. **Amenities:** bar; pool; Wi-Fi (free).

Villa Brunella ★★ Flower-filled terraces spilling down the hillside from Via Tragara seem to pull you right into the magic of Capri, with eye-popping sea views from all of the airy, tile-floored guest rooms. Ambience hovers between cozy, old-fashioned Italian hospitality and romantic getaway, with some nice antiques and overstuffed armchairs in the bright rooms and plenty of bougainvillea-scented nooks and crannies on the pine-shaded grounds. A pool sparkles on a welcoming patio, and guests have access to a beach club at Marina Piccola. The Terrazza Brunella provides excellent food in elegant surroundings for those occasions when even the short walk into town seems like an effort.

Via Tragara 24, Capri Town. www.villabrunella.it. ℭ**081-837-0122.** 20 units. 190€–270€ double. Rates include buffet breakfast. Closed Nov–Apr. **Amenities:** Restaurant; bar; pool; room service; Wi-Fi (free).

INEXPENSIVE

Hotel Tosca ★ You don't have to break the bank to stay on the island or even sacrifice style at this pretty little retreat on the quiet side of Capri Town, near the Gardens of Augustus. Many of the bright, whitewashed rooms have sea views, some have terraces, and all look over lush gardens and have arches, some vaulted ceilings, and tile floors that create the ambience of a simple-yet-tasteful island house. Breakfast is served on a breezy sea-view terrace.

Via Dalmazio Birago 5, Capri Town. www.latoscahotel.com/. ℭ **081-837-0989.** 11 units. 75€–160€ double. Rates include buffet breakfast. **Amenities:** Wi-Fi (free).

Where to Eat

EXPENSIVE

Grottelle ★ CAPRESE A trek along the southern side of the island is rewarded with a stop at this delightful lair tucked onto a ledge above the Arco Naturale. A cave etched out the limestone cliffs and a panoramic terrace provide plenty of ambience that will probably be a lot more memorable than the meal itself, though simple dishes like *zuppa di fagioli* (bean soup) and spaghetti *con pomodoro e basilica* (with fresh tomatoes and basil) are perfectly fine accompaniments to the views that extend across the blue sea to the Amalfi Coast. To find this memorable spot, wander east from Punta Tragara; it's about a 20-minute walk from the Piazzetta.

Via Arco Naturale 13, Capri. ℭ**081-837-5719.** Main courses 15€–30€. Fri–Wed noon–3pm and 7–11pm. Closed Nov–Mar.

Ristorante Aurora ★★ CAPRESE You'll get a taste of Capri's high life at the island's oldest eatery, where photos of celebrities hang above the white banquettes. A few may also be sitting around you in the minimalist main dining room or on the terrace facing Capri Town's main thoroughfare. Despite all the glitz, the third generation of the D'Alessio family sticks to the basics, serving simple island classics that include the trademark pizza *all'acqua* (a thin crust sprinkled with mozzarella and hot peppers), *sformatino alla Franco* (rice pie in prawn sauce), and spaghetti *alle vongole* (with clams).

Via Fuorlovado 18. www.auroracapri.com. ℭ **081–837–0181.** Main courses 12€–22€. Apr–Dec noon–3:30pm and 7:30–11pm.

MODERATE

Gelsomina ★ CAPRESE The sparkling swimming pool is a tempting draw on a warm summer day at this countryside retreat outside Anacapri. You can come for the day, to swim, have lunch, and maybe walk to the Beledere della Migliera viewpoint just down the road. It's also a popular evening spot. Dining is on a large terrace overlooking the sea, and the food is a perfect complement to the low-key surroundings, with a lot of the ingredients coming right from the surrounding gardens. Homemade *ravioli di caprese* is delicious, light as a feather and stuffed with tomatoes just plucked from the vines and delicious ricotta from a local producer. Anacapri is about 15 minutes away on foot, along lanes that slice through vineyards and garden plots. Free shuttle service is available. Several simple guest rooms (from 115€–190€) are above the restaurant.

Via Migliara 72, Anacapri. www.dagelsomina.com. © **081-837-1499.** Main courses 10€–18€. Daily noon–3pm and 7–10:30pm. Closed Nov–Mar.

INEXPENSIVE

Pizzeria Materita ★ PIZZERIA/CAPRESE All the warmth of little Anacapri comes to the fore in this busy local favorite on an animated square overlooking the church of Santa Sofia. Pizzas from the wood-fired oven and the palatable house wine are the crowd pleasers, though the simple pastas (including some laden with seafood) are solidly tasty, too. The busy waiters will also usually come around with a fresh fish that will soon reappear perfectly grilled with island herbs.

Via Giuseppe Orlandi 140, Anacapri. © **081–837–3375.** Main courses 8€–18€. Wed–Mon 12:30–3:30pm and 6:30–10:30pm.

Pulalli Wine Bar ★★ CAPRESE To find a hideaway in the jam-packed Piazzetta, just look up, to this little terrace next to the clock tower. A bird's-eye view comes with wine, a selection of cheeses, or a meal—the *risotto al limone* (lemon-flavored risotto) is especially transporting in this magical setting, especially since it's served in a hollowed-out lemon.

Piazza Umberto I 4, Capri. © **081-837-4108.** Main courses 10€–25€. Wed–Mon noon–3pm and 7pm–midnight. Closed Nov to just before Easter.

A Meal & a Swim

Some of Capri's most beloved institutions are the *stabilmenti balneari,* beach clubs, where you can eat well and begin or end a meal with a swim and some lounging. A day at one of these charming places is, like so much else about Capri, one of those simple pleasures with a glamorous twist.

Addio Riccio ★★★ SEAFOOD The cliff-side pavilion that serves as the informal beach bistro of the Capri Palace (see above) is done in soothing shades of blue and crisp white and hangs just above the Grotta Azzurra, bathed in the same mesmerizing light. The setting is so delightful that you won't want to leave after feasting on a fish lunch, and you don't have to—the top level is a sunning platform, filled with lounges and umbrellas, while, better yet, stairs and a path descend to wave-washed swimming platforms below. Lunch draws crowds even from the mainland, and dinner is also served in busy summer months, making this the prime spot on the island for a romantic evening. The kitchen does wonderful things with what's said to be the freshest seafood on Capri, turning out turbot baked in a salt crust and platters dished up from counters heaped high with mysterious denizens of the deep. The

Capri

Addio Riccio.

spaghetti with urchin roe is so good you'll wonder why you've been missing out on this treat all your life. Buses from Anacapri to the Grotta Azzurra stop just outside the door, as do shuttles from the Capri Palace.

Via Gradola 4, Grotta Azzurra. www.capripalace.com. ℰ **081-837-1380.** Main courses 20€–40€. Daily 12:30–3.30pm and 8–11pm. Closed Nov–Mar.

La Canzone del Mare ★ SEAFOOD/CAPRESE   The British music hall star Gracie Fields came to Capri in the 1930s and decided she would be the happiest woman on earth if "one small blade of grass on this wonderful, gentle place could belong to me." She eventually bought Il Fortino, a house fashioned out of a ruined fort at Marina Piccola. Over the years she carved bathing platforms out of the rocks, installed a saltwater swimming pool shaped like the island, and built terraces and lounges that would accommodate a restaurant, an American bar, and a few guest rooms, as well as living quarters that served as an informal retreat from life at her villa in Anacapri. Fields died of pneumonia after performing on the Royal Yacht anchored offshore, but her bathing establishment and restaurant still flourishes. A meal of fresh vegetable and seafood pastas is lot more expensive than you might expect from the simple surroundings, but the atmosphere is fun and eccentric and Fields is still a presence. Five rooms, named after Elizabeth Taylor and other famous former guests of the past, provide sleeping quarters about as close to the sea as you can find on Capri, aside from a berth on a yacht.

Via Marina Piccola 93. www.lacanzonedelmare.com. ℰ **081–837–0104.** Main courses 20€–40€. Daily 12:30–3.30pm and 8–11pm. Closed Nov–Mar.

La Fontelina ★★ CAPRESE/SEAFOOD   Many travelers spend the winter months dreaming of a summertime lunch on the rocks at the base of the

Faraglioni, where a meal comes with a swim in one of Europe's most legend-ary seaside settings. A fruit-loaded sangria is the house drink; the Caprese salad—with *mozzarella di bufala* and just-off-the-vine tomatoes—is legend-ary; and fish is so fresh you might think it jumped right out of the sea that laps at your feet onto your plate. Lunch is the only meal served, and it's necessary to reserve one of the two seatings, at 1 and 3pm. Most guests come early and hang around long after a meal to lounge on the rocks and dip into the crystal-line waters.

Via Faraglioni. www.fontelina-capri.com. ✆ **081–837–0845.** Main courses 20€–40€. Daily noon–7pm. Closed Nov–Mar.

Lido di Faro ★ CAPRESE   The cove at the far western end of the island, the Punta Carena, is an ideal spot for a swim—the wave action and warm water create the sensation of being in a big, natural Jacuzzi. Adding to the experience is a meal or snack at the lively restaurant, bar, and swimming pool tucked away on the jagged rocks just below the lighthouse (*faro*). You can eat lightly on a good selection of salads and omelets. Sunset views from the ter-races and bathing platforms are the best on the island, making this a choice spot for an evening swim and an *apertivo*.

Punta Carena, Anacapri. www.lidofaro.com. ✆ **081-837-1798.** Main courses 12€–25€. Daily noon–sunset. Closed Nov–Mar.

Shopping for Local Crafts

Every glitzy retailer in Italy, and beyond, seems to have an outlet in Capri Town. But the island also turns out some high-end products of its own mak-ing. **Carthusia,** scent maker to the rich and famous, has been concocting unique perfumes from local herbs and flowers since 1948. You can take a whiff at the **laboratory,** Viale Matteotti 2d (www.carthusia.it; ✆ **081-837-0368;** daily 9:30am–6pm) or pop into one of the island outlets: Via Camerelle 10, Capri Town (✆ **081-837-0529**); Via Federico Serena, Capri Town (✆ **081-837-5335**); and Via Axel Munthe 26, Anacapri (✆ **081-837-3668**).

Stylish sandals (handmade, of course) are the stock in trade of **Amedeo Canfora ★,** Via Camerelle 3, Capri (www.canfora.com), ✆ **081-837-0487;** and at Antonio Viva's **L'Arte del Sandalo Caprese ★,** Via Giuseppe Orlandi 75, Anacapri (www.sandalocaprese.it; ✆ **081-837-3583**). The island also has an ages-old jewelry-making tradition, with some of the finest examples filling the shelves at **La Perla Gioielli,** Piazza Umberto I 21 (✆ **081-837-0641**).

Capri After Dark

The **Piazzetta** is the epicenter of island nightlife, and an evening in a cafe watching wafer-thin models and balding boulevardiers strut back and forth usually suffices for a night on the town. The **piano bars** in the **Grand Hotel Quisiana** and in the **Capri Palace** are a bit more exclusive, while **Anema E Core,** Via Sella Orta 39/a, Capri (www.anemaecore.com; ✆ **081-837-6461**) is the closest the island comes to having a nightclub, with live music of the easy-listening genre, but no dancing and no food.

ISCHIA ★★

30km (18 miles) NW of Capri; 42km (26 miles) NW of Naples; 20km (13 miles) W of Pozzuoli

While Capri is swathed in glamor and sophistication, Ischia (pronounced *EES*-kee-a) is scented with sulfur, rising off hundreds of thermal hot springs. These wellsprings have been the island's calling card ever since the ancient Romans stepped ashore and discovered the pleasures of a long, soothing soak. Monte Epomeo, the island's 788m-high (2,585-ft.) dormant volcano, still has enough life in it to feed the mineral hot springs and produce therapeutic muds that are the stock in trade for 150 spas and thermal establishments on the island. In a rather optimistic appraisal of the waters' alleged curative properties, Ischia is often called the "island of eternal youth." That moniker more aptly refers to the young Neapolitans who alight every summer and peacock around cafes and bronze themselves on the many beaches. Ischia is also known as the Isola Verde (Green Island), not, as some assume, for its verdant slopes, but for the green-tinged karst (limestone) that underlies much of the landscape. Even so, Ischia *is* refreshingly green with forests, orchards, and vineyards, and the towns that ring its 37km (23 miles) of shoreline are laid back, pleasant places that might lack the sophistication of Capri or the Amalfi Coast, but for many admirers are all the better for it.

Essentials

GETTING THERE   Ischia's three main harbors—Ischia Porto (the largest), Forio, and Casamicciola—are well connected to the mainland, with most ferries leaving from Pozzuoli and Naples's two harbors of Mergellina Terminal Aliscafi and Stazione Marittima. Both ferry and hydrofoil (*aliscafi*) services are frequent in summer but slow down during the winter, when hydrofoil service is sometimes suspended altogether because of rough seas. **Medmar**

Ischia.

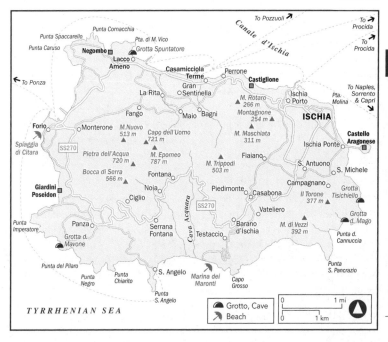

(www.medmargroup.it; ℂ **081-333-4411**), **Caremar** (www.caremar.it; ℂ **199-116655** in Italy), and **SNAV** (www.snav.it; ℂ **081-428-5555**) offer regular service from Napoli, Pozzuoli, and Procida to Ischia Porto and Casamicciola. **Alilauro** (www.alilauro.it; ℂ **081-497-2222**) runs hydrofoils from Naples (Mergellina and Molo Beverello) to Ischia Porto and Forio; **NLG-Navigazione Libera del Golfo** (www.navlib.it; ℂ **081-552-0763**) operates from Salerno to Ischia; and **Alicost** (www.lauroweb.com/alicost.htm; ℂ **089-234892**) offers connections from Salerno, Capri, Amalfi, and Positano to Ischia Porto. *Note:* During high season, car access to the island is restricted and the number of car slots is limited; if you are planning to bring your car, check with the transport company and make your reservations well in advance.

GETTING AROUND Public transportation on Ischia is excellent, with a well-organized **bus** system with EAV (ℂ **800-053-9309** toll-free in Italy). One line circles the island in a counterclockwise direction (*circolare destra,* marked CD), and one in a clockwise director (*circolare sinistra,* marked CS), plus a number of other lines crisscross the island among its major destinations. Tickets cost 1.90€ and are valid for 90 minutes (a daily pass costs 6€); they are on sale at bars, tobacconists, and news kiosks). You can get a printout of the bus schedule from the tourist office (see "Visitor Information," below).

Taxis wait at stands strategically located around the island, including Piazza degli Eroi (✆ **081-992550**) and Piazzetta San Girolamo (✆ **081-993720**) in Ischia Porto; Piazza Bagni (✆ **081-900881**) in Casamicciola; and Piazza Girardi in Lacco Ameno (✆ **081-995113**).

You can **rent motor scooters, bicycles,** and **cars** on the island from a number of agencies, including **Autonoleggio In Scooter** in Forio (www.autonoleggioinscooter.it; ✆ **081-998513** or 320-421-8039) and **Island Center,** Via V. Di Meglio 161 in Barano (✆ **081-902525**).

VISITOR INFORMATION   The **AACST tourist office** (www.infoischia-procida.it; ✆ **081-507-4231**) is at Via Sogliuzzo 72, Ischia Porto, where you'll find free maps of the island as well as information and brochures. In summer an information booth operates at Piazza Antica Reggia 11, Ischia Porto.

Exploring the Island

Ischia is large as far as its neighbors in the Bay of Naples go, about 46 sq. km (18 sq. miles). Most of its main settlements—Ischia Porto, Casamicciola, and Lacco Ameno—are on the north shore, with Forio holding down the west coast. Boats call at Ischia Porto, with the island's one great historic landmark, the Castello Aragonese; Casamicciola, a famous spa town; and Forio, surrounded by beaches and the beautiful gardens at La Mortella. Lacco Ameno is the island's most sophisticated resort. Wherever you settle, you won't be too far from the other island sights. A road follows the coast around the island, and buses make getting from one town to the other easy.

ISCHIA PORTO & ISCHIA PONTE ★★

The island's two main settlements, one the principal port and the other a yacht haven and fishing village, are linked by a seaside promenade that stretches for 2km (1¼ miles). Islanders often lump them together as "Ischia." The busy harbor of Ischia Porto is a volcanic crater that was once landlocked, until 1854, when Bourbon King Ferdinand II had a channel cut to the sea. He created one of the most thrilling sea entrances anywhere, as ferries and yachts navigate the impossibly narrow cut and emerge into a becalmed lake surrounded by colorful waterside cafes and green hillsides carpeted with the island's distinctive white, flat-roofed houses. The king used to soak his creaky bones in the town's municipal baths, now housing government offices and a spa for soldiers.

Smaller, quieter Ischia Ponte (Bridge) takes its name from a wooden causeway erected in the mid–15th century, linking the rest of Ischia with a rocky outcropping to which part of the picturesque settlement clings. The massive Castello Aragonese (see below) overshadowing the little shops and snug harbor is not so much a castle as it is a vast medieval military complex. Formidable as the walls and turrets are, they provided a place of refuge to islanders in 1301, when an eruption of nearby Mt. Epomeo sent them scurrying to the gates of the fortress, where they eventually established a village within its walls.

The Castello Aragonese.

Castello Aragonese (Aragonese Castle) ★★★ HISTORIC SITE

Greeks settled this rocky islet as early as the 5th century B.C., building watchtowers to keep an eye on enemy fleets moving through the sea lanes. The fortifications atop 91-m (300-ft.) cliffs have been a plum for invaders ever since, from ancient Neapolitans and Romans to Goths to Normans. King of Naples Alfonso I gave the walled complex its present form in the mid–15th century as a defense against pirate raids, shoring up watchtowers and walls, as well as installing churches, terraces, and little squares that give the walled compound a villagelike air. At one time more than 17,000 people sheltered within the walls, among them nuns, monks, and soldiers from a military garrison. The British shelled the compound during the Napoleonic Wars in 1809, and they did a pretty good job of it, though enough remains to give an idea of the onetime might of the citadel.

Many of the islet's churches still stand, in various states of repair. The frescoed crypt is about all that remains of the Cattedrale dell'Assunta, while the Chiesa dell'Immaculata and hexagonal San Pietro a Pantaniello are fairly intact. A somber if not downright macabre presence is the small Cimitero delle Monache Clarisse, attached to the island's convent. When the inhabitants breathed their last they were left sitting on stone chairs as a reminder of what becomes of our earthly presence—the spooky-looking seating arrangement is still in place, minus the bones.

You can ponder all this as you make a circuit of the breezy ramparts, a vertigo-inducing lookout hundreds of feet above the crashing waves. An elevator whisks visitors up the rock face to the castle entrance, though the climb up the stairs and ramps that Alfonso installed provides a more authentic experience.

Piazzale Aragonese, Ischia Ponte. www.castelloaragoneseischia.com. ℂ **081-992834.** Admission 10€ adults, 6€ youth 10–14; free for children 9 and under. Daily 9am–sunset.

CASAMICCIOLA TERME ★

6 km (4 miles) W of Ischia Porto

This tidy little town facing a pretty harbor is not the frivolous seaside resort that it might appear to be. It's devoted almost entirely to the healing arts, and the island's largest concentration of spas lines the squares and streets. Patients at the now derelict seaside charity hospital of Pio Monte della Misericordia led the way, when they began showing signs of improvement after a spa was installed in 1604. Ever since, arthritic, gouty, and otherwise ailing travelers have found their way here from around Europe. Many of the grand establishments survived the violent earthquake that shook the town in 1883, but the rocking and trembling diminished some of the Belle Epoque grandeur that once greeted travelers who stopped to take the waters as part of the Grand Tour. Among them was Norwegian playwright Henrik Ibsen, who came for a cure in the 1860s, with time off from treatments to read the works of existential philosopher Soren Kierkegaard and write his famous verse drama *Peer Gynt*. He's honored with a plaque in Piazza Marina, near a statue of King Vittorio Emanuele II.

LACCO AMENO ★★

8km (5 miles) W of Ischia Porto

Ischia ramps up its glamour quotient in this picturesque port that stretches along the sandy coast at the foot of Monte Epomeo. Looming just offshore is the Fungo, a mushroom-shaped lump of wave-sculpted tufa that is as iconic to Ischia as the Faraglioni are to Capri. Also reminiscent of that glitzier, more fabled place are the yachts in the harbor and the well-dressed and tanned cafe sitters along pedestrian-only Corso Rizzoli. This low-key street skirting the bay is named for publishing magnate and film producer Angelo Rizzoli (1889–1970), who put what had been an unassuming fishing port on the map in the 1950s. The arrival of Richard Burton and Elizabeth Taylor in 1963 to shoot the barge scenes from the blockbuster film *Cleopatra* ensured the town's celebrity. The quiet little backwater became a jet-set hotspot when newspapers around the world ran candid paparazzi photos of the adulterous lovers yachting and swimming just offshore.

Lacco Ameno.

Museo Civico Archeologico di Pithecusae ★ MUSEUM   Villa Arbusto, the onetime summer home of wealthy publisher Angelo Rizzoli, shows off Ischia's ancient past. A long and very ancient past it is, as the eight rooms display Greek pottery from as early as the 8th century B.C. Some "newer" pieces are from the period around 474 B.C., when Greeks from the Sicilian colony of Siracusa arrived on Ischia in force to help the city of Cuma across the bay (see p. 91) fight off Etruscan invaders. The prize is the Nestor Cup, a drinking vessel from 725 B.C. that is inscribed with what's believed to be a reference to the *Iliad*. This makes it one of the oldest examples of the Greek alphabet and maybe Europe's first literary reference. The meaning of the text will continue to be the subject of scholarly dissertations for years to come as classicists debate the meaning of the lines, "Nestor's cup I am, good to drink from. Whoever drinks from this cup, him straightaway the desire of beautiful-crowned Aphrodite will seize." The connection with the *Iliad* comes into play with the mention of Nestor, the aged king of Pylos who appears in the epic poem. One of the more intriguing theories about the meaning of the seemingly disjointed lines is that they were written as part of a drinking game. Each player added a rhyming bit, and the ditty ends with an elegant and eso- teric suggestion that wine will sexually arouse them, hence the reference to Aphrodite, goddess of love.

The villa guesthouse is a shrine to Rizzoli, who made his fortune as a pub- lisher and went on to produce some of Italy's most iconic films, including Federico Fellini's *La Dolce Vita* (1960) and *8 ½* (1963). Thousands of photo- graphs are a tribute to those glory days of Italian cinema.

Corso Angelo Rizzoli 210. www.museincampania.it. ✆ **081-900356.** Admission 3€. Sum- mer, Tues–Sun 9:30am–1pm and 4–8pm; winter Tues–Sun 9:30am–1pm and 3–6:30pm.

Museo e Scavi Santa Restituta ★ MUSEUM   Restituta, a 3rd-cen- tury Christian from Carthage in North Africa, is honored in her namesake church. Legend has it that Restituta's tormentors set her afloat in a burning boat but she failed to burn or drown. She did, however, die at sea, and the boat containing her perfectly preserved body came ashore on Ischia. An angel came to an islander in a dream and directed her to Restituta. She and other Christians buried the saint at the foot of nearby Monte Vico, and a church was built in Restituta's honor. As if to prove that you never know what lies just under your feet, 1950s renovators of her church opened a Pandora's box when they removed an 18th-century tile floor in the 1950s. Below it was a floor from the 15th century, and beneath that the floor of a Roman cistern and remains of an early Christian church. They kept going and hit more pay dirt, the remains of an early Greek factory where ceramic pots were made and fired and shipped all over the Mediterranean. Scattered among the excavations are amulets, pottery, and a reconstruction of an ancient Greek home, with a loom equipped with the weights used to warp yarn and a charming collection of toys that kept ancient kids amused.

Piazza Santa Restituta. ✆ **081-980161.** Admission 3€. Apr–Oct, daily 10am–1pm and 4–7pm.

FORIO ★
13km (8 miles) W of Ischia Porto

Sprawling, sloppily built Forio compensates for its lack of beauty with some spectacular stretches of sand, a lively resort scene, and some extremely palatable wines from the surrounding vineyards. **Il Torrione,** a solid, late-15th-century watchtower, adds a bit of historic charm. An even more enticing seaside presence is the tiny, whitewashed **Madonna del Soccorso ★★,** officially the church of Santa Maria delle Neve, on a headland jutting out to sea just to the west of the town (Via Sorccoso, usually open for 8pm mass only). The nickname, Our Lady of Assistance, becomes obvious in the simple tile-floored interior. Walls are covered with models of ships and paintings of shipwrecks that sailors have offered to the Madonna as thanks for her help in their safe return from perilous sea voyages. The 15th-century crucifix is a bit of flotsam that conveniently washed up on shore just outside the church.

La Colombaia ★ ARCHITECTURAL SITE/GARDEN   The great film director Luchino Visconti (1906–76) spent his summers in this Moorish-style villa tucked away amid exotic seaside gardens on the Monte Vico promontory. The airy white rooms now house a rather disjointed collection of photographs documenting Italian cinema, but it's wonderful to share the spaces, even vicariously, with the pioneer of neorealism and the director of such classics as *The Leopard* (1963), *The Damned* (1969), and *Death in Venice* (1971). As you climb into the tower and catch a glimpse of the sea from one of the many terraces, it's easy to imagine the hot summer nights when the cultured and privileged Visconti, the son of a duke and pharmaceutical heiress and himself a count, entertained his lovers, actor Helmut Berger and director Franco Zeffirelli, and such luminaries as Maria Callas.

Via Francesco Calise 73. ⓒ **081-333-2147.** Admission 4€. Mon–Sat 9:30am–12:30pm and 3:30–6:30pm.

Villa La Mortella ★★ GARDEN   Sir William Walton (1902–83), one of the greatest English composers of the 20th century, and his Argentine wife Susana Walton (1926–2010) settled on Ischia in 1949. Walton found the peace and light conducive to composition, and Susana became enchanted with the idea of creating a garden at their home, La Mortella (the Myrtles) on the west side of the Monte Vico promontory outside Forio. She worked with the great landscape designer Russell Page throughout the 1950s to landscape the Valley Garden, filling it with rare Mediterranean and South American species; great sweeps of orchids and other flowers; and fountains, ponds, and brooks. Walton could control the valves from his study and turn off the jets when the gurgling disturbed him. Lady Walton designed the sunny, view-filled Hill Garden as a tribute to her husband in the 1980s, working in the soil herself well into her later years. The exotic romance of the gardens is an apt tribute to the Waltons, who married just a few months after meeting at a reception in Buenos Aires. As soon as Walton, a notorious womanizer, laid eyes on Susana, he supposedly told fellow composer Benjamin Britten, "I think I'll marry that girl over there." He proposed every day for the next two weeks, and when Susana finally accepted, her father was so upset that he spent her entire dowry on champagne for the wedding guests. A Greek theater tucked into the hillside is the setting for summer concerts. It's customary on a walk along the garden paths to wave at the palms, following Lady Walton's belief that "You have to wave at them when you go by because they think you haven't paid attention."

Via Francesco Calise 39. www.lamortella.it. ℂ **081-986220.** Admission 12€ adults, 10€ children 8–16 and seniors over 60, 6€ children 5–7. Apr 1–Nov 15 Tues, Thurs, and Sat–Sun 9am–7pm.

Sant'Angelo ★★
11km (7 miles) SW of Ischia Porto

The southern side of Ischia is agricultural, and mountainsides are carpeted with orchards and vineyards surrounding small, terraced villages. There's only one town of any size, and it's a beauty. Sant'Angelo's tidy little houses cling to the base of a towering rock that's connected to the shore by a sandy isthmus 100m (328 ft.) long. Just east of town is one of the weirdest sights in Ischia, so-called **Fumarole beach.** Hot underground vapors heat the sand to such high temperatures that islanders come here to bury chicken and fish in aluminum foil and splash around a bit as they wait for their food to cook. The sands also provide welcome relief to arthritis sufferers, who plonk down on the warm grains and let the heat penetrate their aching joints. Just offshore, geysers bubble up to create natural hot-tub–like pools. A flotilla of little boats ferry passengers from the town marina to this otherwordly seascape, about 5€ each way, and it's easy to reach on a seaside path.

Beaches

Ischia has a commodity that's the envy of Capri and towns along the Amalfi Coast: some long stretches of sand. They're especially pleasant in May and September, but in the dog days of summer the sands are jam-packed with a mixed crowd of islanders, day-tripping Neapolitans, and Germans and Russians who are drawn to Ischia by the combined allure of thermal baths and beaches. The island's most beautiful beach is **Spiaggia dei Maronti ★★★,** stretching for about 2km (1¼ miles) east of the village of Sant'Angelo. South of Forio is the **Spiaggia di Citara ★★,** with hot mineral springs that flow out to sea at its southern edge. The lovely beach on the bay of **San Montano ★★** is tucked onto the flanks of the promontory of Monte Vico near Laco Ammeno. If you're staying in or near Ischia Porto or Ischia Ponte and can't wait to get in the water, your best bet is **Spiaggia dei Pescatori ★,** where local fishermen beach their boats; it's just west of the Aragonese Castle.

Getting Active

Ischia is good hiking territory. The island's most popular hike is the trek up the slopes of **Monte Epomeo,** starting from the main square in the small town of Fontana (well served by public buses). The well-signposted path is steep in places, but for the most part the hike is a pleasant amble through lush greenery and vineyards, with remarkable views of the island and over the Bay of Naples to Capri and Procida along the way. You can reward yourself at the top with a drink and snack at the bar/restaurant. A satisfying **coastal walk** takes you east from Sant'Angelo for about 3km (2 miles) to Maronti beach, passing Fumarole beach on the way, so you can combine the easy trek with some swimming and time on the beach. A good source of other walking routes on the island is at www.ischiareview.com.

Spas & Thermo-Mineral Treatments

Ischia's *terme,* or thermal baths, have been popular since ancient Greeks sat in the island's natural hot springs to soak their weary bones. Elaborate thermal parks are top among the island's many attractions. Some are attached to hotels and a perk for guests only, and others are fun zones where the public happily spends the entire day soaking, swimming, dining, drinking, and, at some, undergoing massages, mud baths, and other spa treatments. Many have beaches, and most set their pools within verdant gardens. Pools are fed by thermal springs that ensure water temperatures that range from refreshing to downright hot and are embellished with waterfalls, underwater jets, whirlpools, and some jazzy features like submerged lounge chairs in which, like a hedonistic Roman emperor or empress, you can recline in warn water as you're massaged with soothing jets.

Many patrons get their money's worth and idle away the entire day. Novel as the experience is, you can go limp as a limpet after soaking in all that warm water after a couple of hours. Most facilities offer slightly lower rates after mid-afternoon, so you can save some euros and opt for a late entrance and a sunset soak.

Parco Termale Castiglione ★★ SPA/THERMAL BATH   Low-key might not be quite the right word for a place that splashes out with ten pools, but they're tucked into delightful, tastefully designed seaside terraces laced with all sorts of quiet nooks and crannies. If the pool temperatures get to be a bit too relaxing—they range from 82° to 104°F (28° to 40°C)—a stone jetty is well poised for a dip in the sea. The absence of a beach, and some serious mud and thermal treatments, makes the park more popular with a sedate crowd than it is with families, so screaming kids aren't likely to disturb the peace.

Shore road, btw. Ischia Porto and Casamicciola. www.termecastiglione.it. © **081-982551.** Admission 27€ a day, 23€ after 1pm, 9€ children 2–12; 2€ more in Aug. Apr–Oct 9am–7pm.

Parco Termale Giardini Poseidon ★ SPA/THERMAL BATH   Everything about Ischia's largest spa is over the top, with 22 pools, a large private beach, acres of tropical gardens, and several restaurants. The kitsch quotient runs high, with toga-bedecked statues and colorful mosaics. It's hard not to feel like a figure of ancient legend in the complex's nicest feature, an eons-old

Parco Termale Negombo.

natural thermal cave etched out of a cliff. It's a toss-up who enjoys these elaborate surroundings more, Germans and their kinder or Italian families, so be prepared for a crowd.

Via Giovanni Mazzella, Citara Beach, near Forio. www.giardiniposeidon.it. © **081-908-7111.** Admission 32€ a day, 27€ after 1pm, 16€ children 4–11; 2€ more in Aug. Apr–Oct, daily 9am–7pm.

Parco Termale Negombo ★★★ SPA/THERMAL BATH   If you have time and/or inclination to visit only one thermal establishment on Ischia, make it this delightful spot on the island's most picturesque cove, San Montano. Gorgeous gardens, laid out by botanist Duke Luigi Camerini, surround 12 pools and facilities that include saunas, steam rooms, and massage cabins. While waterfalls and luxuriant plantings provide a transporting getaway atmosphere, just as alluring is the beach of fine sand out front. You could happily spend a day traipsing back and forth between the warm pools and the refreshing sea, with some nap time in the shade next to one the garden's beautiful, albeit ersatz, waterfalls.

San Montano beach, on the promontory of Monte Vico near Lacco Ameno. www. negombo.it. © **081-986152.** Admission 32€, 26€ after 1:30pm, 22€ after 3:30pm, children less than 4½ ft. and more than 3¼ ft. tall, 22€, 20€ after 12:30pm, 18€ after 3pm. Late Apr–mid-Oct, daily 8:30am–7pm.

Where to Stay
EXPENSIVE
Hotel Regina Isabella ★★   Film producer and publishing magnate Angelo Rizzoli created this glamorous getaway in the 1950s, and plenty of

Fruit of the Vine

The Romans called Ischia "Enaria," or "Land of Wine," and the island still does a good job of living up to the reputation. The slopes of Monte Epomeo, with their fertile volcanic soil and gentle sea breezes, have been especially favorable to growing grapes. Ischia whites and reds are similarly respectable. White grapes are Biancolella and Forastera, both yielding straw-colored, slightly floral wines. Red grapes are Guarnaccia and Piedirosso ("Red Foot," often called Per' e Palumm, "Pigeon's Foot"), and both produce wines that are ruby red and floral. Per' e Palumm Passito is a dark-red dessert wine. You'll encounter these wines in restaurants all over Ischia, and drinking them close to the source is one of the island's great pleasures.

dolce vita pampering still shines through. Former guests Elizabeth Taylor and Richard Burton may as well be sitting next to you in the chic retro bar and palatial lounges or bobbing around the private cove in one of the hotel's trade-mark floating chairs. In the sumptuous guest rooms, a tasteful smattering of antiques sit on hand-painted ceramic floors and terraces overlook the sea and lush gardens. Thermal springs heat the swimming pools and supply the mud for all sorts of soothing treatments at the island's classiest spa.

Piazza Santa Restituta 1, Lacco Ameno. www.reginaisabella.it. ℓ **081-994322.** 126 units. 340€–460€ double. Rates include buffet breakfast. Free parking. Closed Nov–Mar, but open 1 week over the New Year. **Amenities:** 2 restaurants; 2 bars; babysitting; concierge; 3 pools; room service; spa; tennis courts; Wi-Fi (free).

Mezzatorre Resort & Spa ★★★   A former fortress at the end of a rocky promontory provides a sense of privileged escape. You will be excused for feeling like a feudal lord or lady if you choose to survey the sea and the 17 acres of pine-scented gardens from one of the beautifully appointed rooms in the dark-red, 15th-century watchtower. All of the airy, view-filled accommodations are spectacular, including the spacious quarters in the low, modern annexes scattered among the gardens, and all are stylishly done in bright Mediterranean color schemes and a chic mix of antiques and contemporary pieces. Thermal pools tucked onto seaside terraces, a hot springs and spa, and private beach ensure that you can partake of a wellness regimen without ever leaving the property.

Via Mezzatorre, 80075 Forio. www.mezzatorre.it. ℓ **081-986111.** 60 units. 440€–580€ double. Rates include buffet breakfast. Free parking. Closed Nov–Apr. **Amenities:** 2 restaurants; bar; babysitting; concierge; health club; 3 pools; room service; spa; outdoor tennis courts; Wi-Fi (free).

MODERATE

Park Hotel Miramare ★★   Sant'Angelo is the prettiest village on the island, and the picturesque setting for what must be Ischia's most attractive and distinctive inn, run by the same family since 1923 and hosting guests who come year after year. The old-fashioned rooms are a delight, tastefully done with wrought-iron bedsteads, bright fabrics, and gleaming tile floors, and each has a sea-facing terrace. Part of the private beach is reserved for nudists, and guests have use of the **Aphrodite-Apollon** thermal park, with 12 pools.

Via Comandante Magdalena 29, Sant'Angelo. www.hotelmiramare.it. © **081-999219.** 50 units. 250€–420€ double. Rates include buffet breakfast. Closed mid-Nov to early Apr. **Amenities:** 2 restaurants; bar; babysitting; children's program; concierge; spa; beach; access to attached thermal park; Wi-Fi (free).

INEXPENSIVE

Albergo Il Monastero ★★ The courtyards, labyrinth of stone-walled, arched passageways, and arbor-shaded seaside terraces of this former monastery are enticing in themselves, all the more so since the old premises are set within Ischia's spectacular Aragonese Castle (p. 193). Whitewashed guest rooms carved out of the former monks' cells are spacious and soberly stylish, with handsome dark furnishings and knockout sea views from most. A huge panoramic terrace atop the castle walls is the setting for breakfast and delicious dinners, made in part with produce from the hotel's garden. The hotel is only accessible by foot, and accommodations are reached by what can seem like endless staircases.

Castello Aragonese. www.albergomonastero.it. © **081-992435.** 20 units. 120€–160€ double. Closed Nov–Mar. **Amenities:** Restaurant; Wi-Fi (free).

Hotel della Baia ★ At this delightful little getaway tucked onto the myrtle-clad hillside above San Montano Bay, a bar and lounge is shaded by lime trees, and all the simple but chic rooms open to bougainvillea-filled terraces. Just down the road are two of the island's best places to swim and lounge, a sandy beach in a beautiful cove, and Negombo, the nicest of Ischia's thermal parks (see above).

San Montano beach, on the promontory of Monte Vico near Lacco Ameno. www. negombo.it. © **081-986150.** 16 units. 100€–120€ double. **Amenities:** Bar; pool; beach; Wi-Fi (free).

Hotel Villa Melodie ★ Umbrella pines shade the large swimming pool and terrace to create quite a splashy welcome, and everything about this pleasant little villa seems geared to warm hospitality. For some extra soothing, an indoor thermal pool is tucked into a stone grotto. Bright, appealing, whitewashed rooms have glistening tile floors, terraces, and a view toward the sea or over luxuriant greenery. The beach is an easy walk away, as are the shops and restaurants of busy Forio.

Via Capizzo 6, Forio. www.melodie.it. © **081-998364.** 33 units. 100€–120€ double. Rates include buffet breakfast. Closed mid-Oct to mid-Apr. **Amenities:** Restaurant; bar; concierge; pool; Wi-Fi (free).

Where to Eat
EXPENSIVE
Umberto a Mare ★★ CAMPANIAN/SEAFOOD The bright, airy dining room with a wave-splashed terrace tucked into the sea wall above the Bay

of Citara is as much a landmark as the adjacent Santuario del Soccorso. The currently presiding Umberto is the grandson of the founder, and he continues to serve the traditional seafood preparations that are mainstays of a leisurely lunch or romantic evening. *Tartare di palamito al profumo d'arancia* (tartar of local fish with citrus) or any of the other marinated raw fish dishes are gourmet odes to freshness, while *paccheri dolcemare*, pasta with squid, sultanas, pine nuts, and a touch of cinnamon, is an exotic prelude to the catch of the day, grilled or served *all'acqua pazza* (in a light herb broth).

Via Soccorso 2, Forio. www.umbertoamare.it. © **081-997171.** Main courses 25€–36€. Daily 12:30–3pm and 7–11:30pm. Closed Nov 5–Dec 28 and Jan 7–late Mar.

MODERATE

Trattoria il Focolare ★★★ CAMPANIAN   Head inland from Casamicciola and you'll soon find yourself among vineyards and forests. The cuisine changes, too, from surf to turf, from seafood to hearty meat- and game-based mountain dishes like these, served in a stone-vaulted room and on a timbered Alpine-style porch. You can take a cholesterol-inducing plunge by beginning with *tagliatelle al ragu di cinghiale* (pasta with wild boar ragout), or maybe ease into a meat fest with ravioli stuffed with endive. Follow-ups that bring carnivores from all over Ischia are *tagliata* (steak) and *coniglio all'Ischitana* (a local rabbit dish with tomatoes, garlic, and herbs). Desserts take their inspiration from Naples and include a delicious *pastiera* (pie filled with ricotta and orange peels).

Via Cretajo al Crocefisso 3, Barano d'Ischia. www.trattoriailfocolare.it. © **081-902944.** Main courses 8€–25€. Daily 7:30–11:30pm; Fri–Sun 12:30–3pm and 7:30–11:30pm. Closed Wed Nov–May.

INEXPENSIVE

Da Ciccio ★★ SEAFOOD   A seat on the little terrace in front of a half-a-century-old island favorite comes with killer views of the Aragonese Castle (p. 193). That's about as showy as it gets at this little hole in the wall, where Ciccio and his son Bruno focus on fresh seafood in some memorably delicious preparations: Thick mussel soup is steeped with mountain herbs and topped with fried bread; squid is stuffed with bread crumbs, raisins, and chopped fish; and linguine is laden with clams.

Via Luigi Mazzella 32, Ischia Ponte. © **081-991686.** Main courses 10€–15€. Wed–Mon noon–2.30pm and 7–11pm.

La Brocca ★★ SEAFOOD   Lacco Ameno might be the toniest town on the island, but simple old-time ways still hold sway at this no-frills spot facing the sea and Il Fungo. The friendly family could be the town's goodwill ambassadors as they rush between the dining room and terrace to serve straightforward and delicious preparations of fresh-off-the-boat seafood. Any of the pastas *alla pescatora* (with seafood), washed down with a chilled carafe of the house white, deliver a memorable feast.

Via Roma 28, Lacco Ameno. © **081-900051.** Main courses 8€–15€. Daily noon–2.30pm and 7–11pm.

Ischia After Dark

The island has a fairly lively cultural scene, with a summertime musical season at **La Mortella** (www.lamortella.it; ✆ 081-986220), the seat of the William Walton Foundation. The **Ischia Film Festival** (www.ischiafilmfestival.it) takes place in early July each year, with most screenings in the Castello Aragonese in Ischia Ponte. The island's most colorful event is the **Festival of Sant'Anna** (patron of pregnant women) on July 26, celebrated with fireworks and a procession of torch-lit boats around the Castello Aragonese.

Harbor-side cafes around the island are prime perches for summertime nightlife. Some standouts are **Da Lilly,** a shack on the rocks, with a simple terrace overlooking the **Spiaggia dei Pescatori** (p. 197) in Ischia Ponte, and **La Tavernetta del Pirata** (✆ 081-999251), overlooking the little harbor at Sant'Angelo. At **Bar Franco,** Via Roma 94, Lacco Ameno (✆ 081-980880), you can sit at the pleasant outdoor terrace facing the beach and supplement your drink with a dish of the excellent house-made ice cream. **De Maio,** Piazza Antica Reggia 9, Ischia Porto (✆ 081-991870), serves the best ice cream on the island; with 80 years of experience, the shop makes wonderful creamy flavors. **Da Ciccio,** a few doors away at Via Porto 1, is also excellent and creative. The two are beacons to summer-evening crowds, who include a stop at either or both in their promenades around the picturesque town.

PROCIDA ★★

32km (20 miles) NW of Naples; 12km (8 miles) W of Pozzuoli; 8km (5 miles) W of Ischia

Just looking at the facts, the smallest island in the Bay of Naples seems like it might be a bit of a pass-by. Procida happens to be the most crowded island in

A bird's-eye view of Procida.

Europe, or almost anywhere, with 10,000 islanders squeezing onto a hunk of rock of a little more than 3 sq km (2 sq miles). Even Neapolitans complain about the traffic on the island's one main road—justifiably, though most of the vehicles involved are motor scooters. But approach on a boat from Pozzuoli on the mainland just 12km (8 miles) across the water or another port in the Bay of Naples, and the little charmer will captivate you even before you step ashore. Tall stacks of pastel-colored houses seem to rise right out of the sparkling blue sea, and above them are crumbing, ruined watchtowers, craggy cliffs, and green hillsides. Procida turns even the most reluctant photographers into obsessive shutterbugs, and painters have flocked to the island for centuries. The island is small enough that you won't feel cheated if you have only a couple of days for a visit. Even a brief stop will give you enough time to wander down shady lanes past sun-bleached houses and tiny garden plots, take in the few sights, soak in the fishing-harbor ambience, and lie on one of the black-lava beaches.

Essentials

GETTING THERE & AROUND Medmar (www.medmargroup.it; © 081-333-4411); **Caremar** (www.caremar.it; © 199-116655), and **SNAV** (www.snav.it; © 081-428-5555 or 081-428-5500) offer ferry and hydrofoil service from Napoli, Pozzuoli, and Ischia.

Given Procida's diminutive size, it's easy to see the island **on foot.** Four **public bus** lines run by **SEPSA** (© 081-542-9965), all starting from Marina Grande; tickets are 1€ per ride. **Taxis** meet the ferries, or you can call one for pickup (© 081-896-8785). You can also get around the island by boat, or at least do a circuit to take a look at the seaside sights. You can rent a boat at any of the three harbors on the island, Marina Grande, Marina della Corricella, and Marina di Chiaiolella. Expect to spend about 25€ for a 2-hour trip with a boat and skipper.

VISITOR INFORMATION The tourist office is at Via Marina Grande near the ferry dock (www.infoischiaprocida.it; © 081-810-1968). It is open May to September, Monday to Saturday from 9am to 1pm and 3 to 7pm; the rest of the year it's only open mornings. The travel agency **Graziella,** Via Roma 117 (www.isoladiprocida.it; © 081-896-9594) is another good resource for help with hotel reservations and boat rentals.

Exploring Procida

The island is really just one sprawling village, a colorful cluster of houses that climbs and falls over volcanic outcroppings. Rather surprisingly, given the almost Manhattan-like density of the place, tucked in among the tall, pastel-hued houses and narrow streets are citrus groves, gardens, and the occasional vineyard. The fortified old town, Terra Murata, clings to a bluff atop cliff-like slopes at the western end of the island; the rest of Procida hugs the shoreline, where the three picturesquely fading port towns—Marina Grande, Corricella, and Chiaiolella—cluster around their chaotic, ramshackle quays. The only real way to see the island is on foot, and the best experience you can have is simply to wander from one town into the next. Amid the jumble of peeling facades and vine-covered garden walls you'll never forget you're on an island. You'll often catch some glimpses of the blue sea between the houses, and occasionally get a peek at the profile of Ischia in one direction and the slope of Vesuvius in the other. It's only about 3km (1¾ miles) from one end of the island to the other, an easy walk of an hour or so, though one that might require some artful scooter dodging.

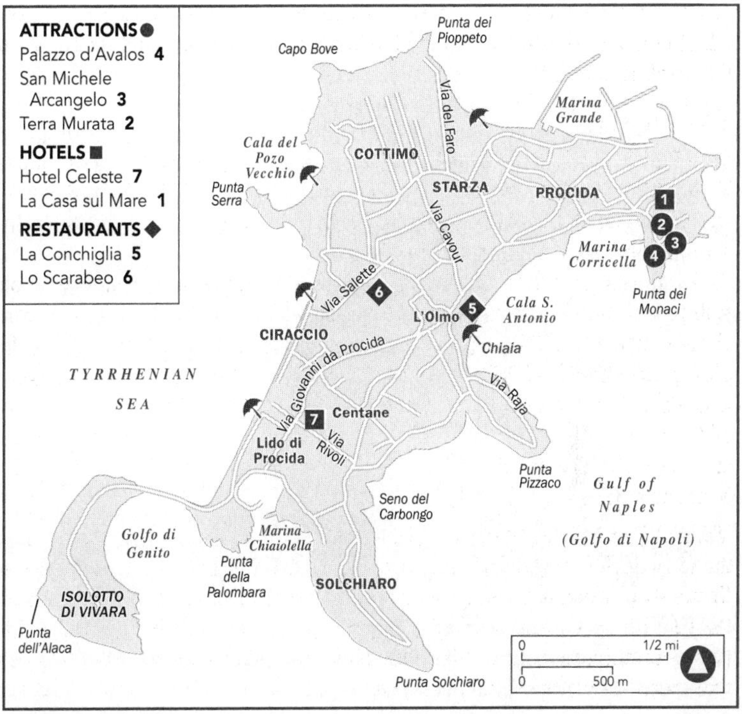
ATTRACTIONS ●
Palazzo d'Avalos 4
San Michele Arcangelo 3
Terra Murata 2
HOTELS ■
Hotel Celeste 7
La Casa sul Mare 1
RESTAURANTS ◆
La Conchiglia 5
Lo Scarabeo 6
Punta dei Pioppeto
Capo Bove
Via del Faro
Marina Grande
Cala del Pozo Vecchio
COTTIMO
Punta Serra
STARZA
PROCIDA
Via Cavour
Marina Corricella
Via Salette
Punta dei Monaci
L'Olmo
Cala S. Antonio
CIRACCIO
Via Giovanni da Procida
Chiaia
TYRRHENIAN SEA
Via Raja
Centane
Via Rivoli
Lido di Procida
Punta Pizzaco
Gulf of Naples
(Golfo di Napoli)
Seno del Carbongo
Golfo di Genito
Marina Chiaiolella
Punta della Palombara
SOLCHIARO
ISOLOTTO DI VIVARA
Punta dell'Alaca
Punta Solchiaro
0
1/2 mi
0
500 m

MARINA GRANDE

Locals call the main port Marina di Sancio Cattolico, dialect for "safe harbor." From all the old wheezes fussing around their bobbing boats you may rightfully assume that fishing is still the island's mainstay. Streets that end in staircases lead from the ramshackle quayside to **Piazza dei Martiri,** the main square, then continue up to **Terra Murata,** the crumbling old town fortified by 16th-century walls. The gloomy old Castello, also known as Palazzo Reale, is officially Palazzo d'Avalos, for the 17th-century cardinal who once lived in the now-abandoned shell. Its melancholy appearance stems in part from its later use as a prison, where inmates enjoyed bird's-eye views of the island and bay that hundreds of artists, with whom the island is especially popular, have worked so hard to capture.

San Michele Arcangelo ★★ CHURCH Benedictine monks wisely built their abbey on a cliff 90m (280 ft.) above the sea to keep out of the way of harm as inflicted by North African pirates who raided the coast with alarming frequency and efficiency. Those islanders who could afford to do so followed suit and settled into *palazzi* that are now falling into melancholic, overgrown ruins. As a little extra reassurance, the monks also built a grand church teetering on the cliff face to honor the island's patron, San Michele (St. Michael). The saint, a handy fellow to have around on any occasion, is the protector of mariners as well as policemen, firemen, and soldiers. He allegedly saved the island during a 1535 pirate raid when he appeared above the masts of the ships of the invaders and sent them scurrying. One crew didn't even have time to weigh the anchor that's displayed near two paintings depicting the miraculous scene. One, below a beautifully coffered ceiling, is by Luca Giordano, a 17th-century Neapolitan master also known as *Luca fa presto*, or "Luca paints quickly," for his speedy craftsmanship and ability to master almost any style. He does justice to the scene with geographic accuracy, showing the profile of nearby Ischia in the background.

Via Canalone 1. © **081-896-7612.** Admission 2€. Daily 9:45am–12:45pm and 3:30–6pm.

MARINA DELLA CORRICELLA ★★

The charms of the colorful panache of pastel houses and sparkling blue waters of the small port are much appreciated, even by those who have never set foot on Procida. Moviegoers were treated to sweeping views of the pretty cove, the atmospheric quay, and jumble of stone houses that are stacked along narrow staircase streets in the films *Il Postino* and *The Talented Mr. Ripley.*

MARINA DI CHIAIOLELLA ★★

Procida comes to an end at this crescent-shaped, marina-filled harbor that was once the crater of one of four now-submerged volcanoes whose eruptions over the ages formed little Procida. Floating in the sparkling waters is tiny, half-moon–shaped **Vivara,** what's left of the rim of an ancient volcano. The islet is a wildlife reserve, connected to Procida by a 362m (1,188-ft.) bridge.

Beautiful Procida.

Beaches

The longest and often most crowded beach on the island is the one at **Chiaiolella,** with stretches of black sand backed by open-air bars. **Chiaia,** west of Corricella, is at the bottom of a cliff, reached by steep steps from the road above or by boat from Corricella. Views across the shallow bay all the way to hilltop Terra Murata are especially pleasant when floating on your back in the calm, shallow water.

Where to Stay & Eat

Hotel Celeste ★★ Trim, white, and pastel-hued rooms are airy and refreshing, and they all open to a terrace next to a fragrant orange grove or a breezy veranda. A stay in this trim little oasis, tucked in amid the crumbling facades and laundry-strung lanes behind the main port, plunges you right into the rhythms and charms of island life. In August, Signora Concetta requires that her guests take lunch or dinner, for an extra 20€ a head, but that's not such a bad idea at any time.

Via Rivoli 6, Marina Grande. www.hotelceleste.it. ✆ **081-896-7488.** 34 units. 70€–90€ double. Rates include buffet breakfast. Closed Oct–Mar. **Amenities:** Restaurant; bar; bike rental; Wi-Fi (free).

La Casa sul Mare ★★ Marina della Corricella looks especially picturesque from these elegant, tile-floored guest rooms of a traditional, 18th-century island home, perched just high enough up to provide stunning bird's-eye views across the length of the island. Pleasant guest quarters are some of the nicest on the island, with handsome iron bedsteads and some lovely old pieces; all open to sea-facing terraces. Breakfast is served in a lovely, shaded garden, and a shuttle will take you to the beach at Chiaia, though it's only short walk away.

Salita Castello 13, Corricella. www.lacasasulmare.it. ✆ **081-896-8799.** 10 units. 170€ double. Rate includes buffet breakfast. **Amenities:** Bar; bike rental; concierge; Wi-Fi (free).

La Conchiglia ★★ SEAFOOD Views from this beachside perch outside Corricella are worth the effort to get here, by boat (free, but runs every 2 hours) from Corricella or a bit of a climb down and back up steep steps from the road. Once you've settled onto the terrace, soak in the views of Corricella gleaming in pastel hues across the water and enjoy a long, lazy meal. Menus change with the catch, but *spiedini di mazzancolle* (prawn skewers) are usually on offer, and pastas are reliably brimming with *aragosta* (local lobster) and *vongole* (clams).

Via Pizzaco, Chiaia, Corricella. ✆ **081-896-7602.** Main courses 12€–23€. Apr and mid-Sept to Oct daily 12:30–3pm; May to mid-Sept daily 12:30–3pm and 7:30–11pm. Closed Nov–Mar.

Lo Scarabeo ★ ISCHITANO You can't help but to think of lemons in this charmer tucked away on old lanes, where lemons will be knocking you in the forehead as you take a seat in the shady arbor. There's only one way to begin a meal here, and that's with the refreshing *insalata di limoni*, a Procida specialty where chunks of local lemons are mixed with fresh mint and chili, then dressed with olive oil. Some delicious homemade pastas, groaning with seafood or fresh island vegetables, accompany the house specialty, *totani ripieni* (stuffed squid).

Via Salette 10, Marina Grande. ✆ **081-896-9918.** Main courses 10€–18€. Dec–Easter Sat–Sun 1–3pm and 7:30–11pm; after Easter–Oct Tues–Sun 1pm and 7:30–11pm. Closed Nov–Dec 20.

SALERNO WITH PAESTUM, PADULA & THE CILENTO

While it might seem as if it would be hard to top the Amalfi, by many accounts the most beautiful stretch of coastline in Europe, the lands to the south make a valiant effort. The ruins at Paestum, the sandy and, in places, empty beaches of the Cilento, and the wild, mountainous interiors are certainly spectacular in their own right. These sights of the southern stretches of Campania are less polished and sophisticated than the towns along the Amalfi Coast and, for better or worse, they lack the urban buzz of Naples. But travelers who venture into them will enjoy the pleasure of discovering a stretch of Italy that's well off the beaten tourist track.

Salerno is the jumping-off point into the region. While the busy port city might come in handy for an overnight between train or bus connections, after a quick look around, jump you should. Nearby are the spectacular ruins at Paestum, and beyond them the Cilento, where most of the mountainous terrain and cove-etched seacoast is protected as a national park. The coast here is the lure—especially for Italian families in August—but venture inland on twisting roads to explore one of Italy's wildest, most remote regions with mountaintop villages and a remarkable monastery, the Certosa di San Lorenzo, tucked into the hillside.

SALERNO ★

55km (34 miles) SE of Naples

When it comes to scenery, this modern, gritty port city pales in comparison to its picturesque neighbors along the Amalfi Coast, and when it comes to monuments and street life, it doesn't hold a candle to boisterous, theatrical Naples just to the north. Even so, busy, sunny Salerno has some charms of its own and a heady

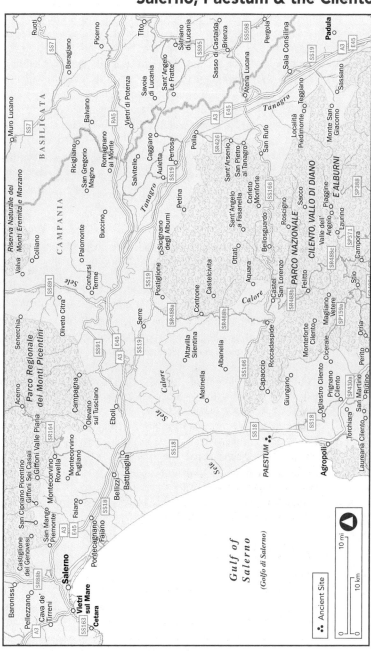

history, having been a colony for Etruscans, Greeks, and Romans, and, from the 11th century, a capital for the Normans, then powerful Italian Sanseverino lords. Salerno eventually lost its prominence to Naples, and the city got the bad end of the deal again in 1943, when the Allies landed nearby and began their German-routing march through Italy. Salerno very briefly became the capital of liberated Italy, but fighting and bombing left the city in ruins. Heavy-handed post-war rebuilding accounts for the fairly mundane appearance of modern Salerno, though the waterfront and historic center deliver all the beauty and charm you've come to expect from this part of the world.

You'll probably just pass through Salerno. It's a convenient gateway to towns along the eastern end of the Amalfi Coast, and for the remarkable Greek ruins at Paestum and the beautiful Cilento region just to the south. Take time out, though, for a walk through the *centro storico* and a look at magnificent Duomo.

Essentials

GETTING THERE   Salerno lies on the main north–south rail corridor so is well served by **trains,** with frequent connections with other Italian and European cities from its train station (*stazione*) on Piazza Vittorio Veneto. As the end of the line for Italy's high-speed rail network, Salerno is less than 15 minutes from Naples. This makes it a convenient gateway to the eastern end of the Amalfi Coast, with frequent bus service to and from towns between Salerno and Amalfi—reaching them through Salerno rather than Sorrento can save quite a bit of bus travel. Trains, high-speed and otherwise, leave Naples every 10 to 30 minutes for the trip to Salerno. Contact **Trenitalia** (www.trenitalia.it; ℭ 892021 in Italy) for more information.

Ferry travel is a good option in the summer, when the SS 163, the Amalfi Drive, can be jammed. Salerno is a major sea terminal, and ferries arrive here from other ports in the Mediterranean. Local ferries connect Salerno to nearby harbors: **Alicost** (www.alicost.it; ℭ 089-234892) and **Alilauro** (www.alilauro. it; ℭ 081-497-2238) with Capri, Amalfi, Positano, and Ischia; **Travelmar** (www.travelmar.it; ℭ 081-704-1911) with Positano, Amalfi, Minori, and Maiori; and **Cooperativa Sant'Andrea** (www.coopsantandrea.it; ℭ 089-873190) with Amalfi, Capri, Minori, and Sorrento.

Salerno is also well connected by **SITA** (www.sitabus.it; ℭ 089-405145), with frequent **bus service** between the city and Naples, as well as to towns on the Amalfi Coast and the Sorrento Peninsula. For Ravello and towns west of Amalfi, you will change in Amalfi. **CSTP** (www.cstp.it; ℭ 089-252228 or 800-016659 toll-free in Italy) serves Salerno, Pompeii, Paestum, and the Cilento. The **bus terminal** is in Piazza della Concordia, near the train station.

By **car** from Naples and points south, Salerno is easy to reach on autostrada A3; take the exit marked SALERNO and follow signs for the city center. Once there, follow signs for **public parking;** the town center is pedestrian only.

Salerno

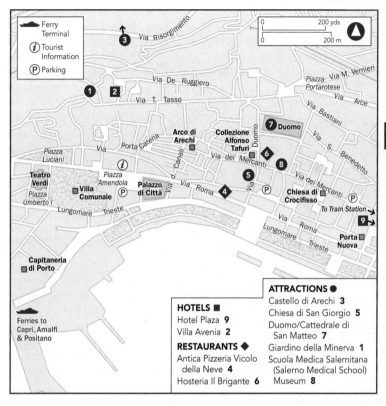

Map legend and labels:

Ferry Terminal
(i) Tourist Information
(P) Parking

0 – 200 yds
0 – 200 m

Via Risorgimento
Via De Ruggiero
Via T. Tasso
Piazza Portarotese
Via M. Vernieri
Via Arce
Via Bastiani
Piazza Luciani
Via Porta Catena
Arco di Arechi
Collezione Alfonso Tafuri
Duomo
Via S. Benedetto
Teatro Verdi
Piazza Amendola
Via d. Canali
Via dei Mercanti
Piazza Umberto I
Villa Comunale
Palazzo di Città
Via Roma
Chiesa di Crocifisso
Via dei Mercanti
To Train Station
Lungomare Trieste
Via Roma
Lungomare Trieste
Porta Nuova
Capitaneria di Porto
Ferries to Capri, Amalfi & Positano

ATTRACTIONS ●
Castello di Arechi **3**
Chiesa di San Giorgio **5**
Duomo/Cattedrale di San Matteo **7**
Giardino della Minerva **1**
Scuola Medica Salernitana (Salerno Medical School) Museum **8**

HOTELS ■
Hotel Plaza **9**
Villa Avenia **2**

RESTAURANTS ◆
Antica Pizzeria Vicolo della Neve **4**
Hosteria Il Brigante **6**

VISITOR INFORMATION The regional tourist office is at Via Velia 15, 84100 Salerno (www.eptsalerno.it; ⓒ **089-230401**). You can also get some good information online at www.turismoinsalerno.it.

Exploring Salerno

Salerno looks its best along the palm-tree shaded **Lungomare Trieste,** a lovely seafront promenade where you can turn your back on the modern sprawl behind you and forget all about 21st-century concerns. The old-world charm extends into the pleasant and orderly gardens of the **Villa Comunale** (Piazza Amendola) and adjacent, 1872 **Teatro Verdi** (Piazza Luciani; www. teatroverdisalerno.it; ⓒ **089-662141**). A strikingly contemporary waterfront addition, a free-form ferry terminal by internationally renowned architect Zaha Hadid, will also be a stunner when completed.

Allied bombers flattened much of Salerno during World War II to retake Italy from the Germans, though much of the medieval core remains intact behind the waterfront. The historic district is off limits to cars and stretches

Salerno cityscape.

from the train station, on **Piazza Vittorio Veneto,** to Piazza Amendola, at the western edge of the medieval center. The center of the old city is the charming **Piazza Sedile del Campo,** the medieval market square, where the little **Fontana dei Delfini (Fountain of the Dolphins)** gurgles away. Some of Salerno's oldest churches line the lanes just off the lively square—**Sant' Andrea de Lama,** with a 12th-century bell tower, is on Via Roteprandi, and just beyond is 10th-century **Sant'Alfonso.** From Piazza Sedile del Campo, **Via dei Mercanti,** Salerno's main shopping street since medieval times, leads through the old center.

Castello di Arechi ★★ LANDMARK Residents of Salerno are used to casting an eye up toward this formidable, looming presence, a reassuring landmark on the heights 300m (990 ft.) above the old city since 800. That's when Duke Arechi II, part of the Germanic dynasty that ruled southern Italy until the 11th century, embellished an earlier Byzantine fortification. (The duke was apparently a bit of a pro at appropriating old structures for his own use—he also converted a Roman bathhouse and early Christian mausoleum in the town below into a palace; it's now the **Palatine San Pietro a Corte** church on Vicolo Adalberga, with some touchingly primitive 11th-century frescoes.) Subsequent rulers have made their own additions to the extensive fortifications. You'll appreciate the strategic position as you approach the thick walls rising from the mountaintop on the 45-minute uphill trek from the Duomo, though the less sporting trip up on the number 9 bus is similarly rousing. The partially restored ruins are now used for special exhibitions and are occasionally the setting for concerts, though the eagle's-eye views across Salerno and far out to sea are reason enough to make the ascent.

Via Benedetto Croce. © **089-496-4015.** Free admission. Daily 9am–1 hr. before sunset (hrs. vary; check with tourist office).

Chiesa di San Giorgio ★ CHURCH Salerno's most beautiful baroque church is a monument to the Solimenas, father and son who made their names in Naples. The younger Francesco (1657–1747) soon outshone his father, Angelo, with sumptuous canvases full of light and shadows and dramatically poised figures in flowing robes. Francesco's lavish style, a trademark of Neapolitan baroque painting, comes to the fore in the large fresco of St. Michael over the fourth altar on the right. Some of the lovely architectural elements, including a peaceful atrium at the entrance, seem refreshingly restrained by comparison.

Via Duomo 19. © **089-228918.** Free admission. Daily 9:30am–12:30pm.

Duomo/Cattedrale di San Matteo ★★ CHURCH The bell tower of Salerno's beautiful cathedral rises high above the old city, a powerful presence of vaulted arcades and mullioned windows. Below is a stage set of an entrance: A sweeping staircase leads to an atrium, surrounded by a portico with 28 arches supported by columns salvaged from the Roman city, and a set of massive bronze doors cast in Constantinople in 1099. If all this grandeur doesn't instill good behavior in the faithful, the large marble pulpit might. It's decorated with mosaics showing a snake biting a sinner in the breast, as an eagle digs his talons into the unfortunate fellow's head for good measure.

The Castello di Arechi.

Actually, by tradition Salerno is tolerant of those who fall by the wayside. The Duomo is dedicated St. Matthew the Evangelist, the apostle who once worked as a tax collector, a less than honorable profession in the 1st century. When Christ was criticized for joining Matthew and his coworkers in a meal, he rejoined "I did not come to call the righteous, but sinners to repentance." Matthew, of course, did repent, and became a zealous Christian and author of the first gospels. His remains are stashed in the vaulted crypt beneath colorful frescoes that portray stories from the Gospel of St. Matthew, including touching scenes of Christ praying in the wilderness as the devil shows up to tempt him. The church is also the final resting place of Gregory VII, an 11th-century pope who spent much of his highly effective but embattled papacy enforcing such unpopular doctrines as chastity and poverty. Gregory was eventually forced to flee from Rome to Salerno, where he died in 1085. His wax effigy is creepily encased behind glass among frescoes and mosaics in the **Cappella delle Crociate** (**Chapel of the Crusades**), where Crusaders once had their weapons blessed before sailing for the Holy Land.

Piazza Alfano I. ℂ **089-231387.** Free admission. Daily 7:30am–noon and 4–7pm.

Giardino della Minerva ★ PARK/GARDEN   The Giardino dei Semplici (Garden of Simples) that physician/instructor Matteo Silvatico of Salerno's acclaimed medieval medical school created behind his house in the 13th century is Europe's first known botanic garden. Silvatico was widely known for his expertise in healing plants, the only known medical arsenal against disease at the time. "Simples" refers to a few plants, noted by plaques in the garden, which were the cornerstones of most remedies. Silvatico was also a clever engineer, and the gardens are set out in multilevel terraces watered by a network of channels fed by a cistern the top. A 17th-century addition is a staircase that mounts the city walls, from which you can enjoy a pleasing view over the old town and the harbor.

Via Ferrante Sanseverino 1. www.giardinodellaminerva.it. ℂ **089-252423.** Admission 2€. Tues–Sun 10am–1pm and 5pm–sunset.

Scuola Medica Salernitana (Salerno Medical School) Museum ★ MUSEUM   The world's first medical school was founded in Salerno in the 9th century and flourished throughout the Middle Ages. Practitioners and instructors had access to a vast library of texts from ancient Greek and Arabic physicians, and Salerno became known as the Town of Hippocrates in honor of the great 4th- to 5th-century B.C. man of medicine who established a clinic and school on the Greek island of Kos. Travelers came to Salerno from all over Europe looking for cures and to learn at the feet of the famous instructors. Among the lecturers and practitioners was the first renowned female physician, 12th-century Trota of Salerno, whose gynecological texts circulated widely and were the bible for treating women for many centuries. A small collection in the former St. Gregorio Church shows off some historical documents and terrifying early medieval instruments that will make you feel fortunate to be alive now rather in the Middle Ages.

Via dei Mercanti. ℂ **089-257-6126.** Free admission. Mon–Sat 9am–1pm and 4–7pm and Sun 9am–1pm.

Where to Stay & Eat

Salerno hotels have a rough time of it, with so much competition just up the Amalfi Coast. Plus, the town is definitely a pass through, a transit point between the picturesque coastal towns to the west and the ruins of Paestum and the beaches and wilds of the Cilento to the south. Even so, if you're here for part of a day or a night, you'll find some nice places to sleep and dine in the historic center, within easy reach of the train station.

Salerno's Welcome Invasion

Salerno is now a prime spot on a beach-goer's map for its strategic location between two of Italy's most popular seaside getaways, the Amalfi Coast to the west and the Cilento coast to the south. But in September 1943, Salerno was in the crosshairs of Allied military commanders who were planning Operation Avalanche, the invasion of Italy. By the morning of September 9, more than 450 Allied warships had assembled off the coast of Salerno and troops began coming ashore on beaches south of the city, around Paestum. Between that morning and the end of the month, 190,000 troops, 30,000 vehicles, and 120,000 tons of supplies came ashore at Salerno. More American troops were on European soil than at any time since 1918. Operation Avalanche came to an end when the Allies took Naples on October 1, 1943. American casualties numbered 12,500 (2,000 killed, 7,000 wounded, and 3,500 missing). After a bitter winter of intense fighting, the Allies broke through German lines and entered Rome on June 5, 1944.

Hotel Plaza ★   Location is what this serviceable stop just across from the train station is all about. Public lounges and the smallish guest rooms could use some freshening, but they're spotless and kept in tip-top shape. The absence of a beach, pool, and other amenities most have come to expect on the Amalfi Coast is offset by the lively buzz of the old center just outside the doors. The neoclassical facade is a welcome sight after a late-night train arrival, and the ferry and bus terminal are also a short walk away for easy access to the rest of the region.

Piazza Vittorio Veneto 42. www.plazasalerno.it. © **089-224477.** 42 units. 90€ double. Rate includes buffet breakfast. Parking 15€. **Amenities:** Bar; Wi-Fi (free).

Villa Avenia ★★   Salerno looks especially fetching from the terraces and gardens of this comfortable old villa on a hillside above the city center. Just as welcoming as the many shady bowers are the quirky, charmingly decorated guest rooms, filled with old family pieces and a lot of homey conveniences. Many have views of the bay. Among the neighbors is Giardino della Minerva, the city's famous botanic garden, and the Castello di Arechi looms just above. While this atmospheric lair is a pleasant alternative to the city's plainer accommodations, it's also convenient: An elevator that connects the hillside with Piazza Aiello in the old town below is just down the street, putting the train station and port within easy reach on foot.

Via Porta di Ronca 5. www.villaavenia.com. © **089-252281.** 8 units. 90€ double. Rates include breakfast. No credit cards. Parking in nearby garage 12€. **Amenities:** Bar; Wi-Fi (free).

Antica Pizzeria Vicolo della Neve ★★   PIZZERIA/SALERNI-TAN   Salerno's oldest restaurant, and one of the city's best-loved institutions, sports a lot of worn stone and brick to show off its 200-year-old history. Pizzas and calzones are the menu staples, but the few other Southern Italian dishes on offer are delicious, too, with *pasta e fagioli, ciambotta* (vegetable stew), and salt cod and potatoes providing simple and hearty sustenance.

Vicolo della Neve 24. www.vicolodellaneve.it. © **089-225705.** Pizzas from 6€; main courses 7€–10€. Thurs–Tues 7–11pm.

Hosteria Il Brigante ★ SALERNITAN   Attempts at decor don't get much fancier than wooden benches and etchings of the namesake bandits who once roamed the surrounding hills, service is informal at best, and menus are handwritten or scribbled on the tables. Instead, the focus at this little place tucked away in an alley in the historic center is on straightforward preparations of local favorites. Kicking off a meal are some excellent pastas, many with fish and seafood or loaded with fresh vegetables, such as spaghetti *alici, pinoli, uva passa e pomodorini* (seasoned with anchovies, pine nuts, raisins, and cherry tomatoes) and *sangiovannara* (with eggplant and mozzarella). Seafood dominates the few main courses on offer, often fresh fish baked and served alongside roasted vegetables, and anchovies fried with bread crumbs. The house specialty is *maiale ubriaco,* "drunken" pork, roasted with sweet wine, *vin santo.*

Via Fratelli Linguiti 4 (behind the Duomo). © **089-943-8729.** Main courses 7€. No credit cards. Tues–Sun 12:30–3pm and 8:30–11pm. Closed 2 weeks in Aug.

WEST OF SALERNO

Salerno is the eastern gateway to the fabled Amalfi Coast, though the first towns you'll encounter as you head west along the coast road, SS 163, are hardly typical of the picturesque and glamorous resorts farther along. Vietri and Cetara are both workaday towns, one devoted to ceramics, the other to fish.

Essentials

GETTING THERE   Coming from Salerno, Vietri is the first town along SS 163. **SITA buses** on the Salerno–Amalfi route stop frequently at Vietri and nearby Cetara.

VISITOR INFORMATION   In Vietri, the tourist office (© **089-211285**) is in the Municipal Building on Piazza Matteotti. In Cetara, the tourist office (www.prolococetara.it; © **089-261593**) is at Corso Garibaldi 15.

Vietri sul Mare ★★

5km (3 miles) W of Salerno on SS 163

Merchants in this busy, overbuilt town (which is really a suburb of Salerno) have discovered that there are ways to lure tourists other than quaintness and sea views. Instead, all of Vietri is one big china shop, and colorful facades are emblazoned with the ceramics that have put the town on the map ever since the 15th century. Even the Duomo gets into the act with an enchantingly tiled cupola.

Vietri makes it easy to seek out its famous products. Main drag Via Madonna degli Angeli is closed to car traffic and lined with shops. Most artists sell directly from their workshops here, or along Via Enrico De Marinis in the nearby suburb of Molina, due north past the train station. These are some of Italy's most distinguished ceramics, created by artists with their own distinctive patterns and color palettes. The most famous of the ceramic shops is the impossible-to-miss **Ceramica Artistica Solimene Vincenzo,** Via Madonna degli Angeli 7 (www.solimene.com; ✆ **089-210243**), housed in a remarkable free-form building with ceramics embedded in the walls. Architect Paolo Soleri, a student of Frank Lloyd Wright, designed the studios and factories in the early 1950s. His time working with ceramics in Vietri had a big influence on his career, and he continued to work ceramics into his highly praised designs in the United States, including his most famous project, Arcosanti, an experimental town in Arizona.

For an overview of the local industry, head inland about 2km (1¼ miles) to **Raito** ★, a picturesque little village of whitewashed houses and gardens (take SP 75 off SS 163). The **Museo della Ceramica,** Via Nuova Raito (✆ **089-211835**) pays reverence to the 500-year old local industry with religious items and other works, but most intriguing are the avant-garde pieces by foreign (mainly German) artists who worked in Vietri between 1929 and 1947 (admission is free; the museum is open Tues–Sun 8am–7pm). The little town is also the unlikely setting for a chapel in the 16th-century church of **Madonna delle Grazie** ★, filled with the delightfully showy, lively works by Luca Giordano (1634–1705). The Neapolitan master, most famous for the work he did for Florence's Medici family, was known as "Luca fa presto" (Luke work fast) and "The Thunderbolt" for his lightning speed and deft handiwork.

Cetara ★

6km (3¾ miles) W of Vietri; 15km (9⅓ miles) E of Amalfi

The name says it all: Cetari means seller of large fish, and ever since the 9th century this tidy little village has made its living off tuna. These days the undertaking is a bit less colorful than it once was, now that fishing is done on huge factory ships that indiscriminately take young fish and are more or less depleting the Mediterranean populations. Cetara has also turned its attention to anchovies and makes a wicked *colatura,* a salted fish sauce that is more or less the same as the *garum* that appeared on every table in ancient Rome. In Cetara, anchovies are caught in spring and early summer, salted, pressed, and exposed to sunlight for almost 6 months, and reappear as much-desired sauce in late fall. Fishy business aside, Cetara is a delightful, relatively unspoiled place, where the main attraction is a pebbly beach that stretches beneath a watchtower that was constructed after Turkish slavers carried off most of the population in 1534.

Where to Eat

If you don't like anchovies, you might change your mind by the time you get out of Cetara, where they're roasted, grilled, deep-fried, and lovingly preserved in salt and oil or chopped into a savory fish sauce. You might want to enjoy a seafood meal at one of the town's excellent restaurants or buy some of the local products to take home at **Pescheria Battista Delfino,** Via Umberto I 78 (© **089-261069**), or at **Pescheria San Pietro,** Via Umberto I 72 (© **089-261147**).

Ristorante Pizzeria Al Convento ★AMALFITAN/PIZZA   The frescoed cloisters of a former convent and breezy, arbor-covered terrace are atmospheric spots to tuck into the local specialties, maybe starting with the classic spaghetti *alla colatura di alici* (seasoned with anchovies) and moving on to *tonna alle erbe* (strips of lightly grilled tuna with mountain herbs). Come evening, another taste sensation is on hand: Pizza is served *al metro* (by the yard).

Piazza S. Francesco 15. www.alconvento.net. © **089-261039.** Main courses 12€–18€. Thurs–Tues 12:30–4pm and 7pm–2am (open daily May 15–Sept 30).

San Pietro ★AMALFITAN   On the shady terrace and simple yet elegant dining room, anchovies vie with views over the stage-set town square. Fish wins out in a multitude of creative preparations, such as vermicelli *con colatura di alici* (with anchovy essence), and some refreshing takes on fried or marinated anchovies. Other fish and seafood, including a delightfully simple grilled fish with lemon sauce, are also available.

Piazza San Francesco 2. www.sanpietroristorante.it. © **089-261091.** Main courses 15€–30€. Wed–Mon noon–3pm and 7–10:30pm (open daily in summer). Closed 2 weeks in Jan–Feb.

THE RUINS OF PAESTUM ★★★

35km (22 miles) S of Salerno; 100km (62 miles) SE of Naples

South of Salerno, soaring seaside cliffs and forested mountains give way to a wide, flat, agricultural plain. As uninspiring as the dull, grassy landscapes might seem to be, rising from them is an amazingly dramatic sight: three honey-colored temples, some of the best-preserved remains of the ancient world. The scene is especially lovely in spring and early summer, when poppies and wildflowers surround the ruins. Adding to a sense of timelessness is the presence of Italian water buffalo, which have grazed the low-lying grasslands for the past 1,000 years or so. The huge, sluggish beasts are not only tried-and-true draught animals, but they also produce the milk that yields the region's deliciously rich and creamy *mozzarella di bufala.*

Essentials

GETTING THERE   **Trains** stop at two train stations near the ruins: **Capaccio-Roccadaspide** and **Paestum,** only 5 minutes from each other. Either station is only about a 10- to 15-minute walk from the archaeological area, with Paestum being the more convenient. Via Porta Sirena leads from Paestum train station to Via Magna Grecia, which cuts through the middle of the archaeological site. The trip to either is about 30 minutes from Salerno and 90 minutes from Naples, though you can shorten the journey from Naples by taking the high-speed train to Salerno and connecting to the local train there.

Paestum

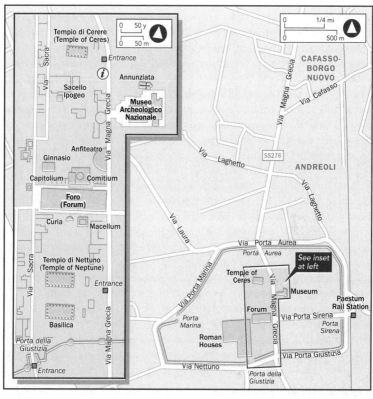

Contact Trenitalia (www.trenitalia.it; ✆ **892021** in Italy) for fares and information.

Paestum is well connected to Salerno by bus. **CSTP** (www.cstp.it; ✆ **089-252228** or 800-016659 toll-free in Italy) has regular service to Paestum from Napoli and Salerno (both line 34), with both lines continuing on to Agropoli and Acciaroli, in the Cilento (see below). **SITA** (www.sitabus.it; ✆ **089-405145**) makes runs from Salerno to Capaccio Scalo and Paestum; and **Autolinee Giuliano Bus** (www.giulianobus.com; ✆ **0974-836185**) has several lines between Naples, Salerno, and the Cilento, making stops in Paestum and Capaccio Scalo (lines 3, 4, 5, 6, 7, and 10).

By **car,** take autostrada A3, exit at BATTIPAGLIA onto SS 18, and follow the brown signs for Paestum.

VISITOR INFORMATION   You'll find a tourist office information point (www.infopaestum.it; ✆ **0828-811016**) at Via Magna Grecia 151, by the Archeological Museum, not far from the main entrance to the temples (daily 9am–1pm and 2–4pm).

Exploring the Ruins

Greek explorers realized their good fortune when they stumbled upon what is now Paestum in the 7th century B.C. Not only did natural deposits of travertine supply plenty of building materials, but the fertile plains extending around the banks of the River Sele were well suited to growing grain and other crops, and fresh water was plentiful. Ironically, they called their settlement Poseidonia, in honor of the sea god, though the sea lay on the other side of a freshwater lagoon and the town never had a large harbor. Romans overran the town in 273 B.C. and the colony they called Paestum flourished for almost six centuries, growing wealthy from agriculture and trading. Eventually, though, deforestation caused marshes to form along the banks of the River Sele, and these became breeding grounds for malarial mosquitoes that more or less rendered Paestum uninhabitable. While the forum and other parts of the town have been reduced to rubble, Paestum's three magnificent temples, rediscovered and excavated around 1750, are remarkably intact. So are parts of the circuit of massive defensive walls, 5m (16½ ft.) thick on average, 15m (50 ft.) high, and 4,750m (15,584 ft.) in length, with 24 square and round towers along their length. At the monumental western gate, **Porta Marina,** you can climb the walls and walk on the patrol paths, enjoying excellent views over the ruins and coast. Bourbon government laborers destroyed one of the four gates, the Porta Aurea, during 1828 roadwork, along with large sections of the southern walls. Part of the site was destroyed in the name of progress again in 1930, when engineers removed much of the amphitheater to build another road. The archaeological area is not huge, but the temples are spread far enough apart that you'll do a bit of walking. Wear comfortable shoes and bring a sun hat and water. Allow at least an hour to see the temples and another hour to visit the museum (see below).

Archaeological Area of Paestum ★★★   The enclosed site contains the three temples (all built facing east) and a number of other ruins that were part of the sacred area at the center of the ancient Greek town. The **Via Sacra (Sacred Street)** runs straight through the length of the site, connecting all three temples, its Roman pavement laid over the original Greek road. When it was built, the road continued for about 12km (7½ miles) to connect the Greek town of Poseidonia with the Sanctuary of Hera on the coast (see below).

The archeological area of Paestum.

Tempio di Hera (Temple of Hera) ★★★   The oldest of Paestum's three temples was built in 550 B.C. with a monumental portico that's still supported by 50 columns. Worshippers also attended

The Temple of Neptune.

rites in front, gathering around a partially ruined sacrificial altar and a square *bothros*, a sacrificial well where the remains were thrown. The temple is believed to have been part of a huge complex dedicated to Hera, wife and sister of Zeus and the goddess of fertility and maternity (who is also honored in the Sanctuary of Hera Argiva, see below). It was never, as 18th-century archeologists assumed, a Roman basilica, or civil building, though the temple is still confusedly referred to as "the basilica."

Tempio di Nettuno (Temple of Neptune) ★★★

The best example of a Doric temple in the world dates from around 450 B.C. and is lined in travertine stone that glows a magical gold color when hit by the sun's rays. Perfect proportions lend a slender elegance, while thick, closely spaced columns give the temple a powerful presence. It is also the best preserved of Paestum's temples: Only the roof and the internal walls are missing. The name is a misnomer, as the temple was probably also dedicated to Hera. In front are two sacrificial altars; the smaller one is a Roman addition from the 3rd century B.C.

Tempio di Cerere (Temple of Ceres) ★★

The smallest of the three temples, at the northern end of the site, was built at the end of the 6th century B.C., probably in honor of the goddess Athena. Under the Romans it was dedicated to Ceres, their goddess of agriculture and fertility, and three Christian tombs in the portico suggest later use as a church.

Main entrance Via Magna Grecia 917; secondary entrance Porta della Giustizia (Justice Gate, off Via Nettuno; for ticket holders only). www.infopaestum.it. © **0828-721113.** Admission 10€. Daily 9am–6:45pm (last admission 60 min. earlier); closed 1st and 3rd Mon of month.

National Archaeological Museum of Paestum ★★ MUSEUM

Star of the show among the artifacts from centuries of excavations is the sole figure of a young man taking a swan dive into a rushing stream from the so-called Tomb of the Diver, probably dating to around 470 B.C. The meaning of the simple, powerful image has long been the subject of debate, though the most reassuring suggestion is that the fellow is graciously making the transition from earth into the other world. The young man was clearly an athletic sort, as flasks filled with the oil he used to prepare himself for wrestling matches were found next to a skeleton assumed to be his. Four other frescoes from the same tomb complex depict scenes of a symposium—more or less a drinking bash—probably meant to give the deceased a good send-off. These images are unique, the only tomb frescoes from the ancient period that depict human figures. A frieze from the Sanctuary of Hera Argiva (see below) gives a close-up look at some of the mythological scenes that would have delighted a 6th-century-B.C. audience. A perennial crowd pleaser tells the story of Hercules and the Kerkopes. As legend has it, the hero had fallen asleep when two scamps snuck up on him and stole his weapons. Hercules awoke, captured the miscreants, and tied them upside down to a pole that he carried over his shoulder. The Kerkopes started laughing and Hercules demanded to know why. They told him they were laughing at his hairy backside, so he started laughing, too, and set the boys free (Zeus was less amused by their antics and later turned them into mon-

A carved temple decoration of a lion.

keys). Another delightful scene depicts two lithe and gleeful maidens running, their finely sculpted robes flowing around them—the joy of these images suggests just how light-hearted ancient Greek religion could be.

Via Magna Grecia 918 (across from the entrance to the temples). ℂ **0828-811023.** Included with admission to temples. Daily 9am–6:45pm (last admission 45 min. earlier). Closed 1st and 3rd Mon of month.

Sanctuary of Hera Argiva (Heraion) ★   The Via Sacra once led the 12km (7½ miles) from Paestum to the mouth of the River Sele and the Heraion, a sanctuary to the goddess Hera that was one of the most famous temples of antiquity. Archeologists brought the complex to light in the 1930s, unearthing the scant remains of the main temple, parts of a smaller *thesaurus* (treasury), and a portico that led to outlying buildings. Most impressive of the remains are the glorious meteope friezes and votive statuettes that are in the National Archaeological Museum of Paestum (see above). The complex was one of several around the ancient world to honor Hera, wife and sister of Zeus; goddess of agriculture, fertility, matrimony, and navigation; and someone on whose good side any god or mere mortal would want to remain. Hera was frighteningly vengeful to anyone who crossed her and spent much of her time plotting against the maidens who flirted with her husband—she famously cursed Echo, who had been concealing Zeus's many affairs from her, so the poor woman could only repeat the words of others. Christianity adopted some of the better sides of the powerful goddess in attributes of the Virgin Mary, who, like Hera, is sometimes depicted with a pomegranate, a symbol of fertility.

The **Museo Narrante del Santuario di Hera Argiva ★**, in a restored farmhouse near the ruins, presents an excellent multimedia installation describing the discovery of the ruins and the function of the sanctuary; it's closed as we go to press but slated to open soon, so check with the information desks at the sanctuary or Paestum before heading out there.

Ruins: Near the mouth of the River Sele, about 1.5km (1 mile) inland from the sea and 11km (6¾ miles) north of Paestum. Museum: Masseria Procuriali, Via Barizzo, Foce Sele Capaccio, about 2km (1¼ miles) from the ruins and 9km (5½ miles) from Paestum. ✆ **0828-861440.** Free admission. Ruins daily 9am–7pm (July–Sept until 10pm). Museum Tues–Sun 9am–4pm.

Where to Stay & Eat

The place to taste the region's famous *mozzarella di bufala* is **Tenuta Vannulo,** Via Galileo Galilei, Contrada Vannulo, Capaccio Scalo (www.vannulo. it; ✆ **0828-727894**), a buffalo farm near the ruins. You can try the delectable product, meet the providers (two- and four-legged—the beasts are soothed with recorded Mozart concertos), and enjoy utterly delish buffalo-milk gelato as well. The cheese wins out, though: Tasting it fresh at the source is like eating a cloud.

Il Granaio dei Casabella ★   The former granary of an old farm across the road from one of the gates of ancient Paestum would be a delightful retreat even without its famous neighbor. The large gardens are tailor-made for lounging over morning coffee or a glass of Prosecco in the evening, while open fires blaze in atmospheric, tile-floored lounges in the colder months. Many of the delightfully old-fashioned beamed guest rooms overlook the ruins, some from balconies. Dining is on an enclosed veranda, and a seafood lunch here is a perfect respite from exploring the ruins.

Via Tavernelle 84 (off Via Magna Grecia). www.ilgranaiodeicasabella.com. ✆ **0828-721014.** 14 units. From 120€ double. Rates include breakfast. Free parking. Closed Nov–Feb. **Amenities:** Restaurant; bar; Wi-Fi (free).

La Locanda del Mare ★★   These whitewashed bungalows tucked into a pine forest are some of the most stylish accommodations on this part of the coast, with simple and attractive furnishings and bright splashes of color and pleasant terraces that open to lush gardens. Topping it all off is the sparkling blue sea and 14km (9-mile) stretch of sand at the end of the garden path, so a day of visiting the nearby ruins (a 5-minute drive away) can begin with a swim and walk on the beach. A pleasant restaurant serves simply prepared meals that make the most of local produce.

Via Linora. www.lalocandadelmare.net. ✆ **0828-811-1162.** 16 units. From 60€ double. Rate includes breakfast. Free parking. **Amenities:** Restaurant; bar; beach; Wi-Fi (free).

Nonna Sceppa ★★ SALERNITAN   No need to settle for the cafeteria grub amid the ruins when homemade, traditional meals, as satisfying as the ones served in this cozy room and nice terrace, are so close at hand. Summer menus lean toward seafood while wintertime specials focus on game and hearty meat ragouts. The signature pastas with seafood, including spaghetti *con l'aragosta* (with spiny lobster) are usually available any time of year. Any meal should begin with a serving of the delectable *mozzarella di bufala* provided by the hairy beasts just down the road.

Via Laura 45, Capaccio Scalo. www.nonnasceppa.com. ✆ **0828-851064.** Main courses 12€–25€. Oct–May Fri–Wed 12:30–3pm and 7:30–10pm; June–Sept daily 12:30–3pm and 7:30–10pm. Closed 3 weeks in Oct.

PADULA & CERTOSA DI SAN LORENZO ★★★

98km (59 miles) SE of Salerno

For the Carthusian monks of St. Lorenzo, obviously bigger was better. The monastery they assembled on the slopes of a hill outside the little town of Padula is one of the largest in the world, a work of architectural splendor that, on first glance, might lay asunder any notions of the simple, contemplative life.

Essentials

GETTING THERE & AROUND Trenitalia (www.trenitalia.it; ✆ **892021** in Italy) offers direct connections from Naples and Salerno to Battipaglia, where you will need to switch to a shuttle bus (which runs on schedule with the trains) to Padula and the monastery. You can also take a **bus** directly from Salerno: **Lamanna** (www.autolineelamanna.it; ✆ **0975-520426**) makes runs to Padula from Piazza della Concordia near the train station. By **car,** take the exit marked PADULA-BUONABITACOLO off the A3 to SS 19, and follow the signs for PADULA.

VISITOR INFORMATION The tourist office is at Via Italo Balbo 45 (www. prolocopadula.com; ✆ **0975-778611**).

Exploring Padula & the Monastery

Padula is a pretty little hill town, though its old streets and stone houses are overshadowed by its super-sized monastery. From April through June, another big attraction is the so-called Valley of the Orchids outside nearby Sassano, when more than 180 wild species bloom.

Certosa di San Lorenzo ★★ MONASTERY Everything about this massive complex, established in 1306 and

A grand stairway at the Certosa di San Lorenzo.

Mindful Monks

While it would be easy to write off the San Lorenzo monastery as a bit of ostentatious showiness, like the McMansions of modern suburban life, the vast complex is a fine showplace of Carthusian values. Carthusian monks were the thinkers of the Middle Ages. Much of a community like the one at San Lorenzo was comprised of hermit monks, who spent a life of contemplation. The two-floor "cells" surrounding the huge cloister at San Lorenzo are typical of Carthusian living arrangements. They opened off long corridors, and next to each door was a small revolving compartment, a "turn," through which meals and other items could be delivered without disturbing the occupant. The lower floor was for wood and tool storage and accommodated a workshop where the monks could engage in woodworking or some other form of craftsmanship or manual labor. Upstairs was a room for prayer, study, sleeping, and eating. Each cell opened to a walled garden for growing flowers and vegetables. The monks ate alone, and left the cell only three times a day for prayer. Once a week they took a countryside walk, on which they were allowed to speak, and they joined the community, in silence, for meals on Sundays and feast days. Supporting the hermit monks was a large community of lay brothers who mastered everything from cooking and farming to selling the community's produce. As you'll learn on a tour of San Lorenzo, they could spare a thousand eggs to make a single omelet, which indicates that someone was also quite skillful at raising chickens.

expanded over the next several centuries, is a bit over the top, more like a showy palace than a religious institution. Sprawling over 168,963m (554,341 sq. ft.) are 320 halls, 52 staircases, 100 fireplaces, 13 courtyards, and 41 fountains. As you begin to take it all in, it becomes clear that the Carthusian community is organized in typical monastic fashion to accommodate work and facilitate contemplation. Near the entrance are storerooms, an olive press, stables, laundry, and other necessities. The kitchens are so vast it really doesn't seem all that surprising that the monks once impressed Holy Roman Emperor Charles V by whipping up a 1,000-egg omelet. (They might have been helped along in the venture by the monastery's namesake St. Lawrence, patron of chefs.) Contemplative quarters are deeper within the complex, with a richly decorated church and a tall library in which a carved staircase spirals from one level to another. Most impressive of all is the main cloister, the largest in the world, where two levels of porticos supported by a forest of columns surround 1.2 hectares (3 acres) of lawns and gardens. Opening off the carving-lined walkways are the monks' "cells," three- and four-room affairs with cozy little studies/workshops, private porticos for fresh-air contemplation, and garden plots. The **Festival di Ravello** (Ravello Music Festival; p. 161) occasionally stages concerts in the cloisters, and it would be hard to find a more evocative setting.

Viale Certosa 1. www.magnifico.beniculturali.it/certosa.html. © **0975-77745.** Admission 4€. Daily 9am–8pm. Last admission 1 hr. earlier.

Where to Eat

Taverna Il Lupo ★★ CILENTAN   The vaulted, stone-walled dining room seems refreshingly homey after the excesses of the monastery—just the place to enjoy the rustic cuisine typical of the surrounding mountains. Surprisingly, the emphasis is on garden-fresh vegetables, with a memorably filling *pasta e fagioli* (pasta with white beans and onions) that suffices as a meal in itself.

Via Municipio. ✆ **0975-778376.** Main courses 7€–12€. Tues–Sat noon–2:30pm and 7–10pm, Sun noon–3pm.

THE CILENTO

110km (68 miles) S of Naples

From the shores of the Gulf of Salerno, the Cilento region extends 100km (62 miles) south to Campania's border with the Basilicata region. Shorelines are laced with miles of beaches, where sand is littered not just with beach towels but with *primula di Palinuro*, a rare dune flower, while behind the coast two mountain ranges, the Alburni to the north and Monte Cervati to the south, rise and fall across the forested interior. Stone villages crown the occasional hilltop, and ancient ruins litter coastal plains. The Cilento is one of Italy's wildest, most remote regions, and much of it is protected as a 180,000-hectare (444,790-acre) national park, Parco Nazionale del Cilento, Vallo di Diano e Alburni. For anyone who's been lulled by the picturesque stage sets of the Amalfi Coast, the rough-around-the-edges expanses of the Cilento will come as a bit of a jolt, and maybe a welcome escape, too.

Essentials

GETTING THERE   The towns of the Cilento are well connected by public transportation. Even so, you will want a car to explore the region in depth and to get easily from one sight to another.

Direct **trains** link Naples and Salerno to Agropoli/Castellabate, Pisciotta/Palinuro, and Vallo della Lucania. Contact **Trenitalia** (www.trenitalia.it; ✆ **892021** in Italy) for fares and information.

Towns and villages in the park are served by **bus** from Naples, Pompeii, Salerno, and Paestum: **CSTP,** Piazza Matteo Luciani 33, Salerno (www.cstp.it; ✆ **089-252228** or 800-016659 toll-free in Italy) runs several lines from Napoli, Pompeii, Paestum, and Salerno to Vallo della Lucania, Agropoli, Santa Maria di Castellabate, Acciaroli, and Pollica. **Curcio Viaggi** (www.curcioviaggi.it; ✆ **089-254080**) offers lines from Rome and Salerno to Sicignano degli Alburni, Scario, and Polla. **Autolinee Giuliano Bus** (www.giulianobus.com; ✆ **0974-836185**) runs from Naples and Salerno to Roccadaspide, Agropoli, Vallo della Lucania, and Pioppi. Finally, **SITA** (www.sitabus.it; ✆ **089-405145**) operates service between Salerno and Pertosa and Polla.

VISITOR INFORMATION   The park's Visitor Center (www.cilento ediano.it; ✆ **0974-719911**) is on Piazza Santa Caterina 8, 84078 in **Vallo della Lucania,** the eastern gateway to the park.

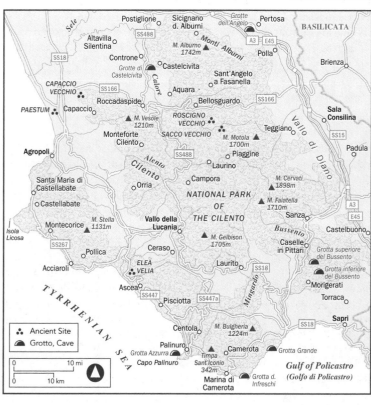

Ancient Site
Grotto, Cave

Gulf of Policastro
(Golfo di Policastro)

Exploring the Park

From Paestum, the SS 267 heads south into the park, following the coast for part of its length before meeting up with SS 447 for the swing inland to Vallo della Lucania (90km/54 miles southeast of Salerno, 45km/27 miles southeast of Paestum), where park headquarters are located.

In **Agropoli,** about 14km (8½ miles) south of Paestum, scruffy modern outskirts surround a well-preserved medieval citadel and a partially ruined castle that overlooks a small fishing harbor. As at other castles up and down the coast, the sturdy towers allowed sentries to keep an eye out for a steady stream of pirates and Moorish invaders. On a clear day, you can see all the way to Capri.

The lonely, sturdy medieval fortress town of **Castellabate,** 20km (13 miles) south of Paestum, clings to a craggy outcropping and is also topped with a castle. Just below on the sea is the delightful little **Santa Maria di Castellabate,** where old palazzos and simple fishermen's houses surround a sandy

Cilento in Full Color

Among the many attractions of the Cilento is a profusion of wildflowers. In April and May, hillsides are ablaze with broom and heather, and throughout the warm months the landscapes are scented with lentisco, a shrublike ever-green. In the Valley of the Orchids in Sassano, just outside Padula (see p. 224), 180 species of wild orchids bloom from April to June. From January through March, the coast is ablaze with primula Palinuri, a rare dune flower. The blooms are especially prevalent around Palinuro (see below).

beach. A nearby promontory, Punta Licosa, is named after the Siren Leucosia, who, as legend has it, came here and threw herself to her death from the cliffs after she become despondent when she failed to lure Odysseus and his crew to their deaths on the rocks off present-day Positano (see p. 133).

The colorful little fishing harbor of **Acciaroli** (42km/25 miles south of Salerno) was a hideaway of American novelist Ernest Hemingway in the 1950s. The fishermen who still set out to sea to net a bounty of fish and sea-food supposedly inspired his 1952 masterpiece *The Old Man and the Sea.*

The coast is especially rugged and beautiful around **Palinuro,** another 50km (30 miles) south of Acciaroli. It's said the popular resort (surrounded by coves for an easy getaway) is named after one of the sailors who, in Roman author Virgil's *Aeneid,* accompanied Aeneas in his flight from Troy to Italy but fell overboard here. Even so, the clean waters are some of the most inviting in the Mediterranean. Inland, the Cilento is much wilder, riddled with gorges and caves (see below) and carpeted with forests.

Grotte dell'Angelo ★★ NATURAL WONDER Parts of these caverns, extending for at least 3km (2 miles), are underwater. In fact, a visit begins with a ride on a raft across the first chamber. How much you see depends on the tour you choose: the Inferno (60 minutes), the Purgatorio (75 minutes), or the Paradiso (90 minutes); you'll probably see enough of the underworld to satisfy any subterranean cravings on the 60-minute tour. All show off magnificent rock and crystal formations, and it is easy to see why the supernatural-seeming surroundings became places of worship for the region's Greek, Roman, and medieval inhabitants. Experienced spelunkers can explore less accessible parts of the grottoes, including the dank, dark, and creepy vaults that open off the subterranean stream. To reach the grottoes, follow the signs for PERTOSA on SS 19; the parking area is a short distance off the road to the left. Pertosa is 68km (41 miles) east of Paestum and 74km (44 miles) southeast of Salerno; it is just off the A3.

Pertosa. www.grottedellangelo.sa.it. ⓒ **0975-397037.** Three guided tours 10€, 13€, and 16€. Mar–Oct daily 9am–7pm, Nov–Feb daily 10am–4pm. Thurs and Fri when school is in session, access to the grottoes is reserved for classes; they open to the public at 2pm.

Grotte di Castelcivita ★ NATURAL WONDER It's said that the escaped gladiator Spartacus and his fellow rebels hid in this vast cave system when they were fleeing from the Roman legions during a 1st-century B.C. slave uprising. That's probably no more true than the claim that Spartacus also hid in the crater of Mt. Vesuvius. But the galleries and natural halls extending for more 5km (3 miles) under the Alburni mountains would certainly be a good hideout if you had half the Roman army on your heels in hot pursuit. Spartacus claims aside, the caves were inhabited by ordinary mortals as far back as 10,000 years ago, and even without a human legacy, their multicolored rock formations are simply stunning and worth a visit. The caves are outside Controne, 57km (34 miles) southeast of Salerno and 35km (21 miles) northeast of Paestum; Controne is on SS 488.

Controne. www.grottedicastelcivita.com. ℂ **0828-777-2397.** Admission 10€. Accessible by guided tour only, every 90 mins., Mar 16–Sept 30 10:30am–6pm; Oct 1–Mar 15 10:30am–3pm.

Velia ★ RUINS The ruins of this once great city in hilly terrain near the coast are not nearly as well preserved or as well known as those at Paestum, 43km (26 miles) north, but they're evocative and storied nonetheless. They are what remain of the Greek colony of **Elea,** once the seat of the famed Eleatic school of philosophy. Greeks fleeing a Persian invasion of modern-day Turkey are thought to have settled the town around 540 B.C. Traveling with them was the philosopher Xenophanes (570–475 B.C.). He spent much of his long life traveling throughout the Greek world but remained in Elea long enough to leave his mark. In doing so he was living up to his self-prediction that his "fame that will reach all of Greece, and never die while the Greek kind of songs survives." By the time the Romans took over, the town Elea had grown into such a beacon of Greek culture that it was allowed the privilege of maintaining Greek as its official language. Some portions of the 5km (3-mile) circuit of walls, a stretch of pavement arched by the impressive Porta Rosa (Pink Gate), and fragments of a bath and theater remain. The beauty here, though, is in the details: Aside from locally quarried limestone, much of the town was constructed of distinctive bricks fired on-site. You'll come to the ruins as you follow the coast road south from Acciaroli; they are about 17km (10 miles) south of Acciaroli.

Ascea Marina. ℂ **0974-971409.** Admission 3€. Daily 8:45am–sunset.

Getting Active

The best of the many **hiking trails** in the park are those that ascend **Monte Cervati,** the region's highest mountain that soars to 1,898m (6,227 ft.). The mountain rises just outside Vallo della Lucani, where park headquarters can provide hiking maps. However, the ascent is via two trails from the town of **Sanza,** 60km (37 miles) east on SS 517. Both trails climb through extensive lavender fields and the round-trip on either takes about 6 hours.

Beaches

Italian families descend on Cilento beaches from mid-July through August, transforming normally quiet strands into noisy playgrounds. A good bet for solitude at any time is **Palinuro,** 50km (30 miles) south of Acciaroli, a fishing and resort harbor set among olive groves in a picturesque bay. Cliffs rising from the sea on both sides of town are studded with secluded coves and caves. The most beautiful of them, the **Grotta Azzurra ★★,** is far less mobbed than its more famous cousin in Capri, yet its water takes on magical colors, especially around noon and sunset. You can explore it, and the rest of the shoreline, in one of the little boats, with or without crew, for rent in the harbor. The little fishing harbor of **Marina di Camerota,** 12km (7 miles) farther south, is surrounded by coves and sandy and rocky beaches.

Santa Maria di Castellabate, 20km (12 miles) north of Acciaroli, is tucked onto the coast below the old hilltop town of Castellabate (see above) and is blessed with two beautiful beaches: The one to the north, the largest, has unusually fine sand, while the smaller one to the south is backed by a shady pine grove. The stretch of coast here, around **Punta Licosa,** is protected as a marine park, with excellent **snorkeling** and **scuba diving. Cilento Sub,** Via Roma 3, Santa Maria di Castellabate (www.ascilentosub.com; ✆ **0974-961628**), provides guides and equipment.

Where to Stay

Agriturismo Le Favate ★★   A 400-year-old farmhouse on 100 hectares (247 acres) hidden away in the countryside, just above the coast near Ascea, is a memorable introduction to the rural pleasures of the Cilento, with a lot of luxury thrown in. You can lounge by a sparkling pool with the sea in the distance, seek out the shade on stone porticos, or walk amid the vineyards and olive trees. Rustic, wood-beamed guest rooms are filled with handmade furnishings and equipped with fireplaces or ceramic stoves. The farm's wine, olive oil, cheese, and other produce appear in delicious dinners, served family style on a terrace in good weather. Ascea is near the coast, 78km (47 miles) south of Salerno.

Contrada Favate, Ascea. ✆ **0974-9773-1090.** 14 units. 90€–110€ double. Rates include breakfast. **Amenities:** Bar; restaurant; pool; Wi-Fi (free).

Palazzo Belmonte ★★★   Principe Angelo di Belmonte graciously shares his 17th-century stone palazzo and surrounding estate with guests, and you'll feel quite privileged when you step through the gate into the 2 hectares (5 acres) of palm-shaded gardens and sea-facing lawns. Comfortably elegant, bright accommodations, simply but carefully done with homey old pieces, are scattered throughout the palazzo and other houses on the grounds; all are just a stroll away from the large pool and private beach. The pleasant seaside village of Santa Maria di Castellabate is just 5 minutes down the road, and Paestum and many other sights are within easy reach, making this pretty getaway 70km (42 miles) south of Salerno an exceptional base for exploring the region.

Via Flavio Gioia 22, 84072 Santa Maria di Castellabate. www.palazzobelmonte.com. ℗ **0974-960211.** 50 units. 186€–427€ double. Free parking. Closed Nov–Apr. **Amenities:** Restaurant; bar; concierge; pool; private beach; Wi-Fi (free).

Residenza d'Epoca 1861 ★★★   The laid-back resort of Santa Maria di Castellabate seems especially pleasant from this character-filled seaside mansion perched just above the beach. The animated little town buzzes around you, while the spacious, light-filled, tile-floored rooms are oases of calm—and most are well suited for viewing the town's famous sunsets. Excellent meals are served in the stone-walled restaurant. Santa Maria di Castellabate is 70km (42 miles) south of Salerno.

Lungomare Perrotti, Santa Maria di Castellabate. residenzadepoca1861.it. ℗ **0974-961454.** 6 units. 90€–150€. Rates include breakfast. Closed Jan–mid-Mar. **Amenities:** Restaurant; bar; Wi-Fi (free).

Where to Eat

Il Ceppo ★ CILENTAN/SEAFOOD   An ordinary-looking modern trattoria on a busy side street in this bustling resort town delivers exceptional seafood, along the lines of a delicious *tagliolini con gamberi, fiori di zucca e vongole* (fresh pasta with clams, shrimp, and zucchini flowers). The fish, best simply grilled, is reputed to be the freshest on the coast, so reliably good that locals have been flocking to the plain dining room and pleasant terrace for decades. The 20 clean, basic guest rooms (65€–90€ double) are comfortable but less inspiring.

Via Madonna del Carmine 31, Agropoli. www.hotelristoranteilceppo.com. ℗ **0974-843036.** Main courses 10€–21€. Wed–Mon 12:30–3pm and 7:30–10:30pm (also Tues in Aug). Closed 10 days in Nov.

La Taverna del Pescatore ★ CILENTAN/SEAFOOD   The kitchen at one of the top seafood spots on the coast can be delightfully creative. Owner-waiter Roberto prides himself on serving dishes that these days you'd be hard-pressed to find elsewhere, such as spaghetti *ai ricci di mare a crudo* (with raw sea urchins). Should you wish to play it safer with something more traditional, the *zuppa di pesce* (fish stew) is delicious and similarly memorable. The terrace and pleasant dining room can get crowded and service can be slow, so order one of the excellent local wines and prepare to linger.

Via Lamia 31, Santa Maria di Castellabate. ℗ **0974-968293.** Main courses 11€–18€. Apr–June and Sept–Oct Tues–Sun noon–3pm and 7:30–11pm; July–Aug Tues–Sun 7:30–11pm. Closed Nov–Mar.

FARTHER AFIELD: CASERTA, CAPUA & BENEVENTO

9

The shores of the Bay of Naples and the islands have always basked in the limelight. They're the parts of the region that the Romans called *campania felix,* or "fertile land." The rugged inland landscapes are a different place altogether: dry, sun-backed, traditionally poor, and a lot less traveled than the coast. Venture east, though, even on a day trip from Naples, and you'll see there's a lot to discover.

Romans put the inland region on the map when they settled Capua, a city that was once second only to Rome, with a huge amphitheater to show for its prominence. Romans also settled Benevento, an important crossroads at the junction of two of their most important roads, the Via Appia and the Via Traiana (Appian Way and Trajan Way). Bourbon King Carlo III made the move off the coast in the mid-18th century and built the largest palace in Europe, the Reggia, at Caserta. These places might be off a bit off the radar, but they're not too far off the beaten track and easy to reach by train from Naples.

CASERTA ★★

17km (11 miles) NW of Naples

Residents of this busy, modern, uninspiring town may or may not realize it, but had world events taken a different turn, they could be living in one of the great world capitals. Caserta had its moment of glory in the mid-18th century, when the new Bourbon king Carlo III decided to move his court here from Naples, in part as insurance against sea attacks and also to remove himself from the dust, grime, and hoi-polloi of the city. The palace he built was designed to rival Versailles, and around it was to burgeon a grand new town. Though Carlo left for Spain before the palace was even completed and his

Caserta, Capua, and Benevento

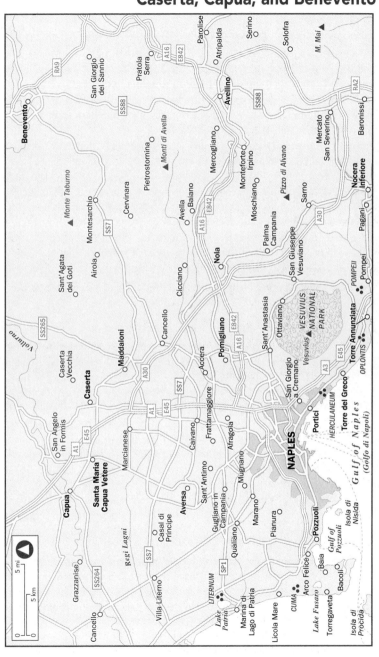

successors did not share his vision of a royal court at Caserta, at least part of the king's grand plans came to fruition: The palace he commissioned is one of the great monuments of Italy and the largest royal residence in the world.

GETTING THERE   Caserta is easily reached by train from Naples. Trains leave Napoli Stazione Centrale every 10 to 20 minutes for the 30-minute trip. Contact **Trenitalia** (www.trenitalia.it; ✆ **892021** in Italy) for fares and information. Caserta is also served by **Metro Campania Nord-Est** (www.eavsrl. it; ✆ **800-053939** toll-free in Italy) from Naples. Trains arrive at Caserta's **railway station** in Piazza Giuseppe Garibaldi, only a few steps from the Reggia, on the other side of Piazza Carlo III.

By car, from either Rome or Naples, take autostrada A1 to the exit marked CASERTA NORD and follow the signs for CASERTA CENTRO. Coming into town, you will see signs for SAN LEUCIO, CASERTA VECCHIA, and REGGIA. The Reggia (Royal Palace) is in the center of town. CASERTAVECCHIA, the medieval town, is about 10km (6 miles) up the hill from the Royal Palace; head northeast and follow the signs. To reach the Belvedere, head northwest from Piazza Vanvitelli, following the signs for SAN LEUCIO. Bus no. 110 leaves from Piazza Garibaldi, in front of Caserta train station, Casertavecchia.

VISITOR INFORMATION   The tourist office has a booth at Corso Trieste 9, at the corner with Piazza Dante and Via Douhet (www.eptcaserta.it; ✆ **0823-321137**). It's open Monday to Saturday 9am to 7pm.

Exploring the Palace & Other Sights

Though Carlo Borbone has faded into relative obscurity, no one could accuse him of not thinking big. His plan was to build a palace to rival Versailles and create around it a city that would hold its own against Paris, Vienna, and other European capitals. The scheme required the services of thousands of laborers and craftsmen, for whom Carlo's architects and engineers created a makeshift town, now the heart of modern Caserta, next to the palace grounds. They constructed an aqueduct to water the magnificent gardens, and Carlo's successors eventually established a silk factory to create a flourishing local industry to support all these enterprises. While many of these plans came to naught—a monumental avenue to link the palace with Naples never got off the drawing boards—the palace, gardens, and a few other remnants suggest what might have been. Carlo never spent a night at his palace. He moved on to a better job as king of Spain, and the palace wasn't fully completed until the 1850s, a century after work began.

Though the palace is conveniently located next to Caserta's train station, a visit involves a lot of walking. The palace is wheelchair accessible through a private elevator in back of the ticket booth, and golf carts are available for visits to the gardens; call in advance to make arrangements. A shuttle bus is provided between the palace and the entrance to the English Gardens; ask at the ticket booth when you arrive.

You will find a **cafeteria** inside the Reggia, at the end of the main gallery just before the exit to the gardens; it's open during all visiting hours. In

Caserta

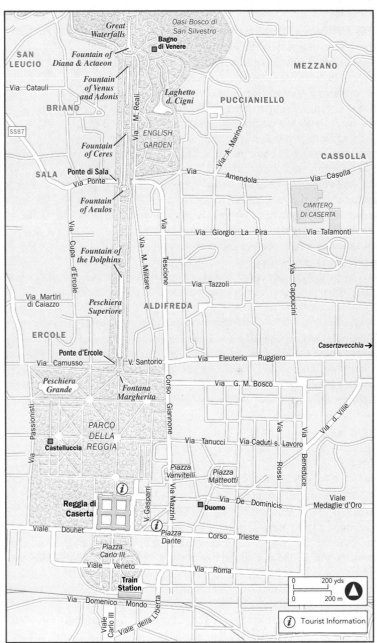

Oasi Bosco di
San Silvestro

Great
Waterfalls

Bagno
di Venere

Fountain of
Diana & Actaeon

SAN
LEUCIO

MEZZANO

Fountain
of Venus
and Adonis

Via Catauli

Laghetto
d. Cigni

PUCCIANIELLO

BRIANO

Via M. Reali

ENGLISH
GARDEN

SS87

CASSOLLA

Fountain
of Ceres

Via A. Marino

Via

Amendola

Via Casolla

SALA

Ponte di Sala

Via Ponte

CIMITERO
DI CASERTA

Fountain
of Aeulos

Via M. Militare

Via Tescione

Via Giorgio La Pira

Via Talamonti

Via Cupa d'Ercole

Fountain of
the Dolphins

Via Cappucini

Via Tazzoli

Via Martiri
di Caiazzo

Peschiera
Superiore

ALDIFREDA

ERCOLE

Ponte d'Ercole

Casertavecchia →

Via Camusso

V. Santorio

Via Eleuterio Ruggiero

Peschiera
Grande

Fontana
Margherita

Via G. M. Bosco

Via Passionisti

Corso Giannone

Via Benedice

Via d. Ville

PARCO
DELLA
REGGIA

Via Tanucci

Via Caduti s. Lavoro

Castelluccia

Via

Piazza
Vanvitelli

Piazza
Matteotti

Via Rossi

Viale
Medaglie d'Oro

Reggia di
Caserta

V. Gasparri

Via Mazzini

Duomo

Via De Dominicis

Viale Douhet

Piazza
Dante

Corso Trieste

Piazza
Carlo III

Viale Veneto

Via Roma

Train
Station

0   200 yds

0   200 m

Via Domenico Mondo

Viale Carlo III

Viale della Libertà

ⓘ Tourist Information

235

summer, you'll find a temporary snack bar at the entrance to the English Gardens.

Royal Palace & Gardens (Reggia di Caserta) ★★★ PALACE/GARDENS King Carlo III Bourbon gave his architect Luigi Vanvitelli a tall order: to build him a palace and gardens that would make him the envy of all the other courts of Europe. Vanvitelli dedicated the last 20 years of his life to the project, creating a grandiose masterpiece of harmony that measures over 45,000 sq. m (484,376 sq. ft.), and is divided into four wings, each surrounding a separate courtyard. The palace has 1,200 rooms, 134 windows on the main facade alone, and 34 staircases, all beneath a central cupola and complemented by a park and garden of 120 hectares (297 acres).

The Reggia di Caserta.

Vanvitelli, a capable engineer with a well-developed sense for visual drama, had a good track record for grandiose design. Among his credits were Roman monuments that include the handsome facades of the basilica of San Giovanni in Laterano and the Palazzo Poli, the dramatic backdrop to the Trevi Fountain. Vanvitelli fulfilled the king's request and created a palace that not only resembles Versailles, the gold standard for palace builders across 18th- and 19th-centuy Europe, but exceeds its French counterpart in size and possibly pomp. Little wonder that the king gave Vanvitelli an encouraging pat on the back by telling him that the design filled him with emotion "fit to tear my heart from my breast."

THE PALACE

Having grown up in Madrid's Palazzo Reale, Carlo had some pretty high expectations for a royal residence. Vanvitelli wisely took his inspiration from the great monuments of Europe, modeling the theater after the Teatro San Carlo in Naples, the octagonal vestibule after the basilica of Santa Maria della Salute in Venice, and the Palatine Chapel after the one built for Louis XIV at Versailles. Even the most confident prince or cardinal could feel like a country bumpkin on the long climb up the double set of 116 steps of the vast main staircase, swathed in marble and flanked by statues. At the top are 40 frescoed staterooms designed to flaunt the power and grandeur of the Bourbon monarchs, who are pictured in the lineup of medallions depicting the 46 kings of Naples in the gilt and stucco throne room. As if to suggest that comparison with mere mortals could never suffice, frescoes in the nearby Sala di Marte celebrate the regime's military might with frescoed scenes of epic, divinely influenced battles of the *Iliad*.

Some corners of the **Royal Apartments** almost come close to suggesting a note of domestic coziness. A walk through the so-called *appartamento vecchio* ("old" apartment) is a delightful seasonal romp, with frescoes capturing spring in the reception room, intended to get a state visit off on a hopeful note; summer in the sitting room; fall in the dining room; and winter in the smoking room, as if smokers of the day were relegated to the chilly perimeters like their counterparts today. Especially engaging are canvases by **Jakob Philipp Hackert** (1737–1807), a German-born artist whom the Bourbons kept busy, not just giving drawing lessons to the young royals but also capturing the scenes of the kingdom's harbors and other holdings now hanging in the king's study. German man of letters Goethe befriended the artist on a 1786 journey through Italy and was so impressed with Hackert's prolific output on behalf of the Bourbon patrons that he called him an "inveterate hard worker." Quite fittingly, the magnificent *presepio reale* (royal nativity scene) on display in the nearby Oval Hall is undoubtedly the largest and most lavish Christmas creche you'll ever see.

THE GARDENS

Some of the most celebrated Italian gardens in the world stretch from the palace to the nearby hills along a central path 3km (2 miles) long, graced with sumptuous fountains and pools. At the end of the vista is the water feature extraordinaire: A majestic waterfall cascades 150m (495 ft.) into a huge basin where two groupings of baroque statues enact the mythical story of Diana and Actaeon. In one tableau the goddess of the hunt bathes with her nymphs as the mortal youth Actaeon comes upon the scene; in the other grouping Diana has transformed the unfortunate boy into a deer and his own hounds are setting upon him. Architect Luigi Vanvitelli engineered the Carolino aqueduct to bring water all the way from Monte Taburno, 40km (25 miles) away, to feed these elaborate waterworks. The **English Garden,** created by Carlo Vanvitelli, son of architect Luigi, is relatively sedate by comparison, a romantic bower with a lake, a spring, a small temple, and some lovely plantings. It paid to be in the employ of a Bourbon monarch when it came time to acquire garden ornaments—statues lining the charming paths are ancient Roman originals purloined from the ruins of Pompeii.

Viale Douhet. www.reggiadicaserta.beniculturali.it. ℂ **0823-448084** or 0823-277111. Admission 12€ apts and gardens. Audio guides 7€, or 10€ for 2. Bus shuttle to English Garden 1€. Apts: Wed–Mon 8:30am–7:30pm; last admission 30 min. earlier. Gardens: Wed–Mon 8:30am–sunset; last admission 2 hr. earlier.

Casertavecchia ★★

King Carlo III Bourbon didn't have to worry about a workforce when it came time to build his palace. He simply emptied out the original town of Caserta, pressed the residents into service, and moved them closer to his worksite. Inadvertently, he created a treasure: Casertavecchia, on a hilltop about 10km (6 miles) outside the modern town, is now one of the best-preserved medieval precincts in Italy. Narrow streets, arches, and houses richly ornamented with stone detailing are picturesquely poised beneath the ruined 11th-century **Norman Castle.** Amid all of it, rising from Piazza Vescovado, is a 12th-century **cathedral,** a fantasy-like creation with Arabesque arches and a marble facade crawling with a stone bestiary of lions and other creatures. Inside is a forest of columns taken in part from Roman temples. Off to one side, a sturdy bell tower is pieced with an arch, through which passes the main street of town (© **0823-371318;** free admission; daily 9am–1pm and 3:30–6pm, till 7:30pm in summer).

San Leucio ★★

In 1778 King Ferdinand IV converted his hunting preserve, on a hill northwest of the Royal Palace, into a silkworm farm and a weaving factory. Ferdinand and his liberal minister Bernardo Tanucci not only built three industrial buildings housing silkworm rooms and spinning and dyeing facilities, but also enacted a series of progressive laws and labor practices. Education was obligatory and free from the age of 6 up, with schoolrooms on the premises and housing provided for teachers. Workers wore uniforms to strip away any sense of sartorial one-upmanship and men and women were treated equally. Women were provided with dowries when they married a coworker, and a portion of the profits was set aside for those who were unable to work due to poor health or old age. The factory became famous for its precious fabrics and still operates privately, and expert artisans keep the tradition alive by weaving damasks, brocades, and other fine fabrics. Visitors can stroll through the original workers' village that grew up around the factory, where orderly rows of stone houses line tidy streets. The dwellings were equipped with running water and indoor toilets, progressive innovations in the late 18th century. A small palace, **Casino Reale di Belvedere ★★,** is adjacent to the colony on Piazza della Seta and houses the **Museo della Seta (Silk Museum).** The factory's original 18th-cenutry weaving machinery is on display and still in working order—you can ask to see one in action. A rather jarring contrast to Fernando's experiments with progressive labor practices are the **Royal Apartments,** richly frescoed with allegoric scenes (© **0823-273151;** admission 6€; open Wed–Mon, 9:30am–6pm).

Where to Eat

Antica Hostaria Massa ★ CASERTAN/PIZZA   Caserta's favorite lunch spot is well poised near the palace for a break from all the pomp in a welcoming vaulted dining room and arbor-covered patio. Pizzas are a big draw, but the kitchen also turns out some excellent pastas and a delicious secondi of grilled local sausages.

Via Mazzini 55, Caserta. www.ristorantemassa.it. © **0823-456527.** Main courses 10€–25€. Mon–Sat 12:30–3pm and 7:30–11:30pm–10:30pm; Sun 12:30–3pm. Closed 10 days in Aug.

Antica Locanda ★ CAMPANIAN/CASERTAN   This is a great stop for lunch if you're visiting the silk factory and worker's village in San Leucio, but you won't eat lightly. The handsome dining room, opening off the picturesque main piazza, is known for its large portions of traditional favorites, including some excellent risottos, such as *porcini e provola* (porcini mushrooms and local smoked provolone) and *scialatielli ai frutti di mare* (homemade eggless pasta with seafood).

Piazza della Seta 8, San Leucio. ℓ **0823-305444.** Main courses 10€–16€. Tues–Sat 12:30–3pm and 7–10:30pm; Sun 12:30–3pm.

Cca' sta' O Masto ★ CASERTAN/PIZZA   This simple little hole in the wall is popular for its pizzas and hearty pastas, like the light-as-a-feather *gnocchi* in a simple sauce of butter and sage. But the crowds really pour in on Fridays, the only day seafood is served, when the kitchen turns out heaping platters of *frittura* (deep-fried calamari and shrimp).

Via Sant'Agostino 10, Caserta. ℓ **0823-320042.** Main courses 6€–12€. Tues–Sun 12:30–3pm and 7:30–11pm.

SANTA MARIA CAPUA VETERE ★★

7km (4 miles) W of Caserta; 24km (15 miles) NW of Naples

A suburb of Caserta is littered with the remains of an ancient city that, in its heyday, was second only to Rome. The ancient city was then known as Capua, while the modern city of Capua, 5km (3 miles) northwest, was originally Casilinium, the Roman harbor.

Essentials

GETTING THERE   Trenitalia (www.trenitalia.it; ℓ **892021** in Italy) serves Santa Maria Capua Vetere's **train** station with routes from Rome, Caserta, and Naples. The station is also a stop on the **Metro Campania Nord-Est** line (www.eavsrl.it; ℓ **800-053939** toll-free in Italy) from Naples and Caserta. From Caserta you can also take a **taxi.** By **car,** exit autostrada A1 at CASERTA NORD and take SS 7 (Via Appia). From Caserta and the Royal Palace, take Viale Douhet west; when it turns into SS 7, follow signs for SANTA MARIA CAPUA VETERE. Two parking lots are off the main road on the left, one behind Piazza San Pietro and another off Via F. Pezzella, which you can access from Corso Garibaldi.

GETTING AROUND   Santa Maria Capua Vetere is small enough to explore **on foot;** its most important attractions are along the ancient Appian Way, which is called Corso Aldo Moro.

Exploring the Roman City

The modern Corso Appia follows the route of the ancient Via Appia, the Appian Way, from the Arco di Adriano (**Hadrian's Arch),** still an imposing majestic triumphal monument though its marble finish and two of its three arches have long since disappeared. Capua was such an important city that the Appian Way was begun in 312 B.C. to link it with Rome. Farther along, at Corso 210, are the remains of a 1st-century B.C. Roman house, **Casa di**

spartacus, CAPUA'S REBEL SLAVE

One of the discoveries you'll make in Capua is that Spartacus, leader of the famous 1st-century B.C. slave revolt, was a gladiator in the arena. A teacher at the city's famous gladiator school bought Spartacus at a slave auction in 73 B.C. Spartacus and two fellow gladiators at the school stole kitchen knives and made an escape. The men soon came upon a stash of gladiatorial weapons and armed themselves. So equipped, and with their well-honed combat skills, they were easily able to fend off soldiers who tried to stop them. Legend has it that the men took refuge in the crater of Mt. Vesuvius, fashioning vines into ropes to navigate the slippery slopes. With the army in pursuit, the rebels made their way north, picking up other slaves as they went. Soon Spartacus was in command of more than 70,000 men, but the greatly reinforced army had them on the run. In a final decisive battle as the men tried to reach Sicily, more than 12,000 slaves were killed and 6,000 were captured. The prisoners were crucified along the Apian Way between Capua and Rome. Spartacus was not among them, and his fate is unknown. The story made it to the big screen in the 1960 Stanley Kubrick classic, *Spartacus*, with Kirk Douglas in the title role. *Spartacus: War of the Damned* (2010–13) brought the story to television, with Liam McIntyre playing our hero.

Confuleio Sabbio (discovered by chance during construction in 1955). The modest dwelling was the home of a freedman, a merchant specializing in the production of *sagum:* the heavy woolen cape worn by soldiers and—in a less-refined version—by slaves and paupers. The **Duomo,** off Piazza Matteotti on Via Sirtori 3, is a repository of the city's distant past, built in A.D. 432 over early Christian catacombs, with five Renaissance naves supported by columns topped with Corinthian capitals taken from the amphitheater and Roman temples (② **0823-846640;** free admission; open daily 9am–12:30pm and 4:30–6pm).

Anfiteatro Campano ★★★ AMPHITHEATER The city's majestic amphitheater (only the one in Rome was larger) was probably built around A.D. 3 and enlarged a century later by Emperor Hadrian. The giant arena has a maximum length of about 170m (558 ft.) and its now ruined seating could accommodate more than 60,000 spectators. Much of the marble, stone, bronze, and lead has been carted off over the centuries, but from what remains, it's easy to imagine the sheer magnificence of the structure when the four-story height was covered in gleaming travertine stone and embellished with marble busts of the gods. The likenesses served as keystones for each of the 240 arches on the lower floors, and full-length statues stood under the arches of the second and third floors. Only the busts of Ceres and Juno remain, carved over the main entrance—the two were undoubtedly reassuring presences, Ceres being the goddess of agriculture and fertility and Juno being the patron and protector of the Empire. The well-preserved labyrinth of corridors below the arena led to the "locker rooms" for gladiators and the bestiary,

Santa Maria Capua Vetere

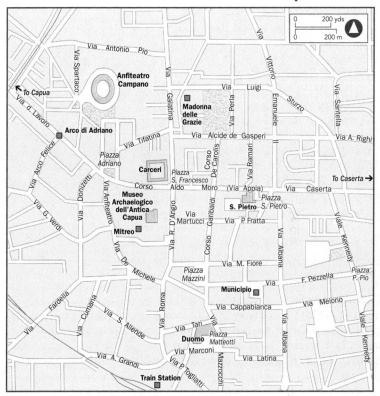

where the fighting animals were stabled. Tucked into a niche are some faint frescoes, what remains of a Christian oratory eked out of the space in the 9th century. Littering the grounds in front of the arena is a delightfully random array of statues, lintel, columns, and other bits and pieces collected from throughout the Roman city. Among the fragments is a playful 2nd-century mosaic in which Nereides and Tritons, mythical mermaid-like sea creatures, splash in the sea. The adjacent **Museo dei Gladiatori (Gladiators' Museum)** ★ shows off four complete suits of gladiator armor, while a model reconstruction of the amphitheater and a thrilling animation of a gladiatorial fight bring the days of violent blood sport to life. Capua claims the rebellious slave Spartacus as a native son. As a student at the coliseum's famous gladiator school, Spartacus led a revolt when he and 80 other slave gladiators broke out of the compound and, gathering men and weapons, gave the Roman legions a run for their money (see box, above).

Piazza Ottobre (off Piazza Adriano). ✆ **0823-798864.** Admission 2.50€ includes Museo Archeologico dell'Antica Capua and Mitreo. Tues–Sun 9am–5:30pm.

Museo Archeologico dell'Antica Capua ★ TOWER Capitals, columns, and other remains of the Roman city fill a space that's an attraction in itself, the Torre di Sant'Erasmo. The tower was built to defend the town against an invasion by the Longobards, the Germanic tribe that overtook Italy in the 6th century. The star attraction here is the **Mitreo,** just behind the tower on Vicolo Mitreo. The well-preserved temple, built between the 2nd and 3rd centuries, is one of hundreds of shrines to the sun god Mithras found throughout the former empire. The cult was especially popular among soldiers and involved elaborate initiation rites that took place in frescoed stalls in the temple, with each of the seven stages accompanied by an elaborate banquet. The vaulted ceiling is decorated with a

The impressive ruins of Santa Maria Capua.

large fresco of the central image of the cult, in which Mithras is born from a rock and sacrifices a white bull. By some interpretations, the god was born on December 25 and is a precursor of Jesus Christ. (The temple can be visited by guided tour only, included in the price of admission; sign up at the ticket booth of the Anfiteatro Campano, above).

— Via Roberto D'Angiò 48 (off Corso Aldo Moro [Via Appia]). ℗ **0823-844206.** Admission 2.50€ includes access to Anfiteatro Campano and Mitreo. Tues–Sun 9am–6pm.

Exploring Capua

This sleepy village on a picturesque bend in the Volturno River began as the Roman harbor of Casilinium; it was an important river crossing on the Appian Way. Just to confuse matters, the town took its name from the ancient Roman city 5km (3 miles) to the southeast, whose residents fled here after a Saracen raid in A.D. 840. So, Casilinium became Capua, and Capua became Santa Maria Capua Vetere.

Capua still retains some of the fortifications that defended the Roman harbor and the bridge that carried the Appian Way across the Volturno River (the bridge was perfectly functional until it was bombed in 1943, as Allied forces moved up the peninsula to retake Italy from the Germans). As you stroll along Corso Appio (the original Appian Way), you'll notice a liberal sprinkling of Roman artifacts, including a bas-relief at Via Pier delle Vigne 26 (just off Corso Appio) and six marble busts gracing 16th-century **Palazzo del Municipio** on Piazza dei Giudici, also off Corso Appia. They were taken from the Anfiteatro Campano of Santa Maria Capua Vetere (see above). The **Cattedrale di Santo Stefano e Sant'Agata,** on Piazza Landolfo, is also liberally sprinkled with columns, capitals, and bas-reliefs from Roman Capua, and the

Santa Maria Capua Vetere — FARTHER AFIELD: CASERTA, CAPUA & BENEVENTO

11th-century atrium is composed almost entirely of ancient elements (© **0823-961081;** free admission; open daily 8–11am and 5:30–7:30pm).

Basilica di Sant'Angelo in Formis ★★ CHURCH   Diana, the Roman goddess of the hunt, was often considered to be aloof and mysterious, preferring to reside in high mountains and dark, sacred woods. So it's only fitting that this exotic hillside basilica built over the remains of one of her temples should also be otherworldly. Flooring, columns, and other elements of the slightly Moorish-Arabaesque landmark come from Diana's temple, while the 11th-century frescoes that almost completely cover the walls of the arched portico and the three naves are exotically Byzantine. Artists imported from Constantinople decorated the basilica, rebuilt from a 7th-century church that rose over the site of the temple. The colorful works depict the life of Christ and other scenes from the Old and New Testament, in color-rich panels that are divided by columns or paintings of trees. The Archangel Michael, to whom the basilica is dedicated, floats over the entrance, while a terrifying scene of the Last Judgment fills the west wall. A good tonic to the swirling visions of angels and devils, saints and sinners, is the view from the front of the basilica, across the countryside and sea all the way to Ischia on a clear day. You can easily reach the church by buses that depart from in front of Capua's train station. The village of Formis is also a stop on the **Metro Campania Nord-Est** line (www.metrocampanianordest.it; ✆ **800-053939** toll-free in Italy) **By car** from Capua, take Via Roma out of town following signs for S. ANGELO IN FORMIS.

Piazza della Basilica di Sant'Angelo, Formis. ✆ **0823-960492.** Free admission. Summer Mon–Sat 9:30am–noon and 3–7pm, Sun 10am–4pm; winter Mon–Sat 9:30am–12:30pm and 3–6pm, Sun 10am–4pm.

Museo Campano ★ MUSEUM   Among Etruscan pottery, Roman mosaics, and some unremarkable medieval paintings are the intriguing **Le Madri (The Mothers)** in rooms five through nine. Excavations in a field outside ancient Capua that began in 1845 unearthed a monumental altar flanked by these haunting statuettes, carved in tufa stone, of women holding as many as six swaddled infants in each arm. They were probably offerings to a divinity known as Mater Matuta, dedicated to motherhood, fertility, and peace. One of the figures holds a pomegranate in one hand and a dove in the other, symbols of fertility and peace, and other statues are of afflicted body parts, suggesting the ill and injured also came here to leave votives in the quest for a cure.

A walk through the medieval holdings provides a good look at the man who is one of the most influential and fascinating figures of European history, Federico II. In 1239, Federico commissioned the statues that are now in room 26 for his castle in Capua. The unknown sculptors obviously thought it prudent to cast their patron in a good light and make him appear handsome. Federico was one of the greatest of medieval rulers, king of Sicily at the age of 4 and Holy Roman Emperor at 18; so competent and forceful he was known as Stupor Mundi ("wonder of the world"). But in real life, the one quality the enlightened and intelligent Federico lacked was good looks. One contemporary said he "was covered with red hair, was bald and myopic. Had he been a slave, he would not have fetched 200 dirhams at market."

Via Roma 68 (off Via Duomo). ✆ **0823-961402.** Free admission. Tues–Sat 9am–1:30pm; Sun 9am–1pm.

BENEVENTO ★

51km (31 miles) E of Caserta; 86km (53 miles) NE of Naples

Pleasant as this pretty hilltop town is, it's been destroyed time and again over the centuries. The busy town's long past begins in the 7th century B.C. and includes a prosperous period as flourishing Roman marketplace and military outpost, then as a privileged papal possession. Romans changed the original name, Maleventum, "site of bad events," to the more-promising Beneventum, "site of good events," but to no avail. Barbarians swept through town during the Dark Ages, an earthquake leveled Benevento in 1688, and U.S. bombers repeated the almost-total destruction in 1943. That so many well-preserved Roman and medieval monuments remain is really rather remarkable.

Benevento

Tourist Information
Parking

Essentials

GETTING THERE   Benevento is well connected by **train,** with frequent service from Naples and Caserta. Contact **Trenitalia** (www.trenitalia.it; ☎ 892021 in Italy) for fares and information. Benevento is also served by the **Metro Campania Nord-Est** line (www.eavsrl.it; ☎ 800-053939 toll-free in Italy) from Naples. Trains arrive at Benevento's **stazione** located in Piazza Colonna 2, to the north of town.

By **car,** take the autostrada A16 to the exit signed BENEVENTO and continue on the short stretch of highway to the town.

GETTING AROUND   The center of Benevento is relatively small and accessible **on foot;** however, since the town is built on a steep hillside, you might want to take a **bus** from the hub across from the train station to the top and walk down. Lines 1 and 7 both pass by Trajan's Arch, going up to the Rocca dei Priori in the heart of the historic district. Buy bus tickets at a tobacconist or a newsstand before boarding; tickets cost 1€ and are valid for 90 minutes. **Taxis** wait at the **stand** on Piazza Colonna, across from the railway station (or call ☎ 0824-50341).

Benevento has long been associated with dark magic, and little wonder. The Romans started the bad rap with their Temple to Isis, the powerful Egyptian goddess with the power to cast spells and work miraculous cures. The Germanic Longobards who took Benevento in A.D. 571 brought with them adoration of the god Wotan, who counted sorcery among his many talents. Legend has it that his followers met beneath a walnut tree on the banks of the River Sabato for nocturnal rituals. For better or worse, Benevento's reputation for harboring black-magic covens spread throughout the Middle Ages, and the witches of Benevento became infamous. Word was that the town was the launching pad for nightly excursions via broom into surrounding villages, where the witches inflicted ailments on the unsuspecting, stole newborns, and created all sorts of other mischief. Benevento persecuted hundreds of witches. During their trials the accused were said to utter "Unguent, unguent, carry me to the walnut tree of Benevento, Above the water and above the wind, And above all other bad weather." By the 18th century or so it became better known that unguents, so called "flying powders," were actually hallucinogens, and that many women accused of witchcraft were suffering from psychological disorders. Even so, some say witches can still sometimes be seen on the banks of the Sabato at night. You can engage in a bit of black magic by tasting Strega, the local liqueur made from a secret mixture of 17 herbs and spices. It's potent, and you might not be surprised to learn that *strega* is also the Italian word for "witch."

VISITOR INFORMATION The excellent local tourist office is at Via Nicola Sala 31, 82100 Benevento (www.eptbenevento.it; © **0824-319911**).

Exploring the Town

Benevento commands a hilltop high above a green valley and tumbles down the slope from the **Rocca dei Rettori,** on Piazza IV Novembre. The war-prone Samnites, an ancient Italian tribe, dug out defensive terraces up here in the 7th century B.C., the Romans constructed waterworks on the hilltop, and papal governors built the lavish palacelike fortress that now houses government offices. The fortress grounds and the adjacent gardens of the **Villa Comunale** provide some nice glimpses of the valley below. It's easy to pick out the arteries that made the town so important for such a long time: The Calore and Sabato rivers merge nearby, as do the Via Appia and Via Traiana (Appian and Trajan ways), two major roads of the empire. Benevento was an important overland crossroads at the western terminus of the Via Traiana (see Arco di Traiano, below). The Ponte Leproso, the bridge the Romans built to carry the Via Appia over the Sabato River, is still in use today. When you visit the Teatro Romano, take a short walk west for a look.

Arco di Traiano (Trajan's Arch) ★★★ MONUMENT One of southern Italy's best-preserved and most magnificent Roman monuments was built between A.D. 114 and 117 to honor Emperor Trajan (reigned A.D. 98 to 117).

Trajan's Arch.

The graceful monument marks the western terminus of the Via Traiana (Trajan Way), a relatively level and quick route between Benevento to the Empire's Eastern Mediterranean port at Brindisi. Carved reliefs celebrate the deeds of Trajan, and there is much to boast about. The enlightened and illustrious leader enlarged and strengthened the empire while implementing generous social reforms that included providing funds to poor children, allotting grain to the poor, and (that age-old popularity booster) lessening taxes. Benevento has gotten good use out of the arch, and in the Middle Ages made it the main gate, Port'Aurea, in the city walls. The nearby 10th-century church of **Sant'Ilario a Port'Aurea,** Via San Pasquale, houses an illuminating exhibit on the arch and Roman life under Trajan.

Free admission; daily 10am–1pm, in winter also 3–6pm, fall–spring 4–7pm, summer 5–8pm.

Duomo ★ CHURCH   What was once considered the finest Romanesque church in Italy, with bronze doors as beautiful as those on the baptistery in Florence, was blown to smithereens during U.S. bombing raids in 1943. Enough remains to suggest the church's onetime grandeur. The elegant marble facade is embellished with arches, a loggia, and—tucked into a niche on the right—the statue of a knight placed here after his eternal rest was disturbed when World War II bombs destroyed his tomb. One of the bronze doors has been restored, and the 72 intricately etched scenes depict scenes from the life of Christ and portray some plump and smug-looking local bishops. Fantastic monsters, half-man, half-beast, surround the massive door handles, probably there to ward off evil spirits and keep them away from the sacred precincts within.

Piazza Duomo. Free admission. Daily 9am–12:30pm and 5–7pm.

Museo del Sannio ★ MONASTERY   The former monastery of Santa Sofia (below) houses artifacts that begin with some tomb markers of the namesake Samnites, the fierce and combative tribe that lived in the region as early as the 7th century B.C. and hung around long enough to give the Romans a hard time. Elegant though headless statues of Trajan and his wife, the treacherous and aptly named Plotina, are probably from the nearby Arco di Traiano. Another emperor, the deeply religious and mystically oriented Domitian (reigned A.D. 81 to 96), allowed construction of a cult-oriented Temple to Isis, the Egyptian goddess of nature and magic, in Beneventum. Art from the temple includes a portrayal of Domitian, himself a cult personality, in Egyptian garb. Part of the collection spills into the monastery cloister, a lovely spot with an exotic blend of Moorish arches and Romanesque columns, carved with intriguing vignettes of boar hunts and pilgrimages. The monastery was a powerhouse

Benevento

A detail from one of the columns of Santa Sofia.

of medieval Italy, famous throughout Europe for disseminating manuscripts in an elegant script, "scriptorium Beneventanum."

Piazza Santa Sofia. ② **0824-21818** or 0824-28831. Admission 4€. Tues–Sun 9am–7pm.

Santa Sofia ★★ CHURCH Duke Arechi II, part of the Germanic dynasty that ruled southern Italy until the 11th century, made Benevento his headquarters for part of the 8th century. One of the ways he left his mark was with this extraordinary star-shaped church that surrounds a central hexagon, covered by a dome. Supporting it all is a forest of columns, some of them repurposed from the Roman town's Temple to Isis (see above). As if the odd shapes and intriguing perspectives of this architectural tour de force weren't enough, some faded fragments that once covered the entire interior charmingly depict the moment the Virgin Mary learns she is about to become the mother of Christ and other Christian scenes. The monastery attached to the church now houses the Museo del Sannio (see above).

Piazza Matteotti. ② **0824-21206.** Free admission. Daily 10am–noon and 4:30–7pm.

Teatro Romano ★★ THEATER One of the better-preserved Roman theaters in Italy was completed in the first part of the 2nd century A.D. As many as 15,000 spectators could squeeze into the sizeable semicircular space—and still do. While only one tier remains of the three levels of 25 arches that once covered the facade, much of the structure is amazingly intact, largely because it was buried sometime around the 8th century. Original entrances and corridors lead to some intact stone seats, still used for summertime performances of opera and classical dramas.

Via Port'Arsa. ② **0824-47213.** Admission 2€. Daily 9am–1 hr. before sunset.

Where to Eat

Nunzia ★ BENEVENTAN This institution that's as much a part of the local scene as witchcraft prides itself on homey preparations of traditional favorites, served in plain, cozy surroundings near the Arco di Traiano that will make you think you've stumbled into a Beneventan home. Soups (*cardone* is a delicious concoction of chicken stock with meatballs) and pastas, including tasty spaghetti *e piselli* (with peas) and linguine *al nero di sepia* (with black squid ink) are lovingly made and followed by such house specialties as *baccalá con capperi e olive* (salt cod in an olive-and-caper sauce). A meal is pleasantly inexpensive.

Via Annunziata 152. ② **0824-29431.** Main courses 6€–12€. Mon–Sat 1–3pm and 8–11pm. Closed 2 weeks in Aug.

PLANNING YOUR TRIP

This chapter provides planning tools and information on how to get around and make the most of local resources while you're in the region.

One of the two most important things to consider is when to go. See "When to Go" in chapter 2 for specific advice, but the main consideration is that many businesses, including hotels and restaurants, close between November and March. The other factor to keep in mind when planning is that the laid-back *dolce vita* reigns here, so you don't want to put too much on your plate, unless it's the local food.

GETTING THERE
By Plane

Campania is served by Naples's **Capodichino Airport** (www. gesac.it; ⓒ **081-7896111** or 848-888777 toll-free in Italy); its international airport code is **NAP.** It's fairly easy to reach the rest of the region from the airport.

The only intercontinental nonstop flights to Naples are those offered by **Meridiana** in the summer from New York (www. meridiana.it; ⓒ **718-751-4499** in the U.S., **0789-52682** in Italy). With other carriers, you'll most likely be touching down in Italy at Rome's Fiumicino-Leonardo da Vinci Airport (international airport code **FCO**) or Milan Malpensa (MXP). You can fly on to Naples from those airports or use the country's high-speed train network (see "By Train," below). Naples is only 50 minutes by air from Rome and about 90 minutes from Milan; the train trip is a little more than an hour from Rome and a little more than 4 hours from Milan. Flights into Milan are often so much less expensive than those to Rome that the extra travel time may well be worth it.

Another option is to fly into another European city and connect to Naples from there. Among the major airlines offering flights to Naples from their European hubs are Alitalia, Air France, Aer Lingus, Austrian Airlines, British Airways, Iberia, and Lufthansa.

FROM THE AIRPORT   The airport is about 7km (4 miles) from Naples's city center. The **Alibus shuttle bus** (www.unicocampania. it; ⓒ **081-551-3109**) to Naples departs every 20 minutes, with stops

10

on Corso Garibaldi near Napoli Centrale train station and in Piazza Municipio at the heart of the historic district. The fare is 3€. Shuttle bus service to Sorrento and towns on the Amalfi Coast is also available (see chapter 6). The flat rate is 19€ for Naples, 100€ for Sorrento, 120€ for Positano, 130€ for Amalfi, and 135€ for Ravello. Most hotels and resorts along the coast offer airport pickup: For a limousine booked through your hotel, you'll pay about 30€ for Naples, 90€ for Sorrento, and 115€ for Amalfi. You might get better rates contacting a car service directly (see "Getting Around: By Car," later in this chapter).

By Train

Naples is on Italy's main southern corridor, making the city easily accessible from other Italian and European towns. Most of your travel around the region will probably be by suburban train lines, as well as by bus and boat (see "Getting Around," later in this chapter).

The national railroad company **FS-Trenitalia** (www.trenitalia.it; ℂ **892021** from anywhere in Italy, 39-06-6847-5475 from abroad) offers service on regional trains as well as the faster Intercity (IC) trains and even faster high-speed *le frecce* network. To make matters a little more confusing, high-speed trains are sometime referred to as Eurostar. High-speed trains offer two types of service—Frecciarossa, traveling up to 360km/h, and Frecciargento, traveling at speeds up to 250km/h. These trains can make the trip between Rome and Naples in 1 hour and 10 minutes and between Milan and Naples in 4 hours and 10 minutes. On all high-speed trains in Italy it is necessary to make a seat reservation when you buy a ticket. Travelers with rail passes (see below) must also make a seat reservation, for a 10€ fee, before boarding. High-speed trains have four classes of service: Standard, Premium, Business, and Executive. Standard is perfectly comfortable, even for longer journeys, with plenty of leg room. If you have an aversion to riding backward, you may be out of luck. Seating faces forward and backward, and trains switch directions leaving various stations as they travel the north–south corridor. So, you may be facing forward between Florence and Rome, then backward between Rome and Naples.

A private company, **Italo** (www.italotreno.it), also operates on the high-speed lines, offering similarly comfortable service at competitive rates.

Fares for fast trains are not cheap, but fares are almost always lower if you book online, especially in advance, on the **Trenitalia** website (www.trenitalia. it). Children ages 5 to 11 receive a discount of 50%, and children age 4 and younger travel free with their parents. Seniors and youths age 25 and under can purchase discount cards.

Intercity (IC) trains are one step down from the *frecce*, but they are comfortable, reasonably fast, and can be less expensive. The slower Regionale (R) and Regionale Veloce (RV) trains make many more stops and offer the lowest prices. However, high-speed service has replaced much of the IC, R, and RV service on the main north–south routes. Since most investment has been in the impressive high-speed network, many of these other trains, especially those on R and RV lines, are poorly maintained and can be quite run-down and dirty.

If you do not have a seat reservation, you must validate your ticket at the little yellow box before boarding the train. You can be fined heavily if you board a train without a seat reservation or a validated ticket. Should you find yourself on a train without either, seek out the conductor, who might be a little more forgiving since you've gone to the trouble of making the situation known.

In stations, schedules are printed on large placards—yellow for departures, white for arrivals. Arrival and departures, with the number of the track (*binario*), are also posted on monitors throughout stations. You can also check schedules and buy tickets at www.trenitalia.com. Automated ticket machines in stations are easy to use and present an alternative to waiting in long lines. You can also use them to check schedules anywhere on the network, even if you're not buying a ticket. If you do wish to see an agent, in most stations (Naples included) you will take a number from a machine and wait for the number to appear on a screen. The Naples train station is clean and well-run, and equipped with ATMs, restaurants, and shops. Luggage-storage lockers are available.

If you plan to travel extensively in Europe by train, it may be cheaper to purchase a **Eurail Pass,** offering unlimited travel for a set number of days within a 2-month period. For more information and a look at the many options, contact **Rail Europe** (www.raileurope.com; ✆ **877-272-RAIL** [7245]). Remember, though: If you are traveling mostly in the Naples and Amalfi Coast region, you will not be doing much train travel aside from some jaunts on suburban lines, on which the passes are not valid.

By Boat

Naples and Salerno are well served by international ferries and regular stops on many cruise-ship lines. Arriving in Naples by ship is a magnificent experience. You'll land at **Stazione Marittima,** at the edge of the historic district.

Many major ferry companies offer regular service between Naples and other Italian and European ports (see "Getting Around" later in this chapter for local service between Naples and the Amalfi Coast, Capri, Ischia, and Procida). Companies include **Siremar** (www.siremar.it; ✆ **199-118866**), with service to and from the Aeolian Islands and Sicily (Milazzo); **SNAV** (www.snav.it; ✆ **081-428-5555**), with boats to Sicily, Sardinia, and the Aeolian and Pontine islands; **Tirrenia** (www.tirrenia.it; ✆ **892123** or 02-2630-2803), with boats to and from Sardinia (Cagliari) and Sicily (Palermo); and **TTTLines** (www.TTTLines.it; ✆ **800-915365**), with ships to and from Sicily (Catania). Major companies operating from Salerno are **Caronte & Tourist** (www.carontetourist.it; ✆ **800-627414** toll-free in Italy, or 089-258-2528), with boats to and from Sicily (Catania and Messina); and **Grimaldi Lines** (www.grimaldi-ferries.com; ✆ **081-496444**), with regular service to and from Spain (Valencia), Malta (La Valletta), Tunisia (Tunis), and Sicily (Palermo).

By Car

To drive a car in Italy, technically you are required to have an **International Driving Permit (IDP),** which is an official translation of your license. You will most likely be able to rent a car without an IDP, but you will be probably be asked to present one if you're stopped by the police or are involved in an accident—and you can be fined if you don't have it. Apply in the United States at any **American Automobile Association (AAA)** branch; or contact **AAA's national headquarters** (www.aaa.com; ℭ **800-222-4357** or 407-444-4300). Canadians can get the address of the nearest **Canadian Automobile Association** by visiting www.caa.ca or calling ℭ **613-247-0117.** An international permit is valid only if physically accompanied by your home country–issued driver's license and only if signed on the back.

Most rental companies require a minimum age of 23 or 25, but a few will rent less expensive models to drivers who are at least 21. Most rental companies will not rent a car to drivers 76 and older. Insurance on all vehicles is compulsory and can be purchased as part of your rental package. You will also usually need a valid credit card (not a prepaid or debit card) for a standard model and two credit cards for a deluxe model; cash payments will not be accepted.

Prices vary with car size and special offers, but a compact car will generally rent for between 60€ and 100€ per day. You will usually get a much better deal if you book far in advance. To keep costs down, opt for the smallest models with manual transmission and pickup and return at the same location. Cars with automatic transmission are often not available and can be extremely expensive to rent. Package discounts are sometimes available when you book your car together with your flight.

All of the major international rental companies serve Naples and the Amalfi Coast. You may also want to check the prices of such Europe specialists as **Auto Europe** (www.autoeurope.com; ℭ **800-223-5555**); **Europe by Car** (www.europebycar.com; ℭ **800-223-1516,** or 212-581-3040); **Kemwel Holiday Auto** (www.kemwel.com; ℭ **877-820-0668**); **Maggiore** (www.maggiore. it; ℭ **199-151120** toll-free in Italy); and **Sixt** (www.sixt.com; ℭ **888-749-8227** in the United States; 199-100666 in Italy). Renting online usually will get you the best prices, but it is worth checking with the local rental office for a better deal. Also, ask when you book if your American Automobile Association (AAA) or AARP membership will give you a discount.

Limited-access express highways in Italy are called *autostrada* and numbered from A1 on. They sometimes are also marked with the European number, starting with the letter E. North of Naples, *autostrade* are toll roads; they are extremely well maintained and have excellent signage and modern gas stations and service centers at sensible intervals. Tariffs depend on the size of your vehicle and the type of road. To give you an example, Rome-Salerno will cost you a minimum of 16.70€. The official website, www.autostrade.it, is equipped with an excellent tool to help you determine the best routes and calculate your costs.

The Autostrada del Sole A1 from Milan to Naples is the main highway to Campania. From Naples, the A3 leads to Salerno. Driving from Milan to Naples will take you about 9 hours on average, and about 10 hours to Sorrento.

GETTING AROUND

By Train

Local train lines serve much of the region. **Alifana** (www.eavsrl.it; ✆ **800-053939**) covers Benevento and surrounding areas; **Circumvesuviana** (www.vesuviana.it; ✆ **800-053939**) connects Naples with Herculaneum (Ercolano), Pompeii, Castellammare di Stabia, Sorrento, and other towns around the east side of the bay; and **Metronapoli** (www.unicocampania.it; ✆ **800-053939**), connects Naples with Pozzuoli and the Phlegraean Fields. Fares on local trains are cheap, service is frequent, and you don't need advance reservations. You can buy your tickets at the automatic machines inside the stations and hop on the train, but be sure to validate them at the little boxes on or near the platforms; failure to validate a ticket can result in a steep fine. Rail stations are usually in the center of towns, within walking distance of many major attractions and well connected by public transportation. You will find more information in the "Getting There" and "Getting Around" sections at the beginning of each chapter.

By Bus

Local bus companies operate throughout Campania. You'll probably be using the bus to travel along the Amalfi Coast, a welcome alternative to driving the traffic-choked, winding coast road. SITA (see below) schedules numerous runs between Salerno, Naples, and Sorrento, with extra lines between Amalfi, Positano, and Sorrento, as well as secondary lines from Amalfi to Ravello and from Amalfi and Sorrento to minor destinations along the coast. These provide not only convenient but also cheap transport, and you can buy a single pass valid on public transportation in the region. The Unico Costiera covers all the towns along the Sorrento and Amalfi coasts, from Meta di Sorrento to Salerno. The best deals are the 24-hour pass and the 3-day pass (7.60€ and 18€, respectively). The Unico is also available in 45-minute and 90-minute increments (2.50€ and 3.80€, respectively). Any of the passes will allow you unlimited rides on SITA buses and the Circumvesuviana trains connecting Meta with Sorrento and stations in between. For more information, visit www.unicocampania.it.

The leading bus operators in the region are **CSTP** (www.cstp.it; ✆ **800-016659** or 089-487001), with buses in Salerno, Paestum, and the Cilento; **CTP** (www.ctpn.it; ✆ **800-482644**), serving Naples and linking it with neighboring towns; **SEPSA** (www.sepsa.it; ✆ **081-552-5125**), serving Pozzuoli, Baia, Cuma, and Miseno, as well as Procida and Ischia; and **SITA** (www.sitabus.it; ✆ **089-053939**), serving the Sorrento Peninsula and the Amalfi Coast.

For more information, see the "Getting There" and "Getting Around" sections throughout this book.

By Ferry

Ferries are a handy option, particularly during the summer, when the narrow coastal roads become terribly congested. Several companies connect the region's top destinations. Hydrofoil service is the fastest, but is suspended in winter and operates only between selected harbors—chiefly Naples, Capri, Ischia, Sorrento, Positano, Amalfi, and Salerno. Other options include large ferries with transport of vehicles, and smaller motorboats, which can reach smaller harbors. All companies charge similar rates for similar service. The only relevant difference is the time schedule.

Naples's two harbors—Stazione Marittima, downtown, and Terminal Aliscafi, in Mergellina—along with **Salerno**'s, are the region's main hubs, followed by **Amalfi, Sorrento,** and **Pozzuoli.** All offer multiple daily connections to the islands (**Capri, Ischia,** and **Procida**) and the smaller towns of the Amalfi Coast, including **Positano.**

Companies offering local service are **Alilauro** (www.alilauro.it; ✆ **081-497-2222**), with hydrofoils to Ischia and Positano; **Caremar** (www.caremar.it; ✆ **199-116655**), with ferries and hydrofoils to Ischia, Capri, and Procida; **Medmar** (www.medmargroup.it; ✆ **081-333-4411**), with ferries to Ischia; **NLG** (www.navlib.it; ✆ **081-552-0763**), with hydrofoils to Capri; **SNAV** (www.snav.it; ✆ **081-428-5555**), with hydrofoils to Ischia, Capri, and Procida; and **Volaviamare** (www.volaviamare.it; ✆ **081-497-2211**), with fast boats between Naples, Sorrento, Amalfi, Positano, Salerno, Ischia, and Capri.

By Limousine/Car Service & Taxi

A good alternative to renting a car is using a **taxi** or a **car service**—make sure they use cars and minivans with air conditioning (very important in summer), as well as trained, English-speaking drivers. Even so, given the ease of getting around the region via public transportation, moving around this way is a luxury and an unnecessary expense for anyone watching the pocketbook. Official taxis are at the airport and the train station. They are white and have a taxi sign on the roof, a city logo, and a card clearly detailing the official rates inside. The Municipality of Naples has established flat rates for major tourist destinations in the region. These rates are cheaper than if the meter was used, and you have to ask for them before departure. A round-trip to Herculaneum with a 2-hour wait (during which you visit the ruins), is 70€; Pompeii with a 2-hour wait is 90€; a round-trip tour of the Amalfi Coast (Positano, Ravello, Amalfi, and Sorrento) for an entire day is 220€; a round-trip to Mt. Vesuvius with a 2-hour wait is 90€; a round-trip to Baia (Scavi Archeologici) and Solfatara with a 3-hour wait is 85€; and a tour of Naples is 70€.

Some well-established, Naples-based taxi companies with good reputations are **Cooperativa Partenopea** (www.radiotaxilapartenope.it; ✆ **081-551-5151,** or 081-556-0202); **Consortaxi** (consortaxi.com; ✆ **081-2222**); **Radio Taxi La 570** (www.la570.it; ✆ **081-570-7070**); and **Radio Taxi Napoli** (www.consorziotaxinapoli.it; ✆ **081-8888**). Taxis operate from the airport or

Getting Around

PLANNING YOUR TRIP

various taxi stands at major destinations in and around the city. You can just go to one of these stands and grab a taxi, but book in advance for longer excursions.

There are several car sevices that provide service on the Sorrento Peninsula and Amalfi Coast, with drivers acting as guides. Among them are **Cuomo Limousine** (www.carsorrento.it), **Paolo Bellantonio** (www.bellantoniolimo service.com), based in Sorrento; **Benvenuto Limos & Tours** (www.benvenuto limos.com), based in Praiano; and **Avellino Car Service** (www.amedeo avellino.com), based in Vico Equense.

By Car

Unless you are planning to explore some the farther-flung reaches of the region, such as Cilento National Park, you probably won't need a car. You'd be insane to try to drive in Naples, and a car is nothing but an impediment on the Amalfi Coast. Traffic can be at a standstill, most towns are closed to cars, and parking is scarce and expensive. Just consider that while driving from Sorrento to Amalfi in the off season will take you less than an hour, with summer traffic, a 2-hour ride is typical, and at some traffic-heavy times cars are made to wait until congestion clears before entering the road. You aren't allowed to bring a car to Capri or Procida, nor to Ischia in high season. Gasoline prices and parking fees are steep.

Neapolitans, especially, have a well-earned reputation for aggressive and daring driving, disregarding speed limits and traffic lights with abandon. Motor scooters are extremely prevalent and their drivers often don't even make the slightest pretense of obeying traffic laws, so be mindful of them as they zoom and swerve between cars.

RULES OF THE ROAD   In Italy, driving is on the right-hand side of the road. Unless otherwise marked, **speed limits** are 50 kmph (31 mph) in urban areas, 90 kmph to 110 kmph (56–68 mph) in suburban areas, and 110 kmph to 130 kmph (68–81 mph) on limited-access highways. Speed limits for trailers, or towed vehicles, are lower: 70 kmph (43 mph) outside urban areas and 80 kmph (50 mph) on autostrada (100 kmph/62 mph for auto-caravans, or mobile homes). Automatic speed controls are installed on most roads, and you may be ticketed for driving faster than the posted limit.

It is mandatory to have your **headlights** on at all times outside urban areas and to use **seat belts** (front and rear) and age-appropriate **car seats** for children. High-beam headlights are sometimes used to signal to fellow drivers: If you are in the left passing lane and a driver flashes you from behind, you need to move out of the way. If an oncoming car signals you, it means that some danger is ahead, so slow down. If cars ahead of you put on their hazard lights, slow down—the traffic is completely stopped ahead. Horns cannot be used in urban areas except in an emergency.

Drinking and driving is severely punished, and there are fines for talking on your mobile phone while driving and for illegal parking.

FINDING YOUR WAY   Road signs are posted with one sign about 1.6km (1 mile) before an exit, and then another right at the exit. Destination signs are blue for local roads and green for the toll highway. Destinations of cultural interest are posted on brown signs. Often, only the major town on a local road is marked, while smaller towns and villages on the way will not be posted.

GASOLINE   Gas stations are distributed along local roads at sensible intervals; however, large stretches of countryside are without stations. Pumps are generally open Monday to Saturday from 7 or 8am to 1pm and 3 or 4pm to 7 or 8pm (some have a self-service pump accessible after hours). On toll highways, gas stations are positioned every 32 or 48km (20 or 30 miles) and are open 24 hours daily. Most cars take unleaded fuel (*benzina senza piombo*) or diesel (*diesel* or *gasolio*). Among diesel cars, only the newest models take the ecofuel labeled blue diesel (*blu diesel*). Be prepared for sticker shock every time you fill up as fuel is priced throughout the country at around 1.80€ per liter (diesel is a little cheaper, selling around 1.70€ per liter); a gallon equals about 3.8 liters. Make sure the pump registers zero before an attendant starts filling your tank: A common scam involves filling your tank before resetting the meter (so that you also pay the charges run up by the previous motorist), and it is still performed by some dishonest attendants.

BREAKDOWNS & ASSISTANCE   Roadside aid in Italy is excellent. For 24-hour **emergency assistance,** contact the national department of motor vehicles, **Automobile Club d'Italia** (www.aci.it; ⓒ **803116** toll-free in Italy).

PARKING   Parking is always limited, particularly during the high season and near major attractions. Parking lots and areas are indicated with a square sign bearing a large white p on a blue background.

Parking spots are marked on the pavement with painted lines of various colors depending on the type of parking: Yellow is for reserved parking (deliveries, drivers with disabilities, taxis, and so on); white is free parking (very limited—you won't find many of those on the Costiera); blue is paid parking. Rates vary as they are established by each municipality: Check the signs at the beginning and end of the stretch of parking spots and the sign on the automatic parking machines (usually located at a more or less reasonable distance from your parking spot; look for a gray/white box on a post or on a wall). Many machines accept only coins (some will take credit and debit cards), so come prepared (prices usually range from 1€–3€ per hour). The timer shows the current time, and as you insert money, it will show you what time you are paid through. When you're done, press the green button, collect the receipt, and place it on your dashboard in a visible spot. Do not even think about skipping this, particularly in tourist areas—authorities are very vigilant.

The alternative is a private parking lot. These are usually located near the historic district (or attractions) in most towns. They are often underground, and attendants will park your car for you. Expect to pay 20€ to 50€ per day, depending on the location.

TOURS

Cultural Trips

Context Travel (www.contexttravel.com; ✆ **800-691-6036** toll-free in the U.S., or 215-392-0303) arranges walks and excursions with local experts. Itineraries in Naples might include a look at the works and influence of Caravaggio or the charms and quirks of Neapolitan life.

Adventure & Wellness Trips

Breakaway Adventures (www.breakaway-adventures.com; ✆ **800-567-6286**) organizes cycling and walking tours on the Sorrento Peninsula and along the Amalfi Coast as well as in the Cilento.

Food & Wine Trips

Dolce Vita Wine Tours (www.dolcetours.com; ✆ **888-746-0022**) organizes walking food- and wine-oriented tours that focus on Capri and the region around Mt. Vesuvius.

Sorrento Cooking School (www.sorrentocookingschool.com; ✆ **081-878-3255**) runs a varied program that ranges from daily excursions to longer tours lasting up to 8 days, and includes cooking classes and wine tours.

Mami Camilla, Via Cocumella 06, Sant'Agnello di Sorrento (www.mami camilla.com; ✆ **081-878-2067**) is a family-run business with a focus on the cooking of southern Italy and a mission to introduce guests to the charms of the region.

[FastFACTS] CAMPANIA & THE AMALFI COAST

Area Codes **081** for the province of Naples (including Sorrento, Pozzuoli, Ischia, and Capri); **082** for the provinces of Caserta, Benevento, and Avellino; **089** for the province of Salerno (including the Amalfi Coast); and **097** for the Cilento. To call to and from this region, see "Telephones," later in this section.

Automobile Organizations **Automobile Club d'Italia (ACI;** www.aci.it; ✆ **803116** toll-free in Italy) provides roadside assistance

throughout the country. Their offices also help with car insurance, registration, and other regulation-related issues. **Touring Club Italiano** (www.touringclub.com) publishes maps and guides, and maintains useful databases of services for car travelers. Most rental agencies provide roadside assistance, with emergency contact numbers. Be sure to ask when renting.

Business Hours General business hours are Monday through Friday 8:30am to 1pm and 2:30 to

5:30pm. Banks are open Monday through Friday 8:30am to 1:30pm and 2:30 to 4pm. Some banks and businesses are also open on Saturday mornings. Shops are usually open Monday through Saturday from 8 or 9am to 1pm and 4:30 to 7:30 or 8pm, with one extra half-day closing per week at the shop's discretion. A growing number of shops in tourist areas stay open during the lunch break and on Sunday.

Customs Rules governing what tourists can bring

in duty-free are detailed at www.agenziadogane.it (click on "Traveler's customs card"). While there is no limit on how much you can take out of Italy, certain items are restricted; in particular, art objects: You'll need special permits for the export of objects more than 50 years old. As well, the purchase and export of protected species is prohibited. So is the purchase and export of copies of fashion items (think Vuitton, Chanel, and the like) and other copyrighted material. The fines are steep; do not break the law!

Disabled Travelers

Laws in Campania and in Italy have compelled train stations, airports, hotels, and most restaurants to follow a stricter set of regulations for **wheelchair accessibility.** Museums and other attractions have conformed to the regulations, which mimic many of those presently in effect in the United States. Even so, much of this region is not easily accessible to travelers with limited mobility. Many streets are paved with uneven cobbles and are stepped, while some restaurants and hotels cannot be fitted with the equipment required to make them wheelchair-accessible. Always call ahead to check on accessibility in hotels, restaurants, and sights you want to visit.

Local resources include **Accessible Italy** (www. accessibleitaly.com), a nonprofit association based in

San Marino (the mini-state in central Italy), which offers specialized tours as well as assistance for independent travelers, including rental of equipment and lists of accessible accommodations and other services.

Drinking Laws There's

no minimum drinking age in Italy. Alcohol is sold day and night throughout the year, and the only limitations are the operating hours of bars and shops (see "Business Hours," above). The law is extremely tough, though, on drunken behavior, and disturbance of the *quiete pubblica* (public peace) while inebriated is punished with stiff fines and jail time. Driving under the influence is severely penalized and can result in jail time as well as loss of your driver's license.

Electricity The electricity in Italy is an alternating current (AC), varying from 42 to 50 cycles. The voltage is 220. Laptop computers usually have converters built into the cord. Italian plugs have prongs that are round, not flat; therefore, an adapter plug is needed. You can purchase one in any hardware store, and hotels usually have some on hand to lend to guests.

Embassies & Consulates Embassies are located in Rome, but you'll find most consulates in Naples: The **U.S. Consulate** is at Piazza della Repubblica 2 (http://naples. usconsulate.gov; ☎ **081-583-8111**), and the **Canadian Consulate** is at Via

Carducci 29 (www.canada.it; ☎ **081-401338**). British subjects should contact the U.K. embassy in Rome, Via XX Settembre 80a (http://ukintaly.fco.gov.uk; ☎ **06-4220-0001**).

Emergencies Dial ☎ **113** or 112 for the police, ☎ **118** for an ambulance, and ☎ **115** for a fire. For road emergencies, dial ☎ **803116.**

Etiquette & Social Customs Italians are pretty forgiving about the social behavior of foreigners, and if you are observant and mold your behavior to Italian customs, you'll avoid most blunders.

Appropriate Attire: Italians tend to dress more formally than Americans do, particularly in urban settings. Shorts and tank tops are reserved for the beach. Women tend to dress more conservatively in general, particularly if they are alone. Churches usually have strict dress codes: no showing of shoulders or legs above the knee in a *chiesa* or on sacred ground.

Courtesy: On public transport, offer your seat to the elderly and to pregnant women, or anybody carrying a small child; men are expected to open doors for women and the elderly. Don't cut in line: Italians might not queue in an orderly manner like the English do, but they respect the order of arrival at an establishment, from the ice-cream counter to the post office. Always acknowledge people when entering and exiting a place, such as a shop, with "Buongiorno" and "Grazie."

Eating & Drinking: It is customary for two parties to "argue" over the dinner bill, and you are expected to offer to pay, even if you won't be allowed. If you have been taken out for a meal, then it is good manners to return the invitation. If that is impossible, a small gift (flowers, for example) sent to their home (if it was a private party) or a thank-you note (if it was a business meal) will do the trick. If you are invited to someone's home, never go empty-handed: Flowers, pastries, chocolates, a bottle of wine, or a small gift for the children is the right way to go.

Gestures & Contact: Italians do gesticulate a lot, but pointing at someone with your index finger is considered rude. Shake hands with your right hand. Hugging and kissing on the cheek among friends is common.

Photography: It is forbidden to take photographs of military, police, or transport (including subway and airport) facilities.

Family Travel The whole country, especially southern Italy, is completely welcoming to children. Italians love kids and take theirs with them wherever they go. However, don't expect special amenities: Playrooms, babysitting programs, and kiddie areas with small tables and crayons are not commonplace.

Most hoteliers will add a cot to your room for your child for free, and most have special rooms or suites designed for families with children. Many attractions offer discounts to children, though in state-run museums, only E.U. citizens ages 17 and under are admitted free.

Campania is particularly well suited for a vacation with children. The ancient sites and castles stimulate children's imagination while the many beaches and resorts are a perfect place for them to vent their energy.

The key to a successful family vacation in Italy lies in some smart planning: Involve your children in both the research and the decision-making process; schedule your visits alternating "adult" attractions with those in which your kids will be interested; and plan to make lots of gelato (ice cream) breaks.

See chapter 1 for some family-specific suggestions, and in chapter 3 you'll find an itinerary mapped out especially for families.

Gasoline (Petrol) Gasoline sells on average for 1.80€ per liter and diesel for about 1.70€ per liter, with small variations depending on the location. Taxes are already included in the printed price. One U.S. gallon equals 3.8 liters or .85 imperial gallons.

Health There are no particular health concerns in Campania, though you'll

want to protect yourself from mosquito bites.

Availability of Health Care: You'll find English-speaking doctors in most hospitals and clinics, and pharmacists often speak English as well. The largest hospitals in the region are in Naples, but you'll also find hospitals, excellent private clinics, and smaller facilities in more remote places.

Before leaving home, find out what medical services your health insurance covers. Medicare and Medicaid do not provide coverage for medical costs outside the U.S. To protect yourself, consider buying medical travel insurance (see "Insurance," below). Emergency rooms will always provide treatment, regardless of your insurance coverage.

Over-the-counter medicines are widely available in Campania. However, a pharmacy can only fill prescriptions written by a physician in Italy or elsewhere in the E.U. A prescription from the U.S. will probably not be honored, and you will have to consult a local doctor to write prescriptions for medication refills you might need—so plan accordingly and bring an adequate supply with you. However, some medicines that are available only by prescription in the U.S. are available over the counter in Italy. Names of products will be different, so make sure you know the active ingredient of your brand. If you are bringing **prescription medications** with you, pack them in your carry-on luggage, and carry them in their original containers, with pharmacy labels—otherwise they might not make it through security.

Contact the **International Association for Medical Assistance to Travelers (IAMAT;** www.iamat.org; © **716-754-4883,** or 416-652-0137 in Canada) for tips on travel and health concerns in the countries you're visiting, and for lists of local, English-speaking doctors.

Sun Exposure: Do not underestimate the strength of the sun. Wear a hat, sunscreen, and carry water when you visit outdoor attractions and archaeological areas such as Pompeii and Herculaneum.

Insurance Trip-cancellation insurance can be a good investment if you are spending a lot of money on your trip and you have made plans way in advance. Relatively safe as this region is, setbacks do happen, from auto accidents to lost luggage, so some general traveler's insurance coverage can be a good idea, too.

Internet & Wi-Fi You'll find Wi-Fi hotspots all over the region, and even the most modest hotels often offer free Wi-Fi. Many hotels also have computers or iPads for guests who are traveling without their Wi-Fi–equipped devices. For a directory of cybercafes in the region, check www.cybercafe.com.

Legal Aid If you are pulled over for a driving offense, you'll have the choice to settle the fine right there on the roadside (you will be given a copy of the fine and an official receipt) or pay it at the post office (you will be given a form to fill out). If you are taken to the police station, you can ask for a translator to be sure you understand the situation. If you are actually arrested, the consulate of your country is the place to turn for legal aid, although offices can't interfere in the Italian legal process. They can, however, inform you of your rights and provide you with a list of professional attorneys. If you're arrested for a drug offense, the consulate will notify a lawyer about your case.

LGBT Travelers Since 1861, Campania and Italy have had liberal legislation regarding homosexuality. Ischia and Capri have long been gay meccas, and you'll find a somewhat active gay life in Naples. Still, open displays of same-sex affection are sometimes frowned upon in the highly Catholic country (despite the fact that people in Campania are very physical, and men and women alike embrace when saying hello and goodbye).

ARCI Gay (www.arcigay.it) is the country's leading gay organization, with branches throughout Campania. Another major organization is **Gay.it** (www.gay.it), which maintains a search engine for gay-friendly bars,

restaurants, and the like, and a specialized tour operator, **Gayfriendlyitaly.com** (www.gayfriendlyitaly.com).

Mail International and internal mail is now all sent at the *Posta Prioritaria* rate. Your letter will take 3 to 8 days, depending on the destination. Postcards and letters weighing up to 20 grams cost .85€ for Europe; 2€ for Africa, Asia, and the Americas; and 2.50€ for Australia and New Zealand. You can buy stamps at all post offices and at *tabacchi* (tobacconist) stores.

Maps Tourist offices are the best places to find user-friendly local maps, usually available for free or for a small fee. Most hotels also dispense town maps. If you are driving, the best maps are available from Touring Club of Italy (www.touring.it); buy directly from their website, at bookstores abroad, or from most bookstores and newsstands in Italy.

Mobile Phones If you have a dual-band or triband GSM phone, it will work in Italy and all over Europe. The bandwidth used in Europe for GSM phones is 900–1800 hertz. Just call your wireless operator and ask for "international roaming" to be activated on your account. Unfortunately, charges can be high—anywhere from $1 to $5 per minute. However, many U.S. carriers offer "travel bundles" that provide free calling and texting for a set amount of time (often 100 minutes for each), with lower-than-average per-minute costs beyond the limit. You will also get much cheaper rates by renting or buying an Italian SIM card. You will need to have your phone unlocked by your provider at home so that it will function with any SIM card and network. You can buy an Italian prepaid SIM card, called *scheda prepagata,* in mobile phone shops, which you'll find in most towns throughout the region. Major networks that have excellent local coverage in the region are Telecom Italia (TIM), Vodafone, Wind, and H3G. The SIM is encoded with the phone number that will be yours for the time of your stay. The *scheda pre-pagata* costs 25€, 50€, 80€, 100€, or 150€.

Another option is to rent a phone with the bandwidth used in Europe and a local SIM card. A number of companies offer mobile phones for rent, and you may also be able to add a phone to your car rental. You might also want to consider buying a phone, for as little as 30€, for use during your stay.

In North America you can rent Europe-ready phones from InTouch USA (www.intouchglobal.com; ☏ **800-872-7626**) or Road-Post (www.roadpost.com; ☏ **905-272-5665**).

Money & Costs
The currency conversions quoted below were correct at press time. However, rates fluctuate, so before departing consult a currency exchange website such as **www.xe.com** to check up-to-the-minute rates.

ATMs (automated teller machines) are common and present in all but the most remote localities in the region. The **Cirrus** (www.mastercard.com; ☏ **800-424-7787**) and **PLUS** (www.visa.com) networks are the most common. Be sure you know your daily withdrawal limit before you depart. Many banks impose a fee every time you use a card at another bank's ATM, and that fee can be higher for international transactions (up to $5 or more). In addition, the bank from which you withdraw cash may charge its own fee. For international withdrawal fees, ask your bank.

Most ATMs accept **four-** and **five-digit codes;** six digits may not work, so if you have a six-digit code, go into your bank and get a new PIN for your trip.

Credit and debit cards in Italy have chips instead of a swiping magnetic band, but "swipe" cards are widely accepted. Do keep cash on hand, as many shops have a higher minimum than in the U.S. for credit card use (most often they will not accept credit or debit cards for amounts below 15€).

Passports
You'll need a **valid passport** to enter Italy. The passport should be valid for at least 3 months beyond the period of your entry and should have at least two empty visa pages. American, Canadian, Australian, New Zealand citizens, and those from a few other countries (check the list at www.esteri.it/visti) can stay up to 90 days without a visa; citizens from a country belonging to the Schengen area (the 26 countries that have abolished passport and border controls) can enter with a simple identification card; other E.U. residents need a passport.

Police
Dial ☏ **113** or 112 for emergencies.

Safety
Campania is generally safe, though one of the biggest risks in the area is road accidents. Always be vigilant, particularly as a pedestrian, when crossing

THE VALUE OF THE EURO VERSUS OTHER POPULAR CURRENCIES

Euro	US$	Can$	UK£	Aus$	NZ$
1€	$1.10	C$1.40	£0.70	A$1.45	NZ$1.65

Campania is still an affordable destination in Italy: The cost of traveling is lower than Tuscany or Milan, and quite a bit lower than such northern Europe destinations as London, Copenhagen, and Amsterdam.

WHAT THINGS COST IN NAPLES	EURO [€]
A metro or city bus ride	1.50
Soda standing at bar	2.00
Scoop of gelato	2.00
Cocktail in nice bar	6.00
Caffè lungo (American-style espresso)	1.00
Ticket to the National Archeological Museum	8.00
Taxi from the airport	19.00
Moderate three-course dinner for one without alcohol	20.00
Moderate hotel room (double)	125.00
Liter of house wine in a restaurant	8.00
First-class letter to the United States	2.00

the street (especially in Naples) or walking in a narrow street with no sidewalk.

The crime rate in Campania is generally low outside Naples, and most crimes occur in certain urban areas, such as near Naples's Stazione Centrale and in the poverty-stricken neighborhoods of the city's suburbs. Stay away from the dark, narrow streets of Naples's historic district and from poor neighborhoods at night.

The most common menace for the average tourist, especially in Naples, is the plague of pickpockets and car thieves. Pickpockets are active in all crowded places, particularly tourist areas. Note that they are sometimes dressed in elegant attire, and often work in pairs or groups, using various techniques, from distraction routines to razor blades to cut the bottom of

your bag. As beautiful and rewarding as Naples is, even savvy travelers must be vigilant and put a full arsenal of safeguards into effect: Do not carry a lot of cash; unless you are planning on using credit cards or debit cards, leave them, along with passports and other valuables, in the safe in your hotel room or in the hotel safe; do not wear valuable jewelry; when walking, carry a purse of other bag on the inside, away from the street, to prevent ride-by snatching; carry money and cards in an inside pocket, preferably one that zips shut, or in a money belt—pickpockets can do some incredibly deft handiwork. Finally, it's not unusual, especially at the train station and ferry terminal in Naples, for individuals to befriend travelers at stations, airports, and bars, then take advantage of their lower level of vigilance:

Choose your friends carefully.

The city center is also where most car thefts occur, although vehicles are always at risk, except in the most remote rural areas. Never leave valuables inside your car, never travel with your doors unlocked, and always park in a garage with an attendant. Be careful when traveling on highways at night, as robbery scams often involve staging fake breakdowns. Instead of stopping, call the police from your mobile; they'll send a car. Also, if you rent a car, make sure there is no rental sticker on the car that could make you a target (tourists often have expensive gear, such as cameras and electronic devices). Make sure, too, that no luggage or other items are visible inside the car, and do not open your trunk and display the contents in the parking spot where you're planning to leave your car unguarded. Get what you need from your luggage ahead of time.

It's a good idea is to make photocopies of your important documents: tickets, passport, credit cards, and IDs. Make sure you keep them in a different pocket or bag than the originals.

One further concern is ATM skimming. Attached to legitimate bank ATMs usually located in tourist areas, electronic devices can capture your credit card information and record your PIN through a pin-hole camera. Always use ATMs at banks and other reputable institutions.

To keep on the right side of the law, if you make any kind of purchase, from a cafe, to a meal in a restaurant, to a handbag, the vendor is required to give you an official receipt. You are required to keep it with you for a few hundred yards after coming out of the shop.

Smoking Smoking is still very common in the region, but is forbidden in restaurants, bars, and other enclosed public spaces, except those with separate ventilated smoking areas. If you decide to eat al fresco on a terrace, you will often be placing yourself in the smoking section. Many hotel rooms are nonsmoking.

Taxes Taxes in Italy are usually included in the prices quoted, but some luxury hotels will show taxes separately on their bills.

VAT, Value-Added Tax (called IVA in Italy) is imposed on most goods and services; the rate depends on the item and varies from 4% for basic food items to 20% for accessories and clothing. VAT is used in Italy for social purposes and, as a foreigner, you can ask for a refund: Non-E.U. (European Union) citizens are entitled to a refund of the VAT for purchases over 154.94€ before tax at any one store, on those goods you will take out of the country. To claim your refund, request an invoice from the cashier at the store and take it to the Customs office (*dogana*) at the airport to have it stamped before you leave.

Note: If you're going to another E.U. country before flying home, you can have it stamped at the airport Customs office of the last E.U. country you'll be in (for example, if you're flying home via Britain, have your Italian invoices stamped in London). Once you're back home, mail the stamped invoice (keep a photocopy for your records) back to the original vendor within 90 days of the purchase. The vendor will send you a refund of the tax that you paid at the time of your original purchase. Reputable stores view this as a matter of ordinary paperwork and are businesslike about it. Less-honorable stores might "lose" your file. It pays to deal with established vendors on large purchases. You can also request that the refund be credited to the card with which you made the purchase; this is usually a faster procedure.

Many shops are now part of the "Tax Free Shopping" network (look for the sticker in the window). Stores participating in this network issue a check along with your invoice at the time of purchase. After you have the invoice stamped at Customs, you can redeem the check for cash directly at the Tax Free booth in some international airports (in Rome, it's past Customs; in Milan's airports, the booth is inside the duty-free shop). Or, mail it back in the envelope provided within 60 days. Global Blue (www.globalblue.com) lists shops that participate in the Tax Free Shopping program and provides other information.

Telephones Pay phones are not as commonplace in Italy as they once were, but you'll still see them (especially in railway stations and airports) and they can come in handy if you're not using a cell phone overseas. They require prepaid telephone cards, called a *carta* or *scheda telefonica,* which you can buy at a tobacconist (*tabacchi,* marked by a sign with a white T on a black background), bar, or newsstand. The local Telecom card is available for 3€ and 5€: The duration depends on the place you are calling (within Italy or abroad) and are valid for 1 month from the first time you use them. The card has a perforated corner that you need to tear off before inserting it into the phone slot.

To make international calls, you need to purchase an international prepaid card. The cards are sold at tobacconists and some bars and newsstands. They usually allow from 200 to 700 minutes call time for 5€. You need to scratch the back to reveal the secret code and dial it after the access code indicated on the card; then dial the number you want to call.

More convenient but not necessarily cheaper is to have: (1) your own calling card linked to your home phone, or (2) a prepaid calling card that you pay monthly by credit card; both are good options. Some calling cards offer a toll-free access number in Italy, while others do not; the first kind is obviously more convenient. When calling from a public phone booth, you sometimes need to put in money or a *carta telefonica* just to obtain the dial tone, even if you are using a prepaid card; you may be charged only for a local call or not at all. Check with your calling-card provider before leaving on your trip.

You can also make collect calls directly by calling the operator (see below) or through a telephone provider in your country. For AT&T, dial ✆ **800-172-4444;** for MCI, dial ✆ **800-905825;** and for Sprint, dial ✆ **800-172405** or 800-172406.

Remember that calling from a hotel is convenient but usually very expensive.

To call Italy:
1. Dial the international access code: 011 from the U.S.; 00 from the U.K., Ireland, and New Zealand; or 0011 from Australia.
2. Dial the country code for Italy: 39.
3. Dial the local area code and then the number. Telephone numbers in Italy can have any number of digits depending on the location and the type of telephone line, which can be very confusing to foreigners. The amount of numbers can range from five (for special switchboards of hospitals and other public services, such as the railroad info line of Trenitalia, ✆ **892021,** for example) to a maximum of 10 (for some land lines and all cellular lines). Telephone numbers always include the area code, which can have two or three digits. Area codes begin with 0, for land lines, or 3, for cellular lines; you always need to dial the 0 in an area code.

To make international calls: First dial 00 and then the country code (U.S. or Canada, 1; U.K., 44; Ireland, 353; Australia, 61; New Zealand, 64). Next, dial the area code and number. For example, if you wanted to call the British Embassy in Washington, D.C., you would dial 00-1-202-588-7800.

For directory assistance: Dial ✆ **1240.**

For operator assistance: Dial ✆ **170;** the service is

available only from 7am to midnight.

Toll-free numbers: Numbers beginning with 800 or 888 within Italy are toll-free, but calling a 1-800 number in the States from Italy is not toll-free: It costs the same as an overseas call.

Time Italy is 6 hours ahead of Eastern Standard Time in the United States and 1 hour ahead of Greenwich Mean Time in the U.K. (GMT+1). Daylight saving time in Italy is from the last Sunday in March to the last Sunday in October.

Tipping Tipping is not required, as service charges are usually included in your bills. It is customary, though to leave a small tip if you are satisfied with the service: Give your hotel maid .50€ to 2€ per day, the doorman (for calling a cab) .50€, and the bellhop or porter 1€ to 5€ for carrying your bags to your room. In cafes, you usually leave a small tip, such as .10€ if you had a coffee. In restaurants, your menu or your bill should say if the service charge is included; if you're not sure whether it is, ask, "È incluso il servizio?" (ay een-*cloo*-soh eel sair-*vee*-tsoh). If it is not included, add 10% to 15% to your bill. An additional tip isn't required, but it's customary to leave a couple of euros if you've been pleased with the service. Checkroom attendants expect .50€ to 1€, and washroom attendants should get at least .50€. Taxi drivers can be tipped 10% of the fare, or round up the fare to the nearest euro and add a euro for good measure.

Toilets Restrooms (*toilette*) can be few and far between, so make use of facilities at restaurants and cafes when you can. You will usually pay .50€ to use toilets at train stations, while those at museums and archaeological areas are overseen by attendants who expect a tip of about the same amount. Usually restrooms are designated WC (water closet) and bear international symbols or the signs DONNE (women) and UOMINI (men). A designation of SIGNORI (gentlemen) and SIGNORE (ladies) can be confusing, so watch that final i and e! It's a good idea to carry some tissues in your pocket or purse—they often come in handy.

Women Travelers
Naples used to be on the black list for women travelers, but conditions have improved enormously. Even so, women often have to fend off the proffered "friendship" of local men. Most often, ignoring remarks, avoiding eye contact, and proceeding on your way as if you hadn't noticed anything is the best approach.

Always dress appropriately. Italian women dress more conservatively in urban areas than their counterparts in the United States: Reserve your strappy tanks and short shorts for the beach, ladies.

Should you ever perceive a real threat, immediately request assistance from a police officer, a storekeeper, or even a passerby (elderly women are usually perceived as particularly forbidding by young Italian males). In general, avoid seedy neighborhoods where you don't see many women strolling around, and above all, use your common sense.

USEFUL ITALIAN PHRASES
GENERAL

English	Italian	Pronunciation
Thank you	Grazie	**graht-tzee-yey**
You're welcome	Prego	**prey-go**
Please	Per favore	**pehr** fah-**vohr**-eh
Yes	Sì	**see**
No	No	**noh**
Good morning or Good day	Buongiorno	**bwohn-djor-noh**
Good evening	Buona sera	**bwohn-ah say-rah**
Good night	Buona notte	**bwohn-ah noht-tay**
It's a pleasure to meet you	Piacere di conoscerla	**pyah-cheh-reh dee koh-nohshehr-lah**
My name is_	Mi chiamo ____	**mee kyah-moh**
And yours?	E lei?	**eh lay**
Do you speak English?	Parla inglese?	**pahr-lah een-gleh-seh**
How are you?	Come sta?	**koh-may stah**
Very well	Molto bene	**mohl-toh behn-ney**
Goodbye	Arrivederci	**ahr-ree-vah-dehr-chee**
Excuse me (to get attention)	Scusi	**skoo-zee**
Excuse me (to get past someone)	Permesso	**pehr-mehs-soh**

GETTING AROUND

English	Italian	Pronunciation
Where is . . . ?	Dovè . . . ?	*doh*-vey
the station	la stazione	lah stat-tzee-*oh*-neh
a hotel	un albergo	oon ahl-*behr*-goh
a restaurant	un ristorante	oon reest-ohr-*ahnt*-eh
the bathroom	il bagno	eel *bahn*-nyoh
I am looking for . . .	Cerco . . .	*chehr*-koh
the check-in counter	il check-in	eel check-in
the ticket counter	la biglietteria	lah beel-*lyeht-teh-ree-ah*
arrivals	l'area arrivi	*lah*-reh-ah ahr-*ree*-vee
departures	l'area partenze	*lah*-reh-ah pahr-*tehn*-tseh
gate number	l'uscita numero	loo-*shee*-tah *noo*-meh-roh
the restroom	la toilette	lah twa-*leht*
the police station	la stazione di polizia	lah stah-*tsyoh*-neh dee poh-lee-*tsee*-ah
the smoking area	l'area fumatori	*lah*-reh-ah foo-mah-*toh*-ree
the information booth	l'ufficio informazioni	loof-*fee*-choh een-*fohr*-mah-*tsyoh*-nee
a public telephone	un telefono pubblico	oon teh-*leh*-foh-noh *poob*-blee-koh
an ATM/cashpoint	un bancomat	oon *bahn*-koh-maht
baggage claim	il ritiro bagagli	eel ree-*tee*-roh bah-*gahl*-lyee
a cafe	un caffè	oon kahf-*feh*
a restaurant	un ristorante	oon ree-stoh-*rahn*-teh
a bar	un bar	oon bar
a bookstore	una libreria	*oo*-nah lee-breh-*ree*-ah
To the left	A sinistra	ah see-*nees*-tra
To the right	A destra	ah *dehy*-stra
Straight ahead	Avanti (or sempre diritto)	ahv-*vahn*-tee (*sehm*-pray dee-*reet*-toh)

DINING

English	Italian	Pronunciation
Breakfast	Prima colazione	*pree*-mah coh-laht-tzee-*ohn*-ay
Lunch	Pranzo	*prahn*-zoh
Dinner	Cena	*chay*-nah
How much is it?	Quanto costa?	*kwan*-toh *coh*-sta
The check, please	Il conto, per favore	eel kon-toh *pehr* fah-*vohr*-eh

A MATTER OF TIME

English	Italian	Pronunciation
When?	Quando?	**kwan**-doh
Yesterday	Ieri	**ee-yehr**-ree
Today	Oggi	**oh**-jee
Tomorrow	Domani	doh-**mah**-nee
What time is it?	Che ore sono?	kay **or**-ay **soh**-noh
It's one o'clock	È l'una	**eh loo**-nah
It's two o'clock	Sono le due	**soh**-noh leh **doo**-eh
It's two-thirty	Sono le due e mezzo	**soh**-noh leh **doo**-eh eh **mehd**-dzoh
It's noon	È mezzogiorno	**eh** mehd-dzoh-**johr**-noh
It's midnight	È mezzanotte	**eh** mehd-dzah-**noht**-teh
in the morning	al mattino	ahl maht-**tee**-noh
in the afternoon	al pomeriggio	ahl poh-meh-**reed**-joh
at night	di notte	dee **noht**-the

DAYS OF THE WEEK

English	Italian	Pronunciation
Monday	Lunedì	loo-nay-**dee**
Tuesday	Martedì	mart-ay-**dee**
Wednesday	Mercoledì	mehr-cohl-ay-**dee**
Thursday	Giovedì	joh-vay-**dee**
Friday	Venerdì	ven-nehr-**dee**
Saturday	Sabato	**sah**-bah-toh
Sunday	Domenica	doh-**mehn**-nee-kah

MONTHS & SEASONS

English	Italian	Pronunciation
January	gennaio	jehn-**nah**-yoh
February	febbraio	fehb-**brah**-yoh
March	marzo	**mahr**-tso
April	aprile	ah-**pree**-leh
May	maggio	**mahd**-joh
June	giugno	**jewn**-nyo
July	luglio	**lool**-lyo
August	agosto	ah-**gohs**-toh
September	settembre	seht-**tehm**-breh
October	ottobre	oht-**toh**-breh
November	novembre	noh-**vehm**-breh
December	dicembre	dee-**chehm**-breh
spring	la primavera	lah pree-mah-**veh**-rah
summer	l'estate	lehs-**tah**-teh
autumn	l'autunno	low-**toon**-noh
winter	l'inverno	leen-**vehr**-noh

NUMBERS

English	Italian	Pronunciation
1	uno	*oo*-noh
2	due	*doo*-ay
3	tre	tray
4	quattro	*kwah*-troh
5	cinque	*cheen*-kway
6	sei	say
7	sette	*set*-tay
8	otto	*oh*-toh
9	nove	*noh*-vay
10	dieci	dee-ay-chee
11	undici	*oon*-dee-chee
20	venti	*vehn*-tee
21	ventuno	vehn-*toon*-oh
22	venti due	*vehn*-tee *doo*-ay
30	trenta	*trayn*-tah
40	quaranta	kwah-*rahn*-tah
50	cinquanta	cheen-*kwan*-tah
60	sessanta	sehs-*sahn*-tah
70	settanta	seht-*tahn*-tah
80	ottanta	oht-*tahn*-tah
90	novanta	noh-*vahnt*-tah
100	cento	*chen*-toh
1,000	mille	*mee*-lay
5,000	cinque milla	*cheen*-kway *mee*-lah
10,000	dieci milla	dee-ay-chee mee-lah

Useful Italian Phrases

PLANNING YOUR TRIP

Index

Accommodations

Restaurants

Photo Credits